Lower and Middle Palaeolithic artefacts
from deposits mapped as Clay-with-flints

Lower and Middle Palaeolithic artefacts from deposits mapped as Clay-with-flints

*A new synthesis with significant implications
for the earliest occupation of Britain*

J. E. Scott-Jackson

Oxbow Books
2000

Published by
Oxbow Books, Park End Place, Oxford OX1 1HN

© J. E. Scott-Jackson 2000

ISBN 1 84217 005 8

This book is available direct from
Oxbow Books, Park End Place, Oxford OX1 1HN
(Phone: 01865–241249; Fax: 01865–794449)

and

The David Brown Book Company
PO Box 511, Oakville, CT 06779, USA
(Phone: 860–945–9329; Fax: 860–945–9468)

or from our website

www. oxbowbooks.com

Printed in Great Britain at
The Short Run Press
Exeter

Contents

Preface

Lower and Middle Palaeolithic artefacts found in relation to the deposits mapped as Clay-with-flints, which cap the highest hill-tops and plateaux on the Chalk Downlands of southern England, afford an exciting area of study for archaeologists, geologists and sedimentologists and one that has been largely overlooked – despite its importance to our understanding of the earliest occupation of Britain and north-west Europe. Indeed, prior to this research, artefacts from these high-level deposits were effectively excluded from the British Palaeolithic archaeological record.

The great variability of the deposits mapped as Clay-with-flints and the existence and differing condition of the numerous Palaeolithic stone tools found in association with these deposits, were for me, not adequately explained and could not, despite pressure to the contrary, be ignored. Therefore, in 1989, I began compiling a Gazetteer of Lower and Middle Palaeolithic artefacts found in relation to deposits mapped as Clay-with-flints.

Amongst the two thousand or so entries in this ongoing project there are a few references to stone-tools having been found actually 'embedded' in the underlying various Clay-with-flints deposits when for one reason or another the top-soil has been removed. A comprehensive review of these 'embedded' Palaeolithic sites is included in this book. Embedded artefacts are particularly important as the majority of these finds have proved to be discreet assemblages that are indicative of *in situ* sites. One such embedded assemblage was discovered in 1984/85 on Wood Hill – a small hill, near Deal in East Kent.

The excavations and investigations which I directed on Wood Hill in 1993 and 1994, established the *in situ* status of this Lower Palaeolithic site and marked the first attempt using rigorous modern scientific methods, to address the fundamental questions and hypotheses posed by the surviving presence of Palaeolithic stone tools on the highest hill-tops and plateaux in areas mapped as Clay-with-flints on the Chalk Downlands of southern England.

As a 'Case-study' site, Wood Hill afforded an ideal framework for this pioneering multidisciplinary research. Although this book provides detailed guidance and ideas for the specialist, it is nevertheless written for the general reader, albeit with a grounding in archaeology and/or earth sciences. Arguably, it will be of the greatest value to the Palaeolithic field archaeologist as the emphasis is on the application of new detailed methodologies and geologically founded techniques to solve the archaeological problems associated with these high-level artefacts. However, it also provides important theoretical frameworks for the analytical archaeologist or pre-historian specialising in the Palaeolithic. Many of the recommendations and practices set out here would also be applicable to excavations and investigations in a different geological context and/or later periods where the need for meticulous detailed recording may still be critical.

As so much of the information embodied in this book is new, or a structured exposition of existing but so often convoluted data, it has been necessary to include two 'Explanatory' Sections which provide a theoretical analysis of the processes that have formed and changed both the Chalk Downlands and the deposits mapped as Clay-with-flints, and which over geological time have been instrumental in retaining on these high-levels evidence of the activities of Palaeolithic people in the form of stone tools. Also contained in the Explanatory Sections is a 'Benchmarks' system which provides a unique means of identifying possible *in situ* Palaeolithic sites.

Investigating and excavating Palaeolithic high-level sites on deposits mapped as Clay-with-flints is difficult, very detailed work, requiring great patience and restraint. It is therefore impossible to stress sufficiently, just how important it is to adhere to the principles, methodologies, techniques and recommendations that I have set out in this book – failure to do will result in valuable irreplaceable data being lost and the integrity of both the sites and the artefacts compromised. Scientific progress has always depended on individuals not being content with existing explanations. Invariably new ideas generate contention. Some may therefore disagree with the interpretations and conclusions that I have set out here. Given that the arguments are based on similarly detailed analysis of similarly sound data, then these contributions to the debate are to be welcomed. As an early explorer in this neglected field of study, I look forward to the new insights which I hope future researchers will add to our understanding of both the deposits mapped as Clay-with-flints and the associated Palaeolithic artefacts, for as this research has shown, Lower and Middle Palaeolithic artefacts found in relation to deposits mapped as Clay-with-flints are, after all, a major component of the British Palaeolithic archaeological record. If we are to understand the movements and activities of Palaeolithic people, at any one point in time, we must consider the landscape as a whole and the relationship that exists between both high-level and low-level sites, as no one site can provide all the answers.

Finally, any student or researcher who feels that their work is unacknowledged, or ignored, can take heart from this book which proves that it is still possible to overcome the natural conservatism of established theory given a firm case, a sound argument, courage and good, repeatable, testable data. The most encouraging reaction to any new idea is when people start to see how obvious it was all along!

Julie E. Scott-Jackson
October, 1999

Unit for the study of Palaeolithic artefacts
and deposists mapped as Clay-with flints (PADMAC),
Donald Baden-Powell Quaternary Research Centre,
Pitt Rivers Museum
University of Oxford

Acknowledgements

Writing this book has been a long journey over many years, a journey that has taken me through a variety of different disciplines, some very familiar, some less so. The assistance which I received along the way is greatly and gratefully acknowledged but if any errors remain, I have only myself to blame.

To the tenacious Wood Hill 1993 and 1994 excavation and survey teams; the staff at the Sites and Monuments Records offices, museums, libraries, local archaeological groups, all who have worked with me on my Gazetteer and to my colleagues at the Donald Baden Powell Quaternary Research Centre, University of Oxford, I extend special thanks.

I am also especially indebted to Mr. G. Halliwell and Mr. K. Parfitt who allowed me access to the Wood Hill 1984/85 site archive and whose help has been invaluable, during and since the 1993 excavation.

Specialist technical expertise was provided by many people at the University of Oxford in the Department of Earth Sciences, School of Geography, Department of Statistics and The Research Laboratory for Archaeology and the History of Art. Their work is acknowledged as appropriate in the text.

I am exceedingly grateful to Prof. D.A. Roe, Dr. R.B.G. Williams and Prof. R. Dennell for reviewing the original text in all its various forms and for their valuable comments; to Prof. J.A. Catt, Dr. S.N. Collcutt, Prof. C.S. Gamble, Mr. R.J. MacRae, Dr. J. Mitchell, Dr. I. Slipper, Dr. S. Stokes, and Dr. J.J. Wymer for their academic input, encouragement and support and to both Mr M.H.R. Cook (now sadly deceased) and Mr. J. Wallis for the line drawings of the Wood Hill artefacts.

Finally, most sincere thanks to my funding body, 'The C.S.A. Fund for Palaeolithic Archaeology', for their support and courage in funding such a neglected area of research and the means to establish a Unit for the study of Palaeolithic Artefacts and associated Deposits Mapped as Clay-with-flints (PADMAC) at Oxford University.

General Introduction

The Lower and Middle Palaeolithic in Britain and Europe

Climatic changes and tectonic activity in Europe during the Middle and Upper Pleistocene (approximately 780,000–10,000 years B.P) produced conditions of which there is no real equivalent today. During the glacial periods, huge ice sheets formed which moved relentlessly southwards, gradually covering vast areas of land, capturing rivers and lowering sea levels. Beyond these fully glaciated areas, a 'periglacial' landscape of ice and tundra and sparse forests existed. Then, as the climate ameliorated during interglacial periods, the ice sheets retreated, meltwater swept across the land removing and depositing debris, the sea levels rose and deciduous forests appeared. As the sea levels fluctuated, the small landmass (which is now Britain) appears to have alternated between being a peninsula of Continental Western Europe and an island.

With only a few possible exceptions, the earliest traces of Lower Palaeolithic human activity in Continental Europe occur somewhere around 700,000 years B.P. (the beginning of the Middle Pleistocene). Many Lower and Middle Palaeolithic sites have been found in Europe; often they have yielded a substantial amount of archaeological material in the form of stone tools, animal and plant remains and, occasionally, hominid remains and structural traces such as hearths and shelters, allowing archaeologists to distinguish between 'kill' or 'butchery', 'stone working' sites and 'homebase camps'. By comparison, the evidence for the presence of hominid groups in Britain during the Lower and Middle Palaeolithic periods (around 500,000–35,000 years B.P.) is almost entirely derived from the many stone tools that have been recovered from a variety of locations in the southern half of Britain. Actual hominid remains also exist in Britain, but are extremely scarce, to date, having been found at only three sites (Swanscombe, Pontnewydd cave and Boxgrove). Perhaps this scarcity is to be expected, as Britain was situated at the extreme north-west edge of the Palaeolithic world. However, the key component in determining the patterns of Lower and Middle Palaeolithic occupation in Britain over geological time, may well have been the regulating effects of marked climatic change on both the sea-levels and the migration of flora and fauna. This generated a situation conducive to intermittent, rather than continuous occupation. The Lower and Middle Palaeolithic periods, as represented in the British archaeological record, are therefore, a discontinuous record of change.

No satisfactory or generally agreed correlation appears to exist between the different industry-types of stone tools and the various species of *Homo*; nevertheless enough is known to provide a general picture. It is not possible to say with any certainty whether the Lower and Middle Palaeolithic peoples who visited Britain, at any one time during the middle and upper Pleistocene, were Archaic *Homo sapiens* or Neanderthals (*Homo sapiens neanderthalensis*), with specific clinal characteristics). However, the hominid tibia found at Boxgrove (site date – around 500,000 yrs. B.P) has been assigned to *Homo cf heidelbergensis* (Roberts *et al*. 1994), and the Swanscombe skull (site date – around 400,000 yrs B.P.) has certain cranial skeletal characteristics usually associated with the Neanderthals.

The British Lower and Middle Palaeolithic industries/technique(s)

Stone tools represent the oldest traces of human presence and manufacturing activity in southern England: the same is true for many other parts of the world. The Lower Palaeolithic period (in Britain) extended from approximately 500,000 years B.P. to around 180,000 years B.P., a date which is generally considered to mark the end of the Lower Palaeolithic and the beginning of the Middle Palaeolithic. No sharp divisions exist anywhere between the Lower and Middle Palaeolithic; the distinction is always blurred. The Middle Palaeolithic period (in Britain) lasted from around 200,000 years B.P. until 40,000 years B.P. As the distinction between the British Lower and Middle Palaeolithic periods is ill defined, with the industries showing both continuity of development over time, and fragmentation in industry-type occurrence. The term 'Lower and Middle Palaeolithic' is used here as an inclusive term to avoid creating distinctions that do not exist. However, in specific instances where the industry-type is known, both it and the period is stated. Any object made by a human may be referred to as an artefact, so this term obviously includes stone tools. When the more specific term tool (or implement) is used here, it implies that the artefact in question has been deliberately shaped into a form intended for use in some task or tasks by humans. Many flakes of various sizes are struck from the parent material in the production of such stone tools and these waste flakes can also quite correctly be referred to as artefacts. Sometimes a struck flake that has not been otherwise modified or retouched may have been used repeatedly or for a substantial period. Flakes such as these are categorised as 'utilised pieces' or 'utilised waste' while the unused knapping debris is usually referred to as 'waste' or 'debitage'. More specific items of waste can sometimes be recognised, such as core-rejuvenation flakes, or handaxe trimming flakes.

Therefore, it has often been thought possible to identify and categorise artefacts as belonging to either the Lower or Middle Palaeolithic periods by certain aspects of their morphology or technology: for example, the precise manner in which flakes are struck from the parent material to produce blanks for the stone tool. These different methods are sometimes used to define 'industry-types'. The names given to these often quite distinctive ways of making artefacts are usually derived from particular sites where this type of artefact was first found (i.e. the type-site). The majority of the Lower and Middle Palaeolithic type-site names are French as most of the relevant discoveries were made in France. Within what is designated as the Lower Palaeolithic period, there are a number of general industry-types, namely

- 'Clactonian' (after Clacton), whether the Clactonian should be considered as an industry-type or a technique is, at present, the subject of considerable debate;
- 'Acheulian' (after Sant-Acheul);
- 'Levallois' technique (not an industry-type), industries specialising in artefacts made by the Levalloisian technique may, sometimes be separate from the Acheulian sequence;
- 'Micoquian' (after La Micoque).

The British Earlier Acheulian industries were originally characterised by heavy, crude handaxes, however, the discoveries at High Lodge (Ashton *et al.* 1992) and at Boxgrove (Roberts and Parfitt,1999) have

led to a reappraisal of this sub-division. As a result, typology, the once unquestioned 'tool' for characterising and dating assemblages, is now widely regarded as inadequate and even dangerously misleading for this purpose. The early Acheulian industries include some consisting entirely of finely made ovates with advanced flaking techniques. Conversely, the Clactonian industries lack handaxes and appear to consist only of flakes and cores. Middle Acheulian industries are somewhat variable, tending to specialise in 'pointed' or 'ovate' handaxe types, sometimes incorporating sporadic use of Levalloisian technique. In Britain, the Late Acheulian/Micoquian is a rather sparsely represented phase, with industries that include technologically distinctive plano-convex pointed handaxes. The gradual change from Lower to Middle Palaeolithic was marked by a long overlap between the Late Acheulian and Micoquian industries; the presence of fine flake tools in certain Acheulian industries and the association of the Levalloisian technique with handaxe forms that are similar to those found in the Middle Palaeolithic.

Many Lower and Middle Palaeolithic artefacts have been found in Britain both as excavated artefacts and surface-finds. A high proportion of the excavated finds were made during commercial gravel or brickearth extraction and in a few cases it has been possible to determine their age by relative and/or absolute dating of the Pleistocene deposits that contain them, or of other contents of those deposits such as bones or shells. Limitations inevitably exist, however, where surface-finds are concerned, as it is only possible to suggest relationships between find-spots by virtue of perceived similarities in the industry-types. The term FIND-SPOT refers to a spot where one or more artefacts were found, not necessarily in their original context, whereas the term FIND-SITE refers to an area where evidence suggests artefacts may have been made or used – a crucial difference in terms of interpretative significance.

It is not possible to ascribe an actual date to any surface-find, only a broad geological period associated with that industry-type.

The association of Lower and Middle Palaeolithic artefacts and areas mapped as Clay-with-flints

During the compilation of the Gazetteer of Lower and Middle Palaeolithic find-spots in North Hampshire (Scott-Jackson, 1991b), it became apparent, not only that so many of the finds on the Downlands came from the highest hilltops and plateaux, but also that these same Chalk high-levels were overlain with clayey, superficial deposits mapped as Clay-with-flints (Figure 1) – a distinctive reddish brown, highly

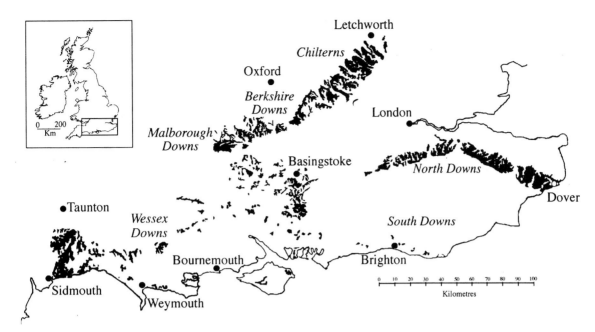

Figure 1. Generalised distribution map of deposits mapped as Clay-with-flints in southern England (based on the Atlas of Great Britain and Northern Ireland, Superficial Deposits, Clarendon Press, 1963, with modifications).

tenacious clay, which often contained many flints and pebbles. The association of Palaeolithic artefacts and deposits mapped as Clay-with-flints has been confirmed by further extensive research and the high-level finds from all the Downland counties of southern England catalogued in the 'Gazetteer of Lower and Middle Palaeolithic artefacts found in relation to deposits mapped as Clay-with-flints on the Chalk Downlands of southern England' (Scott-Jackson,1999). The term 'Clay-with-flints' has been used as a 'blanket term' by many people (including map makers) to include all the different components that make up these superficial deposits, for example: Clay-with-flints *sensu stricto*; Clay-with-flints *sensu lato*; deposits which are also classified as Plateau Drift; waterlain and windblown Brickearths. The origins, definitions and many variations of the deposits mapped as Clay-with-flints are discussed in Explanatory Section 2. The problem is that these deposits are not well understood even on a general level. Furthermore, the deposits mapped as Clay-with-flints exhibit a great deal of variation both between the very large areas (i.e. counties) and within even very small localised areas.

Here therefore, strict scientific rigour will apply; the term 'mapped as Clay-with-flints' will be used as a general description, when referring to areas shown as Clay-with-flints on the geological maps. However, where the particular variation and type of Clay-with-flints (e.g. *sensu stricto* or *sensu lato*) is known, this will be specified if and where necessary. This unavoidable use of the somewhat cumbersome term 'mapped as Clay-with-flints', in place of the more general term 'Clay-with-flints', is but a small price to pay for accuracy and clarity.

Stone tools and deposits mapped as Clay-with-flints

During the past hundred years or so, a great many Lower and Middle Palaeolithic artefacts have been collected as surface-finds from the hill-tops/plateaux in areas mapped as Clay-with-flints. These surface-finds are often single isolated artefacts, but it is important to note that substantial numbers of stone tools have sometimes also been found, in what appear to be discrete assemblages: that is, they have been discovered as a group of artefacts located close together within a single high-level field. However, due to a lack of appropriate research it is rarely known whether such finds represent single-period artefact groups or a palimpsest of occupations of various ages brought together by ploughing or natural processes. Very occasionally, stone tools have been recovered from below the top-soil, actually embedded within the Clay-with-flints deposits themselves (these artefacts and the context in which they were found are fully discussed in Sections 4 and 5).

The significance of sites on deposits mapped as the Clay-with-flints

The Palaeolithic archaeological record in Britain is based almost exclusively on archaeological material found in a very few caves, and in many riverside, lakeside and valley sites, which have been revealed during commercial exploitation of the gravels and brickearths. Most of these finds are derived or in a secondary context: that is, the stone tools had not been made where they were actually found, but have been transported or disturbed by geological processes. The amount and type of wear on these artefacts often indicates that they have moved substantial distances. In many cases, particularly in southern England, the deposits that make up valley floors and river-beds are composed of material that has been washed down from higher levels. It therefore seems to me not unreasonable to suggest that a proportion of the Palaeolithic artefacts found at the 'low-level' sites are highly likely to have descended from 'high-level' working sites in areas mapped as Clay-with-flints as essentially part of the same process.

The lack of academic interest in these high-level finds is linked to the arguments and reservations which can be traced to the reverberating effect of what has, since its occurrence at the turn of the century, generally become known as the Eolith debate, in which violent confrontations took place between the supporters of Benjamin Harrison (1837–1921), who believed his later high-level surface-finds from North Kent to be the work of Palaeolithic people, and those who questioned the authenticity of these simply flaked 'stone tools' (see E. Harrison, 1928). But it is the general misunderstanding and much confusion caused by the misinterpretation of statements made by Wooldridge and Linton (1955) and later workers, regarding the nature of the Clay-with-flints deposits and the effects of climatic change on the Downlands over geological time (see Explanatory Section 1) that has discouraged the serious study of the relationship between the deposits mapped as Clay-with-flints and the related Lower and Middle Palaeolithic artefacts. The main reasons for the previous lack of attention to the high-level finds seem to be:

– that none of the assemblages, however apparently discrete, can be considered in any way to be *in situ*;
– that it is impossible to date this material either by relative or absolute dating methods; and
– that processes operating in cold and temperate environments have effectively removed any useful stratigraphic or environmental evidence that might have existed.

However, as the results of this research show, these objections are no longer valid.

Here, then, is the paradox: The large amount of Lower and Middle Palaeolithic artefacts found on hilltops and plateaux capped with deposits mapped as Clay-with-flints are effectively excluded from the Palaeolithic archaeological record, while the probably derived material found at the lower levels are not. The presence of so many Palaeolithic artefacts (both as surface finds and actually within the deposits) on the high-level areas mapped as Clay-with-flints clearly confirms that the presence and activities of Palaeolithic hunter/scavengers and gatherers were not restricted to low-level sites. It is therefore surely necessary to consider the landscape as a whole, the high-levels, the hilltops and plateaux and the low-levels, the riverside, lakeside, beach and cave sites, if we are to increase our understanding of how Palaeolithic hominids operated.

Patterns of occupation and population density in Palaeolithic Britain

Earlier, it was noted that climatic changes and fluctuating sea levels appear have restricted the movements of Palaeolithic people to and from Britain (the north-west extremity of the Palaeolithic world), thereby producing a pattern of intermittent rather than continuous occupation of the island. This knowledge, combined with the fact that there is a scarcity of hominid remains in Britain has led many to assume that Britain was very sparsely populated during the Palaeolithic period. This may indeed have been the case, but it must also be remembered that the survival and indeed the fossilisation of material depends on a whole variety of accidental and specific circumstances (e.g. falling into a peat bog; being covered up and 'sealed in' by the 'right sort of sediments'). Furthermore, much of what were the actual Palaeolithic landsurfaces, have over geological time, been battered and broken up by glacial action; washed away when the ice melted or buried beneath redeposited sediments. The Palaeolithic material/artefacts that remains today may well be but a fraction of the total amount that once existed in Britain.

Estimations of population density in Palaeolithic Britain have been based on: the number of sites which form the British Lower and Middle archaeological record; the surviving hominid remains and the effects of climatic changes in the Pleistocene. However, an inherent problem exists with this line of investigation as little account appears to have been taken of the very many Lower and Middle high-level sites on deposits mapped as Clay-with-flints – sites which, as we have seen, because of their position and geology are not included in the British archaeological record. As both the high-level and the low-level sites mark the activities of Palaeolithic people, the inclusion of these high-level sites would clearly establish the use of the landscape as a whole by the

Palaeolithic people. Therefore, estimates of Palaeolithic population density in Britain (at any one time) may need revising, as the question now posed is – do these sites indicate a greater number of Palaeolithic people *per se*?

Glaciation limits and the ancient landsurfaces of southern England

The importance of the presence of Lower and Middle Palaeolithic stone tools in areas mapped as Clay-with-flints is further underlined, if one considers that the Downlands of southern England, were above and beyond the reach of meltwater when the ice-sheets withdrew at the end of the Anglian and subsequent glacial maxima (see Figure 2). Although the higher plateaux and interfluves of the Downlands capped with deposits mapped as Clay-with-flints will certainly have undergone the effects of both periglacial and temperate conditions, they may still be considered to be landsurfaces which have been subjected to only 'restricted change'. I have devised the phrase 'restricted change', to allow for limited changes within the deposit, in place of the word 'stability',[1] which infers no change and generates misunderstandings as it crosses different disciplines and is used in various concepts and theories. Therefore, areas mapped as Clay-with-flints have been subjected to only restricted change since approximately the end of the Cromerian i.e. a date at least as old as 500,000 yrs. B.P. and probably substantially earlier (see Explanatory Section 1). As the earliest evidence of hominid occupation in Britain (based on the Boxgrove material) is also currently thought to date from the late Cromerian, a date of around 500,000 years B.P It is likely therefore, that some of the Clay-with-flints assemblages may also be pre-Anglian.

The relationships between the Downlands of southern England, the superficial deposits mapped as Clay-with-flints which cap the highest hilltops and plateaux, and the surviving presence of Lower and Middle Palaeolithic artefacts on these same high-levels have not previously been investigated using modern scientific methods. Indeed, it could be argued that these high-level palaeoliths represent the

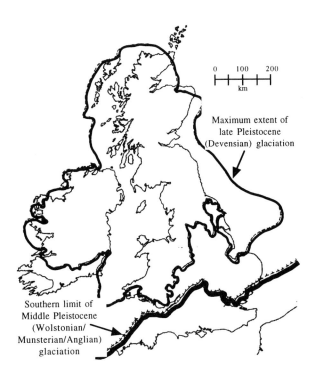

Figure 2 The limits of glaciation in the British Isles in the Devensian and earlier cold stages. After Bowen et al. (1986) in Avery (1990).

most neglected realm of British Lower and Middle Palaeolithic research. Therefore, wherever possible, I have used methods more commonly associated with detailed geological, geomorphological and sedimentological research in order to provide the level of resolution needed to address the following three questions (a, b and c) and three consequential hypotheses (1, 2 and 3).

Questions:
(a) How could Lower and Middle Palaeolithic artefacts become incorporated into, and/or remain on the surface of, the deposits mapped as Clay-with-flints over hundreds of thousands of years?
(b) From the time Lower and Middle Palaeolithic peoples manufactured and deposited their artefacts on the Palaeolithic high level land-surfaces, southern England has undergone many

---

[1] Goudie (1988: 403-4) states that the term 'stability' was originally used to describe,'the ability of an ecosystem to maintain or return to its original condition following a natural or human-induced disturbance'. However, although this concept has been widely used, many other meanings have been become attached to the term 'stability'. Goudie (*op. cit.*) continues: 'For example the term 'stability' has been used in reference to constancy or persistence of species, populations or ecosystems. Two major aspects of ecosystem stability in relation to disturbance have received attention. Even in this context a confusing variety of terms have been used. The first property which is labelled 'resistance' is the ability of a system to remain unaffected by disturbances. This property is referred to as 'inertia' by Orians (1975) and Westman (1978) and as 'resilience' by Holdings (1973). The second attribute is usually termed 'resilience' and is the ability of a system to recover to its original state following a disturbance. The more general term stability has also been applied to this property by May (1973) and Hollings (1973)'.

climatic changes associated with both glacial and temperate periods. What has happened specifically to the superficial deposits mapped as Clay-with-flints on these high-level areas where the artefacts are still to be found?

(c)   As the deposits mapped as Clay-with-flints are highly variable both within even small areas and between large areas, is there a correlation between particular facies of deposits mapped as Clay-with-flints and the occurrence of Lower and Middle Palaeolithic artefacts?

Hypotheses:
1.   Given the state of restricted change of the deposits mapped as Clay-with-flints which cap the Downlands of southern England, *in situ* Lower or Middle Palaeolithic sites should exist on some of the high-levels.
2.   Some current models used to explain patterns and levels of erosion and deposition on the hilltops and plateaux capped with deposits mapped as Clay-with-flints may require substantial adjustment.
3.   There are a number of factors that would indicate whether any given high-level capped with de-

posits mapped as Clay-with-flints would warrant detailed archaeological survey or excavation. Some examples of these factors are: the presence or absence of surface-finds of stone artefacts on the hill-top/plateaux itself; the shape and location of the hill-top/plateaux, as a feature of both the ancient and modern general topography of the immediate area; the geographical relationship between the various hill-tops/plateaux capped with deposits mapped as Clay-with-flints that have produced surface finds of stone artefacts within a specific area; the pattern of distribution of these high-level surface-finds relative to the local distribution of Palaeolithic finds at lower levels and the proximity of essential resources for Palaeolithic people such as good quality flint and/or fresh water.

I am confident that this research is the first step towards explaining the relationships between Lower and Middle Palaeolithic artefacts, the deposits mapped as Clay-with-flints and the Chalk Downlands in southern England. However, as there is much work still to do, a full and final definitive explanation may yet lie many years ahead.

The Chalk Downlands of southern England

Chalk Downlands cover a large area of southern England, extending through Devon, Dorset, Wiltshire, Hampshire, Berkshire, Oxfordshire, Bedfordshire, Buckinghamshire, Hertfordshire, Surrey, Sussex and Kent. The topography ranges from upland plateaux and escarpments, often rising to over 200m (Inkpen Beacon, Hampshire, at 305m. is the highest Chalk hill in England), through to undulating lowland plains. Chalklands can also be found in East Anglia, and north-east England; however, as these areas have been directly affected by glacial and alluvial activity during the Anglian glacial maxima, they are not included in this research. A 'typical' Chalk downland landscape generally consists of convex slopes, with fairly steep valley sides often asymmetric in cross-section and trough-shaped valleys. However, in some places the valleys can also resemble steep gashes, while in others they are wider and more shallow.

Over the past hundred years or so, the Geological Survey of Great Britain has produced many geological maps of southern England. Many of these maps can only be used as a general guide to the geology of a particular area; they cannot be used to provide detailed information on the type, or exact distribution of particular deposits at specific places. The only way to obtain detailed data of the latter kind is by comprehensive field investigations – a fact which assumes important implications in this research, as there is a close relationship between the deposits mapped as Clay-with-flints and the survival of Lower and Middle Palaeolithic artefacts.

The relationship between the Chalk Downlands and the deposits mapped as Clay-with-flints

In order to explain the continuing presence of Palaeolithic artefacts on the Downland hill-tops and plateaux, it is necessary to consider the relationships that exist between the Chalk and the deposits mapped as Clay-with-flints, and why presence of the latter implies only restricted change. This requires a brief examination of the origins of both the Chalk Downlands and the superficial deposits mapped as Clay-with-flints, along with a variety of processes that have acted upon them to produce the Downlands as they are seen today; processes acting over many hundreds of thousands of years, during both glacial and temperate environments, and in a great many different climates, (for many of which, as previously noted, there are no modern equivalents). However, it is the processes acting upon the Chalk Downlands during the Quaternary period, and the preceding Tertiary period, rather than the formation of the Chalklands during the Cretaceous period, that command the greater emphasis in this research.

The evolution of the Chalk Downlands of southern England

Many different theories have been proposed to explain the evolution of the Chalk downlands in southern England and the processes that have produced the characteristic landforms seen today, (see for example: Whitaker, 1867, 1889; Woodward, 1887, 1912; Bull, 1936, 1940; Wooldridge and Linton, 1955; Te Punga, 1957; Sparks, 1949, 1960; Small, 1961: Hodgson, Catt and Weir 1967; Hodgson, Rayner and Catt 1974; Catt and Hodgson, 1976; Jones, 1974, 1980, 1981; Williams, 1971, 1980, 1983, 1986).

However, it is generally agreed that towards the end of the Cretaceous period (approx. 70–100 million years B.P.), tectonic uplift caused a major regression of the sea over much of north-west Europe, including what is now southern England. The Lower Chalk, Middle Chalk and Upper Chalk beds, which had been laid down following a series of marine transgressions over the earlier Gault and Greensand deposits, were uplifted and tilted, becoming exposed to subaerial erosion. As a result, the earliest Tertiary (Palaeogene) rocks rest on different horizons of the Chalk at different places (see for example: Gallois and Edmonds, 1978; Melville and Freshney, 1982).

A consequent drainage system then developed, with many large rivers draining primarily towards what is now the North Sea (Goudie, 1990: 10). Wooldridge and Linton (1955) suggested that the open sea occasionally returned to cover the whole area, but only for short periods, and that these landforms were further modified by tectonic activity in the Miocene (25 million years B.P.). By the Pliocene (5 million years B.P.), the area had been substantially eroded to form a peneplain and the remains of this peneplain survived in some areas to heights of over 300m. They also suggested that the so-called 'drift deposits' on the peneplain were Eocene deposits dating from around 53 million years B.P. This statement by Wooldridge and Linton generated much discussion and caused confusion, as it was *interpreted by many* to imply that the superficial deposits mapped as Clay-with-flints, many of which seemed to derive from various Eocene beds (for example, Thanet Beds, Woolwich and Reading Beds), had remained on the Downlands, unchanged in their original form, for 53 million years – *a situation which of course could not be so.*

During the Quaternary, subaerial stream erosion at increasingly lower levels on the Chalk dip-slope, during both temperate and periglacial periods, exposed and cut into the sub-Tertiary surface. When the basal Tertiary deposits at any locality became thin enough to be permeable, temperate subaerial erosion ceased, and the remnant veneer of Tertiary sediments was gradually changed (Figure 3) to the superficial deposit known as 'Plateau Drift' (Catt, and Hodgson 1976: 190), a form of Clay-with-flints *sensu lato*. This superficial deposit must once have covered a area far greater than that which survives in southern England today. Any extensive cover that might have existed on the Chalk in northern England was almost completely removed by glacial erosion in the Anglian and later cold periods according to Catt (1986a: 151).

The processes that effectively change the Tertiary sediments into Plateau Drift are karstic disturbance (a situation where groundwater makes its way through rocks and dissolves them, and streams flow beneath the surface), weathering and periglacial processes. In addition, insoluble residues from the underlying Chalk, including tabular and nodular flint, were incorporated into the superficial deposit. It is now generally considered that during temperate/warm periods, Clay-with-flints *sensu stricto* developed between the Plateau Drift and the Chalk by the downwashing of clay particles. These clay particles and the insoluble Chalk residue were then redeposited in the spaces provided by the slow dissolution of the underlying Chalk. This solution of the Chalk over geological time has produced solution features in the form of dolines, pipes and 'basin-like' hollows, which have effectively retained the deposits mapped as Clay-with-flints. (Note: Occasionally solution features can be identified from aerial

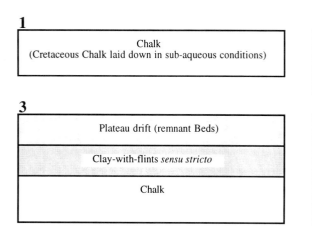

Sub-Palaeogene deposits (now sub-aerial) uplifted by tectonic activity, reworked during Eocene to form Plateau drift, Clay-with-flints *sensu stricto* derived from the Plateau drift and insoluble residues underlying Chalk.

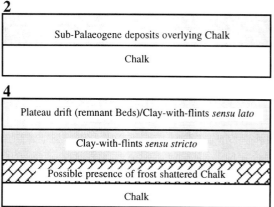

Frost shattering of the Chalk may have occurred before, during or after the Anglian Glacial Maxima.

Figure 3 Idealised schematic diagram showing the formation of Clay-with-flints sensu stricto and sensu lato over geological time.

reconnaissance photographs (see for example, D.R. Wilson, 1982, 'Air Photo Interpretation for Archaeologists') however great care must be exercised when interpreting such photographs as many of the 'hollows' in Downland areas are in fact high-level pits (e.g. Chalk or Brickearth pits).)

Following their investigations into the geomorphological significance of Clay-with-flints on the south Downs, Hodgson, Rayner and Catt (1974: 127) concluded that the unifying feature of remnants of the sub-Tertiary plane in southern England are Clay-with-flints *sensu stricto*, Clay-with-flints *sensu lato*, and other deposits formed by the reorganisation of early Tertiary sediments more or less *in situ*. They also noted that in certain areas it was not easy to distinguish between remnants of the folded sub-Tertiary surface, now covered with Clay-with-flints formed *in situ* and irregularly lowered by dissolution from younger erosion surfaces. Many of these younger surfaces were covered by similar deposits that had also formed *in situ*, but from transported Eocene and/or other material. In addition, deposits derived by mass movement from elsewhere were also present. Therefore, where attempts are made to reconstruct landscape development, as many relevant lines of evidence as possible should be considered. Catt and Hodgson state

> 'it is extremely important to evaluate fully the evidence from the superficial deposits, however thin and dissected they may be' (*op. cit.* 1976: 181).

Where the Downland high-levels are capped by superficial deposits mapped as Clay-with-flints, plateau features are clearly evident. Plateaux are by definition relatively flat surfaces, and high-level flat surfaces in Chalk downland areas imply a modification of the processes of erosion that have produced the usual rounded landforms. Accordingly, where a high-level exhibits plateau features, only 'restricted change' is implied. A full discussion on the nature, origin and geomorphology of deposits mapped as Clay-with-flints is to be found in Explanatory Section 2.

Processes, landforms and the relationship between Chalk and Clay-with-flints

Although the smooth rounded downland hills are often thought to have been produced by surface solution or soil creep (Bull, 1936; Sparks, 1960), Catt and Hodgson (1976: 190) concluded that the 'typical' Chalk landscape is largely the result of solifluction (Williams 1986: 164 adds sheet-wash and rill action) on areas that are, or were, unprotected by a capping of the superficial deposits mapped as Clay-with-flints). A more angular landscape of scarps and dip-slopes occurs where such superficial deposits are present to protect remnants of a sub-Tertiary surface. These interpretations as set out by Catt and Hodgson (*ibid.*) are now generally accepted, although they contrast strongly with, amongst others, the 'classic' works of Sparks (1949), Wooldridge and Linton (1955), and Small and Fisher (1970).

The superficial deposits covering the Chalk appear to have played a protective role in the development of the Chalk landscape during both warm and cold periods. During very cold/periglacial periods, permafrost would have rendered the underlying Chalk and the Clay-with-flints cover (both *sensu stricto* and *sensu lato*) impermeable. The protective cover of the superficial capping deposits modified the landscape by reducing the amount of erosion of the underlying more easily eroded Chalk, in contrast to the unprotected and exposed slopes. In warm periods, the surfaces that were not covered by the superficial deposits seemed to have been lowered more rapidly by dissolution, with the flinty residue being periodically removed, particularly from the side-slopes of the dry valleys by colluviation (a process in which material is transported across, and deposited on slopes as a result of wash and mass movement). Catt and Hodgson (*ibid.*) make the point that this is in direct contrast with surfaces beneath Plateau Drift (i.e., beneath Clay-with-flints *sensu lato*) in which the insoluble Chalk residue was retained as part of Clay-with-flints *sensu stricto*.

Chalk has a very large water-holding capacity, is brittle, and is easily shattered into small fragments by frost (Williams, 1969; 1980). Areas of exposed Chalk, on the hillsides, could accordingly be shattered by frost and the weakened Chalk removed by gravitational downslope movement associated with sheet wash, rill wash and solifluction. This saturated, seasonally thawed composite material known as Coombe Rock (Coombe Deposit), which principally consists of large quantities of chalky mud and rubble mixed with whole and/or broken flints, was transported down the hill-side and deposited on the valley floor (Catt and Hodgson, 1976; Williams, 1986; Goudie, 1988). Periglacial erosion and solution processes have therefore both been instrumental in the formation of the Downland relief, but, although there are considerable volumes of Coombe Deposits to be found in the valleys and on the coastal plain, Williams makes the important point, that it is not always easy to distinguish the effects of periglaciation from those of solution (*op. cit.* 1980, 1986: 163).

Karstic phenomena on the Chalk Downlands – the effects of solution on the landform

The Chalk outcrops of southern England are often considered to lack many characteristic features of karst landscapes. This is a serious misconception, as solution features are many and widespread. Furthermore, the evidence suggests that solution of the Chalk has been a long-continued process (Goudie 1993: 234). The solution process can be defined thus:

> 'Solution erosion and the effect on land surface lowering, that is solutional denudation, is the result of solute uptake. This is the chemical weathering of minerals to release ions into solution, and transportation of those ions away from the locus of solution by water movement... In a geomorphic context the importance of solutional erosion in modelling the landscape lies in the spatial variation of solutional erosion' (Crabtree, 1986: 330).

Two major controls on the distribution of solutional features on the Chalk in southern England have been identified: the lithology of the Chalk itself and the presence of Tertiary Beds or Quaternary superficial deposits on top of the Chalk. Goudie (1993: 234) noted that Edmonds (1983: 264–5) had shown that there is a preferential development of solution features on the Upper Chalk as it is the purest, softest and most porous Chalk, with the fewest restrictions to groundwater flow. However, Goudie considers that the most important distribution control of solution features on the Downlands is the presence of the Tertiary Beds or Quaternary superficial deposits, as they produce a source of acidic water which may be concentrated into particular locations on the Chalk surface.

If we apply the geomorphological soil chemistry-based (two component) model developed by Crabtree (1986: 354) to the Chalk Downlands of southern England, it is clear that the acidic superficial deposits mapped as Clay-with-flints appear to be instrumental in the development of solution features on the Downland hilltops and plateaux. A localised increase in the rate of carbonation resulting from enhanced drainage, perhaps developed at a joint intersection in a specific hilltop/plateau area, would have the effect of concentrating the acidic water derived from the superficial deposits to collect in a localised area and percolate downwards to the soil/bedrock (Clay-with-flints/Chalk) interface. The increase in acidic water flowing though the Chalk in these localised areas would effectively dissolve the Chalk at these points to produce solution hollows and pipes. How quickly the solution features formed in the Chalk would depend on the many factors alluded to by Crabtree (*ibid.*). However, it is clear that the solution features which developed on the hilltops and plateaux were the product of localised vertical (as opposed to lateral) lowering of the Chalk bedrock in these specific areas.

On the slopes, the most commonly reported situation in which pipes can develop is one in which a surface soil cracks as a result of desiccation. During a rainstorm, water infiltrates rapidly down through the cracks and supersaturates a relatively permeable horizon in the subsoil. If lateral seepage is fast enough, particles may be removed and a channel may develop or, if the soil contains dispersible clays, these may lose aggregation. The movement of the water through the subsurface cracks and voids is slow until further down the slope where the water breaks through the soil surface and forms a gully (for detailed discussions see for example: Atkinson and Smith, 1974: 204; Selby, 1982: 113–4; Parsons, 1988: 114–5).

Biological effect on solution processes

The soil is constituted of organic matter, combined with insoluble residues accumulating on the surface as particles. Weathering of the soil is partly mechanical and partly a chemical process. The breaking up of the soil by frost, worm activity and by the penetration of plant roots, are mechanical processes which have the effects of greatly increasing the surface area vulnerable to chemical attack by percolating surface-water, in effect a weak acid, which dissolves basic constituents; chiefly calcium and magnesium carbonates and felspars. The acidity of the surface-water is due partly to complex humic acids formed from the decayed organic matter (including vegetable matter incorporated by worms) in the soil itself and partly to atmospheric carbon dioxide dissolved in rain-water. Where seasonal climates exist, concentrations and total outputs of solutes vary throughout the year. During the growing season, decay of soil organic matter and the production of CO_2 by plant roots increase the bicarbonate content of the soil water in contact with the mineral soil (Selby, 1982: 114). Rather than increasing the rate of weathering of the underlying rock, surface ploughing appears to have the opposite effect, as on cultivated ground the percolation of surface water to the subsoil, on which solution of the Chalk ultimately depends, is inhibited by the evaporation-surface presented by the soil (Atkinson 1957: 231).

Solution denudation rates

Solution processes are generally considered to proceed at a constant rate – a rate that varies with climate and petrography. This has encouraged the backward extrapolation of the present-day solutional erosion rates by some workers, in order to obtain ages for karst landforms. However, the known changes in climate, and hence the hydrology, during the Pleistocene, combined with the paucity of reliable estimates of modern erosion rates and their spatial and temporal variability, makes this 'a hazardous occupation' (Crabtree 1986: 409). A comprehensive list of denudation rates is provided by Goudie (1993: 218–219). The rate at which denudation occurs is commonly expressed as 'm^3 km^{-2}y^{-1}. This gives a mean value for Cretaceous Chalk of 50 (Carboniferous and Jurassic limestone are 55 and 59 respectively). Goudie (*ibid.*) is of the opinion that the available data suggests that the present rates of limestone denudation in Britain are not insignificant. He notes that the solution rate for

- the Berkshire Downs is assessed as 67 (Paterson, 1970);
- the South Downs as 55–65 (Williams and Robinson, 1983) and
- Dorset as 50 (Sperling *et al.* 1977);

The mean solutional denudation rates given for

- the tropics are 45.5 (Smith and Atkinson, 1976);
- for temperate regions 56.9 (*ibid.*);
- for arctic and alpine areas a rate of 61.8.

Goudie (*ibid.*) makes the point that there is an interesting similarity in the values given for the tropics, temperate, arctic and alpine regions to those occurring in Britain. However, the difficulty of applying generalised solution rates is demonstrated by the work of Trudgill (1986); Goudie (1993); Williams (1986) and Thomson (in Potts, Browne and Rendell, 1983).

As solution processes are considered to produce a vertical surface lowering across the Downlands of southern England, a real problem has emerged – attempts made to extrapolate the currently accepted solutional denudation rates produce a Chalk Downland landscape that is much higher and not commensurate with what we see today. Clearly, many changes have taken place to the Downlands over geological time: valleys have been incised, and then often filled in again with 'sludged in' materials; slopes have changed angle, and shape; streams have appeared and disappeared. It is generally agreed however, that the greatest topographic changes to this landscape took place before at least the Cromerian period (around 500,000 yrs. B.P.), and that the Downlands of southern England have escaped landscape modification by two of the most powerful agents of change, namely the scouring movements of ice-sheets as they pass over the land and also the removal and/or deposition of sediments (for example Till and Loess) due glacial outwash, during the various cycles of glaciation and deglaciation. As previously noted, the chalklands further north did indeed suffer in this way.

The key point here is the nature of the change.

Everything is subject to some degree of change, but it is the type and rate of change that is crucial in the development of a specific landform. The propensity for change is inherent in the nature of materials/ substances. It is clear therefore, that the propensity for change and erosion of the Chalk Downlands has been modified by the presence of the superficial deposits mapped as Clay-with-flints. What then is the propensity of the actual Clay-with-flints (both *sensu stricto* and *sensu lato*) for change and erosion? The properties which characterise these deposits produce a material that has the ability, in wet or even very wet weather, to be a highly tenacious sticky clay at the surface-level, but rapidly changing to a solid, 'concrete-like' material just below the saturated surface. In very dry weather, Clay-with-flints deposits develop cracks on the surface but still remain solid as concrete.

Cohesion of the deposits mapped as Clay-with-flints is lost on the steep slopes when erosion forces operate – the material being sludged away. But on higher plateaux and interfluves away from the slope edges, the deposit remains (in the geological sense) *in situ* (see Figure 4)

Changes that have occurred, and are occurring, to the *in situ* deposits mapped as Clay-with-flints should be seen as a succession of adjustments to both general and localised conditions: for example, climatic changes in the northern hemisphere, the direction towards which a slope faces, and the amount and type of vegetational cover. There can be, therefore, many factors operating at any one time, all of which determine just how much disturbance any specific deposits of Clay-with-flints undergo on any specific Downland hill-top. If this line of reasoning is pursued, then it follows that it is most unlikely that all the *in situ* Clay-with-flints capping will have been subjected to the same levels of disturbance, either now or in the past. The approach of previous studies to both the Chalk Downlands of southern England and the capping of deposits mapped as Clay-with-

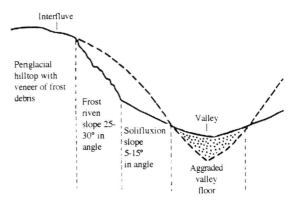

Figure 4 Development of a slope in a periglacial area. After Small (1985) with modifications.

flints has been either to look for and explain evidence of erosion and disturbance, or else to categorise and explain the origins of the deposits mapped as Clay-with-flints. However, detailed investigative work on these widespread and very variable superficial deposits has been very restricted and largely concentrated in roughly the same areas – to date, the deposits mapped as Clay-with-flints are not well understood. Unfortunately, the generalisation of this specific erosion and disturbance data has created severe distortions by emphasising the (presumed) general devastating effects of periglaciation and general erosion across all the deposits mapped as Clay-with-flints. Conversely, this research has examined the evidence that actually indicates how little change has taken place over geological time.

The superficial deposits of Clay-with-flints that survive today may do so either because the depth of the original deposit was such that it has prohibited complete removal to date or else because the deposits are held in solution features. Wind blown materials (that may have included loess or coversands) and waterlain Brickearth, that could delayed erosion by acting as a cover, may in some instances still be present. This cover has, in many cases, eroded away, leaving the underlying Clay-with-flints deposits once again exposed (evidence for the existence of such covers may be derived from soil analysis, see Subsections 6.2 and 6.3). As previously noted, both Clay-with-flints *stricto sensu* and *stricto lato* possess certain inherent properties which require explanations that are, as yet, not forthcoming. The fact that Lower and Middle Palaeolithic artefacts can still be found on and in these the Clay-with-flints capped high-levels, could also be used to support the preceding statements, as these artefacts can, to all extents and purposes, be viewed as both geological and geomorphological process markers – markers which have remained on these hill-tops and plateaux, resisting removal by one process or another over hundreds of thousands of years.

The 'Blanket effect'

Earlier in this Section, it was noted that the deposits mapped as Clay-with-flints overlying the Chalk Downlands appear to have acted as a 'blanket', protecting the underlying Chalk by reducing levels of erosion in those areas during both cold and temperate periods (Catt and Hodgson 1976: 190). One effect of this is the retention of relatively flat surfaces on top of the otherwise typically convex hills. However, the protection an area is afforded by the deposits mapped as Clay-with-flints (and the ultimate survival of the deposits on that hilltop/ plateaux) is linked to the depth of the superficial

deposits which blanket these high-level at any one time, combined with the direction towards which a slope faces. A correlation therefore, appears to exist between the depth of the superficial deposit mapped as Clay-with-flints (at any one time during very cold weather) and the subsequent depth of the frost shattering of the Chalk.

I would suggest that this protective action of the Clay-with-flints deposits implies the existence of measurable erosional features (i.e. frost shattering) of the Chalk, that might indicate, or at least give clues to, the degree of restricted change of a particular area of deposits mapped as Clay-with-flints, based on the morphology of the Chalk as it is today. These ideas will be explored next, using the most comprehensive data available on Chalk weathering and erosion in downland areas, namely the work of Dr. R.B.G. Williams, who has studied weathering and erosion of the Chalk, both in the field and the laboratory, for over twenty years.

Periglaciation and the question of integrity

Earlier in this Section it was noted that is not always easy to distinguish the effects of periglaciation from those of solution. Williams makes the point that

'The abundance of periglacial features makes it tempting to infer that the Chalk landscape was mainly fashioned under periglacial conditions, but this would be to ignore the fact that many periglacial features are little more than surface ornamentation, and are not indicative of any profound degree of land modification. The awkward truth is that it is very difficult to judge the extent to which chalk landforms are the result of periglacial processes' (*op. cit.* 1980: 225).

Much has been made of these periglacial features. So much, in fact, that it has led many Palaeolithic archaeologists to believe that the Downlands of southern England are so cryoturbated that there is nothing to be gained from studying Lower and Middle Palaeolithic artefacts from these areas, or indeed the areas themselves. This view, as this research shows, is no longer valid.

Frost shattered Chalk surface layers on the Downs

It is notable that a number of periglacial features are absent or very rare in the South Downs: for example, giant polygons and stripes, both of which cover large areas of the Chalk outcrop in eastern England (Williams, 1971). Fossil ice-wedges are unknown in the South Downs. Williams (1986: 162) states that this is not surprising, since their occurrence is rare in Chalk anywhere in Britain. No ground-ice hollows have yet been identified on the South Downs (although many well-preserved examples have been found on the Chalk outcrop in East Anglia). However, Williams (*op. cit.*) noted that,

> 'the most widespread yet paradoxically the least discussed periglacial phenomenon is the frost shattering of the surface layers of the Chalk'.

In many places the topmost 0.5 to 2.5m of the bedrock is broken into small fragments which often fit only loosely together. Wetting and drying, and recent frost, may have contributed to some of this breakage, but the bulk of the weathering is likely to be due to the original periglacial processes. Williams also adds that in some parts of the South Downs the shattered zone may be the remains of an active layer that had developed over permafrost, but that shattering must not be regarded as firm evidence of permafrost, since there may have been periods of intense frost in which the bedrock shattered without the temperatures being sufficiently low to allow the formation of permafrost. This frost shattered zone underlies approximately 80 per cent of the land surface of the South Downs (*op. cit.*).

Discussion

Throughout this Explanatory Section, a detailed examination has been made of the various theories and observations that have been put forward to explain the evolution of the Chalk Downlands in southern England, and the processes that have produced the characteristic landforms seen today. However useful as background information to this research this may be, the pertinent question is, have

these observations a practical application in this study? Can they help a field archaeologist searching for Lower and Middle Palaeolithic artefacts buried within the deposits mapped as Clay-with-flints (with or without the presence of surface-finds) quickly assess the suitability of a specific hilltop or an area for further investigations and excavation? I believe they can, and accordingly suggest that, on the Chalk Downlands, two notable features, namely 'frost shattered Chalk' and (to a lesser degree) 'asymmetric valley-side slopes', may be used to provide standard 'bench marks' against which levels of change/ erosion of the Chalk on any specific Downland hilltop or area can be measured, and hence show how much, or how little, the deposits mapped as Clay-with-flints capping have been affected.

In this context, such 'bench marks' should be applicable to all Chalk Downland areas in southern England which may require investigation. They are features which are easily recognisable and measurable, they can provide unequivocal evidence of patterns of erosion of a specific hill or area, and are compatible with both initial and later investigations. Contained in Williams' papers (1971; 1975; 1980; 1986; 1987) are a number of key observations on weathering and erosion of the Downlands that have provided a framework for the development of these 'bench marks'.

The use of the frost shattered Chalk zone as an archaeological 'bench mark'

The use of the 'frost shattered Chalk zone' as a 'bench mark', makes sense only if it is fully appreciated that the frost shattering of the Chalk surface developed *in situ*, (see Figure 5) and that unless the frost shattered Chalk zone is directly exposed to erosion,

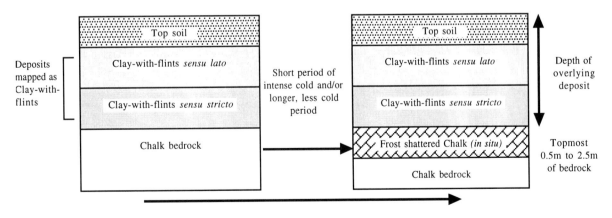

Formation and depth of *in situ* frost shattered Chalk controlled by external temperature (e.g. periglacial processes)
and levels of moisture in the deposit in relation to depth of deposit mapped as Clay-with-flints

Figure 5 Diagram showing the relationship between frost shattered Chalk and deposits mapped as Clay-with-flints.

it remains in place below the landsurface of the Chalk Downlands. Williams (1986: 161) noted that 'On very steep slopes the shattered zone is often poorly developed or even absent'. He concluded that the weathered material was removed by mass movement almost as rapidly as it could form. Clearly, on such slopes one would hardly expect to find Lower and Middle Palaeolithic artefacts *in situ*. Therefore, if Palaeolithic artefacts were found on slopes such as these, it would be reasonable to suppose that they had been 'transported down' from the top of that particular hill (indeed, the presence of such artefacts on the slopes might be indicative of material surviving *in situ* on the top of the hill).

However, where it can be established that there is a frost shattered Chalk layer *in situ* this may be taken to indicate that the specific area has undergone only limited change at least since the cold Zone 3 stage and/or the Last Glacial Maximum (around 20–18,000 yrs. B.P.), and this is a hopeful sign. Williams (*ibid*.) is of the opinion that during the Post-glacial there can have been very little change in the general form of the land surface of the South Downs because the shattered zone is so extensively preserved. Its widespread preservation as a fairly continuous layer suggests that it developed mainly towards the end

of the Devensian. However, there is no way of directly dating the shattering.

Any frost shattering of the surface layers of the Chalk, which occurred during the earlier parts of the Devensian, or indeed previous periglacial periods, would be indistinguishable from later frost shattered layers of Chalk in the uneroded high-level areas, and would subsequently have been lost from the sides of the steep Chalk slopes. The use of simple augering methods, undertaken with the greatest of care (see the important warning in Sub-section 6.6), will allow the archaeologist to locate, and to plot out areas of frost shattered Chalk across the Clay-with-flints capped hilltops. Having located and determined the extent of the shattered Chalk, and the depth of the shattered surface layer on a specific high-level, it may now become possible to extrapolate additional information relating to the levels of change on this particular hilltop/plateau over time, and processes that have effected this change (see Figure 6). It was noted earlier that the frost shattered surface layer of the Chalk is broken into small fragments which often fit only loosely together, so movement within, or of, this surface, however slight, would be expected to have an effect.

As materials (including the shattered Chalk) are

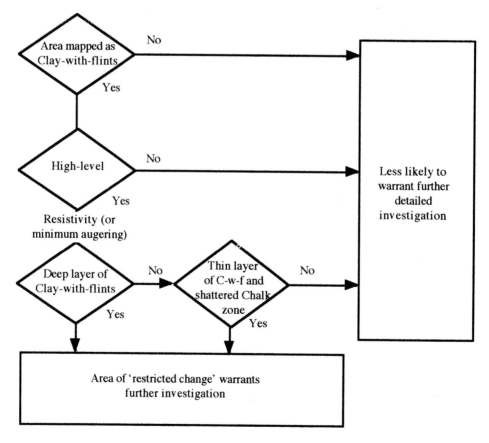

Figure 6 *A simplified decision diagram, based on frost shattered Chalk as a 'bench mark', for the use of field archaeologists looking for in situ Lower and Middle Palaeolithic artefacts in areas mapped as Clay-with-flints.*

removed downslope from the side slopes, the Clay-with-flints capped hills alter shape and size. It would be very useful to have some idea how much movement has taken place on a side slope and also of the direction of the movement, and the processes that have produced this change. These are all crucial considerations from the point of view of the archaeologist in search of *in-situ* Palaeolithic artefacts on Downland hilltops and plateaux capped with deposits mapped as Clay-with-flints, hoping that they have been relatively unaffected by surrounding hillslope processes. The formation of shattered Chalk, its distribution and depth, appears to have been governed by a number of factors, all of which assume great importance in the study of Lower and Middle Palaeolithic artefacts found in relation to the superficial deposits mapped as Clay-with-flints. Williams (1986: 161) describes these factors thus,

(a) 'The shattered surface zone is most clearly developed on relatively flat ground, where the Chalk is bare of all but soil, or has only a shallow covering of superficial deposits.'

(b) 'It is absent where there is a thick capping of Clay-with-flints'

(c) 'The depth of the shattered zone is indicative of the depth of penetration of seasonal freezing and thawing'.

Clearly then, the formation of surface layers of shattered Chalk at any particular area is controlled by the flatness of the land in that area, and the depth of the deposits mapped as Clay-with-flints covering that area. Earlier in this Explanatory Section it was shown that, where high-levels (hilltops and plateaux) are capped with deposits mapped as Clay-with-flints, plateau features are evident and that plateaux are by definition flat surfaces, and flat surfaces on top of the otherwise typically convex Chalk hills imply a modification of the processes of erosion that have produced the usual rounded landform. Accordingly, where a high-level exhibits plateau features, only restricted change is implied. The presence of a shattered Chalk surface layer *in situ*, under the superficial deposits mapped as Clay-with-flints capping a Downland hilltop, confirms that the specific hilltop has undergone only restricted change. However, if a shattered Chalk zone is not found under the deposits mapped as Clay-with-flints, on a Downland hilltop exhibiting plateau features, two possibilities exist.

(a) Following Williams (*ibid.*), that the capping of deposits mapped as Clay-with-flints were too thick to allow the formation of the shattered zone.

(b) That the absence of a shattered Chalk surface layer on a downland hilltop having plateau features, but having only a shallow covering of the deposits mapped as Clay-with-flints, suggests that the present capping is all that now remains of a far thicker cover. Any such loss of the capping material must either have occurred after the end of the Devensian and/or gradually throughout the Devensian but only at a rate that prohibited the formation of a shattered Chalk surface layer.

In situations such as this, it may be possible to assess the amount of change a particular high-level has undergone by examining the side slopes for evidence of shattered Chalk. Without evidence of a shattered Chalk zone, it may be difficult for the field archaeologist to decide (unless detailed investigations are carried out) which area/side of the hill has experienced the least amount of erosion, and to decide on the best areas to investigate/excavate. Reference to any valley side-slope asymmetry existing within the specific area may however provide additional clues to the orientation of maximum erosion.

The use of valley side-slope asymmetry to indicate the maximum erosion orientation of valley side-slope on Downlands capped with deposits mapped as Clay-with-flints

One of the most notable features of many of the dry valleys which dissect the Chalk plateaux and dip-slopes of southern England is valley side-slope asymmetry. Later in this Explanatory Section it will be shown how valley side-slope asymmetry in any particular area of Chalk Downland may provide certain information that could be of use to archaeologists searching for Palaeolithic sites. The valleys are asymmetrical in cross profile (Figure 7).

Typical asymmetric sections of these valleys (generally the middle, and lower parts) are as follows: the gentler slopes (often 7–11 degrees) are longer, and are often dissected by small, shallow tributary dells. The steeper (often 19–23 degrees) and shorter slopes tend to be relatively undissected (Goudie, 1993:184).

Studies undertaken by Ollier and Thomasson, (1957); Smart, Bisson, and Worssam, (1966); French, (1972; 1973; 1976); Williams, (1980) and Goudie, (1993), suggest that the valley side-slope asymmetry pattern of the Chalk downlands in southern England is such that the gentler slopes face north and east, and that these slopes have a tendency to be mantled completely with materials derived by solifluction from the Clay-with-flints deposits on the hilltops. In contrast, slopes facing south and west are shorter and steeper, and lack the solifucted deposits on the

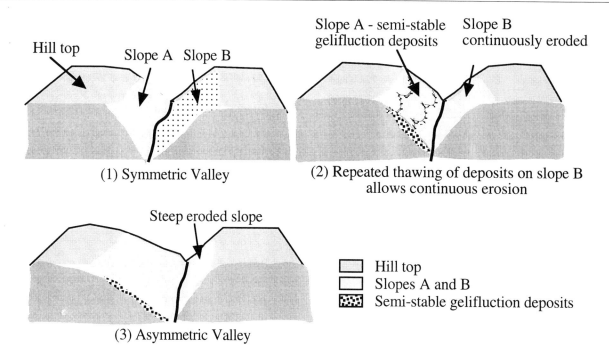

Figure 7 *Formation of asymmetric valley (3) from symmetric valley (1) by unequal periglacial erosion resulting (2) from repeated thawing of slope B valley side and removal of the gelifluction deposits by stream action. After Goudie (1993) and Catt (1986a) redrawn with modifications.*

upper parts of the slopes, although such deposits can be found on the lower part of the slopes and the valley floors. Therefore, asymmetrical valleys, in addition to their slope asymmetry, also possess an asymmetrical pattern of soils, deposits and smaller tributaries (French, 1976: 260). This asymmetry of slopes, and the accompanying asymmetry of periglacial deposits, was also noted by Goudie (1993: 184).

However, the results of further investigations by Williams (1986: 164) on the South Downs, added another dimension to what had been up to then a seemingly clear and uniform pattern of differential erosion to be found in other areas of the Downlands (for example in the Chilterns; Dorset Downs; North Wiltshire Uplands and North Downs. He discovered that the north-and west-facing slopes are invariably steeper (and shorter) than slopes facing south and east. Furthermore, the north and west-facing slopes are usually relatively bare in contrast to the south- and east-facing slopes which are often extensively covered by periglacial deposits.

During the 'bench marks' pilot study, I observed a similar pattern of differential erosion at the Case-study area of Wood Hill, Kingsdown, East Kent, to that recorded by Williams in 1986. It has been suggested that, where studies produce contradictory results, the orientation of the steeper valley side should be plotted against the latitude of its location, as it would seem that some latitudinal grouping of orientation of the steeper valley sides exists (Kennedy, 1976; Parsons, 1988: 61–2; Goudie, 1993: 183).

However, as all the studies of Chalkland valley-side slope asymmetry both in England and France are within the same latitudinal grouping, this line of investigation cannot be applied. Whether Downland valley-side slope asymmetry in southern England is in any way also associated with the tilting in opposite directions either side of the former 'Wealden dome', is a matter of conjecture.

To reiterate, valley side-slope asymmetry is a notable feature of many of the dry valleys that dissect the Chalk plateaux and dipslopes of southern England, and that these valleys are asymmetrical in cross profile. Although there is some variation in the orientation of the asymmetry between the different regions of the Downland, this does not negate the use of valley-side slope asymmetry to indicate the orientation of maximum erosion and removal of debris at any particular point. As we saw earlier, the asymmetrical section of these valleys (generally the middle and lower parts with steep and short slopes, often 19–23 degrees) lack deposits moved by solifluction on the upper parts of the slopes, although deposits can be found on the lower parts of the slopes and the valley floor. In contrast, the gentle slopes (often 7–11 degrees), are longer, and are often dissected by small, shallow tributary dells, and have a tendency to be mantled completely by materials derived by solifluction from the deposits mapped as Clay-with-flints on the hilltops. Therefore, asymmetrical valleys, in addition to the slope asymmetry, also possess an asymmetrical pattern of soil, deposits

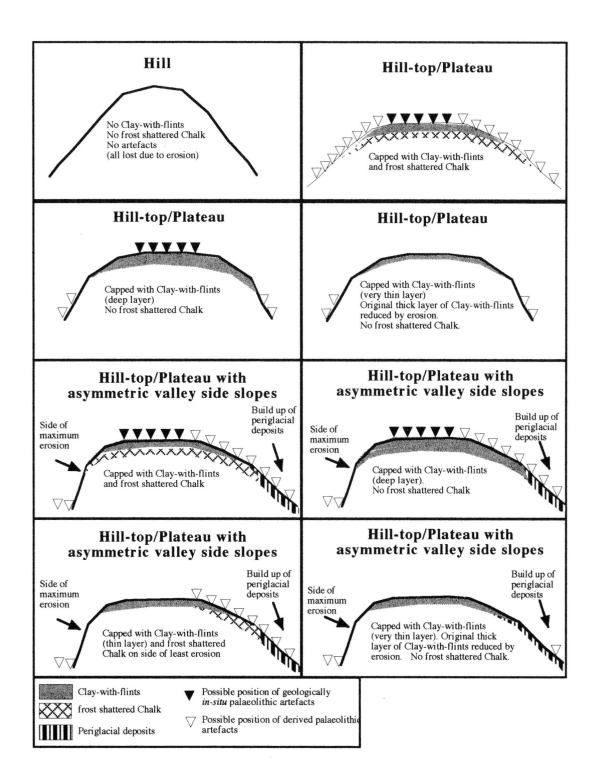

Figure 8 Simplified bench mark diagram for hilltops and plateaux, showing relationships between deposits mapped as Clay-with-flints; frost shattered Chalk; valley side-slope asymmetry and the possible position of Lower and Middle Palaeolithic artefacts.

and smaller tributaries. All of these characteristics reflect the changes in the shape of the hills over time, and the movement of material downslope on the sides of the hills.

As the superficial deposits mapped as Clay-with-flints, which cap the downlands, have undergone only restricted change since at least the late Cromerian, the orientation of maximum erosion of a hill-slope at any one point is of prime consideration to the archaeologists in the search for *in situ* Lower and Middle Palaeolithic artefacts (see Figure 8). As the plateau feature on a Clay-with-flints capped hill-top gives way at some point to a slope profile, it is very important for the archaeologist to be aware of the reason for this change, and to have some idea of the time scale involved in the development of the slope. For example, where the hill-top loses its plateau feature on the side of the hill that has the steeper slopes, it would not be unreasonable to conclude that the change from a plateau to the beginnings of a slope at this point had continued at a faster rate here than on the corresponding areas on the other side of the hill where the slope was gentle. On steep slopes, materials are quickly removed by erosional processes, thereby generating further erosion; hence the lack of deposits to be found on these steep slopes. Conversely, the slower rate of erosion on the gentle slopes facilitated the build-up of deposits on that slope. Identifying the gentle slopes mantled in materials derived from the deposits mapped as Clay-with-flints on the hill-top/plateau may, in a particular area, lead the archaeologist to evidence for a Palaeolithic presence on that hill-top if artefacts are found amongst the slope deposits.

The use of geological and geomorphological data to solve archaeological problems is not new. What is new, however, is the use of frost shattered Chalk, and valley side-slope asymmetry as 'bench marks' for use in an area where there is no existing framework for Lower and Middle Palaeolithic archaeological investigation (Figure 6). Wood Hill, the case-study site (see Section 6.), with its valley side-slope asymmetry, shattered Chalk and Lower Palaeolithic artefacts as surface and embedded finds, provided the ideal area for the 'bench marks' pilot-study.

It is to be understood that results of these initial investigations must not be regarded as providing a definitive answer, so much as a useful 'tool' which enables practical decisions to be made in the field that are based on good scientific data. Data derived from these investigations would then be incorporated in the site-archive.

The superficial deposits mapped as Clay-with-flints

In Explanatory Section 1, the relationships which appear to exist between the Chalk Downlands of southern England and the superficial deposits mapped as Clay-with-flints were examined. In this, the second Explanatory Section, the origins of the Clay-with-flints deposits and the different facies which share this nomenclature are considered, followed by examples of local variations at a range of different scales.

As was previously noted in the General Introduction and Explanatory Section 1: the superficial deposits mapped as Clay-with-flints are not well understood; few investigations of these deposits have been undertaken and many of the results are subjective. Moreover, I am not confident that the results obtained from the localised investigations that have been conducted using scientific methods are in fact, relevant to all areas mapped as Clay-with-flints, since the deposit is highly variable both within areas and between areas. Although an in-depth investigation into the actual origins of these superficial deposits is not relevant here, a general knowledge of the deposits mapped as Clay-with-flints is necessary.

The origins of Clay-with-flints

The amount of information available on the origins of Clay-with-flints is restricted, as relatively few studies on this subject have been undertaken. At the Fourth International Flint Symposium in 1983, Catt presented a paper in which he stated that petrographic studies of the finer fractions (the clay, silt and sand in a deposit) have shown that the Clay-with-flints deposits are derived mainly from a thin remnant veneer of basal Palaeogene (early Tertiary) sediments and that these superficial deposits include materials of differing composition and origin – with the flints ultimately coming from the Chalk. Also, the deposits appear to have undergone many changes during periods of contrasting climates (Figure 9)

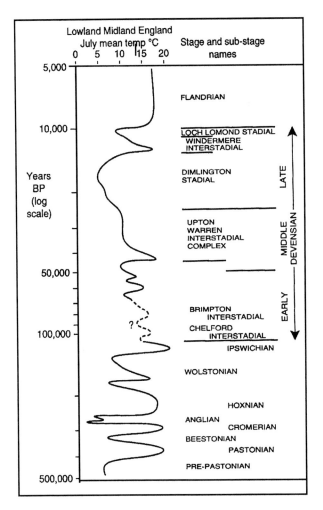

Figure 9 A summary of mean temperatures during the past 500,000 years (recent dating suggests the Hoxnian etc. occurred earlier than shown). After Ballantyne and Harris (1994) with modifications.

which can be explained in terms of the known Tertiary and Quaternary history of southern England (*op. cit.* 1986).

Although the origin of the superficial deposits mapped as Clay-with-flints is varied and uncertain, there is one feature of these deposits that is certain and unique; the northern limits of Clay-with-flints coincides approximately with the inferred southern ice margin of the Anglian and subsequent glacial maxima.

Matthews (1977) noted that small isolated patches of Clay-with-flints do occur beneath the Anglian till in East Anglia and on the chalk in Yorkshire and Lincolnshire Wolds in north-east England. Catt (1986a: 151) however, is of the opinion that glacial erosion operating during the Anglian and later cold periods almost completely removed any extensive cover that might once have existed on the northern chalklands.

To reiterate, the deposits mapped as Clay-with-Flints which cap the highest levels on the Chalk Downlands in southern England, do not seem therefore, to have been directly affected by glacial or alluvial activity during the Anglian and subsequent glacial maxima and appear to have been beyond the reach of meltwater when the ice-sheets withdrew (see Figure 9). Although the hills and the capping deposits have been subjected to processes associated with both periglacial and temperate environments, the superficial deposits mapped as Clay-with-flints, and the landsurfaces, as a whole, may be considered to have undergone no more than 'restricted change' since approximately the late Cromerian – a date of at least 500,000 yrs. B.P.

Clay-with-flints, the problem of definition and identification

As previously discussed in the General Introduction, the term Clay-with-flints has been used as a 'blanket term' by many people (including map makers) to include all the different components that make up these superficial deposits. Confusion exists over the precise terminology of Clay-with-flints/Argile à Silex and associated deposits in both English and French literature. The problem is not so much the literature, but the superficial deposits themselves, as they are neither datable by fossil evidence, nor, as they are superficial, by reference to deposits of known age. (Pepper, 1973: 331) states that

'Field mapping often shows the boundaries between Clay-with-flints and associated formations to be ill-defined, each deposit showing characteristics of the adjacent or subjacent one into which it merges' (see also Avery, 1990).

On the Chilterns, for example, Clay-with-flints encloses areas separated as Pebbly Clay and Sand. In parts of Dorset and Devon, the deposit is mapped as Clay-with-flints and cherts, whereas on the North Downs some of the interfluves (the elevated part of

the landscape that extends between two adjacent valleys, and is normally seen as lying above the steeper slopes of each valley, see figure 4) are mapped as Sand in Clay-with-flints, Head Brickearth, Disturbed Blackheath Beds or Older Gravel. Furthermore, many small and/or thin isolated areas of Clay-with-flints are often not shown on the geological maps. The origins of the deposits mapped as Clay-with-flints have been debated for over a century. The earliest reference to these superficial deposits appears to be by Prestwich (1858). As much of the available data relating to deposits mapped as Clay-with-flints is often presented in a difficult and convoluted manner, I have found it necessary to summarise the many ideas and theories in a greatly simplified form – using Catt's (1986a) paper as a basic framework. Appropriate explanations by others are added in the form of quotes.

A brief chronology of the various ideas and theories that have been postulated to explain the origins, nature and geomorphology of the superficial deposits mapped as Clay-with-flints

1. The superficial deposits in the Chalk areas of southern England were considered by the early geologist to have been formed by the chemical action of rainwater on the Chalk. These deposits were thought therefore, to have been formed by, and consisted simply of, the residue left after a long period of dissolution and weathering of the Chalk.

    However, Catt (1986a: 152) states that the 'very pure Upper Chalk, on which the Clay-with-flints rest, yields an acid-insoluble residue dominated by flint nodules with only trivial quantities of silt and sand'.

2. Whitaker (in Hull and Whitaker 1861) was the first to use the term 'Clay-with-flints' to describe a clay that was of a uniform reddish brown but which often contained black-stained clay with unworn flint nodules. This deposit was observed as forming a thin layer, which rested directly but uncomfortably on the irregular surface of the Upper Chalk of southern England. Whitaker also noted that the deposit filled solution pipes and cavities in the Chalk and that it could contain quartz pebbles and fragments of sandstone. In addition, a few inches of black flinty clay were invariably seen to occur at its base. This stiff brown and red Clay-with-flints deposit containing unworn flints, was commonly overlain by a more heterogeneous drift

deposit of loam and sandy clay. Whitaker named this superficial drift deposit 'Brick-earth', which he interpreted and describes as 'the waste' (a derivative) of Reading Beds sand and clay.

3. Codrington (1866) suggested that the thin basal layer of Clay-with-flints was formed by the clay slowly washing down from overlying hetero-geneous loamy drift deposits. The clay was then redeposited at or near the Chalk junction between the flints released by the dissolution of the Chalk.

4. Whitaker (1889) was of the opinion that 'Clay-with-flints' and 'Brick-earth' could be con-veniently mapped together as' Brick-earth bordered by Clay-with-flints'.
    –   Hodgson, Catt and Weir (1967: 85) stress that 'Many later workers attempted to distinguish the types of drift occurring in this broad mapping unit'.
    –   Catt (1986a: 152) states 'The early (Old Series) geological maps of southern England showed Whitaker's Clay-with-flints and Brickearth separately, the former usually having a narrow outcrop on the upper valley sides where it emerged from beneath the Brick-earth. However, it was later recognised that many of the deposits shown as Brickearth are also flinty and clayey, and because of the difficulties involved in separating the various deposits at the 1:630360 scale they were usually all shown as Clay-with-flints on the later New Series maps'.

5. Reid (1899) thought that the natural dissolution of the Chalk would produce a 'stony desert of angular flints'.

6. Jukes-Browne (1906) agreed with Reid (1899); however, he calculated that Clay-with-flints (in the broad sense current at that time) contained a greater proportion of clay than would be expected in a Chalk residue. He therefore supported the suggestion made by Codrington (1866) that the downwashing of the clay particles from the overlying deposit produced the under-lying thin basal layer of Clay-with-flints. Jukes-Browne was convinced that the Clay-with-flints occurs on

    'a slope which coincides approximately with the inclination of the basal plane of the Reading Beds and that, when allowance has been made for solution, downwash and landslips, the tracts of Clay-with-flints may be regarded as having formed out of so many ancient outliers of Reading Beds'.

7. White (1909) argued that the Clay-with-flints

deposits in the Basingstoke area commonly occur on erosion surfaces that truncate post-Eocene flexures [gentle folds or bends in strata: Watt, 1988] and that the deposit is a mixture of 'the least soluble constituents of the Chalk and the waste of Eocene strata'.

8. Barrow (1919), in addition to supporting Cod-rington's (1866) explanation for the origin of Clay-with-flints, recognised the important dis-tinction that Whitaker (1861) had made between 'Clay-with-flints' and 'Brick-earth'.
    –   Catt (1986a: 152) states that Barrow divided Whitaker's 'Brick-earth' into various types of brickearth ... 'one of which (the 'True Brickearth') was a silty and often almost stone free deposit filling small funnel-shaped depressions (old sinkholes or dolines) pene-trating other interfluve deposits on the Chilterns'.

9. Brajnikov (1937) suggested that the clay is reconstituted at the Chalk junction from silica and sesquioxides, either liberated by alteration of minerals in the Chalk or brought down by percolating waters from a previous cover of loam.

10. Sparks (1949) described a series of erosion surfaces on the Downlands which he called 'flats'. He attributed these 'flats' to marine and subaerial erosion.
    –   Hodgson, Rayner and Catt (1974: 122) in reference to the Sussex Downs, state that 'The presence of Clay-with-flints on the supposed marine 'flats' is incompatible with their suggested origin as remnants of a series of marine platforms. The Clay-with-flints was derived more or less *in situ* from basal Eocene beds, and there are no signs of younger marine deposits'.

11. Wooldridge and Goldring (1953: 117) assumed that 'true Clay-with-flints' is a residual product of Chalk solution.

12. Pinchemel (1954) advanced a similar explanation for the origin of Argile à Silex to that suggested by Codrington (1866) for Clay-with-flints.

13. Wooldridge and Linton (1955: 55–56) main-tained that 'true Clay-with-flints' formed from the residues produced by solution of the Chalk and that on the North Downs the 'true Clay-with-flints' is mainly associated with their sub-aerial Mio-Pliocene surface.

14. Bonte's (1958) suggestions for the origin of Argile à Silex were similar to those suggested by Pinchemel (1954).

15. Avery *et al.* (1959) recognised the importance of the distinction that Whitaker (1861) had made between 'Clay-with-flints' and 'Brick-earth'.

    – Catt (1986a: 152) observed that Clay-with-flints lines solution pipes and cavities that are filled with collapsed Brickearth deposits.

16. Loveday (1958, 1962) confirmed the distinction between 'Clay-with-flints' and 'Brick-earth' as set out by Whitaker (1861). Loveday then re-named Whitaker's 'Clay-with-flints' as Clay-with-flints *sensu stricto* and re-defined the deposit in the petrographic terms which related to its genesis (Catt, 1986a: 152). In addition, Loveday confirmed Codrington's (1866) suggestion for the mode of formation of this layer.

    – Catt (*ibid.*) states 'Mineralogical analysis of the Clay-with-flints *sensu stricto* showed that the small amounts of material coarser than clay were all derived from the Upper Chalk. Together with the unworn flint nodules, they represent the natural residue of the chalk released during the process of subsurface dissolution. However, Clay-with-flints *sensu stricto* is not simply Chalk residue, as the downwashed (illuvial) clay component exceeds this, often by a factor of 5 or more to 1. This mode of origin for Clay-with-flints *sensu stricto* is supported by field observation that the lines of the flint nodules can often be traced from the chalk into the deposit with little disturbance'.

17. Loveday (1962) also examined the petrographic features of the heterogeneous loamy deposit that Whitaker (1861) had named 'Brick-earth' and which could be found, overlying the Clay-with-flints *sensu stricto'*. This led him to re-name the 'Brick-earth' as 'Plateau Drift'. Avery (1959, 1964) and Loveday (1962) had been involved in primary soil mapping of parts of the Chiltern Hills. Avery and Loveday distinguished three main types of 'Plateau Drift'.

    – Catt (1986a: 152) writes

    'The distinction between Clay-with-flints *sensu stricto* and deposits equivalent to Loveday's Plateau Drift can usually be made on the chalk interfluves south of the Chilterns, and whenever the Plateau Drift has been examined petrographically, derivation from basal Palaeogene beds has been inferred'.

18. Sparks (1972) reaffirms Jukes-Browns (1906) ideas on the formation of the Clay-with-flints and states 'Much of the mapped Clay-with-flints is probably a mixture of Tertiary beds resorted by frost heaving or cryoturbation in periglacial conditions'.

19. Other work on the deposits mapped as Clay-with-flints by Hodgson, Catt and Weir (1967); Avery (1969, 1972); Hodgson, Rayner and Catt (1974) and Catt (1986a), amongst others, form the greater part of the more detailed discussion which now follows.

Classification of Clay-with-flints

Based on field characteristics and laboratory investigations by Avery (1958, 1964); Avery, Stephen, Brown and Yaaldon (1959); and Loveday (1958, 1962), the Clay-with-flints deposits in southern England have been classified into two groups; Clay-with-flints *sensu stricto* and Clay-with-flints *sensu lato*. Also associated with Clay-with-flints *sensu stricto* and *sensu lato* are black and green clays with flints, lining pockets in the Chalk (Pepper, 1973; 334).

Clay-with-flints sensu stricto

Loveday (1962: 86–7) describes Clay-with-flints *sensu stricto* in the Chilterns (using the Munsell Color chart) as yellow-red or red-brown ('near' 5YR 5/6), with slight pale yellow mottling and black manganiferous staining specially near the Chalk junction. A more detailed definition is provided by Pepper (1973: 332–3). A Hampshire deposit is described as heavy (65–95 per cent fine earth <0.002 mm), dominantly montmorillonitic clay, often with slickensided structural faces. Clay content may increase near the Chalk, sandy pockets occurring throughout. There are up to 50 per cent flints, broken and corroded in the upper part of the deposit, but commonly unbroken near the Chalk. Other stones may include flint pebbles, quartzites, ferruginous concretions and tabular fragments of secondary silica (chalcedony). Sand mineral contents are low, and include flint chips, quartz grains, chalcedony, manganese segregations and, near the Chalk, collophane and an alteration product of glauconite. In thin section, there is a preferred clay mineral orientation which is strong near the Chalk and is also seen on slickensided surfaces. Shear zones, evidenced for example by fracturing of preferentially oriented clay masses, are often accompanied by heavy black staining. Shrinkage cracks are abundant away from the Chalk, but rare immediately above it. The reverse is true of pores, which can have small clay lobes projecting into them. Thorez, Bullock, Catt and Weir (1971) show that clay appears to replace Chalk by infiltration into the holes left by dissolution. While field mapping on the Downs between Winchester and Basingstoke, Pepper (1973: 333) noted that below the 4-5m of Plateau Drift or 45cm of flinty loam, the Clay-with-flints *sensu stricto* exhibited a considerable variation in thickness, with around 3m recorded on level sites thinning out to approximately 1m on slopes and that the boundary with the undulating Chalk below was sharp.

Subsequently he concluded (Pepper, 1968), that Loveday's (1962: 85) restriction of the term Clay-with-flints *sensu stricto* to 'such deposits as are largely clay and flints; those containing appreciable sand, silt and stones not flints are specifically excluded', is applicable outside the Chilterns. However, he noted variations between the Clay-with-flints *sensu stricto* of level sites and of neighbouring slopes. On level sites it is not only thicker (>1.5 m.) than the slopes (30–60 cm.), but is usually redder (2.5 YR 4/7 and even 10 R 4/6 compared with 7.5 YR 5/7). It is characteristic of the most elevated Chalk surfaces and shows less evidence of mass movement than its hillside counterpart. The relative position and abundant flow structures of the latter (the slopes) suggest that it is at least slightly solifluvted plateau Clay-with-flints, though similar slopes often carry a more heterogeneous brown head deposit which does not meet the requirements of Loveday's Clay-with-flints *sensu stricto*.

Willman and Frye (1970) were able to show that red or brown Clay-with-flints *sensu stricto*, which invariably overlies Chalk and is often overlain by Plateau Drift and/or flinty loam, constitutes a well-defined rock-stratigraphic unit, (i.e. a body of sediments forming a discrete and recognisable unit of reasonable homogeneity defined solely on the basis of its lithological characteristics), and that it makes up a formation with the distinctive and relatively uniform lithological characteristics listed by Loveday (1962).

Clay-with-flints sensu lato

Field studies, (for example, Smart, Bisson and Worssam, 1966; Hodgson, Catt and Weir 1967; Pepper, 1973; Catt, 1979; Catt, 1986a) have shown that associated with Clay-with-flints *sensu stricto* may be a wide range of deposits. Some of these heterogeneous deposits are now classified as Clay-with-flints *sensu lato* but unlike Clay-with-flints *sensu stricto*, ' they do not seem clearly to constitute a rock-stratigraphic unit' (Pepper, 1973: 334). However, solifluction deposits (head) and Plateau Drift occupy well-defined positions, and these are considered by Loveday (1962) to be derived from pre-existing deposits by disturbance and recasting in the Pleistocene. Solifluction (head) deposits of valley sides are sometimes included in the category Clay-with-flints *sensu lato*; however, the deposits shown on the maps are lithologically variable. The deposits are classified as usually brown (7.5 YR 5/7), unmottled, containing angular flints, broken flints, and at lower levels, chalk fragments.

Also classified as *sensu lato* are Clay-with-flints lining Chalk pockets. These deposits are composed essentially of clay and flints and have distinctive and uniform characteristics relative to Clay-with-flints *sensu lato*. The deposits are black (5 YR 2/2) and green (5 Y 5/2) clays occurring as thin bands (normally <45 cm. in depth), always lining Chalk pockets infilled with other material. Thorez *et al.* (1971) noted that, like Clay-with-flints *sensu stricto*, they overlie Chalk and have a variable proportion of little-weathered flints, but they differ in colour, thickness and micromorphological characteristics, and so do not belong to the same rock-stratigraphic unit. Loveday's (1962) paper, 'Plateau deposits of the southern Chilterns hills' contains not only a definition of Clay-with-flints *sensu stricto*, (which, as has been shown, is now the accepted definition), but also a re-assessment of the petrographic features of the often thick and heterogeneous drift deposit that Whitaker (in Hull and Whitaker, 1861) had classed as Brickearth. Loveday (*op. cit.*), considered that this layer was in fact a different type of deposit from that which was generally considered to be 'brickearth' and so renamed it 'Plateau Drift'.

The superficial deposit Plateau Drift can also be classified as Clay-with-flints *sensu lato*. It can be found up to 8m. thick on plateau surfaces and overlying a variety of deposits including Clay-with-flints *sensu stricto*, brickearth, and Eocene sediments. Loveday (1962: 88–90) lists the characteristics of this deposit as: mottled (strong brown 7.5 YR 5/6, yellowish red 5 YR 5/6, yellowish brown 10 YR 5/6, grey 10 YR 7/1–2), heterogeneously textured, from clay through to sand or sandy clay loam (30–70 per cent fine earth is sand, 15 per cent silt, 20-60 per cent clay). The amount of stones within the deposit varies considerably; most are broken flints, but the deposit may also include nodular flints, flint and quartzite pebbles, ferruginous concretions and chalcedony. The sand minerals are mainly quartz with ferruginous concretions. Heavy mineral analysis shows a predominance of zircons, tourmaline, rutile, staurolite and kyanite. The clay fraction in these particular samples (analysis by Loveday (*ibid.*)) is dominated by kaolin and mica. (Marked important and significant differences in the clay mineral domination in other Clay-with-flints areas is discussed later in Sub-sections 6.3 and 6.4).

Loveday (1962) and Avery (1964) distinguished three main types of Plateau Drifts in the south-western Chilterns:

'(a) a reddish brown clay 2–6 m thick with a few angular flints and flint pebbles, occurring on all parts of the dipslope, but only above 200 m O.D.

(b) patches of sand and clay, often with abundant

flint pebbles and sometimes containing blocks of sarsen-stone and Hertfordshire pudding-stone, occurring mainly at heights of 150–200m O.D. (the larger of these patches are separated on geological maps as Pebbly Clay and Sand).

(b) patches of pebbly sand or clay similar to type (b) but containing many pebbles of quartz, quartzite and sandstone, occurring below 150 m O.D. but above the Harefield Terrace'.

Research conducted by Reid (1898, 1903) and, in particular, Jukes-Browne (1906), had shown that on the South Downs and parts of Salisbury Plain, the areas mapped as Clay-with-flints often surround and pass gradually into outliers of Reading Beds, which is the local basal Palaeogene formation. Clark *et al* (1967) noted that, on the Marlborough Downs in Wiltshire the sub-Palaeogene surface shows more than one facet. It is overlain by Reading Beds as far west as the Savernake Forest, but by Bagshot Beds further west. Catt (1986a) states 'in Dorset there is a similar relationship involving westward attenuation and eventual disappearance of the London Clay and Reading Beds beneath the Bagshot Beds'.

John (1980) noted that the Plateau Drift on the North Downs in Surrey resembled Woolwich and Reading Beds. In other areas of Surrey, the basal formation in the main Palaeogene outcrop is a thin representative of the Thanet Beds. On the lowest parts of the Chalk dipslope, adjacent to the main Palaeogene outcrop, a thin sandy drift, petrographic-ally similar to either the Thanet Beds or the Wool-wich and Reading Bottom Bed, covers the Chalk interfluves.

Hodgson *et al.* (1967) concluded that the Plateau Drift in Sussex was derived from Palaeogene forma-tions of mainly Woolwich and Reading Beds. Catt (1986a), who had previously worked with Hodgson (Hodgson *et al.* 1967), writes 'the derivation of Plateau Drift from almost undisturbed Palaeogene formations ... is also indicated by its distribution resembling that expected of a solid formation'. He noted that on the higher parts of the North Downs in east Surrey and north-west Kent, the clayey Plateau Drift is replaced by gravels composed of oval black-coated pebbles which closely resemble Blackheath Beds. The Blackheath Beds in this area probably overstepping both the Thanet and Woolwich forma-tions to rest directly on the chalk' (*op. cit.*: 154).

Most of the interfluves on the eastern parts of the North Downs are covered by the typical clayey Plateau Drift, but in east Kent there are patches of Sand in Clay-with-flints, and Head Brickearth. The sand patches have been linked to the Lenham Beds (Wooldridge, 1927; Smart *et al* (1966), and to the Oldhaven Beds (Whitaker, 1872). Catt, (1986a: 154) suggests that

'until the Sand in Clay-with-flints patches are re-examined petrographically we should not ignore the possibility that they are another example of chalk plateau deposits derived from Palaeogene formations'.

Localised variations in the superficial deposits

It can be clearly seen, from the examples already given, that areas mapped as Clay-with-flints are highly variable, and that this variability exists both between large areas and within very small areas. The specific variations, which may include irregular lateral and vertical changes of colour, texture, and stone content, are often so localised that the details do not appear on even the largest-scale published maps, although these variations have been observed by a number of workers, for example, Smart, Bisson and Worssam (1966) working in Kent, and Hodgson, Catt and Weir (1967) conducting investigations in Sussex. Willis (1947: 253) who worked in North Hampshire, wrote:

'The special geological feature to which attention is called is the superficial drift known as Clay-with-flints, a variable and often puzzling forma-tion. At Brickfield Copse, Ellisfield, it consists of a red-blue mottled clay, indistinguishable from that of Sherborne St.John Brickfield in the Reading Beds, while at Preston Candover it includes shingle and pebbles resembling the bottom bed of this formation.'

Considerable variation in the deposits mapped as Clay-with-flints was also observed by Catt (1986a: 151) in the Chilterns. He records that reddish brown clay or sandy clay, with red and grey mottles in the upper layer and only occasional subangular flint fragments and flint pebbles, is the most common. However, the deposits can also range from heavy reddish brown clays with large unworn flint nodules to almost stoneless yellow or white sands, yellowish to reddish brown silt loams and silty clay loams, brightly mottled (red, lilac, green and white) stone-less clays, and beds of rounded flint pebbles.

Soil classifications

The Soil Survey of England and Wales described soils developed in Clay-with-flints as paleo-argillic. 'Soil' is used here as a general term and does not only apply to the near-surface layers in which plants root (Avery 1980, 1990). These soils are now included in the Luvic Brown Soils classification, (along with other similar sub-groups, see Avery 1990: 211), and are characterised by chromic argillic B horizons (Avery, 1980, 1985, 1990: 109). 'Soil horizons' are layers of soil that are roughly parallel to the surface within a soil profile; the 'soil profile' is a vertical section through the soil at any one place. Soils with B horizons composed mainly or entirely of Loveday's Clay-with-flints *sensu stricto* are mapped as Winchester series (Clayden and Hollis, 1984). They occur mainly at plateau margins, on the upper parts of scarps, and valley slopes. These soils show evidence of interglacial development having characteristic B horizons with strong brown to red colour or red-mottled, at least in the lower part (*ibid.*). The predominately red hues are the result of rubefication, (a process in which haematite is produced in a warm and seasonally humid environment) and significant illuvial clay enrichment and stress reorganisation of clay components (Catt, 1986a: 154; Avery, 1990: 211). Stagnogleyic chromoluvic brown soils, mainly Batcombe series, (there are other soil groups associated with Clay-with-flints e.g. Carsten series) are extensive on Clay-with-flints and deeply weathered plateau deposits (Plateau Drift) (Avery, 1990: 228). These soils have complex microfabrics. Following the work of Bullock and Murphy (1979) and Chartres (1980), Catt, (1986a: 155) stated that these soils

> 'show the complex microfabrics typical of soils dating from these earlier stages' [the stages referred to by Catt are the Hoxnian and Cromerian interglacials], ... 'but more complex microfabrics have not yet been found in these or any other soils in England. This suggests that most of the chalk interfluves have been stable land surfaces only since approximately the Cromerian'.

These ancient Clay-with-flints paleo-argillic and stagnogleyic chromoluvic B horizons, with their very red (strong brown to red or mottled), illuvial clay enrichment and reorganised clay components, which cap the Chalk downland hilltops, are quite different to the younger soil horizons in the Devensian and Holocene deposits and older sediments that have developed on the slopes of the same hills. The soils on sloping sites, subject to Devensian periglacial erosion, have B horizons which contain only small amounts (<8% by volume) of illuvial clay and show little evidence of reorganisation by freeze-thaw action. Typically they posses brown colours, no redder than hue 7.7YR of the Munsell Color chart, and moist values and chromas <4 (Catt, 1979, 1986a: 154).

Attempts have been made by several workers to attribute soil colours to various processes occurring over a specific time period. Kemp (1990: 70) reviewing the work of Bullock and Murphy (*op. cit*) and Chartres (*op. cit.*) notes that Bullock and Murphy (*op. cit.*) reconstructed the developmental history of a soil containing a paleo-argillic horizon at North Leigh, Oxfordshire, and attributed a number of features and soil colours to various 'processes occurring over a time period encompassing at least one glacial and two interglacials prior to the Devensian'. Kemp (*ibid.*) also records that Chartres (*op. cit.*) contrasted the soils on four chronologically-separate terraces of the Kennet River and found that he was able to identify and date relatively in accordance with their superpositions, three types of clay concentration features. On the upper two levels of the terrace, the palaeo-argillic soils contained all three types with the disrupted red coatings predating egg yellow coating, which were themselves fragmented and older than the undisturbed (presumed) Flandrian reddish orange to yellowish brown clay coatings, whereas the soil on the third terrace level contained only egg yellow and reddish orange/yellowish brown clay concentration features. On the lowest terrace only orange/yellowish brown clay concentration features were present.

Using the extremely limited dating evidence and employing a 'counting back' technique, Chartres tentatively assigned ages to each terrace formation and pedogenic phase. As Kemp noted, this work remains one of the few attempts to relate particular pedological features to specific Quaternary stages, in this case, the localised correlation of egg yellow and red clay coatings to Ipswichian and Hoxnian pedogenesis respectively. However, he adds a warning that as no studies have been made to confirm the general applicability of this work, it is hardly tenable to apply this feature/age correlation data to date other soils of unknown age and that as further stages are introduced into the British Quaternary system, any such correlations based on a 'counting back' technique will need to be reassessed (*ibid.*).

That situation has now arisen. The colour/s exhibited by a deposit, in any one area, is/are a record of its past environmental history – the microclimate of that specific area. The value of the 'counting-back' technique would, therefore, appear to lie in its use as a 'marker' of specific localised environmental change, rather than attempts to use it generally as a means of dating sediments.

Conclusion

The superficial deposits mapped as Clay-with-flints cap the highest hills on the Chalk Downlands of southern England. Detailed studies of these complex deposits, of which examples have been given above, indicate that they consist partly of Chalk solution residues, chiefly flint, and partly illuviated clay derived from remains of Tertiary beds or other formerly overlying materials. During the middle and late

Pleistocene, deposits mapped as Clay-with-flints were subject to processes associated with both peri-glacial, and temperate environments. Although these deposits have been studied to a greater or lesser degree since the 19th century, they have been largely ignored in recent decades. Catt (1986a: 158) states that,

> 'this attitude undoubtedly stems from the com-plex, disturbed stratigraphy and lack of fossil-iferous deposits, but also reflects a failure to understand how long-established land surfaces can provide palaeoenvironmental information unavailable elsewhere'.

This failure to acknowledge the significance of the deposits mapped as Clay-with-flints has, in effect, distorted the British Lower and Middle Palaeolithic archaeological record, since a close relationship exists between the presence of the deposits mapped as Clay-with-flints and the occurrence of Lower and Middle Palaeolithic artefacts on the higher plateaux and interfluve surfaces of the Chalk Downlands in southern England. All the research to date has suggested that the areas mapped as Clay-with-flints have undergone only 'restricted change' since approximately the late Cromerian, a date of at least 500,000 years B.P. and are therefore, capable of adding an important dimension to the British Lower and Middle Palaeolithic archaeological record (Catt, 1986a; Scott-Jackson, 1991a, 1991b, 1994, 1996, 1999). This will be discussed in the following Section.

Lower and Middle Palaeolithic artefacts found in relation to deposits mapped as Clay-with-flints

For many years I have been compiling a comprehensive Gazetteer of Lower and Middle Palaeolithic artefacts found in relation to the deposits mapped as Clay-with-flints in the twelve Chalk Downland counties of southern England: Bedfordshire; Berkshire; Buckinghamshire; Devon; Dorset; Hampshire; Hertfordshire; Kent; Oxfordshire (south of Goring Gap); Surrey; Sussex and Wiltshire (Scott-Jackson, 1998). This substantial body of data includes both archaeological and geological details of over 2,000 find-spots/sites of Lower and Middle Palaeolithic artefacts that have been recovered as surface-finds from hilltops and plateaux in areas mapped as Clay-with-flints. The overall picture suggested by the actual figure listed for any area should be viewed with some caution, as the number of artefacts recovered in any particular area may reflect the activities of nineteenth and twentieth century workers and Palaeolithic artefact collectors, rather than the actual occupation patterns of that area by Lower and Middle Palaeolithic peoples.

Occasionally, the collectors of such artefacts were/are experienced and knowledgeable amateurs who concentrated their efforts on particular areas, with detailed reports of their finds being published appropriately. Often, however, artefacts have been picked up as 'casual finds' by individuals while walking or working in fields and gardens. Occasionally, detailed reports of these finds can be found in Museums or County Archaeological Sites and Monuments Records offices for that area, but more often than not, the information available on these Lower and Middle Palaeolithic artefacts is minimal. Without a doubt, many such casual finds remain completely unrecorded.

My initial data collection covered all finds in Downland areas, not just those specified as coming from the deposits mapped as Clay-with-flints. This is important, for as we have seen in the General Introduction and the Explanatory Sections, the deposits exhibit great variation both within and between areas and small and/or thin areas of Clay-with-flints are often not recorded on the geological maps. Also, original descriptions given for the find-spots can be misleading. Furthermore, there may be relationships between finds on the Clay-with-flints capped high-levels, the surrounding Chalk slopes, and the valley bottoms (which themselves may contain a number of different deposits). Subsequent analysis of the original mass of data has relegated many of the find-spots to a state of secondary importance, but they remain on the database pending further investigation.

Data distortions identified

While collecting data for the Gazetteer, I have become acutely aware of the problems that distorted information can create, although positive identification of the source of the distortion may go some way towards reducing its effects. Mistakes in written reports are to be expected but there are other forms of data distortion which are less obvious. These are as follows:

(a) In certain counties, there has been an apparent reduction in the numbers of Lower and Middle Palaeolithic artefacts found (reported) in recent years coming from Downland areas. It is possible that this reflects the increased levels in mechanisation of farming methods over the past thirty years. The farm worker today has little contact with the fields. Tractors move too fast and cabs are too high for the drivers to see flints in any detail. Ploughing may even be carried out at night. The modern practice of deep ploughing turns over the earth in such a way that the deep levels of soil are brought to the surface while the top layers are buried. This method, although possibly exposing more artefacts for collection, also produces shattered flints through the action of the plough and increases the exposure of the flints to freeze-thaw activity. It is possible, therefore, that artefacts are rapidly being destroyed or identification made more difficult, in ways which did not previously apply.

(b) The existence of small woodlands, particularly on hill-tops, areas turned to grass, unploughed fields, changes in farming practice (as for example E.C. 'set aside' regulations), and the selling off of uneconomical land to private owners for paddocks etc., all restrict the opportunities for direct investigation of these areas. This will affect the artefact distribution analysis, producing a distorting effect on find-spots, sites, and the relationships between them.

(c) The effects of a single band of Palaeolithic people visiting an area over many seasons may be archaeologically indistinguishable now from that of many groups visiting the same area intermittently over perhaps hundreds or even thousands of years, if it is the case that they all employed a generally similar technology. This contraction of time is a factor that acquires immense significance when any analysis is attempted of possible relationships between Lower and Middle Palaeolithic artefacts, find-spots and sites in southern England.

Considering the great number of surface-finds from the high-levels in areas mapped as Clay-with-flints, it is perhaps surprising that, during the past 100 years or so, so few palaeoliths have recorded as being 'recovered from under the top-soil' i.e. 'embedded' within the underlying deposits mapped as Clay-with-flints when, for one reason or another, the top-soil was removed. Embedded finds are particularly important as they may represent *in situ* sites. A simple explanation for this may be that in the past where the land is in agricultural use, holes are only rarely dug deep enough to penetrate below the ploughed soil and, if that is the case, any artefacts embedded within the underlying deposit will not be found. By contrast, where deep holes have been dug in the course of extraction or construction work in these areas, the results have been notable, for example where the demand for brickmaking material ('Brick-earth') in the latter part of the last century led to the digging of many small but deep pits in the Dunstable and Luton area on the Hertfordshire/ Bedfordshire borders. These excavations revealed very important *in situ* Lower Palaeolithic high-level sites (W.G. Smith, 1894). Occasional finds in the Brickearth have continued to be made in more recent times, though they have always been scarce (see also Sampson 1978; Wymer 1980).

The problems involved in identifying embedded finds/sites are many and varied as shown by the following example. To date, I have recorded 98 entries for the County of Hampshire (see Scott-Jackson, 1991a, 1999); large areas of Hampshire are mapped as Clay-with-flints – yet the only well documented report of embedded Lower or Middle Palaeolithic artefacts in these deposits, are two flakes which were recovered from a hole dug for a pylon (no. 60913) stay by the local Electricity company near the village of Brown Candover (find date unrecorded; Basingstoke Willis Museum record No. 104, 6/4/1973). In an attempt to discover more about these artefacts, the only recorded embedded finds in Hampshire, I contacted the local Electricity company who then sent me a map of the area which purported to show the position of pylon 60913 – but the grid reference given on the map is at variance with the supposed position of this pylon. More fieldwork is required to determine the exact position of the pylon stay in relation to the geology of the immediate area.

There are, in addition to those already stated, several other factors that may help to account for so few artefacts being reported as coming 'from below the top-soil'. It could be that Lower and Middle Palaeolithic artefacts brought to the surface by deep ploughing (which cuts right down through the top-soil and into the underlying deposit) may be listed only as surface-finds, the ploughing depth being omitted from the records, or that artefacts brought to the surface by modern methods of deep ploughing may have been so damaged that identifying them for what they are has become very difficult.

In the areas mapped as Clay-with-flints, much less commercial construction work appears to take place on these high-level areas than in the valleys. Where road building or developments have cut through Downland areas mapped as Clay-with-flints, the artefacts recovered from these areas are usually listed as surface-finds. Many of these finds have been collected during archaeological rescue programmes which have entailed field-walking of the proposed route of the road or area of development before construction work started. For example, in October, 1992 three handaxes and a flake were found by P. Harding in an area mapped as Clay-with-flints, during fieldwalking along the route of A36 Salisbury bypass at Stapleford, Wiltshire (Southern Rivers Palaeolithic Project Report No. 1 1991–1992). Once the construction work has started, any flint artefacts embedded within the underlying deposits would almost certainly be displaced and damaged. Much time, money, manpower and access to the site during the construction work would be needed to monitor properly the removal of the top-soil and the underlying deposits. However, the value of monitoring is well illustrated by the following example. During the construction of the Eastern by-pass around Dover, excavations for the southern drainage gully cut through an area mapped as Clay-with-flint at Guston. Two fine, sharp and unabraded handaxes were found (at TR322444) in the excavated soil. The condition of these artefacts suggests that they had remained more or less *in situ* until earth moving for the road began in 1975 (Kent Archaeological Review, 1977, No. 48; G. Halliwell pers. comms.). To date, the only certain examples of embedded find-sites that I am aware of (with the proviso of the Guston, Kent and Brown Candover, Hampshire finds) are those:

– On the borders of Bedfordshire/Hertfordshire near Dunstable and Luton at Caddington, Whipsnade, Gaddesden Row, Slip End, Round Green and Mixieshill (Mixies Hill) and Ramridge End. These sites were discovered by Worthington G, Smith over many years from around the middle of the 19th century (Smith, 1894; 1916);

– At Lower Kingswood, in the Banstead and Walton Heaths area of Surrey – a find-site discovered and first described by L.W. Carpenter (1966);

– At Folkington Hill (also referred to variously as 'above Wannock' or 'Folkington') Sussex, the artefacts were recovered and first described by A.E. Todd (1932–34; 1935);

– At Hackpen Hill, Wiltshire, where this hilltop site was excavated by the Reverend H. G O. Kendall (1916);

– At Wood Hill, Kent, excavated by Parfitt and Halliwell in 1984/85 and by the author in 1993 and 1994. As this site is the subject of the 'Case-study' it is discussed separately in Sections 5 and 6.

The high-level sites discovered by Smith in the Dunstable/Luton and the discoveries at Lower Kingswood, Folkington Hill and Hackpen Hill are described and discussed in the following Section.

The Lower and Middle Palaeolithic 'embedded' find-sites in deposits mapped as Clay-with-flints

A number of the embedded sites are well documented and a few have been the subject of re-excavations in recent years, for example: the Cottage sites at Caddington; Bleak Hall at Whipsnade; Gaddesden Row and the Banstead/Walton Heaths area which includes the Lower Kingswood site. The artefacts recovered from these few recorded embedded sites are usually described in detail and well illustrated. This is important as in several instances I have found that the actual artefacts have been lost, mislaid or are extremely difficult to trace. Even in cases where the artefacts are well recorded, information about the site is often less comprehensive than information about the artefacts found there (e.g. Hackpen Hill in Wiltshire). Other embedded sites however, are less well documented and/or the data that exists is more contentious (e.g. Mixieshill pit, Bedfordshire and Folkington Hill, Sussex). The high-level sites and associated embedded artefacts discovered by Smith in the Dunstable and Luton area and the discoveries at Lower Kingswood, Folkington Hill and Hackpen Hill are now considered.

The Lower Palaeolithic sites near Dunstable and Luton

During the latter part of 19th century and early 20th century several very important Lower Palaeolithic *in situ* high-level sites were discovered by Worthington G. Smith (1835–1917) in the vicinity of Dunstable and Luton (see Figure 10). In his book 'Man, the Primeval Savage' Smith states:

> 'Very few antiquaries or geologists would expect to find traces of primeval man at Caddington, or on the other hill-tops east and west of Dunstable. The geology of the hill district is chiefly represented by the Upper Chalk, nearly 400 feet in surface altitude. The chalk at Kensworth Hill is 500 feet above the Greensand on the south-east of Leighton Buzzard, five miles across the valley to

the north-west of Kensworth. In special places, Chalk-with-flints and red Clay-with-flints occur *in situ* at the surface, together with deposits of large extent of brick-earth mixed with Tertiary remains and red clay. In some positions, vast numbers of Tertiary pebbles occur which have been washed into the brick-earth from an old land surface' (*op. cit.* 1894: 67).

These Lower Palaeolithic sites were found in pockets of Brickearth within the deposits mapped as Clay-with-flints which overlie the Chalk hills at the north-east end of The Chilterns (in Explanatory Section 2 it was noted that the areas mapped as Clay-with-flints regularly include various fine-grained deposits, which are described as brickearths). Over a twenty year period Smith (1894), monitored the work of the local labourers as they dug many pits around Dunstable and Luton in order to obtain material for brickmaking (i.e. brick-earth). He records that as they dug out the 'brickearth', the workmen often uncovered sharp edged Lower Palaeolithic artefacts and in some cases animal bones, at specific levels within the deposit. Smith referred to these levels as 'Palaeolithic floors'. At several sites, he noted that the Palaeolithic floors had lain virtually undisturbed since the day when the Lower Palaeolithic peoples had manufactured their stone tools on that very spot, a view that was substantiated by the presence of conjoinable flakes from knapping waste at these sites. He was also of the opinion that these Palaeolithic sites, whether as working-sites or home-bases, were associated with the edges of ponds or lakes which he envisaged (but with little evidence) existing in Palaeolithic times on the top of the Chalk plateau with its capping of the deposits mapped as Clay-with-flints. For comparison, he noted the presence of modern ponds (both natural and artificial) on the hilltops at Caddington, Kensworth, and Whipsnade.

The plateau is divided by deep valleys into roughly rectangular blocks as the tributaries of the Thames cut back north-westwards. The Chalk, with

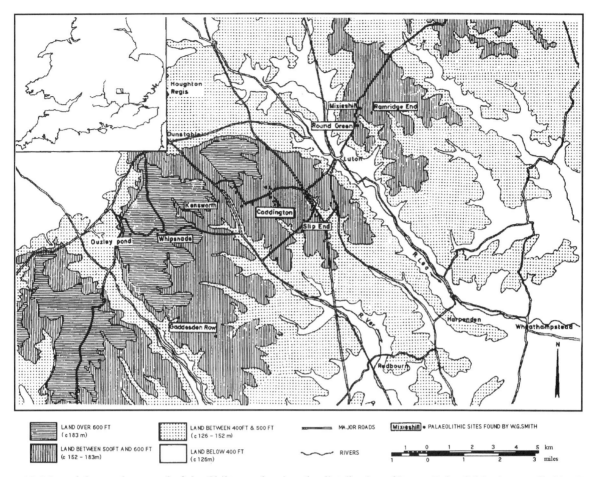

Figure 10 *Map of the northeast end of the Chilterns showing the distribution of Lower Palaeolithic sites studied by W. G. Smith. Inset indicates the locality of the area at the source of the river Lea valley in the northern Thames basin of England.*
After Sampson (1978)

its overlying deposits mapped as Clay-with-flints, dips gently south-eastwards towards the synclinal axis of the London Basin. As a result, a steep scarp slope has been formed facing north-westwards and rising to over 250m O.D. (Figure 11). From the scarp crest, the highest parts of the dip slope plateau lose height fairly rapidly (in a south-easterly direction), falling to about 210m O.D. over a distance of around 2 km. The slope then declines more gently to around 130m O.D. over the next 14 to 18 km.

By careful observation over many years, Smith was able to make a unique record of a total of 14 Palaeolithic find-sites (not all high-level sites) around Dunstable and Luton. However, it seems that many of the records and notes written by him concerning these sites have during the past 100 years been lost or destroyed. This is particularly unfortunate, as there are a number of observations and statements made by Worthington Smith that have been questioned by others. In some cases, their subsequent interpretations of his reports may possibly be their own misinterpretations of the original statements made by him.

On the basis of the information that has survived, the Lower Palaeolithic sites discovered by Smith and relevant to this research are (Figure 10):

– Caddington, Bedfordshire, west of Luton (TL 065176) – The Cottages Site, which includes the sites known as Pit B, Pit C and Pit 3.
– Whipsnade, Bedfordshire, approximately two and a half miles south-west of Caddington Church – were the sites of: Bleak Hall (TL 03351760); Mount Pleasant (TL022199) and Whipsnade Heath (TL018180).
– Gaddesden Row, Hertfordshire, approximately 5 miles in a southerly direction from Caddington – was Butterfield's Brick Yard at Gaddesden Row (TL038133).
– Slip End, Bedfordshire, (TL082188) is one and a half miles south-east of Caddington, and one and three quarters miles south of Luton.
– Round Green, Bedfordshire (TL101227), now a suburb of Luton. Two and a half miles in a south-westerly direction, across the valley is the village of Caddington.
– Mixieshill (also recorded as Mixies Hill) pit,

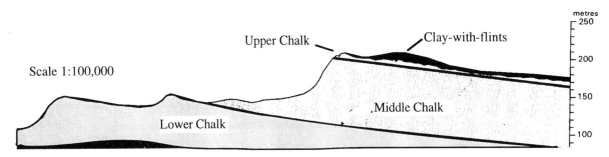

Figure 11 *Generalised vertical section of north-east end of the Chilterns near Dunstable and Luton.*
IPR/22-16 British Geological Survey. © NERC. All rights reserved.

Bedfordshire (TL101229 general), now a suburb of Luton, was a quarter of a mile north of Round Green.

- Ramridge End, Bedfordshire (TL101229 general), now a suburb of Luton, was a quarter of a mile east of Mixies hill pit.

The sites from Round Green to Whipsnade lie approximately on a straight line 5 miles long. Gaddesden Row is nearly 3 miles south of Whipsnade and 7 miles south-west of Round Green. (see Figure 10).

These high-level Lower Palaeolithic sites are now briefly considered: (For a comprehensive review of all Worthington G. Smith's fourteen sites in the vicinity of Dunstable and Luton and the many artefacts recovered from them, the reader is directed to the works of W.G. Smith (1894, 1916); Dyer (1978); Sampson (1978); Roe (1981: 184, 187–8,191–8) and White (1997).

Caddington – Bedfordshire, west of Luton (TL065176) – The Cottages Site, which includes the sites known as Pit B, Pit C and Pit 3

Caddington is situated on top of the plateau, three miles south-east of Dunstable at a height of 580 ft. O.D. To the north-east is the river Lea and to the south-west the Ver valley (Figure 10). As so many of Worthington G. Smith's original reports have been lost, it is now true to say that, of all the sites discovered by him, the best documented is the Cottages Site at Caddington.

Much of what is known about this site has come from his book 'Man, the Primeval Savage' (Smith, 1894). During 1888, Smith located at least seven pits being worked in the Caddington area, these he labelled A to G ('two were probably gravel pits, the rest provided brickearth' Dyer 1978: 162). The first *in situ* artefact to be found by Smith was in pit A. The site has since become known as 'The Cottages Site', and includes Pit B, Pit C and Pit 3 (for plans, site details and stratigraphy, see Sampson 1978).

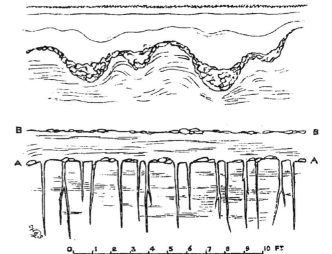

Figure 12 *Section through Palaeolithic land surface showing ancient sun cracks. After Smith, W.G. (1894)*

Excavations at Pit C in the summer of 1890 revealed, 'a remarkable section of a Palaeolithic landsurface' (Smith, 1894: 79). Smith records that the old land surface (shown at A in (Figure 12) 'was seen to have been once full of narrow fissures, ·made perhaps by the sun during a hot summer' (*ibid.*).

Lying on this ancient surface, virtually unmoved since their abandonment by their Lower Palaeolithic manufacturers, were artefacts of all descriptions, together with piles of flint nodules which had been collected to provide the raw material for the implements, and knapping debris (Figure 13). This assemblage included: beautifully made and perfect tools; unfinished, discarded and broken artefacts; waste flakes; cores; hammerstones and punches. (*op. cit.* 114).

The Caddington assemblages were described by Roe as 'an Acheulian industry of Levallois facies' (*op. cit.* 1981: 191). The presence of Levalloisian cores and flakes in the Caddington material was unknown until 1962, when Roe examined the finds. He noted that there were more Levalloisian cores and flakes than there were handaxes and suggested that there were true Levallois flakes present, which he assumed belonged with the handaxes (1995 pers. comms.), although Sampson (1978) seemed subsequently to regard any Levallois as a separate occurrence at the same site. Artefacts are not categorised as 'Levalloisian' in Smith's papers, as he was writing before the term came into use. However, when describing artefacts recovered from a test pit at another of Smith's sites, at Gaddesden Row, Wymer states,

> 'It is unlikely they are faceted as a result of intentional Levallois technique but, as emphasised by Sampson [ibid] in his study of the Caddington material, this was caused inevitably in the later stages of hand-axe manufacture' (*op. cit.* 1980: 2–3).

The artefacts and materials so far described are perhaps the finds one would expect at a Lower Palaeolithic site where the human activities included the manufacture of stone tools. However, an unexpected but common occurrence on this site were very large blocks of flint that had been partially flaked. Smith noted that: some of these blocks weighed ten, twenty or even thirty pounds; that they were often so massive and heavy, that they could not conveniently be taken away by hand and that certain of the larger blocks had been artificially quartered or crushed in Palaeolithic times (*op. cit.* 1894: 114).

The range of materials and the type of artefacts recovered from Pit C indicates a working-site, that is a site where stone tools were manufactured, rather than a living or butchery site. Both pointed and ovate implements were found on the Palaeolithic floor in Pit C and, although some large implements were found, most of the examples were small in size. They do however, vary in thickness, as some were thick and others thin. The importance of this site was further enhanced, and its general nature confirmed, by the ability of Smith to conjoin many groups of flakes or to refit flakes to finished or unfinished implements. The implements found on this Palaeolithic floor (the old land surface) varied considerably in colour

> 'from whitish-grey to dark grey, grey indigo or indigo-blackish. Sometimes they are milk-white, more or less lined blotted or clouded with pale or dark indigo. Others somewhat resemble tortoiseshell in colour, light or dark, a few are semi-transparent. Nearly all the examples are lustrous. A few are lustreless and light or dark grey in colour' (*op. cit.* 1894: 113).

Following the deposition of the artefacts and the blocks of flint on the old land surface (the Palaeolithic floor) and while the fissures in this land surface were still open, 18 inches of watery brick-earth, perhaps brought down by a heavy storm of rain, filled the fissures, covered up the old land surface, and formed the new surface where shown at Figure 13. B, B. (*op. cit.* 1894: 79).

On this second 'floor' in Pit C, Smith reports

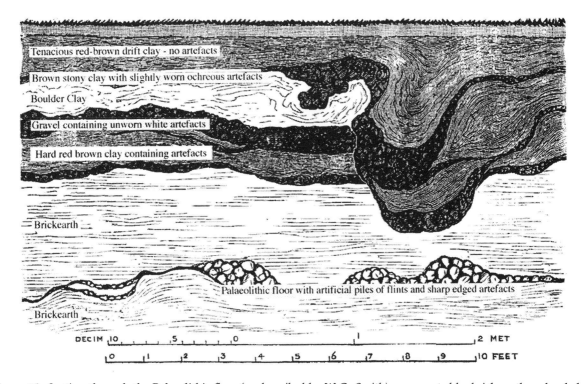

Figure 13 Section through the Palaeolithic floor (as described by W.G. Smith) surmounted by brick-earth and red clay drift in brickfield C, facing south. After Smith, W.G. (1894) with modifications.

finding white or whitish patinated slightly lustrous
artefacts which seldom varied in colour unlike the
artefacts which came from the Palaeolithic floor
below (*op. cit.* 1894: 109). Although the two floors
were separated by a layer of brickearth, Smith
thought that they may have actually formed one
layer as he writes,

> 'The two strata probably coalesce and form one
> stratum at no distance from the excavations made
> by me'. (*op. cit.* 1894: 112).

Palaeolithic artefacts were not only confined to
the two 'floors' in Pit C. However, the artefacts
recovered from the upper levels in all the Caddington pits differed substantially both in colour and
morphology. The colour range included 'yellow,
rusty-brown, deep chocolate-brown, reddish-brown
beautifully speckled and spotted with yellow, or
speckled and streaked whitish, a few are creamy or
ochreous-whitish' (*op. cit.* 1894: 96). The condition of
these artefacts also varied from those found at the
lower 'floor' levels of Pit C. All exhibited varying
degrees of abrasion. More artefacts were recovered
from Pit C than from the other Caddington pits.

A General Discussion of 'The Cottages Site' at Caddington

Smith held the opinion that all the artefacts at
Caddington could be of an identical age and that the
difference in the colour of the patination was due to
the matrix in which the artefacts had been embedded. It would be easy to assume that the ochreous
artefacts found in the top drift layers have little
association with the artefacts found on the Palaeolithic 'floors' low down in the sequences (below the
drift layers). However, this may be shown not to be
so if due regard is paid to both the use of the
landscape as a whole by the Palaeolithic people
themselves and the geomorphological processes that
have operated in the area (see Figure 14).

The 'Brickearth' deposit found in the brick-earth
pits around Dunstable and Luton was a mix of
materials, derived from the Plateau Drift and loess
which capped the hill-tops, that had 'washed-down'
and collected in the solution hollows (Catt, Hubbard
and Sampson, 1978). All the available evidence
suggests that the highest hill-tops and (situated at a
slightly lower level) the depressions and hollows in
the ground that were partially filled with brickearth,
provided ideal areas for Palaeolithic people to work
or camp (see Figure 14.1). At various times brickearth was washed down from the higher levels,
covering and sealing in the Palaeolithic floors in the
hollows (Figure 14.2).

Contemporary or later Palaeolithic people could

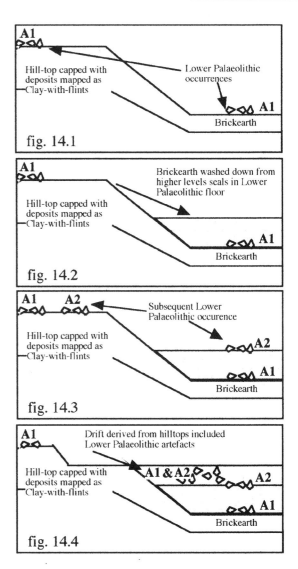

*Figure 14.1–4 Simplified diagram showing possible
relationships between the distribution of Lower Palaeolithic
sites and subsequent landscape development in the
Caddington area.*

also work or camp on the higher levels and also in
the partially filled hollows, if and when they were
dry (Figure 14.4 A2). This layering of Palaeolithic
floors and brickearth could occur more than once.
Eventually, the brick-earth in the solution hollows
was itself overlain by a different deposit, which once
again came from the hill-tops (Figure 14.4). This
deposit, known as 'drift' (or contorted drift when it
had been affected by cryoturbation) was derived
from the Plateau Drift, loess and Clay-with-flints.
Artefacts washed down in the contorted drift from a
previously higher landsurface (A1 and A2) could,
therefore, be found above artefacts (A1 and A2) from
the old Palaeolithic 'floors' (land surface) that existed
in the solution hollow (brickearth pit).

When reporting his observations, and interpreting these observations, Smith makes many references to an association (as he perceived it) between the 'Palaeolithic floors', as he found them in the various brickearth pits, and the presence of water sources in the form of lakes, ponds or rivers in this area during the Palaeolithic (*op. cit.* 1894; 1916). Controversy surrounds a number of his interpretations (see for example, Sampson, 1978; Dyer, 1978; White, 1997). Smith, it is stated, was of the opinion that a substantial layer of brickearth had once covered the whole of the Chiltern Hills forming a continuous 'Palaeolithic floor' on which the Palaeolithic people lived and that Palaeolithic people had camped around a very large lake that had formed on the plateau. Many argue that the brickearth has never existed as a continuous Palaeolithic land-surface covering the whole of the Chiltern Hills, it has only ever existed as an isolated deposit confined to the solution features, that there never was a large lake on the plateau and that Smith was also mistaken in his interpretation of many geological features. The problems of interpreting incomplete records are illustrated clearly as Smith's papers also confirm his view of the existence of many smaller water features

'Palaeolithic man lived by the sides of these lakes or large deep pools or meres, ponds and bogs' (Smith 1894: 64, see also pp. 158–9, 166).

If reference is made to the embedded Lower Palaeolithic sites in other areas mapped as Clay-with-flints (see this Section) certain unifying features are apparent. One particular characteristic of the hilltops and plateaux is the presence of solution features in the form of basins or pipes – which may or may not hold water at any one time.

We can therefore, envisage Smith's Palaeolithic landscape as one of valleys and hills, with high-level ponds and large water features (lakes?) which had formed in *some* of the many depressions and hollows, in the landsurface itself. Clearly, at various times, the areas around these water features, and the other depressions and hollows, when not filled with water, provided ideal places for Palaeolithic people to work or camp.

Over geological time, solution processes would have *gradually* deepened and widened the depressions and hollows in the ground, effectively retaining the artefacts that had been manufactured in them. As solution features often develop basin-like structures (see the Wood Hill Case-study Section 6, Subsection 6.11.), Palaeolithic sites which were once positioned *outside but close to the edge* of a hollow, could conceivably be retained *in situ* but exhibit a tilted stratigraphy as they would now form the edge of the deepened and widened basin (see problems with stratigraphy in Sub-section 6.3).

Although erosional processes have removed much of the superficial deposits which once covered the higher ground around Caddington there is still a chance that a new Palaeolithic site awaits discovery on these high-levels – not just in brick earth pits, as Smith suggests:

'Some of the Palaeolithic men of Caddington made their stone tools on the red clay-with-flints as others did on the brick-earth surface. The implements in the red drift are 'derived' from an old red clay surface ... Red clay-with-flints *in situ* is irregularly spread near Caddington, Kensworth and Whipsnade'... (*op. cit.* 1894: 81).

Cryoturbation

The Caddington area is, of particular interest as it is very close to the northern limits of deposits mapped as Clay-with-flints. Furthermore, during the Anglian glacial maxima, the area which is now the north-east end of the Chilterns lay close to the advancing ice-sheets during the early and middle Pleistocene. Indeed, Catt, Hubbard and Sampson suggest that,

'there were probably several major cold periods when deep-reaching cryoturbation occurred on the Chalk plateau. Probably the most intense of these was when a glacier reached the foot of the escarpment only a few kilometres north of Caddington' (1978: 139).

As previously noted, numerous references have been made by others to the presumed devastating effects of cryoturbation on areas mapped as Clay-with-flints throughout southern England. It could be argued, therefore, that this area, being so close to the ice fronts, constitutes an obvious test case for the maximum devastating effects of periglacial activity on deposits mapped as Clay-with-flints (see Explanatory Sections 1 and 2). Amongst the wealth of geological information in the Rackley report (Sampson, 1978) is an observation (which I have underlined for emphasis) that is of considerable importance to this research. I quote:

'The clay cappings and the clay linings of the pipes (Layer 11) are readily identifiable as Clay-with-flints *sensu stricto*, they lack far-travelled erratics and appear to have formed *in situ* through solution of the underlying Chalk and partly through collapse and solution of the Reading Beds into the pipes. At only a few places in the Rackley south face do they appear to be relatively unaffected by Pleistocene cryoturbation and other weathering processes' (*op. cit.* 1978: 37).

– To find *any* of these features and deposits, even at only a few places, *so close to the ice-fronts reported as being relatively unaffected by Pleisto-*

cene cryoturbation and other weathering processes is indeed worthy of note.

– For if the effects of cryoturbation are not absolute here then *neither were they in the other Downland areas of southern England* well away from the ice-fronts!

Worthington G. Smith was without doubt, an outstanding example of the best of the early amateur collectors. His knowledge of the Luton and Dunstable area was considerable, as his family had been closely associated with it for three hundred years. Every Palaeolithic flake and implement that he found was carefully recorded and invariably drawn, many of these drawing were later engraved and published. Unfortunately, much of Smith's original work was lost during a bombing raid on London during the last war. A concise and scholarly assessment of the fragmented documentation that does exist, is, of course, to be welcomed, but as Smith is not here to clarify his notes and defend his ideas and observations, the greatest of caution needs to be exercised before the ideas and information contained in his work are 'amended', discredited and discarded. For as history often shows, rejected and discredited ideas often become the solid cornerstone on which subsequent knowledge is based. With only marginal success, various investigations have been

conducted in these same areas over the past 40 years in an attempt to find further evidence of the Lower Palaeolithic occupation acutely observed by Smith. This lack of success in the Caddington area may have discouraged some Palaeolithic archaeologists from considering other high-level areas mapped as Clay-with-flints as likely to yield *in situ* Palaeolithic sites. Caddington was just one of Lower Palaeolithic 'embedded' sites discovered by Smith in the Dunstable and Luton area. These other sites are now briefly discussed – beginning with Whipsnade.

The Lower Palaeolithic sites at Whipsnade, Bedfordshire

Approximately two and a half miles south-west of Caddington Church were the sites of Bleak Hall (TL 03351760), Mount Pleasant (TL022199) and Whipsnade Heath (TL018180). The area is approximately 600ft. (183m) O.D. with the river Ver 166ft. (51m) below. Much of what is now known about the Whipsnade site comes from a paper read to the Society of Antiquaries of London by Mr. R.A. Smith (Reginald Smith of the British Museum, who was not related to Worthington G. Smith) in which he states, by way of preface

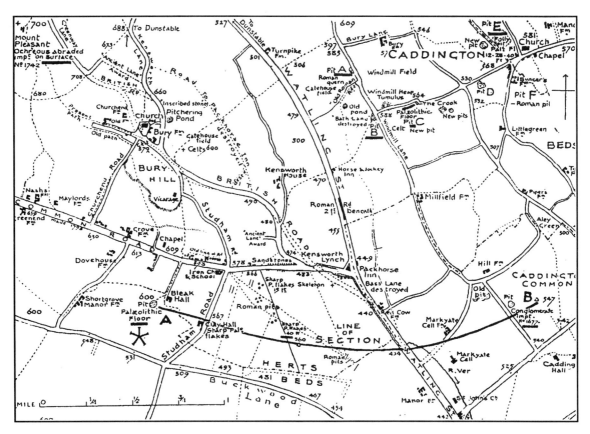

Figure 15 *District of Caddington and Whipsnade (S.W. angle),with sites marked. After Smith, R.A. (1918).*

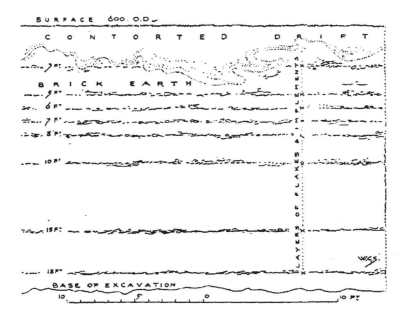

Figure 16 Pit Section at Whipsnade, showing a contorted drift above brickearth.   After Smith, R.A. (1918).

'In fulfilment of a promise to the late Mr. Worthington Smith, I have to communicate to the Society a few notes bearing on his excellent diagrams and drawings of the worked flints found by himself at Whipsnade, Bedfordshire' (1918: 40).

Worthington Smith had died in 1917. The brick-earth pit at Whipsnade was reported to be two and a half miles south-west of Caddington Church, and close to Bleak Hall, Kensworth. At 600 ft. O.D., this is the highest of the four brickearth pits in this part of England in which a Palaeolithic floor is reported to have been found (see Figure 15). The river Ver at this point, is 166 ft below.

Two pit-sections (Figures 16 and 17) are illustrated in R.A. Smith's paper (his fig. 3 and fig. 4) but only one is described. Figure 17 (R.A. Smith's fig. 4) 'shows a pipe in the brick-earth extending 12 ft. below the surface and filled with the contorted drift, Tertiary pebbles, etc., that normally cap the brick-earth' (*op. cit.* 1918: 43).

Reference is also made to a section on the road between Whipsnade and Dunstable Downs in which, under the Tertiary deposits, an horizon of Chalk with large flints and red clay was observed. The flint occurred in large nodules, which are described as very cracked and often deeply stained with oxide of manganese, about 3 ft. from the surface, 'and slight local denudation would have laid the nodules bare on the surface' (*op. cit.* 1918: 43). It appears that there were a number of brick earth pits at Whipsnade, as the Chalk was found at a depth of 3ft to 20ft from the surface, in different excavations. Overlying the Chalk was the brickearth, which had been deposited in horizontal layers forming land-surfaces on which

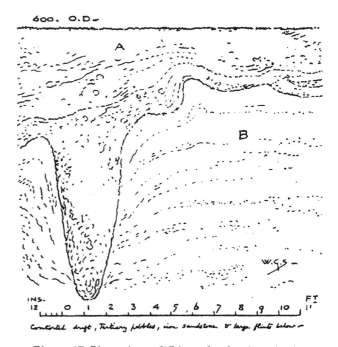

Figure 17 Pit-section at Whipsnade, showing pipe in brickearth. After Smith, R.A. (1918).

the Palaeolithic people had manufactured stone tools. These artefacts were recovered from several feet down (the actual depth is not specified) in the brickearth and are described as having a creamy white patination. Above the brick-earth was a layer of contorted drift or red clay (a feature common in the brick-earth pits as we saw at Caddington). In this layer artefacts were found, many of them were worked and all were patinated in various shades of ochre.

A site at Whipsnade Heath is described as having a layer of drift which varied in depth by many feet and contained, 'flints of large size, large blocks of iron sandstone, often tabular, pieces of soft friable sandstone, and other material' (R.A. Smith, 1918). Here, as in other brick-earth pits, Worthington Smith was of the opinion that the presence of the contorted drift (which had acted as a capping deposit over the brickearth in the solution holes) was due to processes associated with ice. These processes had effectively

> 'brought from a distance, boulders and ochreous implements that formerly lay on the surface, the flints there acquiring the patina that is often associated with the plateau. There are many ochreous flakes from Whipsnade, most with the peculiar white markings commonly seen on plateau specimens, and the contrast to the brick-earth specimens is very striking' (*op. cit*: 45).

The paper read to the Society of Antiquaries by R.A. Smith contains an important statement which is, to a certain degree, at variance with the opinion expressed by Worthington G. Smith himself in his previous papers. R.A. Smith recounted that,

> 'In spite of their colour and rolled condition, the flakes and implements from the contorted drift are older than the creamy white specimens found several feet below them, as is proved incidentally by the discovery in the brickearth at Caddington of a re-chipped ochreous implement from the red-clay drift' (*op. cit.* 1918: 45).

However, Worthington Smith had stated on several occasions (see the discussion in this Section and his paper on Gaddesden Row, 1916: 56) that 'the implements are probably not much older than the implements that occur below'.

As there is no reason to believe that Palaeolithic people restricted their movement only to certain areas of the Palaeolithic landscape, the manufacturing of stone tools could have taken place on the highest hill-tops before, during or after the tool manufacturing activities in the solution hollows. The ochreous artefacts in the contorted drift could therefore be older, contemporary or younger than the artefacts sealed in on the Palaeolithic floor below. Equally, all three time-frames might exist in any one area of contorted drift, but much would depend on the distribution patterns of the Palaeolithic working-site on the highest hills in the local vicinity and the sediment flow patterns in the immediate area of the particular solution feature (see Figure 14).

Artefacts from Whipsnade

From the report as presented by R.A Smith (1918), it is not totally clear just how many pits were excavated at Whipsnade, nor from which pit(s) the artefacts illustrated in the paper come. However, by referring to a catalogue complied by Worthington Smith in which he recorded the serial number of each artefacts (but unfortunately usually no details about the artefact itself); the date on which it was found; measurements and weight; where it was found and occasionally the depth at which it was found (as he often gave artefacts away there is now no record of the whereabouts of many of the artefacts he collected), I was able to identify four areas he had investigated at Whipsnade, namely:

- Whipsnade Heath (NGR. TL018180): cat. no. 1792; found 13 May 1907 (Length 3^7/$_8$", Width 2^5/$_8$"; 6¼ oz.) Given to Henry Dewey, Geological Survey.
- Whipsnade, Kensworth, Mount Pleasant surface (NGR. TL022199): cat. no. 1742; ('Man' 1908: pl. D, fig. 3)
- Whipsnade, Kensworth, South of Bleak Hall (NGR. TL03351760 general) in Mr. Powdrill's pit, cat. no. 1911;
- Whipsnade, Kensworth: Back of Bleak Hall (NGR. TL03351760 general), cat. nos. 1935, 1936, 1941, 1942, 1943, 1951, 1952, 1953, 1954, 1955.

In respect of both artefact types and geological sequence, Whipsnade is similar to Caddington and, as we shall see, to the other high level sites discovered by Worthington Smith (see Figure 18).

R.A. Smith, reporting Worthington Smith's findings, describes undisturbed debris and finished and unfinished implements capable of being refitted which would suggest that the Bleak Hall site at Whipsnade is a manufacturing site. In terms of industry type, the assemblage is all Acheulian (but, according to R.A. Smith, includes a Mousterian side scraper). The assemblage is recorded as predominantly ovate with a few pointed handaxes but, unlike Caddington, no Levalloisian or 'reduced Levalloisian' (Roe 1981: 230) cores or flakes are present.

There are also great similarities in the levels at which artefacts were found at Caddington and Whipsnade (and the other sites discovered by Smith which are discussed later in this Section), including the presence of white artefacts situated between the Palaeolithic floors and the top level of ochreous artefacts, as described below:

A At the highest level, ochreous artefacts in contorted drift
B White flakes in the next layer down (including gravel at Caddington).
C At the deepest level, a Lower Palaeolithic floor with unpatinated artefacts

Sampson *et al.* (1978: 131–133) , in the context of Caddington, considered four alternatives:

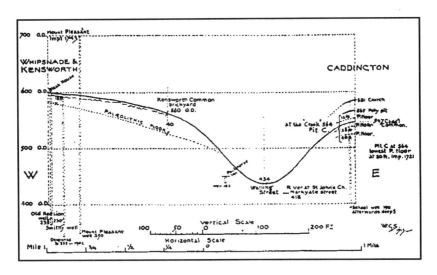

Figure 18 Section along line A to B of Figure 20. After Smith, R.A. (1918)

1. There were two discrete Palaeolithic floors (level B and C).
2. The white, artefacts at B are derived, possibly mixed, from upslope.
3. Both samples were washed downslope from the same knapping area and represent a single, derived assemblage.
4. Some artefacts from the floor were moved upwards by frost action and the two samples are one assemblage, part *in situ*, part derived.

All previous interpretations suggest that the ochreous artefacts were brought in by drift but I could propose at least one other further (fifth) alternative process as follows:

5.1. Lower Palaeolithic floor C was covered by brickearth.
5.2. A later Palaeolithic occurrence produced a discrete floor at A (with artefacts which were at that time, of course, unpatinated).
5.3. Freeze thaw processes subsequently moved some artefacts downwards into the underlying deposit B (brickearth or gravel at Caddington) down to a level where frost action would have a reduced effect. The unpatinated or relatively unpatinated artefacts on the surface would have changed colour to ochreous and the artefacts that had moved down would have acquired various degrees of white/yellow patination. This process would result in a lower layer of whiter artefacts at B above the original Lower Palaeolithic floor at C.
5.4. The artefacts remaining on the surface may well have become ochreous before being covered by drift which subsequently was subject to cryoturbation which, in itself, may have deepened the

colour as well as mixing the artefacts within this upper layer (A).

This alternative does not rely on there having been an upslope Palaeolithic occurrence which, having moved into the lower area, no longer exists.

Sampson *et al.* (*ibid.*) concluded at the Cottage site at Caddington, that the white artefacts at B must have largely moved up from the floor at C. This conclusion was based on their observation that clusters of artefacts found at level B correlated to clusters of artefacts found at level C. If this is true, they considered, then there must be a relationship between the two levels and they cannot be two discrete assemblages, nor can they be derived as this would lead to a random distribution. This view of clustering, however, is based on a covariance of the numbers of finds recorded in given months by Smith, rather than any locational information (which Smith did not record, although he did note some clustering at level C). If the interpretation of clustering covariance is inaccurate then the other alternative interpretations are feasible.

The full effect of the loss of so many of Worthington Smith's original reports is graphically illustrated in this attempt to recount and discuss the Whipsnade site and finds. The available information is limited, incomplete and fragmented. James Dyer, writing in the Bedfordshire, Historical Record Society, Vol. 57, states that

'Smith's last association with palaeolithic implements seems to have been in the Whipsnade clay pit near Bleak Hall at Kensworth Common, where he was still finding specimens in his eightieth year. Though no actual 'floor' seems to have been observed, one must have existed to judge by the material' (*op. cit.* 1978: 173); cf. also R.A. Smith's comment that 'so large a collection of implements from this palaeolithic 'floor' has now been made' (*op. cit.* 1918: 48).

In 1993–4 an excavation was undertaken at Kensworth, under the direction of Dr John McNabb. Many trial trenches were excavated, using a mechanical digger or digging by hand. An area of brickearth was located and one flake was recovered, but no Palaeolithic floor was found (McNabb, pers. comm.).

Approximately 5 miles from Kensworth and Whipsnade (in a southerly direction), across the county boundary but within the same area of deposits mapped as Clay-with-flint, is the village of Gaddesden Row. Smith records finding artefacts in Butterfield's Brick Yard at Gaddesden Row: the site and the finds are discussed next.

Gaddesden Row, Hertfordshire

Approximately 5 miles in a northerly direction from Caddington was Butterfield's Brickyard at Gaddesden Row (TL 038133). The site is at 544ft. (166m) O.D. One mile to the south-west the river Gade is 184ft. (56m) below, and two and a half miles to the north-east the river Ver is 144ft. (44m) below. The village of Gaddesden Row, in Hertfordshire is situated at O.D. 544 ft. in an area mapped as Clay-with-flints (Figure 19).

One mile to the south-west, 184 ft below the village, is the river Gade and two and half miles to the north-east, and 144 ft below, is the river Ver (Figure 20).

The village itself is spread out for 2 miles along a road, which runs from south-east to north-west. Smith describes the Butterfield Brick Yard (at TL 038133) as being at the end of the village adjoining a

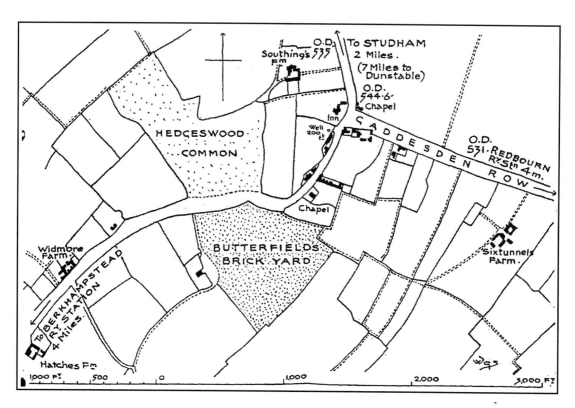

Figure 19 *Plan of Gaddesden Row, Herts, showing Butterfield's brickyard. After Smith, W.G. (1916)*

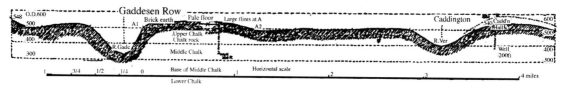

Figure 20 *Section of the Gade and Ver valleys, showing Gaddesden Row and Caddington Hall. After Smith, W.G. (1916).*

chapel at the north-west end, at a turning to the south. He also notes that,

> 'At 1 mile to the north-west the contour line is 600 ft., and at 2 miles the height is 628 ft. The high land at 600 ft., and above, divides the basin of the river Gade from that of the Ver, and 4 miles in the same direction a height of 750 ft is reached. On this level at Kensworth I have found on the surface an abraded ochreous palaeolith and flakes and the 'floor' reaches Whipsnade' (Smith, W.G. 1916: 49).

The brickearth pit at Butterfield's Brick Yard, Gaddesden Row

Butterfield's brick pit at Gaddesden Row was dug to a depth of 45 ft. From the top of the Pit the sequence seems to have been as follows:

- 1ft. of humus (Top-soil).
- 4 ft. of contorted drift. – This contorted drift is described as being of a darker colour than the bulk of the clay, and contained ('as is always the case in implementiferous districts' (op. cit. 1916: 53)) materials that had been derived from the old land surface around Gaddesden Row. It also contained stones both large and small, some of which were considered by Worthington Smith to have been ice-rafted in from more distant places.
- 40 ft. of relaid Eocene clay – (which is the brick-earth), reported as being 'stratified in practically horizontal layers which often undulate slightly, and are rarely somewhat duplicated' (op. cit. 1916: 53).

This brick-earth is thought to have been relaid, and of Eocene or Tertiary origin. Worthington Smith suggested that it had been washed into place in successive periods since the Eocene times and that these incidences may not have been far apart from each other. He was also of the opinion that the brickearth had come, 'from some place in the neighbourhood possibly not far off, where the clay existed in its original position as laid down in Eocene times' (ibid.).

Within the brickearth pit were seven or eight (it is not clear which) strata. In each stratum he found stones, implements and flakes. Smith suggests that at various times after Palaeolithic peoples had left the site, the area was flooded. However, when the flooding ceased they returned to the site, this sequence of events being repeated several times between the 35ft layer and the 20ft layer.

Lower Palaeolithic artefacts from the brick-earth in Butterfield's Brick Yard, Gaddesden Row

Approximately fifty Lower Palaeolithic handaxes and flake tools as well as knapping waste, were recovered from the brick-earth. The implements are described by Smith (op. cit. 1916: 57) as ovate or pointed ovate, thicker at the middle and base, and with cutting edges above. Sharply pointed implements were rare.

> 'Nearly all the implements are ivory-colour or white, others are very faintly ochreous, truly ochreous or brown, and a few dull purplish. They are as a rule sharp-edged, or very slightly abraded, and do not vary in shape from top to bottom of the pit' (ibid.).

There are a few pointed handaxes, as was the case in the Caddington assemblages. However, unlike the Caddington assemblages, there is no record of Levalloisian cores and flakes being identified in the Gaddesden Row materials. Unfortunately, the brick-earth pit did not yield bones or teeth. The 40 ft. of brickearth at Butterfield's pit, in which the Palaeolithic artefacts were found, was not strictly a homogeneous deposit. 'The strata become more and more stony as they ascend, till the culmination is reached at the horizontal palaeolithic floor at 20 ft from the surface' (op. cit. 1916: 55). Lying on this 'floor' were many large flints, which appeared to have been derived from 'adjoining lower places' but adjacent to the 'floor' where the chalk and flints occurred on the surface. Such a position is noted by Smith, where a cross is placed on the horizontal line near the middle of Figure 20. Subsequently, the Palaeolithic floor at the 20 ft. level was covered with water, which deposited more brick-earth, in much the same way as had occurred previously throughout the lower level. However, this time the character of the stratification change is described as

> 'becoming more and more undulating till about 6 ft or more below the present surface. There are streaks of darker coloured clay, seen on the exposed faces as at B, E, and B, B, C' (op. cit. 1916: 56). The streaks are described as varying in colour from light to dark brown. Contained within these levels were 'faintly brownish, somewhat abraded implements ... . A few implements are blackish or purplish, others are variegated. All the implements are coloured within black, blackish, or purplish slate-colour' (ibid.).

Here again this variation in colour is considered by Smith to be 'caused by the differently coloured environment of clay'. The Palaeolithic floors, situated at and below the 10ft. level in the Gaddesden Row pit, were then capped by contorted drift. At Gaddesden Row, unlike Caddington, the contorted drift varied considerably in depth, being shallow ('somewhat feebly developed' *op. cit.* 1916: 56) in places. Sometimes it measured no more than 3ft, whilst in others, it was well developed. The artefacts found in the drift are coloured brownish or faintly liver-coloured and most are somewhat abraded. Smith was of the opinion that the implements recovered from the contorted drift were probably not much older than the implements which occurred below. He envisaged that these artefacts had 'all been swept from higher positions in the neighbourhood, now washed away' (*ibid.*).

The 1975 excavation at Gaddesden Row

During 1975, under the direction of Dr John Wymer, a test section was cut in Butterfield's Pit with the hope of locating the sequence described by Worthington Smith and any archaeological areas, if they had not been worked out. The excavation exposed sediments that were considered to be 'broadly related to those published, although there is a considerable lateral variation in the strata' (Wymer, 1980: 2). Although a few artefacts were found *in situ*, none were considered by the excavators to be in primary context. They therefore concluded that if any 'floor' (as described by Smith) did still exist in the pit, 'it does not do so at this point' (*ibid.*). The test section was sited where 3m of deposits had already been removed commercially. However, it is recorded by Wymer, that over a metre of made ground had accumulated over the undisturbed deposits (*ibid.*).

The recovered assemblage consisted of two small flakes, less than 3 cm long, and one (listed as no. 4) which are described as hand-axe finishing flakes. The remainder were primary flakes. Of these, four flakes and a spall, have plain striking platforms but the remainder have prepared platforms, to some degree (*ibid.*).

Wymer considered that the faceting on the platforms was unlikely to have been produced as a result of intentional Levallois technique, rather it was caused inevitably in the later stages of hand-axe manufacture (*ibid.*). One of the plain-platform flakes is described as considerably more abraded than the others, and is also scratched and stained (*op. cit.* 1980: 3). Artefacts from layer 2 are described as, 'all patinated and weathered to some extent. They are slightly abraded' (*op. cit.* 1980: 2). John Wymer (like Boyd Dawkins before him), in reference to the Hackpen Hill artefacts (see this Section), suggests that the marks on the artefacts appeared

> 'to be the result of soil movement rather than rolling in water or sand abrasion. Edge-chipping

and faint scratches are also present and characteristic of soil movement' (*ibid.*).

Within the deposits of Layer 3 (the brickearth layer), one metre below the gravel, one artefact was found. This is described as 'a crude flake, 9 cm, long with a diffused bulb and negligible striking platform. It is patinated creamy-white but is neither edge-damaged nor scratched' (*ibid.*).

Time, money and a great deal of effort has been directed by a number of people towards finding pockets of brickearth (in the area centred on Caddington) that may have escaped the attention of the brickmakers, in the hope of locating remnants of Smith's Palaeolithic 'floors'. By comparison, however, virtually no time, money or effort has been spent looking for evidence of Palaeolithic sites which might just still exist at the higher levels, in the other deposits mapped as Clay-with-flints in the Dunstable/Luton area. Perhaps they have indeed all been 'washed away' but, as Smith did not look for them and neither has anybody else, the presence or absence of *in situ* Palaeolithic sites on these hilltops (capped with deposits mapped as Clay-with-flints other than 'True brickearth') must remain uncertain. It is unlikely that any of these sites (if they could be found) would provide such a range of material as that recovered from the brickearth pits. The deposits would no doubt be decalcified, which effectively degrades material within them, other than the stone artefacts. However, any artefacts occurring at 'higher levels' than the brickearth pits would certainly provide clues to the distribution and activities of Lower Palaeolithic peoples within this area before the period in which climate deterioration produced the contorted 'drift', so a proper search would be worthwhile. Only thus will we gain a full picture of the early humans exploiting all parts of their topographically varied territory.

Slip End, Bedfordshire

Slip End (TL082188) is approximately one and a half miles south-east of Caddington, and one and three quarters miles south of Luton. The area is around 502ft. (153m) O.D. One and a half miles to the north-east the river Lea is 148ft. (45m) below.

The Lower Palaeolithic sites at both Caddington and Gaddesden Row were capped with a-red-brown drift deposit which contained Lower Palaeolithic artefacts which, it has been suggested, are important because they are derived from sites which are believed to have been situated at an even 'higher' level. Slip-End, in Bedfordshire, provides another such example of palaeoliths embedded in the 'drift'. The only surviving reference to Slip End in the extant literature is the short description given by Smith in his book 'Man, the Primeval Savage' (1894: 95) and a few entries in his catalogue of finds. The entries for Slip End in this catalogue are themselves somewhat confusing, as Smith provides two codes, namely SE for Slip End and SEC for Slip End, Caddington. This suggests that there were at least two sites/pits. Smith records,

> 'I also repeatedly examined the excavations at Slip-End and whenever and wherever a hole was dug or grave made in the churchyard or cemetery, I was usually on the spot to note the nature of the ochreous excavated material. The result to the end of 1893 is that I have found in the tenacious red-brown drift of Caddington and Slip-End about thirty ochreous slightly abraded Palaeolithic implements, and a large number of flakes and cores' (*ibid.*).

It is very unfortunate, that there is not more information about 'the excavation at Slip End'; for here, as in his Gaddesden Row report, Smith makes the point that,

> 'From the slightly abraded condition of the ochreous human relics, it is obvious that, high-level implements as they are, they have all been derived from some still higher position, of which but few traces are now visible' (*ibid.*).

However on searching through the surviving pages of Smith's catalogue I found the following entries:

- Catalogue no. 1513, 27 September 1872 (L 3". W 2¼". 3oz). 'Slip End, 1¾ miles South of Luton, close to and South of Prebendal Farm. Thrown out by a brickmaker from the clay he was using in making brick. Found by me close to brickmaker's temporary shed, with a few flakes – given to Sir J. Evans'
- Catalogue no. 1640, 15 August 1896 (L 5⅝", W 3⅛"; 13¾ oz). 'Slip End, Luton. Found by my grandson Worthington, in brick-earth thrown out by brickmakers. Given to Mr. Bell of Oxford'.

As one aim of this study is to find new Lower and Middle Palaeolithic sites on the deposits mapped as Clay-with-flint, the important question is: where was/is the 'still higher position' from which these 'high-level implements' had been derived? Smith was of the opinion that these 'ochreous' implements were very ancient indeed. He was to some extent influenced by a theory, current at that time but *not* now accepted, which postulated the idea that erosion on the Chalk downlands had since Palaeolithic times, been so great, that the hill-tops which we see today were in fact once valley bottoms. These ancient artefacts were therefore, manufactured by 'river-sides or lake-sides' situated in these former valley bottoms. The water, he suggests, must have drained from the elevations, which have now vanished.

If the Slip End artefacts did come from somewhere 'even higher' then perhaps the place of origin of these artefacts still exists, in the area today; if so, it will be a hill-top, capped with deposits mapped as Clay-with-flints that are held in solution hollows. It is of some interest to note therefore, that just south-east of Dunstable, at Zouches Farm is a radio/TV-mast which at 200m (656 ft.) O.D. marks the highest point in the area. This mast is situated in an area of deposits mapped as Clay-with-flints (see Figure 11), the same spread of deposits which dip down in south-easterly direction and on which in a direct line, Caddington and Slip End are situated (see British Geological Survey Sheets 220 and 238).

Round Green, Bedfordshire

Round Green (TL101227), is at 530ft. (162m) O.D. One mile to the south-west the river Lea is 178ft. (54m) below. Two and a half miles in a south-westerly direction, across the valley is the village of Caddington (see Figure 21). For twenty seven years,

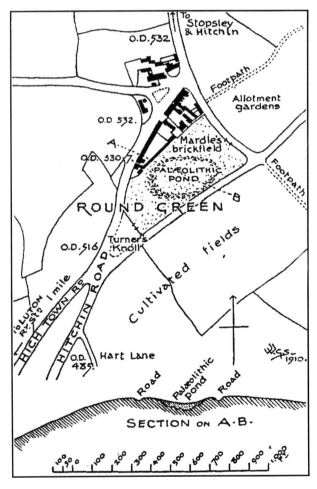

Figure 21 Plan and section of Round Green, near Luton, Beds. After Smith, W.G. (1916).

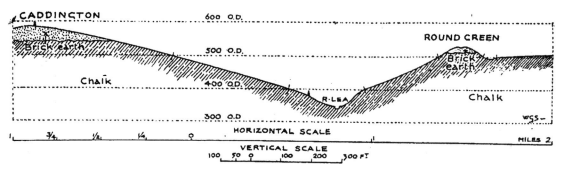

Figure 22 Section showing Lea valley between Caddington and Round Green. After Smith, W.G. (1916).

Worthington Smith monitored the extraction of brickearth from a pit at Round Green. This single pit revealed what appeared to be a Lower Palaeolithic working-site, which had been situated on the edge of a small lake or pond. Subsequent changes in the climate produced various deposits which effectively 'sealed in' the Palaeolithic floor. Round Green, now a suburb of Luton, was a small hamlet at the turn of the century. It is now one mile to the north-east of Luton Town Hall and the area around the site has been developed. The small brickyard at Round Green was in 'a considerable depression on the summit of the hill'. (*op. cit.* 1916: 62). At O.D. 530, the hill is 132 ft. above the river Lea at Luton.

In Smith's time, water from the hill drained into the river Lea on its east side through a farm and into a lake. On the west side, the ground drained somewhat sharply into the Lea valley. To the south, the ground descended steeply into the valley and the town of Luton. The valley at this point is approximately 200ft. in depth. Across this valley, two and a half miles in a south-westerly direction, is the village of Caddington. Round Green and Caddington (as can be seen in Figure 22) are thus at similar levels but on opposite sides of the valley, both being situated on Upper Chalk hills that are capped with deposits mapped as Clay-with-flints. It is not easy to envisage this in the built up landscape of present day Luton.

The deposits at Round Green

The deposits overlying the Chalk in the Round Green area were observed by Smith in various sections exposed during road and house building and in the clay pits (Figure 23).

He describes the exposed sections thus:

– '6 in. to 2 ft. of humus or dark mould; amongst these are broken up flints from Clay-with-flints and the Chalk-with-flints, Tertiary pebbles, pieces of quartz, iron sandstone, Lydian stone and many pieces of Hertfordshire conglomerate. In some places the Chalk-and-flints and Clay-with-flints appear *in situ* on the surface. The brick-earth represents washings of the red Clay-with-flints, and the colour is derived from the iron sandstone in the Tertiaries. Sometimes there are extensive washings of the chalk' (*op. cit.* 1916: 64).

Smith also found traces of highly coloured clays and stones which he assigned to Woolwich and Reading beds and a 'whitish drifted stony boulder clay' (*op. cit.* 1916: 66); the geology of the restricted area of the Round Green brickyard was reported in greater detail. The geology is discussed in reverse order to that which is shown in Smith's diagram, but the key to the deposits is retained and remains the same.

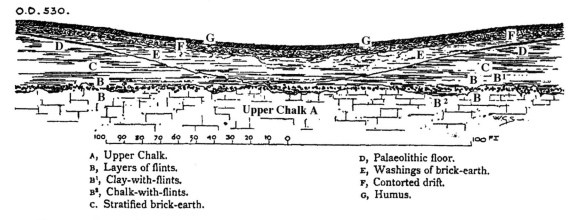

A, Upper Chalk.
B, Layers of flints.
B¹, Clay-with-flints.
B², Chalk-with-flints.
C. Stratified brick-earth.

D, Palaeolithic floor.
E, Washings of brick-earth.
F, Contorted drift.
G, Humus.

Figure 23 Section through pond and Palaeolithic floor at Round Green. After Smith, W.G. (1916).

G. Humus. (Top-soil) thinly scattered with pebbles and stones derived either from boulder clay or Tertiary beds.

F. Contorted drift. This was poorly represented in the Round Green brickyard, although as previously noted, Smith identified drift deposits nearby in sections exposed during construction work.

E. Washing of brick-earth. This deposits must have been (according to Smith) very gently laid down, as none of the Palaeolithic artefacts on the underlying 'floor' were disturbed 'in the slightest degree; this is proved by the fact that some of the flakes were capable of replacement' (*op. cit.* 1916: 65).

D. Palaeolithic floor. Lying on the surface of the stratified brick-earth of (C) were Lower Palaeolithic artefacts that had retained the position they had been left in by Palaeolithic people.

C. Stratified brick-earth. A 12ft. layer of stratified brick-earth covered the underlying undisturbed flint layer (B).

B. 1. Clay-with-flints. Smith stated that where the Clay-with-flints adjoins the area marked B.2. (Figure 23) the layer becomes Chalk-with-flints (*ibid.*)

B. Layers of flints. Both large and small flints were found here. Smith reports that
'This layer at Turners Knoll on the south side of the brickyard is close to the surface with in some places unusually large flints.... Many of the flints were seen to be split whilst still *in situ* [Smith does not state whether this splitting was natural or man made]. All were more or less covered with black oxide of manganese' (*ibid.*).

A. Upper Chalk. (The base level), Smith makes no reference to the Chalk at this level showing any effects of periglaciation, nor does he later when he notes that 'A very short distance to the northeast the chalk appears at the surface' (*ibid.*).

Lower Palaeolithic artefacts from the brick pit at Round Green

The brick pit at Round Green corresponded to the edge of a small pond or lake (approximately 350 ft. long and 250 ft. wide) which, during the Lower Palaeolithic period had evidently provided a suitable place for these early humans to engage in activities which clearly included the manufacture of stone tools. Smith records that the former pond at Round Green was filled to a depth of 14ft. with loam derived

'probably from the red clay-with-flints and the chalk' (*op. cit.* 1916: 64). The Round Green brick pit was eventually dug to a depth of 20ft, however, it

soon became 'waterlogged' which Smith interpreted as 'a modern return to a palaeolithic pond' (*ibid.*).

Smith, who in many ways was far ahead of his time as a Palaeolithic field-archaeologist, considered the artefacts found on the Palaeolithic floor at Round Green to be an occurrence of great integrity and of special interest. He writes, 'During the excavation, the entire stock-in-trade of the pond-side dwellers was exposed, and as far as possible every scrap of worked flint was secured'(*op. cit.* 1916: 68). He also records that;

'twenty-one well-defined sharp-edged implements [handaxes] were found *in situ* on the Round Green palaeolithic floor ... one had been broken into three pieces in palaeolithic times; two of the pieces were found and conjoined, the third was not found. Nine sharp-edged knife forms were found, mostly thin, but a few thick; 261 flakes were collected.... Only one distinct sharp-edged core was met with on the floor. A largish flake was replaced on one of the implements, and a few of the flakes I refitted together' (*ibid.*).

The artefacts from the contorted drift varied in colour from ochre to orange-brown and brown. Here, as at Caddington, Gaddesden Row and Slip-End, the ochreous artefacts recovered from the 'drift' layers are considered by Smith to be 'not necessarily older than those found on the floor, they were probably gathered up by the moving contorted drift from a surface not far distant' (*op. cit.* 1916: 69).

Mixieshill (variously written as Mixies hill/Hill) pit, Bedfordshire

Now a suburb of Luton, Mixieshill pit (TL101229) was a quarter of a mile north of Round Green. The area is at 520ft.(158m) O.D. One mile to the southwest the river Lea is 168ft. (51m) below. No bones or teeth were found in the Round Green pit. However, Smith records finding (in 1886) animal bones, antlers of *Cervus elaphus*, and sharp Palaeolithic flakes in a long disused brickearth pit at Mixieshill, one quarter of a mile north of Round Green at a height of approximately 520 ft. O.D. (Smith states that this would make the Mixieshill pit 10 ft. lower than the Round Green pit). He kept one piece of the bone: the others, which were friable and dark-brown in colour, together with the flakes, he sent to Sir John Evans. These bones were not the first to be found in the Mixieshill pit, Smith notes that

'Other bones and antlers had been found in the pit before I knew the brickyard, but I could not recover them, and immediately after the discovery the pit was closed and abandoned' (1894: 167; 1916: 67).

Mixieshill pit was excavated to a depth of 22ft. and one productive stratum was found about 10ft. to 12ft. below the surface. Smith mentions digging out several flakes from this layer in later visits. Subsequently, he was informed by the kiln builder that the base of the pit at 22ft. had produced many more bones, and that the workmen had taken some of them away. Despite his efforts he was unable to trace the workmen (many were itinerant labourers). In 1905, nine years after Mixieshill pit had closed, Smith met a man who had worked in this pit, who informed him that, in addition to the first group of bones which had been found at a depth of 22ft., the workman had come across more bones. Near to the first group, but not with them were

> 'the bones of a human being extended at full length on its right side, and with all the bones in place, and the head, which was somewhat flattened, to the south-west. He measured the skeleton, which he said was 5ft. 6in. long. The bones were all dark-brown in colour and very friable' (*op. cit.* 1916: 67).

When touched, the skull is reported to have fallen into pieces. Smith states that the colour of the bones agreed with those he had found in the pit and that 'the depth at which the bones had been found precluded any idea of burial' (*op. cit.*, 1906: 10; 1916: 68). Whether these human bones were indeed Palaeolithic will always remain a mystery. If the description is taken at face value, they might have been one of the outstanding hominid fossil occurrences in all Europe, but we shall never know. The find is reminiscent of the Galley Hill, Kent skeleton, long believed to be Lower Palaeolithic, but eventually shown to be a burial of a much later date.

Ramridge End, Bedfordshire

Ramridge End (TL103229 general) now a suburb of Luton, was a quarter of a mile east of Mixieshill. The area is at 520ft. (158m) O.D. Approximately, one mile and a quarter miles to the south-west the river Lea is 168ft. (51m) below. The Ramridge End pit was, like the Mixieshill pit, situated in an area mapped as Clay-with-flints and it also contained bones. Smith states:

> 'I myself saw brown friable bones deep down in this Ramridge End pit. They completely collapsed on being touched. I have a large hacking implement from the Ramridge End pit, which weighs 3lb. 7 oz' (*op. cit*, 1916: 68).

There are no other references to this pit in the 1916 paper, Smith's catalogue of artefacts has provide some additional information. He records finding on

- 18 June 1904, Impey's pit, the discovery of [1 artefact], *in situ* face of pit, 4ft. top of drift.

- 12 August 1905, [1 artefact], 2/3ft.
- 28 February 1913, [1 artefact] 12ft.
- 14 May 1914, [1 artefact]. 'Brick-earth in a horizontal line of small stones, no flakes. I saw this on a shelf in a tomatoe house where the digger who found it had placed it' (*ibid.*).

As so little is known about the Ramridge End pit or indeed the whereabouts of the artefacts found in it, no useful comparisons can be made between it and the other sites discovered by Smith.

General discussion

Since the death of Worthington G. Smith in 1917: the Dunstable and Luton area has become for many a focus of Palaeolithic research. The Lower Palaeolithic *in situ* sites, the artefacts and the bones that Smith discovered in the many brickpits in this area, have perhaps only recently been equalled in quality by those at Boxgrove, Sussex (see for example Roberts *et al.* 1992). As previously noted, in the intervening years since Smith's death, archaeologists have spent considerable amounts of time and money re-examining the old pits and searching for new patches of brickearth in the hope of finding *in situ*, undisturbed Palaeolithic sites – but with very little real success. This lack of success could be contributed to either of two things:

(1) There are in fact no new Palaeolithic sites to be found, as they were all dug out by the brickmakers, or
(2) Sites do still exist in pockets of brickearth, but the archaeologists were not looking in the right place for the brickearth.

Logic and commerce dictate that all the obvious and accessible patches of brickearth would have been removed by the brickmakers, many years ago. But in the light of the following information, it would seem that undiscovered Palaeolithic sites may still exist in well hidden pockets of brickearth. Referring to Round Green, Smith records,

> 'No one would suspect the presence of brick-earth within the boundary of this waste patch, as the outside was chalk-with-flints, red clay-with-flints, almost colourless, translucent sand, and Tertiaries. The presence of the brick-earth was revealed by accident to a master brickmaker. A small excavation or drain was being dug from the inside to the outside of this No-man's-land, and in this little trench the brickmaker saw, to his surprise, water charged with brick-earth trickling along. He had a few test holes dug which revealed the deposit of brick-earth and ultimately brought to light the palaeolithic floor [of Round Green]' (Smith, 1916: 64).

This report is of particular interest as the brick-makers, and indeed Smith himself, possessed much experience and a great deal of knowledge of the brickearth deposits and where to find them. However, it was only by chance that brickearth was found at Round Green and with it the Lower Palaeolithic floor – illustrating both the difficulties and the hopes of the archaeologist searching for Palaeolithic site on deposits mapped as Clay-with-flints. Furthermore, as we saw in Section 3 and earlier in this Section, changes in landuse during the latter part of the twentieth century have added considerably to the problems confronting the Palaeolithic archaeologist.

The artefact assemblages from the various sites discovered by Smith are similar – including flakes, handaxes and debitage. The typology is Acheulian with, in the case of Caddington, possibly some Levallois or 'reduced Levallois' technique. All the sites can be classified as being in the ovate tradition (Group VI and VII according to Roe's 1968 classification) but with some artefacts, for example some of those at Round Green, being more pointed. The technology is again similar with low percentages of twisted handaxes but more frequent evidence of a tranchet finish (Whipsnade seems to have only one tranchet finished handaxe but there are only 10 in total).

We have, then, different 'floors' (occupations) producing similar assemblages but, without firm dating evidence, it is therefore, impossible to show whether these different occupations were close to each other in time or whether the Palaeolithic people concerned were associated in any way.

* * * *

'Embedded' artefacts from deposits mapped as Clay-with-flints at Lower Kingswood, Surrey

Lower Kingswood in Surrey (TQ 245542) is on a plateau of the North Downs at about 170m O.D. and, until World War 1, had been mainly uncultivated heathland (Figure 24).

After the second world war, Walton and Banstead Heaths, which includes the Lower Kingswood area, were cleared and subsequently ploughed. In the early 1950s, this area was the subject of intensive field walking by Mr. L.W. Carpenter. His finds included a large number of Palaeolithic handaxes and flakes, most of which appeared to have been brought to the surface by deep ploughing. After 1956, his field walking was curtailed in this area as cultivation decreased (see Carpenter 1956, 1957). However, in the autumn of 1959 Carpenter made a new and important discovery in an area known as Rookery Farm, Lower Kingswood. He records that

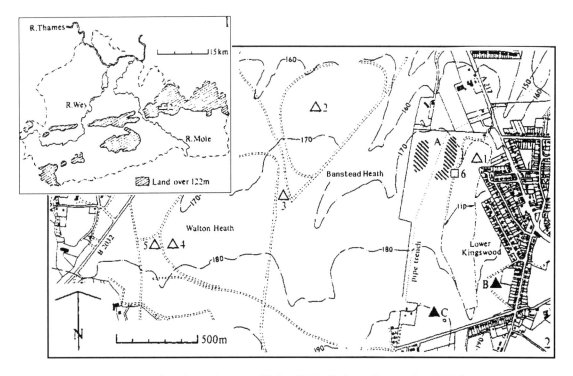

Figure 24 Location maps showing the main area of Palaeolithic finds on Banstead and Walton Heaths, including Lower Kingswood, and the finds by Walls and Cotton (marked A–C). After Walls and Cotton (1980).

'a small dry valley or coombe on the edge of the plateau at Lower Kingswood had all the top soil removed by bulldozers and scrapers. The top soil was heaped up around the perimeter, while the floor of the valley was raised by dumping of ashes, clinker, and hard rubbish and the top soil subsequently re-spread. This soil removal exposed the old Clay-with-flints surface, which seems to lie mainly between 18 inches and 3 feet below the present agricultural surface. The cleared area was carried up to just above the 550 feet contour line. After scouring by autumn and winter rains the surface could be searched for worked flint, ... At first no trace of Palaeolithic worked flint could be found but at length in the S.W. corner of the cleared area and just above the 550ft. contour line I found the ovate, embedded in the Clay-with-flints. An intensive search on this spot soon revealed other specimens and numerous flakes. Most of the illustrated flints and flakes [see Carpenter, 1960] were found embedded in the surface of this corner or were dug from just beneath the surface. Others, of course, may have been scraped off the clay surface and become buried in the soil mounds ... The flints found embedded in this clay are all deeply patinated and frost bleached, and show the characteristic thermal fractures due to the extremes of temperatures encountered during the last great glaciations.' (*op. cit.* 1960: 99–100).

The Rookery Farm, Lower Kingswood assemblage, is described as follows:

- Ovate handaxe, ivory patination, thermal fractures, sharp edges, patches of cortex present on both sides. Bold economical flaking on one side.
- A handaxe (ficron or tongue-shaped) of cherty flint with a basal point, ivory patination.
- Triangular handaxe, ivory patination with a high gloss, thermal fractures. (This carefully finished implement exhibits battering at one focal point).
- A butt of a massive handaxe, ivory patination with a high gloss, thermal fractures (the pointed end has been removed by frost action as the break shows two pot-lid fractures).
- Unfinished handaxe, irregular patination, thermal fractures. (On one side there is initial bold flaking with the median ridge. A similar attempt to prepare the other side, which is rather cherty, has resulted in the removal of a large irregular flake which has caused a cavity and the flint has been abandoned).
- Biconical core with bold flaking, not deeply patinated, thermal fractures.
- Core, not deeply patinated, thermal fractures. (Seems to have been used as a rough handaxe and also a hammer stone).

- Steep-sided scraper, ivory patination but with reddish and purple stains, glossy.
- Flake chopper, irregular patination, very stained, abraded in places.
- Ovate flake, ivory patination (there is secondary flaking and trimming on one side).
- Butt of a small handaxe, irregular patination from ivory to bluish-white.

Few of the 83 flakes showed signs of secondary working. The types varied from neat handaxe finishing flakes to crude specimens, some of which measured between 5 and 6 inches long. A brown quartzite pointed hammer stone measuring three by three and half inches was excavated. Burnt flint was also found, in the shape of a core with an ivory white patination.

Carpenter's observations over the years, had led him to believe that the flints bleached to an ivory shade of patination were those which had in all probability lain on the landsurface, exposed to the 'severities of the Ice Age for at least a considerable period of time' and that much of the natural flint which occurred in thick beds in the clay was also characterised by ivory bleaching with thermal fractures on the upper surface, while frost shattered flint 'of every shape and size is strewn over the whole area' (*op. cit.* 1960).

In a previous article, he had stated (*op. cit.* 1957) that unless the artefacts recovered from the Banstead and Walton Heaths plateau were deeply patinated; frost-bleached and had thermal fractures he was not prepared to accept them as Palaeolithic. However, he subsequently withdrew this opinion after examining two handaxes found at 'Knowlehawe', Tadworth and the artefacts from Lower Kingswood. The two handaxes from Tadworth were in the Clay-with-flints on the edge of the plateau. One of them is described as bleached on one side but only partly patinated on the other, with the original flints surface showing in places. A half completed handaxe, cores and some flakes from the Lower Kingswood site were neither bleached nor deeply patinated, although all exhibited thermal fractures, all these artefacts were buried in the deposits mapped as Clay-with-flints and dug from below the surface. Following this reassessment, Carpenter was then able to write,

'With the recovery of the handaxes and other pieces together with eighty-three flakes from this small site there seems little doubt that here we have the remains of a palaeolithic working floor, one of the several that must have existed on this plateau. The culture would appear to be Middle Acheulian and is probably contemporary with the material which has recently been excavated from the Middle Gravels at Swanscombe' (*op. cit.* 1960: 100).

Further investigations at Lower Kingswood by T. Walls and J. Cotton

The discovery of Lower Palaeolithic artefacts in 1959 by Carpenter at Lower Kingswood inspired T. Walls and J. Cotton to continue investigations in this area. In 1980, Walls and Cotton reported a further series of Palaeolithic finds made in the area. These are listed as a collection of artefacts recovered as surface-finds at A on fig. 2 (see Figure 24) close to Carpenter's 'working-floor' (shown on their map as no. 1, see Figure 24) and several other individual finds from separate locations in the same parish (shown as B and C on Figure 24) (*op. cit.* 1980: 16–7). They also noted that the area in which Carpenter had made his original find of a 'working-floor' had all but been filled in with dumped rubbish but that a small section of its original profile remained, unaltered and unused, at the southern end of Mogador Road. The remaining area had been filled in with rubbish and was now levelled and returned to agriculture. However, the area designated Site A, which overlooked the western slope of this former valley, had not been disturbed by the rubbish dumping. From 1969 onwards, Walls spent time field-walking in the area (see Figure 24 for the relationship between Carpenter's working-floor and Walls and Cotton's investigations). Double-ploughing during 1969 had offered an exceptional opportunity for the retrieval of flint artefacts. A succession of visits to the area had produced;

> 'a number of implements of Lower Palaeolithic type, together with a quantity of waste-flakes and several hammerstones of arguably similar date. Other flints, with traces of fire-crackling [burnt flints] and the remains of surface-patination similar to that of the Palaeolithic artefacts, were also noted and some samples retained. Despite further deep ploughing, recent visits to this site have failed to produce any other Palaeolithic finds, and it would appear that all the surface material has now been picked up' (*op. cit.* 1980: 17).

Following these successes, field-walking was extended onto arable land to the south of the Kingswood site, where various Lower Palaeolithic artefacts were recovered. Further investigations in this area included a small-scale excavation by F.F. Pemberton in an attempt, 'to trace a knapping floor and also to determine the ecological sequence' (*op. cit.* 1971).

In recording the results of his small excavation, Pemberton displays an unfortunate response to the results of his investigations – one that is not uncommon in Palaeolithic archaeology and one that seems to be routed in a lack of appreciation of the value and importance of *all* Palaeolithic material which is found *in situ*. He writes

> 'the results [of the investigations] proved rather negligible, with only a few primary flakes occurring in section [however] a fossil layer containing erratics and patinated frost shattered flints .. was revealed above the natural Clay-with-flints at a similar depth to that at which the original knapping-floor was located' (*ibid.*).

Perhaps, Pemberton's trench was positioned on the periphery of a 'working site' for he records that double-ploughing, in a field adjacent to the site, had recently brought to the surface a number of pointed and ovate hand-axes with a white patina. He considered these artefacts to be similar to those recovered from the original floor.

Although many of the surface-finds from the Lower Kingswood/Walton-on-the-Hill/Banstead area are described as, having being 'torn out' of the underlying Clay-with-flints by deep-ploughing, the only certain embedded artefacts are those from:

– The Blue Anchor Inn, Banstead Newton (TQ 234554) – 1 handaxe dug up from a 91cm deep trench for a water main by A.T. Watson in 1925 (Carpenter 1963).
– Knowlehawe, Tadworth (TQ232559) – 2 handaxes dug up in garden before 1939 and now in the possession of Mr Easton (Carpenter 1957).
- Banstead, Walton on the Hill (TQ234551) – 1 broken handaxe embedded at 2ft below ground surface (Carpenter 1955).
– Rookery Farm (now demolished and used as infill), Banstead Heath (TQ245542) – 1 hammerstone, 1 fire crackled core [burnt flint], 2 cores, 83 waste flakes, 4 handaxes, 3 scrapers, 2 handaxe fragments recovered from Rookery Farm working floor exposed by land clearance in 1959 (Carpenter 1960).
– Rookery Farm (TQ244541) – A few primary flakes – Excavations by Pemberton 1969–70 in the area of Rookery Farm (Pemberton 1971).

Discussion

Carpenter's keen observations and carefully written reports established the importance of the Lower Kingswood artefacts – artefacts whose value would have otherwise be minimised if, like so many other hill-top finds from deposits mapped as Clay-with-flints, they had been consigned to the surface-finds category. Furthermore, this well documented discovery of the Palaeolithic working-floor at Lower Kingswood, inspired Pemberton and Walls and Cotton to continue and expand the area of investigation. All the evidence now available, in particularly the many recorded embedded and recent surface-finds by the local archaeological group, suggests that an undisturbed Palaeolithic floor(s) may still exists in the Walton on the Hill, Kingswood, Banstead area. The importance of these Lower Palaeolithic high-level palaeoliths from Surrey did not go unnoticed by Wymer (1987: 29), as he writes:

> 'The Walton on the Hill – Kingswood – Banstead sites, with hand-axes virtually in primary context in the upper part of the Clay-with-flints, are unique in this respect, for they demonstrate the exploitation of the high Chalk Plateau, well away from contemporary river valleys'.

As we shall see in the detailed discussion in the Case-study Sub-section 6.11, these 'unique' features to which Wymer refers, are characteristic of embedded high-level sites from areas mapped as Clay-with-flints – in whatever county they have been found.

* * * *

Embedded artefacts from the area referred to variously as; 'above Wannock' and/or 'Folkington' (referred to here as 'Folkington Hill') near Eastbourne, Sussex

The site at Folkington Hill (TQ553027), 5 miles NW of Eastbourne at 600ft. (183m) O.D. is on the summit near the edge of the escarpment, from which can be seen Pevensey Bay (see Figure 25). To the SW, the Downs end in sea cliffs, with the town of Seaford on the Cuckmere estuary. Folkington Hill is capped with deposits mapped as Clay-with-flints. The nearest river is the Cuckmere, at a point two and a half miles NW and 600ft. below.

In the 'notes' section of the Proceeding of the Prehistoric Society of East Anglia, is a contribution by A.E. Todd entitled 'Early Flake Implements From Clay-With-Flints On The Eastbourne Downs' (1932–1934: 419–20, Vol. vii), in which he describes three striated flakes from the Clay-with-flints at 600 feet. O.D. on the summit of the South Downs above Wannock, Sussex. A further report by Todd under the title 'Early Palaeoliths from the Summit of the South Downs' (1935: 140–43) describes a number of artefacts found at the same site as the three striated

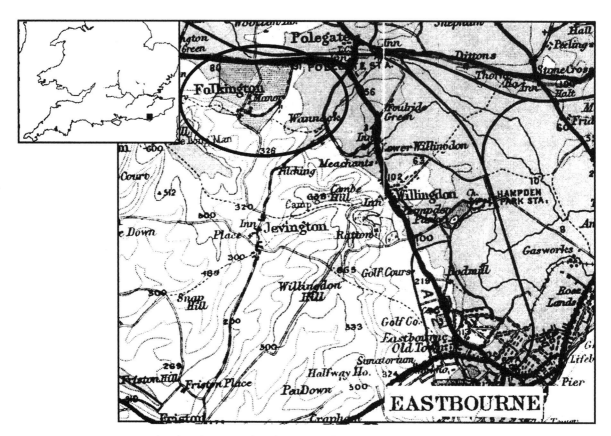

Figure 25 Map showing the area referred to variously as; 'above Wannock' and/or 'Folkington' (referred to here as 'Folkington Hill') near Eastbourne, Sussex.

flakes. All these artefacts were found by him around 1930.

The three flakes described and illustrated in the 1932–34: 419 Proceedings were selected, by Todd, from a number of similar flakes which he had recovered from the Clay-with-flints exposed by ploughing on the summit of the South Downs (600 ft. O.D.). In a subsequent volume of the same Proceedings he writes (1935: 140–143):

> 'I have now to record the discovery on the same site, some 5 miles N.W. of Eastbourne, of four interesting core implements. Adjoining the field of Clay-with-flints' where the flakes were found, there is a mound 13 yards in diameter and 3 feet deep in the centre, which a long time ago may have been thrown out of an adjacent shallow pit ... The mound, beneath a few inches of turf, consists of a mixture of sand, clay, and flints of various shades of brown, similar to those lying nearby in large numbered on the adjoining fields .... I found implements about 2 feet below the surface of the mound. All are abraded and striated'.

These finds occurred in an area where, in the past, many 'Harrisonian eoliths' (see General Introduction for an explanation of the Harrisonian eoliths and associated debate) had been found, but the naturally fractured flint eoliths were very different to the artefacts described by Todd. However, the artefacts recovered by Todd were, where different to other high-level finds. Many of these artefacts are described as black lustrous in colour and striated. These features have often led to the integrity of these artefacts being questioned. I therefore arranged with the British Museum to examine the Todd collection, in the hope of answering the following questions:

- How well do the actual artefacts compare with the illustrations?
- Are they in fact eoliths rather than palaeoliths?
- What are the striations really like?
- How lustrous are they?
- How much edge damage is there? and perhaps the most important question
- If these artefacts were not black, would they fit easily into other Lower Palaeolithic collections and would they then be seen as just 'weathered'?

This is a crucial question, as the colour of an artefact is often determined by the chemical/mineral composition of the soil immediately surrounding it (colouration/staining is discussed later in this Section). On examining the collection, I found that the artefacts collected by Todd were immediately recognisable from the illustrations, but they are not totally black, nor are they eoliths. The general condition of the artefacts is just as they are described and illustrated, the artefacts are indeed striated and

lustrous to varying degrees and are similar, other than in colour, to other Lower Palaeolithic artefacts.

The following descriptions of the Folkington Hill artefacts are Todd's but where necessary and appropriate I have added comments (Note: B.M followed by a number is the British Museum's code for that artefact). Todd (1932–1934: 419–20) describes three flakes thus:

1. 'Flake, unpatinated and black in colour. The surface is highly lustrous but striated on both faces, though more markedly on the upper. All the prominent arretes show signs of abrasion. The flint consists of a large primary flake, showing on the lower face a marked bulb of percussion with eraillure and on the upper face three primary flake scars, one of which shows strongly marked fissures. At the point of impact of the blow which formed the flake, is a small area of cortex. The platform has the appearance of being faceted and secondary flakes have been removed all round the edge of the implement, some of the secondary flaking may be due to natural flaking'.
   - B.M. 1948 5–2 (5): The colour of the cortex is light brown. Some of the secondary flaking does appear to be damage (natural flaking) as Todd suggested.

2. 'Flake, dark patination but flecked and mottled with yellowish markings. The flint shows striations and abrasions similar to No. 1. The lower surface of the primary flake has a bulb and eraillure, the upper retains a considerable area of cortex. There is a certain amount of secondary flaking around the edges, some of which may be the result of natural flaking'.
   - B.M. 1948 5–2 (6): The following additions are made to the previous description. The colour of the cortex is light yellowish brown and dark brown, the striations show as yellow lines on the black surface: the more recent damage shows as white areas. This is a curved flake with a hinge fracture.

3. 'Flake, ochreous patination with white streaks. The primary flake intersections have been smoothed by abrasion (similar to flakes Nos.1 and 2). The lower flake surface shows a prominent bulb of percussion with eraillure and marked pressure rings, the upper surface is divided into five primary flake scars. The striking platform shows no signs of faceting. There is a certain amount of secondary flaking around the edge of the flake, some of which is clearly recent and accidental'.
   - B.M. 1948 5–2 (7): The following additions are made to the previous description. The

colour of the patination is a dull olive/ yellow/yellowish red with the striations show as light brown/white lines, mostly on the ventral surface.

The four artefacts subsequently described by Todd (1935: 140–43) are as follows. Again, I can confirm his basic identifications and have added a number of comments.

1. 'Ovate, 3¾" by 3", lustrous black in colour, striated on both faces, particularly on the lower. The flake ridges are worn and both faces are pitted with percussion marks. The implement is 1⅛" thick at the butt, and is flattened out towards the point for half of its length. The lower face was formed by two blows, one leaving a large negative bulb. The left hand side has been worked on both faces to form a cutting edge, but the right side is blunted. There are two small patches of buff cortex. Ferruginous accretions occur'.

    –   B.M. 1948 5–2 (1): The following additions are made to the previous description. This artefact is lustrous black, but many olive/ yellowish red inclusions are apparent. A number of red lines radiate from the butt (possibly the result of clay minerals crystal- lising in thermal cracks) near a small frost plucked area. There are less striations on the butt end than on either surface.

2. 'Ovate 3¼" by 3". Black lustrous flint with ochreous spots and patches, much striated on both faces, while the worn ridges and innumer- able percussion marks give the implement a very battered appearance. Each face is formed by the removal of a few broad flakes. Left edge blunt; cutting edge on the right produced by secondary work on both faces. There is no cortex, the butt being faceted'.

    –   B.M. 1948 5–2 (2): The following additions are made to the previous description. A large area of olive/yellow/ reddish yellow inclu- sions is concentrated at left edge. There are less striations on the butt end than on either surface.

3. 'A sub-triangular implement, 3½" by 2½". Deep orange in colour with chestnut and olive patches. Flake ridges worn, and both bear striations and percussion marks. Both faces are coarsely worked and are formed by the removal of a few rather thin flakes. The edges are wavy in outline'.

    –   B.M. 1948 5–2 (3): The following additions are made to the previous description. The ventral surface is duller than the distal. The striations appear as reddish-brown lines.

Some ancient damage is present on the distal end, left side.

4. A crudely pointed implement – 'A rostro- carinate implement 4⅛" of the same lustrous black flint as no.1. It exhibits on its flaked surface a large number of striations and some incipient cones of percussion, while its ridges and outstanding portions show considerable abrasion'.

    –   B.M. 1948 5–2 (4): The following additions are made to the previous description. Com- paratively there are fewer striations on this artefact than the others. The ridges may be very weathered.

Five other artefacts from the Folkington Hill site (collected but not illustrated or described by Todd) are held at the British Museum. Two (1950 7–4. 3 and 1950 7–4. 4), may come from the mound, the other three are listed as surface finds. It is not clear, however whether 'surface' in this case refers to flakes recovered from the surface of the Clay-with-flints, as opposed to those from the mound, as Todd writes 'The flake implements illustrated and described in this note are selected from a number of similar flakes obtained by me from the Clay-with-flints exposed by ploughing ….' (Todd 1932–1934: 419–20). I have therefore included brief descriptions of all five artefacts.

–   1950 7–4 (3): Flake, 2½" by 2": the flint is black lustrous with olive inclusions. A number of striations are present on the dorsal surface. This artefact may possibly be a fragment of a handaxe (alternatively it could be just a debitage product). Flakes have been removed from both dorsal and ventral surfaces.

–   1950 7–4 (4): Flake, 3¼" by 2½": the colour of the cortex is grey/white/pale brown: the flint pale brown. There are marked differences in the patina and striations – the ventral surface is dull with large areas of olive/ yellow-pale brown/ reddish yellow/black inclusions, but the dorsal surface is more lustrous, inclusions are not so apparent and far fewer striations are present.

–   1950 7–4. 1: Flake, 3" by 2½". The colour of the cortex is light-brown with yellow patches; the flint lustrous black. Both surfaces are striated, the longest striation is approximately 1cm, but stri- ations are absent on the wide platform.

–   1950 7–4. 2: Flake, 2½" by 2¼". The colour of the cortex is light brown; the flint lustrous black, few striations are apparent.

–   1950 7–4 .5: Flake, 3¼" by 1¾". The colour of the cortex is light brown/pale reddish brown with a small patch of black manganese staining: the flint is pale brown with olive and yellow inclusions.

Discussion

The Folkington Hill artefacts are of great interest. The artefacts divide into two basic groups namely those which are black, and those which are ochreous in colour – the amount of lustre varying from artefact to artefact. The questions, which unfortunately cannot be answered from a simple inspection of the material, are:

- Were the artefacts manufactured from two nodules, inherently different in mineral/chemical composition, the result of which was an eventual difference in the colour of the artefacts?
- Do these artefacts form a single assemblage or
- Do they come from two different levels in the deposits?
- If they come from different levels, would this difference in colour indicate that the artefacts lay in very different local environments?

Even if these questions are unresolved, there are a number of points to be considered. Ochreous artefacts are commonly found on deposits mapped as Clay-with-flints, much less so black. It is interesting to note, therefore, that where very ochreous artefacts with colourful inclusions are found, so are black artefacts (see this Section: the Hackpen Hill discussion and the general Conclusion). The striations and weathering patterns of the artefacts are also interesting. The particular striation patterns observed here and, for example, at Green Lane in East Kent, could be due, not so much to material rolling around, but to soliflucted material moving over the exposed surface of artefacts partially embedded in frozen ground (see also Striations in the general conclusion to this Section). In the quest for a greater understanding of the Lower and Middle Palaeolithic periods in Britain, it has always been the undamaged, perfect specimens of Palaeolithic craftsmanship that have been most generally desired by archaeologists, as perfect specimens may equate to 'primary context' sites (if such things really exist). However, in reality, it is the presence of *any* Palaeolithic artefact found embedded within the deposits mapped as Clay-with-flints that is so important. The rarity of such artefacts elevates their condition to be of diagnostic importance. The artefacts found by Todd in the mound on Folkington Hill may fit somewhat uneasily into the category of 'artefacts found 'embedded' in the Clay-with-flints'. However, the flakes at least, as the reports clearly show, were certainly embedded in the Clay-with-flints. In 1935, Todd wrote,

> 'That these ancient water-worn implements are stranded upon this hilltop, so remote from any existing river system, and so near the denuded Weald, is suggestive'.

Although the deposits mapped as Clay-with-flints are still not well understood, we are now, unlike Todd in 1935, in a position to understand that these artefacts were not, as he implies, 'stranded upon the hilltop'. Rather, they were deposited by Lower Palaeolithic peoples, during the late Quaternary, high up on an ancient landsurface, which had been uplifted from the surrounding Weald during the Tertiary period (refer to Explanatory Sections 1 and 2). Here, therefore, despite their appearance and condition, lies their great value as the colour, patination, striations and abrasions are clues to what has been happening on the summit of this Clay-with-flints capped hill since they were discarded. Such processes, (as discussed in this Section and the Sub-sections) could include solifluction and soil creep, or freeze thaw processes that do not generate substantial lateral transport, but result in movement of the soil around the artefacts.

First we will consider another occurrence, the fascinating site of Hackpen Hill in Wiltshire, where black, ochreous and, a cream patinated artefact were found.

* * * *

Embedded Lower Palaeolithic artefacts from the deposits mapped as Clay-with-flints capping Hackpen Hill, Wiltshire

Hackpen Hill in Wiltshire (see Figure 26) has attracted attention both in prehistory and in recent times. On its summit is the ancient track known as the Ridgeway and, more recently, the deposits mapped as Clay-with-flints which cap the hill have provided a source of material for brick-making. As many Palaeolithic artefacts had been found on the surface of the southern end of Hackpen Hill in the vicinity of a saucer-shaped depression (at SU128726) close to Glory Ann pond, two excavations were conducted by the Rev. H.G.O. Kendall in the depressions from around 1909 and in 1912. A description of the general area and a report of these excavations are included in volume 28 of the Proceedings of the Society of Antiquaries of London (Kendall 1916, 28: 26–48). Kendal had noted that 'a number of chipped flints [Kendall seems to have used this term 'chipped' to mean 'artefacts manufactured by Palaeolithic peoples'] had already been picked up within the hollows, and it was evident they came from a bed occupying parts of the hollows. They occurred numerously there and but sparingly elsewhere; and, in any case, not sporadically, as do the later finds' (*op. cit.*, 1916: 29).

Section 4

The Rev. Henry George Ommanney Kendall, F.S.A. was educated at Magdalen College, Oxford, B.A. 1888; M.A 1893; Leeds Clergy School 1890 and became a Priest in 1893. By 1904 he had become Rector of Winterbourne Bassett. During his twenty years at Winterbourne Bassett he spent the whole of his spare time in the study and collection of Palaeolithic flint artefacts and eoliths, particularly on the Clay-with-flints of Hackpen Hill and the gravels of Knowle Farm Pit. To these localities he added the famous flint mines of Grimes Graves in Norfolk, and he also began the great excavation of Windmill Hill, Avebury. As a result of this concentration of his abilities on this particular branch of Prehistoric archaeology, he was widely recognised as a specialist on stone tools, their manufacture and patination. Kendall was elected a fellow of the Society of Antiquaries in 1913. He also served as President of the Prehistoric Society of East Anglia, in whose Proceedings many of his writings were published.

Misunderstandings, data distortions and prejudice

Before the Palaeolithic site at Hackpen Hill can be considered in any detail here it is imperative that the fundamental data distortions contained in the archaeological record as set out in the Royal Commission on the Historical Monuments of England (RCHME) report regarding Kendall's excavations are exposed and corrected.The salient points to consider are as follows:

– Kendall was a competent archaeologist who, as previously noted, excavated both high and low-level sites;
– The low-level site at the Knowle Farm pit, Savernake (not far from the Ridgeway) is situated in gravel;
– The high-level sites on Hackpen Hill are in an area mapped as Clay-with-flints, Kendall recorded the presence of flint and gravel both as surface finds and during the excavations;
– Both flint and gravel are expected components of deposits mapped as Clay-with-flints;
– Kendall took great pains to establish the integrity of the excavated Palaeolithic artefacts from Hackpen Hill as the Harrisonian 'eolith' debate was raging at this time;
– The grid reference given for Kendell excavations on Hackpen Hill in the RCHME reports is (SU121 726 centrepoint). This grid reference does not relate at all to Kendall's excavations at high-level site in saucer-shaped depression at SU128726 close to Glory Ann pond, but rather to the lower levels of Monkton Down – where many pits have been dug.
– The pits in this low-level Monkton Down area may be the result of flint or gravel extraction or Chalk;
– The RCHME report states that 'there has been considerable flint and gravel extraction in the area in the Post Medieval period ... and ... some of the features may even be natural'

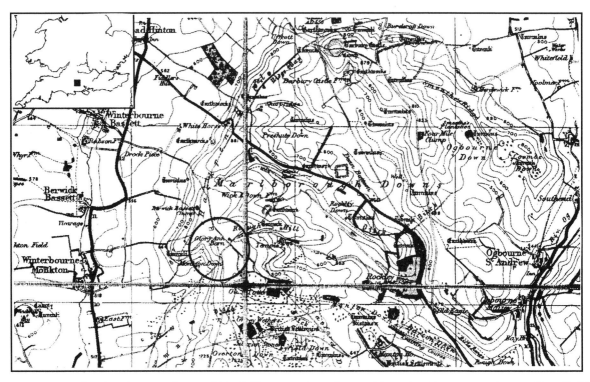

Figure 26 *Map showing the general area of Kendall's excavations close to Glory Ann Barn on Hackpen Hill, Wiltshire.*

Clearly, the RCHME report is misconstrued in its assumption that the hollows Kendell excavated on the high-level site at Hackpen Hill near Glory Ann pond are one and the same place as the low-level pits on Monkton Down where flint digging and gravel extraction is recorded. Kendall's important, and rare, report of embedded Palaeolithic artefacts from this high-level site on deposits mapped as Clay-with-flints is effectively, but mistakenly, dismissed as the following quotes from the report show: 'His [Kendall] excavations at two such depressions in the area indicated the presence of a gravel bed, and the worked flints recovered were compared by him to Palaeolithic material' and 'The discovery of Palaeolithic (and later) worked flint in the Hackpen Hill area is far from unusual, there having been many surface finds'.

The excavations on Hackpen Hill

Hackpen Hill is situated in an area mapped as Clay-with-flints. At 270m (888ft) O.D. it is the highest ridge of the Marlborough Downs, Wiltshire, and also forms their western margin.

The ridge runs in a north-east to south-west direction and is actually the southern end of the great Chalk range which runs diagonally across England. The western face of Hackpen Hill is therefore a steep escarpment consisting largely of Middle Chalk, with a Chalk rock outcrop on the shoulder of the hill. At the top of the hill there is a comparatively thin stratum of Upper Chalk, which in turn is capped with deposits mapped as Clay-with-flints. One mile west of Hackpen Hill, the river Kennet at Winterbourne, is 515ft. above O.D.

In 1912, the Rev. H.G.O. Kendall, accompanied by Mr. W.J. Andrew, began his excavations of Hackpen Hill. The report of these excavations, as presented to the Society of Antiquaries of London, is based on the drawings, measurements and notes which they made 'at the time on the spot'. (*op. cit.* 1916, 28: 26–48). Two excavations (at SU128726) were undertaken, Kendal notes that the excavations were 875ft. O.D. and at the highest point 888ft. O.D. (see Figure 27).

The first excavation consisted of four small pits (see Figure 26) and the second excavation, a single pit, was dug approximately 300 yds away to the north-west from the first site. The excavated areas are described thus:

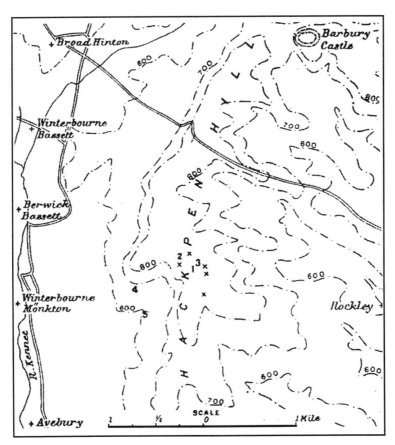

Figure 27 *Map showing sites: 1. 1st excavation; 2. 2nd excavation; 3. Glory Ann Pond where Kendall's fig. 27 was found; 4. Sand-filled rift in the chalk; 5. Sarsen implement (Kendall's fig 26) excavated. Palaeoliths have been found on the spots marked X. After Kendall (1916).*

'Along the top of the hill is a series of hollows, saucer-shaped depressions. They are 20 yds, or more, in diameter, and vary in depth from about 3 ft. to 12 ft. The excavations were made on the less steep slopes of two of these depressions' (*op. cit.* 1916: 28).

Excavation 1

The first site was situated immediately south of the Ridgeway, where it crosses the hill at right angles to the remainder of its course. Some 200 yds away was the barn known as Glory Ann (see Figure 26). Between Glory Ann barn and the depression was a pond, which had resulted from clay-digging for brick-making.

Trial holes were made for the purpose of delimiting a patch of gravel, which proved to be 36 ft. long by 18 ft. at the widest point (see Figure 28). On this first site four small pits were dug.

Pit 1, at the edge of the deeper and inner part of the hollow, but on its least steep slope, was 8 ft. 6 in by 4 ft. by 2 ft deep. A section across it, from the outer towards the inner part of the depression, showed:

– 6 in. Top soil.
– 5 in. to 24 in. (the base being concave); yellow clay, with fractured white flints; depth unknown.

Pit 2, on the rim of the outer and less steep part of the depression, showed ochreous clay only beneath the top soil, and was accordingly abandoned. The clay was in places dark brown and ferruginous.

Pit 3 In the first series of excavations, Pit 3 produced artefacts. A section across the middle of this pit is shown (in Figure 29) and is described as follows:

– 7 in. top soil, with a few stained flints, some chipped;
– 4 in. gravel, the first inch had a little top soil mingled with it. In the remaining 3 in. the flints were embedded in an impenetrable matrix. It was so hard that it could only with difficulty be prised out of the corners of the spade. Pieces of this iron cement, containing flints, were got out several inches in diameter. The iron was frequently found on the chipped surfaces of the flints;
– 4 in. to 6 in. thin gravel in a grey clay matrix;
– 13 in. yellow and grey clay, with a few stained flints;
– yellow clay, depth unknown.

Pit 4, was a small square hole dug in the deepest part of the depression. Here was 3 ft. of mingled clay and humus, with a few stained flints, and very small fragments of chalk in the lowest part. The bottom was not reached, but the chalk was presumed to be not far below. During the excavation heavy rain fell and filled this pit (the first dug) to a depth of about 1 ft. Every drop of this water was held by the sticky clay until the close of the excavation, when the pit was filled in. (Only one of the other hollows on the hill is reported to have held water for more than a few hours, and that was not permanently; *op. cit.* 1916: 28–31)

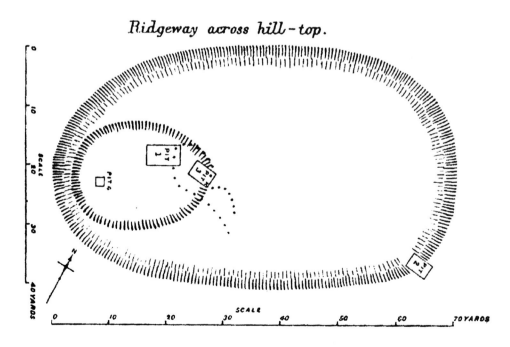

Ridgeway across hill-top.

Figure 28 *Plan of the depression wherein the first series of excavations took place. The dotted line shows the extent of the gravel. After Kendall (1916)*

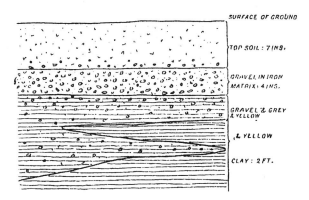

Figure 29 Hackpen Hill section, facing west, across Pit 3.
After Kendall (1916).

Excavation 2

A second excavation on Hackpen Hill was then undertaken by Kendall and Andrew (*op. cit.* 1916: 31). A small trench was dug through the deposits mapped as Clay-with-flints on the 'less steep slope of the hollow to the north-west. The beds were similar to those at the first site, except that the grey and yellow clay was not found, and the gravel rested on yellow clay. Artefacts recovered from the second excavation were similar to those found during the first excavation:

> 'Among the chipped flints, which were of the same industry as at the first site, was a small horseshoe scraper, similar to those of a later date, but somewhat rudely chipped at the end ... A small, whitened, calcined flint was found at a depth of 2 ft. Burnt flints had previously been picked up on the surface at these sites, their fractured and crackled surfaces showing the same yellow staining as do many of the chipped flints' (*ibid.*).

In the detailed discussions which now follow, the Hackpen Hill artefacts are compared and contrasted with each other, and with artefacts from the other high-level sites. Immediately, however, Kendall's own descriptions of the artefacts are given in the order in which they are illustrated in the 1916 report. The original figure number is shown as (Kendall fig. **no.**). As a reassessment of the Hackpen Hill artefacts was made by Lacaille in 1971 and his conclusions discussed in this Section, wherever possible, Lacaille's reference number for the particular artefact is given and shown as (Lacaille, fig. **no.**).

The Hackpen Hill artefacts – as described by Kendall

- Sub-triangular hand-pick or percuteur (Kendall fig. 4); having a blunt point for striking.

- Typical hand-pick or percuteur (Kendall fig. 5); having one side chipped and showing an obtuse point.
- Combined borer and hollow scraper (Kendall fig. 6); it has a bulb partially removed, a facet on the outer face, and very distinct edge-trimming at the base. (Lacaille fig. 2.5.).
- Flat narrow flint, trimmed along sides, with scraping end (Kendall fig. 7).
- Small beak-shaped tool with facets on outer face (Kendall fig. 9).
- Beak-shaped borer, faceted and trimmed round edges (Kendall fig. 10) made on a flake. The excellent edge-trimming, precisely the same in style as on other specimens of the series – all round the neck and up the point (*op. cit.* 1916: 34).
- Earlier implement, Palaeolithic, with facets; stained and striated (Kendall fig. 11); ' it is part of a small ovate implement or just possibly it may never have continued much further, in which case it would form a segmental tool. Eight or nine facets, some small, can be distinguished on its two faces .... One facet has almost corroded away (a not uncommon feature on the anciently broken flints from the plateau' (*ibid.*).
- A rude-pointed implement (Kendall fig. 12).
- A rude-pointed implement (Kendall fig. 13; Lacaille, Fig. 2.8).
- Triangular plane (Kendall fig. 14). This implement, 'is of triangular outline and has an edge at right angles to the surface of the flint, and was no doubt intended for use as a plane. The type continued into neolithic times' (*op. cit.* 1916: 37; Lacaille, fig. 2.10).
- Narrow prismatic tool (Kendall fig. 15); closely resembling the cones and prisms of later periods though of less skilful workmanship (*ibid.*; Lacaille, fig. 2.9).
- Flake with points; edges trimmed (Kendall fig. 16); 'it has a good cone of percussion, and has well-known [*sic*] facets, with eraillures on the outer face' and a trimmed butt (*ibid.*; Lacaille, fig. 2.6.)
- Flake with points, but without bulb or facets (Kendall fig. 17).
- Edge trimmed flint, perhaps of earlier date (Kendall fig. 18).
- Early palaeoliths, almost pebbled, deep brown, striated (Kendall fig. 20; Lacaille, fig. 1.3.)
- Palaeolith, abraded, stained, and striated (Kendall fig. 21); ovate.
- Palaeolith, abraded, stained, and striated (Kendall fig. 22); ovate. (Lacaille, fig. 1.2.)
- Light ochreous flake, with facets and later peak (Kendall fig. 23; Lacaille, fig. 2.7.)
- Dark brown palaeolith, abraded and striated (Kendall fig. 24); this, 'small sub triangular

implement is of somewhat delicate workmanship' (*op. cit.* 1916: 41; Lacaille, fig. 1.6.)

– The Glory Ann Pond slightly abraded palaeolith (Kendall fig. 27; Lacaille, fig. 3.2.) (this artefact is of particular significance in this study: it was not part of Kendall's Hackpen Hill collection, but had been discovered earlier on Hackpen Hill) by Mr. J. W. Brooke).

Some of the small flakes are described as having been used as side scrapers. Kendall records that some borers, scrapers etc were very small indeed, in particular that shown in his fig. 9:

> 'one small tool, $1^3/_8$" long, with a beak-end, has facets on its outer face, and it was made from a flake of which the bulb has been removed. The edge trimming is very neat and extends round the whole circumference. So distinctly human is the work on this and certain other tools that if they were found on the surface, unabraded, and of a different colour, they would be regarded by many as interesting neolithic tools; though there is, as a matter of fact, a difference in the manner of work' (*op. cit.* 1916: 33).

Hackpen Hill artefacts – Patination and condition

Both the excavated artefacts from Hackpen Hill and the artefacts that had been 'torn out of the top of the gravel by the plough etc' are recorded as all showing a red/crimson, yellow or green patination, with the exception of a few artefacts which were black. In addition, a dark brown patina was recorded that 'entered deeply into the flint, which is older than the crimson, of this age are one or two flakes, a few edge-trimmed implements, and two very much abraded palaeolithic implements' (*op. cit.* 1916: 35–6).

The different colours were considered by Kendall to have formed at different times, producing a phenomenon of double and treble patination and invariably in the same succession. Using his fig.11, the part of a small ovate implement, as an example, he noted that it had eight or nine facets, (some small) on both the dorsal and ventral faces, crimson patina and dirty white striations. One facet had been almost corroded away.

> 'Three or four small facets of a greenish yellow have removed parts of the crimson flaking, and are therefore, later. They are slightly striated and less abraded. In addition there are one or two small chips of a clear grey. These have removed part of the greenish yellow, and are later still' (*op. cit.* 1916: 34–5).

Kendall states that it does not matter whether man or nature was responsible for the two later sets of flaking:

> 'The point is that the oldest, or crimson facets, are precisely the same condition as those of other typical palaeoliths from the surface; whilst the second series entirely agrees in appearance with the humanly wrought facets on the flints from the site of the excavation' (*op. cit.* 1916: 35).

> 'The question of patina is a complicated one', writes Kendall, however, he also states that 'in some circumstances patina is of considerable value, and it is evident, in this case, that we are dealing with two distinct periods of patination and two different flint-chipping industries – the typical palaeolithic implements and flakes found on the surface outside the hollows, and the later industry from the site of the excavation.' (*op. cit.* 1916: 35–6).

The differences in patination prompted Kendall to divide the artefacts into two groups and thereby observe notable differences in their shape and condition.

– Group 1. Artefacts: dark brown patina; much abraded and striated (for example Kendall fig. 20). This group had 'coarse edges and a considerable hump near the middle of the stone, yet they are frequently chipped all over and show a lanceolate or sometimes ovate outline (*op. cit.* 1916: 41). (Note – based on typology/condition, group 1 was considered by Kendall to be of a greater age than group 2).

– Group 2. Artefacts: crimson and sometimes a brown patination: much striation, but less than group 1, and fewer points of impact. This group comprised both pointed and ovate implements (Kendall figs. 21 and 22) and flakes (Kendall fig. 23).

The Black artefacts

The black artefacts found at Hackpen Hill are described by Kendall as being easily distinguishable, to the accustomed eye, from the surface tools of later periods. The excavated black artefacts are described as having chipped surfaces that are smoother and more lustrous and there is almost always a tinge of green at one part or another. Furthermore, 'the crust also has a peculiar greyish appearance, and is usually 1 eighth inch thick' (*op. cit.* 1916: 34). The beak-shaped borer (Kendall fig. 10) is just such an artefact; 'it is a most remarkable tool', made on a flake and faceted on the outer face. 'There is excellent edge-trimming, precisely the same in style as on the other specimens of the series – all round the neck and up to the point' (*ibid.*). Kendall considered these black artefacts with their thick greyish cortex to be older than similar artefacts which he describes as 'often red, as though from the clay-with-flints; and frequently very thin' (*ibid.*).

Many times throughout this report, Kendall stresses the genuine nature of the artefacts from Hackpen Hill, for as previously noted, the effects of the 'Harrisonian eolith debate' had cast a shadow on all the high-level finds from the Chalk Downlands of southern England:

> 'The work on the flints of this industry, those excavated as well as those picked up on the surface, is definite and manifestly human; the flakes show bulbs of percussion, and were sometimes struck from the plane surface. One small side scraper shows two bulbs. Some have faceted butts. Both flakes and implements etc. have also well-defined facets caused by flaking' (*op. cit.* 1916: 31)

The Hackpen Hill artefacts – as assessed by A.D. Lacaille

In 1960, many of the Hackpen Hill artefacts, and the area of excavation itself, came under the scrutiny of A.D. Lacaille (see Lacaille 1971). Following these investigations, his considered opinion was that both the artefacts and the site itself were even more interesting and important than they had first appeared, and that, although the number of artefacts was not great or the actual artefacts impressive, it was a comprehensive assemblage. He also noted that various artefacts from Hackpen Hill were apparently unaffected by 'rough transport' but they had not escaped the ravages of climatic alterations since being discarded. In conclusion, Lacaille states that 'none of the palaeoliths can be attributed to workmanship more advanced than the Middle Acheulian' but on page 79 in the same paper, he also suggests that certain artefacts 'could just as well have been fashioned in a highly developed Acheulian, or early Middle Palaeolithic industry.' (*op. cit.* 1971: 71).

In the following discussion the Hackpen Hill artefacts are listed in the same order as they are illustrated in Lacaille's (1971:71–5) assessment. Each artefact is cross-referenced, where possible, to the previously discussed Kendall's (1916) illustrations/descriptions and is shown as (Kendall, fig ...).

Bifaces

The bifaces range in length from 3.55 in. (9 cm.) to 4.55 in. (10.5 cm.); they are made by short flaking on

pebbles, small cobbles, or thick flakes and follow quite usual forms. Ovates and core-tools are also represented (Lacaille, 1971: 71).

- Hand-axe (Lacaille fig. 1.1); made on a pebble, surface scored with short striations.
- Hand-axe (Lacaille fig. 1.2); made on a flake, surface scored with short striations (Kendall, fig. 22).
- Ovate (Lacaille fig. 1.3); heavy, bulging and scratched, with crushed edges and attrite flake-ridges. Smoothed and bruised like water rolled-stones (Kendall, fig. 20)
- Ovate (Lacaille fig. 1.4); overall reduction from an oval to a squarish outline. Smoothed and bruised like water rolled-stones.
- Cordiform tool (Lacaille fig. 1.5); pocked by thermal fractures. Heavily coated, ochreous brown patination (artefact in good state of preservation exhibiting well developed Acheulian workmanship).
- Dihedral (Lacaille fig. 1.6); well-made form. (Kendall, fig. 24).

Flakes and derivatives

Lacaille writes, '[Kendall] showed unusual perspicacity at a time when so many searchers thought only of amassing the finest Lower Palaeolithic tools – mainly hand-axes and the like ... Owing, however, to Kendall's carefulness, worn or worked flakes and pieces were collected [during the excavations on Hackpen Hill]' (*ibid.*).

The Hackpen Hill excavations produced a number of flakes which Lacaille noted were similar to Levalloisian flakes, although he suggest that some of these were waste from bifaces in the making, with a number retaining nodular cortex. Among the residue of hand-axe manufacture were flakes that showed signs of utilisation and trimming (see Lacaille fig. 2.1). Two artefacts (Lacaille fig. 2.5 and fig. 2.6) are considered by Lacaille to resemble finds associated with well-developed Middle Acheulian bifaces and parent cores in the valleys of the Thames, Bristol Avon and the Trent (*op. cit.* 1971: 73).

- Flake (Lacaille fig. 2.1): nodular cortex retained; 'Fine steep dressing along the left edge has converted this flake into a side-scraper'. Its feeble hollow right margin is worked boldly on both faces, the upper showing much wear, not unlike that along the edges of Lacaille fig. 2.2.
- Flake (Lacaille fig. 2.2): nodular cortex retained; upper face shows much wear, which may be due simply to natural bruising against other stones, rather than to use.
- Scraper (Lacaille fig. 2.3): made on a flake;

intentional retouch, but is plain along the short oblique edge on the right side of this squat compound scraper. (The natural roughening of the margin at the base of the high left side compared with the intentional work can be seen in the drawing). This artefact was found 6 to 12 in. (15–30 cm.) below the grass level.

- Scraper (Lacaille fig. 2.4): made on a flake; The bruising along the edge of the pronounced lateral hollow appears to be wear rather than deliberate treatment.
- Scraper (Lacaille fig. 2.5): plain vertical butt (Kendall fig. 6).
- Crenelated scraper (Lacaille fig. 2.6): faceted vertical butt; shows that the basic form of the edge-retouched and worn flake was determined before the slice was struck from the prepared core. 'Upper surface also displays large truncated facets resulting from the working down [reduction] of the original lump [flint nodule] (Kendall fig. 16).
- Scraper (Lacaille fig. 2.7): faceted vertical butt (Kendall fig. 23).

Cores

Kendall recovered a number of different types of cores from the pits on Hackpen Hill, however, Levallois ('tortoise' type) cores were not found.

- Core/artefact (Lacaille fig. 2.8): made on a small cobble; this artefact is scarred bifacially at one end only indicating that the maker intended to use it as an edge-tool. Lacaille suggests that, judging by battered condition of the edge, this implement appears to have been used as a chopper or heavy scraper but in either case it falls into the simplest class of the Middle Acheulian tools deftly struck on corticated nodules. A significant amount of gloss was observed on every long facet of this artefact. (*op. cit.* 1971: 73; Kendall, fig. 13).
- Core (Lacaille fig. 2.9): worn convex edge; this small prismatic piece from which flakes or blades have been detached is described by Lacaille as an 'improvised' tool similar to a core-scraper. (Kendall, fig. 15).
- Core/artefact (Lacaille fig. 2.10): type of plane-scraper (Kendall, fig. 14).
- Core (Lacaille fig. 3.1) multi-faceted, subglobular, of medium size; 'hardly any part has escaped the alternate flaking that shaped and brought it to a circumferential cutting-edge. This mostly retains its pristine keenness, but the flake-ridges are dulled in places and the beds show some lustre' (*op. cit.* 1971: 75).

The circumstances of their discovery convinced Lacaille that none of the Hackpen Hill artefacts could

be regarded as derived and that they had not moved very far from where they had been manufactured or discarded. Furthermore, these Lower Palaeolithic artefacts, like so many of the palaeoliths found on the surface, or just below it, at other high-level sites in southern England and north-west France 'exhibited only signs of weathering, superficial alteration and colouration'. Again, this is a reminder that Palaeolithic people did not restrict their activities to the river valleys, but ventured up to the high-levels. Interestingly, Lacaille notes that in this respect

'the finds recall the collection of Acheulian implements from the surface of the plateaux at over 820 ft. (250 m) above sea-level in the famous Dordogne territory. Below, caves and fluviatile gravels have yielded identical Lower Palaeolithic relics showing with complementary evidence that our remote fore-runners wandered and sojourned where they could' (*op. cit.* 1971: 84–5).

Discussion

There are a number of statements and assumptions contained in the reports so far discussed, which at this stage require additional comments or further examination. Recent advances in British Lower and Middle Palaeolithic archaeology have seen the removal of 'typology' as an effective tool for sequencing palaeoliths. It is therefore, no longer acceptable to consider that roughly/simply made artefacts necessarily belong to an earlier, more primitive, stage of the British Palaeolithic than artefacts which display fine/complex workmanship. The finely made ovates from the pre-Anglian site of Boxgrove made this point admirably, and they are not alone. As typology is no longer the benchmark, it is now possible to re-assess many of the conclusions contained in a number of reports. An alternative explanation for the distribution patterns of palaeoliths recovered from the deposits mapped as Clay-with-flints on Hackpen Hill can now be proposed, one which is based on information contained in the site-report itself, on comments and questions by others to Kendall at the meeting of The Society of Antiquaries (Kendall, 1916) and on Lacaille's (1971) re-assessment of both the artefacts and the site. Working within the typological framework of his time, Kendall (*op. cit.* 1916: 35) concluded that:

'we are dealing with two distinct periods of patination and two different flint-chipping industries-- the typical palaeolithic implements and flakes found on the surface outside the hollows, and the later industry from the excavations'.

Lacaille (1971), who was also constricted by a typological framework, did not disagree with Kendall's conclusions, as he maintains that the sharp and unscathed artefacts, from between 15–30 cms. down in one of the excavated pits, are of a more advanced Palaeolithic age than the blemished and abraded artefacts which constitute the bulk of the Hackpen Hill assemblages. If the constraints of the typological framework are removed, their explanations can be seen to presuppose the sequence in which the hollows on top of Hackpen Hill were formed, the order in which the artefacts were manufactured and the geomorphological processes that have affected the area in question. I suggest that it is equally valid to consider that:

1. Both Kendall and Lacaille were mistaken in their assumptions that, as the Lower Palaeolithic implements excavated from a hollow on the top Hackpen Hill were 'sharp and unscathed', they naturally belonged to a 'more advanced Palaeolithic make', 'possibly a late highly developed Acheulian or even early Middle Palaeolithic', when compared with the 'blemished and abraded artefacts' which make up the bulk of the Hackpen Hill assemblage.

2. All the artefacts belong to the Lower Palaeolithic period and the 'sharp and unscathed implements' could have been made either earlier, later or at the same time as the 'blemished and abraded' artefacts. A direct comparison can be drawn with the W.G. Smith's sites here – the brickearth and 'contorted drift' occurrences being regarded as of similar age (see this Section).

3. The 'sharp and unscathed implements' excavated from a hollow on Hackpen Hill were found *in situ*: That is, they were found where they had been made, or deposited, by Lower Palaeolithic people.

4. This latter suggestion, however, does not depend on the hollow's having been in existence in its present form before the manufacture and/or deposition of the artefacts, as solution processes may have created or deepened this feature in the deposits mapped as Clay-with-flints since the artefacts were deposited (the relationship between solution hollows and *in situ* sites is discussed in Sub-sections 6.6 and 6.11). However, it is not unreasonable to consider the hollows as being available to Lower Palaeolithic peoples, for whom they might have afforded a suitable place (for one reason or another, for example shelter from the wind) for the manufacture/deposition of flint artefacts. It is certainly interesting to note that during the first excavation, Kendall (1971: 31) found a number of small lumps of sarsen stones which he describes as 'suggestive of hammer stones, but the present disintegrated condition of their surfaces

precludes the possibility of determining this'. He also excavated from a depth of 2 ft, 'a small whitened calcined flint'. This was not the first piece of 'burnt flint' to be found on the site. However, 'burnt flint' had previously been found as surface-finds on Hackpen Hill (burnt flint was also found Lower Kingswood, Surrey (see above in this Section) and, as we shall see later, at the Case-study site of Wood Hill, Kent). Kendall noted that 'their fractured and crackled surfaces showed the same yellow staining as many of the other artefacts. The presence of hammer stones (possibly), unstained/unweathered burnt flint and sharp and unscathed implements excavated from the hollow may all be considered as at least suggestive of an *in situ* Lower Palaeolithic working site. The evidence for a Lower Palaeolithic working site is further strengthened by the presence of waste flakes. Lacaille noted that,

'among the flakes from Kendall's excavations on Hackpen Hill are several that could be described as Levalloisian. However, some of these are waste from bifaces in the making, for example, a number retaining nodular cortex such as Fig. 2, nos.1 and 2. Some of this residue of hand-axe manufacture bears signs of the utilisation and trimming' (*op. cit.* 1971: 72–3).

A variety of cores were also found but none of the 'tortoise' type. Lacaille described a number of cores thus,

'an easily held, medium-sized, multi-faceted subglobular core, Fig. 3, no. 1. Hardly any part has escaped the alternative flaking that shaped and brought it to a circumferential cutting-edge. This mostly retains its pristine keenness, but the flake-ridges are dulled slightly in places and the beds show some lustre' and 'a small cobble no.8 is so scarred bifacially at one end only as to indicate that the maker intended to use it as an end tool ... Of small prismatic pieces from which flakes or blades have been detached, one particular, no. 9, is noteworthy for its worn convex edge' (*op. cit.* 1971: 73–5)

5. The cream patinated and almost unblemished handaxe (*ibid.* fig. 3.2; Kendall 1916: 46 fig. 27) from the Glory Barn area of Hackpen Hill may be of greater importance than was suggested by either Kendall or Lacaille. This artefact was found prior to Kendall's 1916 excavations in a clay pit on Hackpen Hill. Kendall and Lacaille found its presence amongst the Hackpen Hill palaeoliths a source of interest, but from markedly different perspectives. Kendall concentrated on its patination and typology, whereas

Lacaille accounted for its presence on the hill by focusing on physical processes that may have brought it to its find-spot, though he also commented on the difference in patination. Kendall states that the handaxe

'was picked by Mr. J. W. Brooke, some years ago, out of the clay dug at Glory Ann for-brick-making. It is cream-coloured and almost una-braded. This patination not infrequently occurs on implements of the Lower St. Acheul Period, to which, by its workmanship, this implement appears to belong. Hence we have on our highest hill-tops in the south of England implements ranging from those of a pre-Chelles or early Chelles Period to perhaps Le Moustier (at Cad-dington) .. a noteworthy fact.' (*op. cit.* 1916: 44).

(Note 'Chellean' as a classification for a Lower Palaeolithic industry-type is no longer used. Attributing an artefact to the Chellean was to suggest that it had been made at the very beginning of the Lower Palaeolithic period. 'Lower St. Acheul' came next in order of age).

Lacaille (1971:79) described the cream-patinated handaxe as,

Found only 200 yds. (183m.) from the principal site ... a cream-patinated and almost unblemished hand-axe from the Glory Ann Barn Pit was picked out of the clay into which it had sunk, probably when the surface was soft. It therefore differs very remarkably from the deeply ochreous-stained, worn down pebbled bifaces which have come from this part'.

In 1894, Smith wrote, 'The white colour [of an artefact] is due to the decomposition of the surface of the artefact brought about by water and the matrix in which the artefact happens to be embedded' (*op. cit*: 109–110). It is now generally agreed that the white patination, which is common on dark flint, often begins with a bluish film, which is often thicker on the upper surface than on the lower ones, and becomes increasingly dull, chalky, and white or cream-coloured over time (see Stapert, 1976: 11–12 and Luedtke, 1992: 108). English Chalk flints are susceptible to such weathering because they generally lie in alkaline soils and because they contain a good deal of chalcedony (Luedtke, *ibid.*). Stapert considers white patina to be highly susceptible to staining by humic substances and iron in ground water but that the presence of iron does not seem to be important for the development of dark patina although some dark patinas may have formed this way' (Stapert, *ibid.*). However, Röttlander (1975), suggests that some dark patinas resulted from oxidation rather than leaching of iron.

Parallels

It is perhaps useful at this point, to refer again to the discoveries of W.G. Smith in the brickearth pits around Dunstable and Luton (this Section). Near to the top of the brickearth pits, in the drift-deposits, Smith recovered Palaeolithic artefacts with dark coloured patinations, which he describes variously as ochreous, yellowish, orange-brown, brown, liver-coloured, purplish and blackish. In addition, these artefacts were often striated and/or abraded. How-ever, this was not the case in the lower sections of these brick-earth pits. The artefacts from these lower layers were invariably patinated in various combina-tions of white, fawn grey and sometimes mottled with indigo (as at Caddington). At Round Green, for example, Smith describes the artefacts found (low down in the sequence) on the Palaeolithic 'floor' as clear ivory-white, a beautiful paleish fawn colour, ivory-grey or grey-fawn (*op. cit* 1916: 68). In his excavations at Gaddesden Row, Wymer (1980: 2) reports finding a 'crude flake 9cm long with a diffused bulb and negligible striking platform. It is patinated creamy-white but is neither edge-damaged nor scratched.' This artefact was found at level 3 below artefacts at level 2 that were not white patinated but were slightly abraded and exhibited edge chipping and faint scratches characteristic of soil movement.

The similarity of the artefacts found at Hackpen Hill to those at Caddington was mentioned by Reginald Smith during the meeting of the Society of Antiquaries of London (Smith R.A. 1916):

'Some of the specimens found on top of the gravel (possibly connected with it) were ochreous and covered with spider-web marking like many from the North Downs and in the 'contorted drift' above Mr. Worthington Smith's 'floor' at Caddington and elsewhere' (*op. cit.* 1916: 47).

It is also of interest to note that the embedded artefacts recovered by Carpenter (1956, 1960); and Walls and Cotton (1980) from the (previously dis-cussed) *in situ* site on North Downs at Lower Kingswood, Surrey, were patinated creamy-white or grey-white with slight purple or orange staining.

The cream-patinated handaxe

All the artefacts recovered from the deposits mapped as Clay-with-flints on Hackpen Hill, whether exca-vated or surface finds, are described as showing variously red, yellow, green, black, crimson and/or dark brown patination. How then do the foregoing observations equate with the presence of the cream-patinated handaxe on Hackpen Hill? Why was only one cream-patinated artefact found? There are, I suggest, a number of possible explanations for this:

- The cream-patinated handaxe may have been introduced onto the hilltop from outside the Hackpen Hill area. This introduction may well have occurred comparatively recently or it may have taken place in the remote past.
- The cream-patinated handaxe may have been 'solifluctd in' from elsewhere on the Hill (as suggested by Lacaille), but there are problems with this explanation. The handaxe is described by Lacaille (1971: 79) as 'almost unblemished'. It is therefore neither very weathered/ abraded, nor is it stained brown or colourfully patinated and in this respect it is, as Lacaille admitted, entirely different from the other Hackpen Hill artefacts.
- Based on facts contained in the reports by: Kendall and Lacaille; the observations of R.A. Smith (1915: 407, 1916: 68) that the artefacts found at Hackpen Hill were similar to those at Caddington; the Palaeolithic sites discovered by Worthington. G. Smith around Dunstable and Luton, and my own fieldwork – there is another explanation, which was not (as far as I can ascertain) considered by either Kendall or Lacaille. However, substanti-

ation would require further excavations on Hackpen Hill. I suggest that perhaps the cream-patinated handaxe found at the Glory Ann clay pit was not as Lacaille believed 'solifluctd in' but that it was discovered in its original place of abandonment, by the workmen digging out the clay used for brick-making. The presence of this handaxe and the difference in patination between this and the other Hackpen Hill artefacts could be explained thus: It may have come from a *lower level* within the deposits mapped as Clay-with-flints on Hackpen Hill than all the other artefacts recovered by Kendall. The site of Kendall's excavation was, as we have seen, situated in a depression south of the Ridgeway and around 200 yds from the barn known as Glory Ann. The Glory Ann clay pit (which later became a pond) was dug between the barn and Kendall's excavations (see Figure 28). Four pits were dug by Kendall and it is clear from his report that these pits were excavated down to around 3 ft without ever locating the Chalk (see Figure 30).

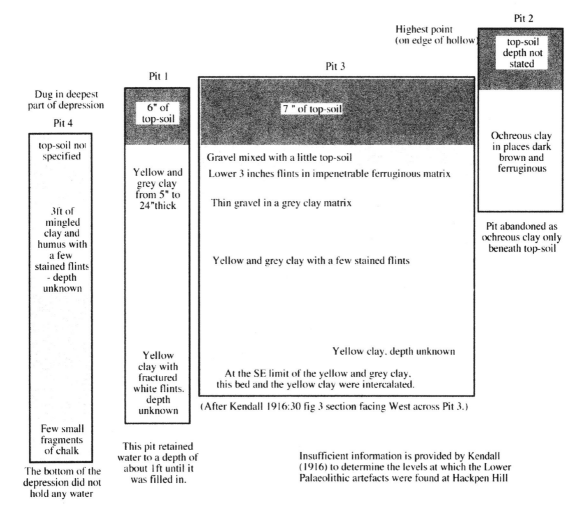

Figure 30. Simplified section diagram showing relationships between the four pits excavated at Hackpen Hill.

What is not clear from Kendall's report is to what depth the workmen may have excavated the Glory Ann pit. It would be reasonable to think that the depth and perhaps area of their excavations exceeded those of Kendall, if they were making bricks commercially. However, it is conceivable that the workmen did not excavate down to the Chalk, as a pond (which is still in existence) formed in the pit, which may not have happened if all the Clay-with-flints deposits had been removed. With the proviso that the underlying Chalk was not totally saturated, the water would perhaps have just drained away if only highly porous Chalk had formed the bottom of the pit.

There is a parallel between the first pit dug by Kendall (pit 1) and the Glory Ann pit (pond). It will be remembered that Kendall wrote:

> 'During the excavations, heavy rain fell and filled pit 1 (the first dug) to a depth of about 1 ft. Every drop of this water was held by the sticky clay until the close of the excavations, when the pit was filled in'.

Significantly, he adds 'The bottom of the depression did not, on the contrary, hold any water. One only of the hollows on the hill holds water for more than a few hours, and that not permanently' (*op. cit.* 1916: 29–30).

Furthermore, there is another reason for believing that the cream patinated handaxe may have come from a low level in the Glory Ann pit. Kendall does not record finding artefacts in pit 1 (his nearest excavation to the Glory Ann pit/pond) but the stratigraphy he found (underlined for emphasis) is described thus:

> 'Pit no. 1, at the edge of the deeper and inner part of the hollow, but on its least steep slope, was 8 ft 6 in. × 4 ft × 2 ft deep. A section across it, from the outer towards the inner part of the depression, showed:
> – top soil, 6 in.,
> – grey and yellow clay, from 5 in. to 24 in., the base being concave;
> – yellow clay, with *fractured white flints*; depth unknown'. (*op. cit.* 1916: 30).

As Kendall uses the prefixes 'chipped', 're-chipped', 'flaked', or 'edge-trimmed' to denote humanly worked material, it must be assumed that the *fractured white flints* from Pit no.1 have not been in any way worked by Lower Palaeolithic peoples. However, much as this may diminish their importance in an strictly archaeological context, it does nothing to reduce their significance from geological and geomorphological perspectives. There are no other references to white or light coloured flints (either natural or as artefacts) being found in any of the other pits that Kendall dug in the deposits

mapped as Clay-with-flints on Hackpen Hill. The presence of these white patinated flints at a low level in the pit can be seen as adding at least circumstantial support to the idea that the Glory Ann artefact did indeed come from the brickearth pit.

The artefacts recovered from the pits in the deposits mapped as Clay-with-flints on Hackpen Hill are described by Lacaille, ' as mostly of a good grade of rich brown and greenish flint, often banded and mottled' (*op. cit* 1971: 70). However, he also noted that there was 'a lack of suitable raw material on the high ground for making large bifacial implements by shallow flaking' (*op. cit.* 1971: 71). As previously noted, artefacts from Kendall's Hackpen Hill excavations exhibit various conditions and colours of patination ranging from brown, crimson, yellow, green and black. However, the 'Glory Ann' pond artefact (see Kendall, fig. 27) was cream-patinated and almost unblemished. That these artefacts differ in degrees and colour of patination is undeniable. The meaning of these variations to the analysis of finds and find-spots/sites may be less clear. This problem was recognised by Kendall as he writes:

> 'The question of patina is a complicated one ... a flint of varying purity will take on different patinas on various of its surfaces at the same time ... in some circumstances patina is of considerable value, and it is evident in this case [Hackpen Hill] that we are dealing with two distinct periods of patination and two different flint-chipping industries ... the typical palaeolithic implements and flakes found on the surface outside the hollows, and the later industry from the site of the excavations' (*op. cit.* 1916: 35–6).

The cream-patinated handaxe, as we have seen, was described by Kendall as being 'picked out of the clay'. From this statement one is led to understand that the handaxe had come out of the clay deposit itself and that it had not at any time been a surface-find which had been introduced secondarily or artificially into the clay at the Glory Ann pit. If this particular cream-patinated handaxe was just one of the surface-finds, then it must have undergone a unique process which resulted in it being the only (recorded) Lower Palaeolithic surface-find of this colour from the deposits mapped as Clay-with-flints on Hackpen Hill.

Therefore, if we set aside the possibility that the cream-patinated handaxe was introduced from elsewhere into the Glory Ann pit on Hackpen Hill, then a series of questions are posed:

1.   Was this handaxe always a single isolated implement lying on the top of the hill? For example, was it discarded independently of other artefacts, for one reason or another, by a Lower Palaeolithic hunter/scavenger/gatherer on the

contemporary landsurface of Hackpen Hill?

2. Was this Lower Palaeolithic handaxe, lying on the contemporary surface of the hill, subsequently 'sealed in' with 'brick-earth' (in the sense of brick-making material)?

3. After digging out the 'brick-making' material, did the workmen stop digging when they came to a different deposit (of no commercial interest), i.e. the Clay-with-flints level? If so –

4. May this one cream-patinated handaxe in fact represent a Lower Palaeolithic assemblage that still waits to be uncovered in the Glory Ann pond area, or elsewhere on Hackpen Hill for that matter?

General conclusion

In this Section, I have reviewed the only certainly embedded Lower and Middle Palaeolithic sites reported (to date) on deposits mapped as Clay-with-flints on the Chalk Downlands of southern England. It will be remembered that, at the beginning of this Section, I took care to list all the positively embedded finds and to suggest the various factors which may account for so few artefacts being reported as embedded finds. Lower and Middle artefacts are common as surface-finds across all the Chalk Downland counties of southern England, but recorded occurrences of embedded finds are very rare indeed. This of course does not mean that embedded artefacts do not exist in these areas. Many artefacts recorded as surface-finds (in the top soil) have simply been released from the deposits mapped as Clay-with-flints by deep ploughing. There is therefore every reason to believe that many *in situ* sites embedded in the deposits mapped as Clay-with-flints remain to be discovered (see especially Section 5 and Sub-sections 6.6 and 6.11).

Many questions have been posed but few answered; nevertheless, contained in these various reports are many observations, whose importance is still not fully apparent to us at the present time. However, as our knowledge of the Lower and Middle Palaeolithic increases, the 'hidden' information contained in these reports is waiting to emerge, allowing problems encountered at one high-level Palaeolithic site on deposits mapped as Clay-with-flints to be tentatively explained by reference to the recorded observations at another Clay-with-flints capped site. For example, in this Section there are references to black-patinated Palaeolithic artefacts being found on deposits mapped as Clay-with-flints capped hilltop site above Wannock, Eastbourne (Todd, 1934: 419; 1935) and on Hackpen Hill, Wiltshire (Kendall, 1916: 34). These artefacts puzzled their finders, this Section is concluded by considering them a little further.

Black artefacts and Glossy patina

From my own personal experience in the field, and with reference to the work of others, it is clear that the patination and colour changes seen on an artefact are caused by that artefact being subject to certain processes (whether rapid or slow), associated with particular environments. Woodcock (1981: 340) suggests that the black patination seen on the Folkington Hill artefacts was probably the product of manganese staining. However, I am not so certain. During the 1993 Wood Hill, Kent Case-study excavation and the 1994 Resistivity survey of the same area (see Section 5 and the Sub-sections), both naturally fractured and humanly struck flakes were recovered from pockets of clay which had a high manganese content, consistent with Hodgson *et al's* (1967: 85–102) findings. The colour/patina of these naturally flakes and the humanly manufactured artefacts (and the nodules) in no way resembles that of the black artefacts from Folkington Hill or Hackpen Hill (see Sub-sections 6.7 and 6.8). I have collected many nodules whose cortex exhibits substantial amounts of manganese/haematite staining, but the flint itself does not resemble that of the black artefacts. Therefore, if manganese staining were the cause of the black colouration of the flint, then surely the cortex of these artefacts would also be black or at very dark also, which it is not.

These black artefacts are described as having a 'glossy patina'. Investigations into the cause of 'glossy patina' has, it seems, been principally directed towards explaining this effect as found on various types of chert. Given the basic similarities between flint and chert (flint is actually a form of chert) much of the research should be directly applicable. The following explanations are taken from various sources:

– Some cherts weather by developing a uniform translucent gloss over their entire surface as a result of silica deposition (Stapert, 1976: 12).

– Some of this silica may have been dissolved in the groundwater, but much of it probably comes from the chert itself (Luedtke, 1992: 109).

– Experiments by Röttlander showed that glossy patina could be produced in the laboratory. During the process, the flint lost weight and silica apparently dissolved from projections on the surface of the flint, which have a high potential energy, and was redeposited in low areas, which have low potential energy (Röttlander, 1975).

– When glossy patina forms [on chert], it seals the cracks and pores and makes the surface resistant to other forms of weathering (Stapert, 1976: 12).

– Glossy patina forms a uniform coating, even into the hollows in the surface of a chert fragment. This appearance distinguishes it from glosses resulting from other processes, including wind and friction (Stapert, 1976: 14–19)

- Wind gloss [on chert] results from mechanical polishing; it tends to have a greasy rather than glassy lustre and generally affects one side of a fragment more than the other (Stapert, 1976: 14–1).
- Friction gloss is apparently caused by siliceous rocks rubbing against one another in the soil, creating small patches of very high gloss [on chert] (Stapert 1976: 29–30).

One or several of the processes listed above could be responsible for the glossy patina to be found on the black artefacts from Folkington Hill and Hackpen Hill. Interestingly, Kendall noted that the artefacts from a low-level site at Knowle Farm, Savernake exhibit certain similarities to those found on Hackpen Hill (*op. cit.* 1916: 41). Kendall worked at both low and high-level sites, which allowed him to make such useful comparisons. His observations support the proposition that high-level sites have a relationship to the low level-sites and an equal place in the Palaeolithic record.

Striations

Several references have been made in the reports discussed in this Section to 'striated' artefacts (for example at Folkington Hill and Hackpen Hill). 'Striations' are scratch marks of varying depth which disfigure the surface of artefacts. They are generally attributed to hill-slope processes that are thought to have moved the artefacts from one place to another (for example solifluction). Following this line of argument, 'striated' artefacts should have been moved some way from where they were originally made or deposited. However, there exists another explanation which may account for some of the scratches to be found on Palaeolithic artefacts. The idea was first put forward (so far as I am aware) by Professor Boyd Dawkins, as reported by Kendall:

'It was alleged that there was something mysterious about the scratches seen on many of the specimens, and that their production had been attributed to ice-action. He [Professor Boyd Dawkins] had carefully examined the Knowle Farm section and noted the festooning and irregularity

of the gravel, marls, and sand, some of the implements being vertical instead of horizontal. It seemed that the gravels had been distributed (*sic*) by the carbonic acid in the rain-water after the beds had been laid down; and in that movement it would have been easy for one flint to press upon another. He [Boyd Dawkins] had himself striated flint by pressing two together with sand in between; hence the striations were of no significance.' (Kendall, 1916: 45).

The possibility that soil movement without substantial lateral transport, rather than rolling in water, or sand abrasion, is responsible for some abraded surfaces is also referred to by Wymer, in his report on the excavations at Gaddesden Row (*op. cit.* 1980: 2 and see also this Section (4) Part 1).

Conclusion

In this Section (4) we have seen that there are several features which the embedded high-level sites on deposits mapped as Clay-with-flints seem to share: hollows filled with brickearth are often present; Burnt flint tends to occur, and the presence of handaxe trimming flakes is quite frequent, suggesting implement manufacture in that particular place from immediately available flint (of these sites Caddington offers the best evidence, with piles of raw material and conjoining handaxe manufacturing flakes). These and other common or recurrent features are discussed in detail in the Case-study Sub-sections.

Having considered the unique and important Lower and Middle Palaeolithic sites which are situated on high-levels in areas mapped as Clay-with-flints in the counties of Bedfordshire, Hertfordshire, Surrey, Sussex, and Wiltshire, and noted that they clearly establish the occurrences of Palaeolithic settlements or occupation sites on the higher ground above the river terraces, we can now turn our attention to the most important site, as far as this research is concerned – a small area of East Kent – the Lower Palaeolithic site at Wood Hill. (see Section 5, for general description and Section 6 Sub-sections for the Case-study format; methodology for excavating a high-level site Palaeolithic site and the required investigations).

The 're-discovery' of a Lower Palaeolithic site at Wood Hill, Kingsdown, near Deal, East Kent – Introduction to the Case-study

Insufficient or inadequate recording of the many Palaeolithic artefacts recovered from the Downlands has generated problems. There are, as we have seen, only a few properly recorded occurrences of the most important artefacts that have been recovered from these high-levels, namely Lower and Middle Palaeolithic artefacts found 'embedded' in the deposits mapped as Clay-with-flints. Sometimes, however, the dearth of information available to a researcher may not be the fault of the original collectors or the museums but rather of those who have the power to publish reports of potentially very important finds – or to ignore them. This Section provides ample evidence of one such occurrence.

The 'rediscovery' of the Wood Hill site

In 1992 I attended a London meeting of the Lithic Society. Here for the first time I met Mr Geoff Halliwell, a member of the Dover Archaeological Group. The Group, as he explained, had over many years, carried out rescue excavations and other fieldwork in the East Kent area whenever the need or the opportunity arose (the Dover/Deal area is rich in archaeological remains which date from many different periods).

When I mentioned my interest in Lower and Middle Palaeolithic artefacts from the Downland hilltops and plateaux in areas mapped as Clay-with-flints, Geoff Halliwell recounted how the Dover Archaeological Group in 1984 and 1985, under the direction of Mr. Keith Parfitt (a professional archaeologist and a Member of the Institute of Field Archaeologists), had the opportunity to focus its attention on a small Downland hill known as Wood Hill (TR 371480, see Figure 31). In the past many stone tools had been recovered from all over the surface of this hill. In order to establish the precise context of the artefacts found on the surface, the Group dug many small trenches (see plan no. 9, Figure 32) on the top of Wood Hill over the two year period.

The excavations followed standard archaeological procedures and a site-archive was produced. However, the stone tools recovered as a result of these excavations all appeared to be Palaeolithic in origin. At that time, both Geoff Halliwell and Keith Parfitt were, as they themselves were the first to admit, not expert in this period and despite their best efforts only a few people showed any interest in these artefacts, as these were hilltop finds. As so little interest and importance was accorded to these finds by the archaeological community in general (see General Introduction) the stone tools and the site-archive were packed away (and half forgotten) – that is until quite by chance I spoke to Geoff Halliwell at the Lithics Society meeting.

A visit to Kent

At the invitation of both Geoff Halliwell and Keith Parfitt I made a field trip to Kent, to visit particular areas where, in the past, the Dover Archaeological Group had found Palaeolithic artefacts (this naturally included the Wood Hill site) and to examine all the artefacts which the Group had recovered during their 1984 and 1985 excavations on Wood Hill. I was also presented with a copy of the Wood Hill site-archive.

Wood Hill

Wood Hill at Kingsdown, near Deal, East Kent (TR 371480) rises to approximately 65m O.D. and is capped by localised deposits mapped as Clay-with-flints over Upper Chalk. This small hill occupies a prominent position at the north-east end of a long ridge of Chalk Downland which is bounded by dry valleys (Figure 33). Within three kms to the east is the sea at Oldstairs Bay (and out to sea, the Goodwin Sands). Open fields lie to the north and west, with Kingsdown Wood covering a substantial area of the hill, to the south.

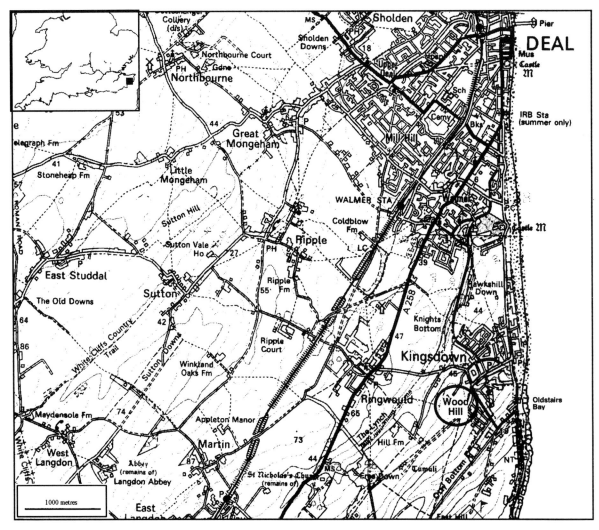

Figure 31 *Map showing Wood Hill, Kingsdown, near Deal, East Kent and surrounding area.*
With kind permission of the Ordnance Survey. Crown copyright. NC/99/179

Over the past 100 years, a number of geological and soil surveys have been carried out in the Wealden District (which includes East Kent). Unfortunately, the Kingsdown area, which includes Wood Hill, is not included in any geological memoirs or soil studies. The only information which is available is to be found on the British Geological Survey map Sheet 290 Solid and Drift Edition. Smart, Bisson and Worssam's (1975) 'Memoir of the Geology of the Country between Canterbury and Folkstone' described the geology depicted on the following British Geological Survey maps: Sheet 289 (Canterbury); Sheet 305 (Folkstone) and Sheet 306 (Dover A) but did not include Sheet 290, which shows the Kingsdown area and Wood Hill. As the Soil Survey and Land Research Centre's Sheet TR35 (Deal) does not cover the area, the related information in Soils of Kent 2, Soil Survey Record No. 15 (Fordham and Green, 1973) and Soils in Kent, Soil Survey Bulletin

No. 9 (Fordham and Green, 1980) is of general interest only as far as this research is concerned. In common with many other geological maps which include areas mapped as Clay-with-flints, Sheet 290 has omissions (see Explanatory Section 2). For example, a small patch of Clay-with-flints, which lies between Wood Hill and Oldstairs Bay, is not shown on Sheet 290. As noted previously (in Explanatory Section 2) many areas of Clay-with-flints deposits are too thin to be mapped and many have been mapped as other deposits, for example, Older gravels, or Blackheath Beds.

A large area of the deposits mapped as Clay-with-flints which cap this hill are covered by Kingsdown Wood (owned by The National Trust). Across the top of the hill is a privately owned concrete track, which runs at right angles to the wood (shown on Figure 34). Access to the wood is from public footpaths to the north-west and south-east.

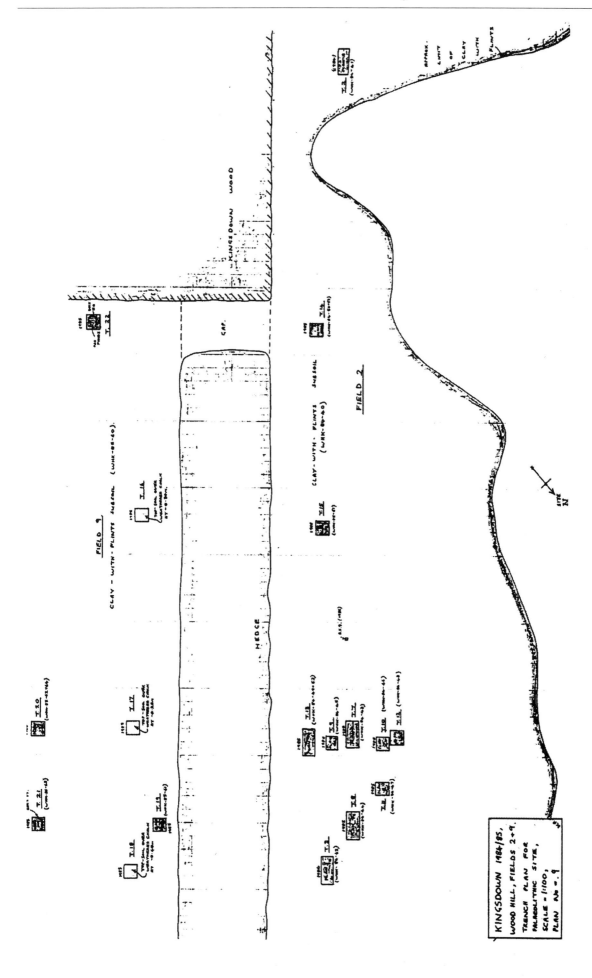

Figure 32 Location of trenches dug by Dover Archaeological Group on Wood Hill during 1984 and 1985. After Parfitt (1985 Wood Hill site archive)

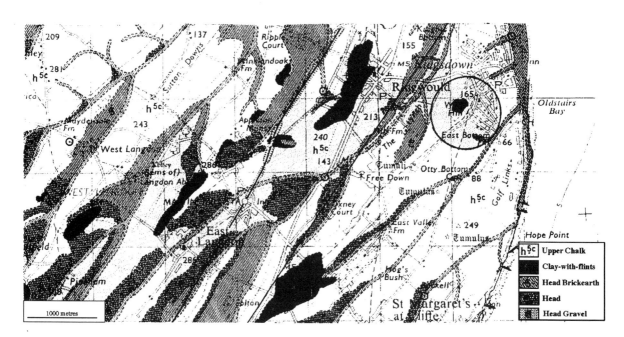

Figure 33 *Map showing Wood Hill in its geological context. IPR/22-16 British Geological Survey.*
© *NERC. All rights reserved.*

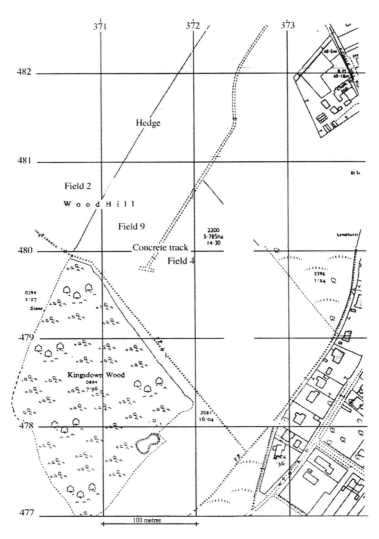

Figure 34 *Map of Wood Hill showing location of concrete track, public footpaths and Fields 2, 4 and 9.*
After Parfitt (1985 Wood Hill site archive)

The Wood Hill 1984 and 1985 excavations – as recorded in the site archive of the Dover Archaeological Group

The 1984 and 1985 excavations at Wood Hill were conducted by the Dover Archaeological Group under the direction of Keith Parfitt and Geoff Halliwell. Over the two year period, a number of small trenches measuring around 2 m × 1m or 1m × 1m were dug to a depth of approximately 1m on top of the hill. Only details of the 13 trenches which yielded artefacts are recorded in the site archive. In many trenches, artefacts are known to have been found in the top soil, but as all surface-finds were only given the site codes W.H.K-84-40 (Field 2) or W.H.K.-85-60 (Field 9) it is impossible to assign this top soil material to particular trenches. The area of excavation on top of the hill was confined to the three fields: namely Field 2, Field 4 and Field 9 (as shown in Figure 34). A trial trench was dug during 1985 in Field 4 but no artefacts were found in the sub-soil. This field was adjacent to a small area of scrub (now a paddock). Artefacts recovered from the top soil of this trench were assigned the site code W.H.K-85-65. Excavations in Field 2 during 1984 and 1985 produced many Palaeolithic artefacts. Field 9, excavated in 1985, also produced a number of Palaeolithic artefacts.

The following descriptions of the trenches and artefacts are a compound of information derived from various tables, sketches and plans in the Wood Hill 1984/85 site-archive and personal communications with Geoff Halliwell. The descriptions of the deposits are based on the rather sparse notes, which occur in the sketches; plans; deposit registers and the tables of flint depths. Information from these diverse sources has been collated in Figure 35 (Wood Hill trench sections – a blue line indicates the levels at which the artefacts were found) and Figure 36 (plan view of the distribution of artefacts in the trenches). More detailed analysis of the relative depths at which the artefacts were found is discussed in Section 6.11 in relation to the 1993 and 1994 excavations. For the sake of clarity, I have found it necessary to introduce the term 'Levels' when describing the deposits. The site archive makes no reference to spits or levels; however, as the site sketches and plans are drawn to scale on graph paper, by measuring where changes in the deposits occur I have been able to assign 'Levels'. The use of these divisions (the 'Levels') allows a virtual framework to be constructed within each trench in order to facilitate discussion and comparisons. Many of the detailed measurements given here (which relate to the deposits) have also been extrapolated from the sketches and plans.

There are a number of entries in the site archive which require clarification, though unfortunately the

necessary information cannot now be supplied (personal communication from Geoff Halliwell). It is, for example, not recorded or remembered what the references written as '+' actually mean in each particular context. In several trenches these very brief descriptions of the deposit are followed by the + sign in reference to pebbles; there is now no way of knowing whether the pebbles formed a layer or were simply scattered throughout the deposit, without any discernible pattern. Where the deposits are described as mottled orange + Lt blue grey clay, it is not altogether clear just how these different coloured clays were distributed through the deposit. The colours ascribed to the deposits were 'as observed' (the Munsell Color chart was not used).

All the artefacts recovered by the Dover Archaeological Group during their 1984/85 excavations on Wood Hill have now been examined by myself and two of the foremost authorities on the British Palaeolithic, namely Prof. Derek Roe and Dr. John Wymer, who both confirmed my conclusions that the artefacts are unequivocally Lower Palaeolithic. The Wood Hill waste flakes (knapping debris) are of many sizes, and include examples produced by both hard hammer and soft hammer techniques. They can be divided into several categories:

- primary waste flakes, from the initial reduction of the flint nodules (with varying amounts of cortex);
- secondary flaking including retouched flakes, handaxe trimming flakes (which were struck off with a 'soft' hammer at a late stage of manufacture;
- blade shaped flakes and fragments of blade shaped flakes. The shape of these flakes may have been accidentally produced as a nodule of an unusual shape was being knapped or, they may have been deliberately struck from a core for a particular use. It is interesting to note that the blade shaped flakes and fragments were found almost exclusively in Trench 13.
- 1 small core and 2 groups of core fragments (one group of which conjoins);
- 2 lumps of burnt flint (see Sub-section 6.11).

These excavated artefacts are patinated white to light grey. Where the cortex is present, it is pale yellow to very pale brown. Many of the surface-finds are also patinated white to light grey; however, other surface-finds have a buff to orange patina, in particular the Dover Archaeological Group's earliest finds on Wood Hill. (Halliwell and Parfitt have observed that ploughing around the edge of the wood often brings fresh patches of clay to the surface and with it considerable numbers of heavily patinated ochreous Palaeolithic artefacts (1993: 83). In the 1984/85 site-archive: the position of the artefacts in the trenches is

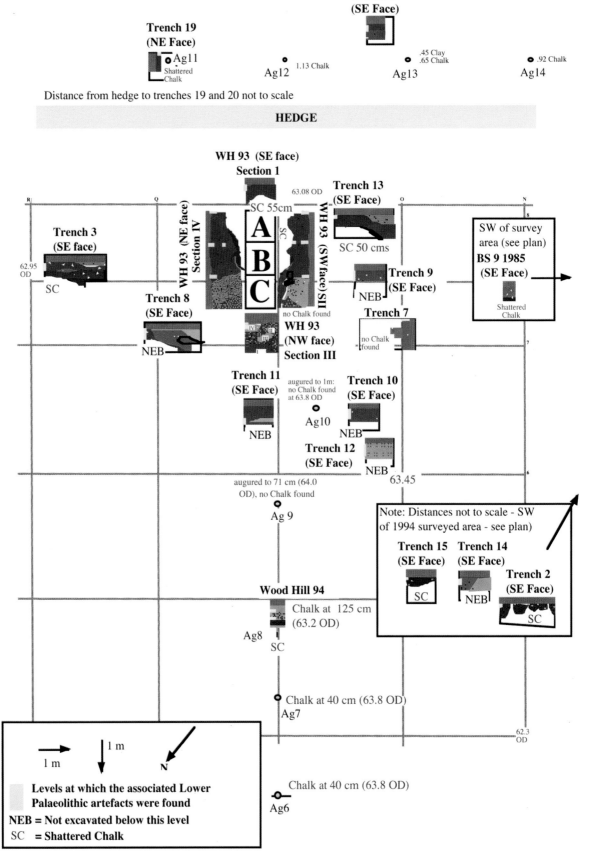

Figure 35 *Diagram showing the Wood Hill 1984/85, 1993 and 1994 trench sections - including levels at which the associated Lower Palaeolithic artefacts were found.*

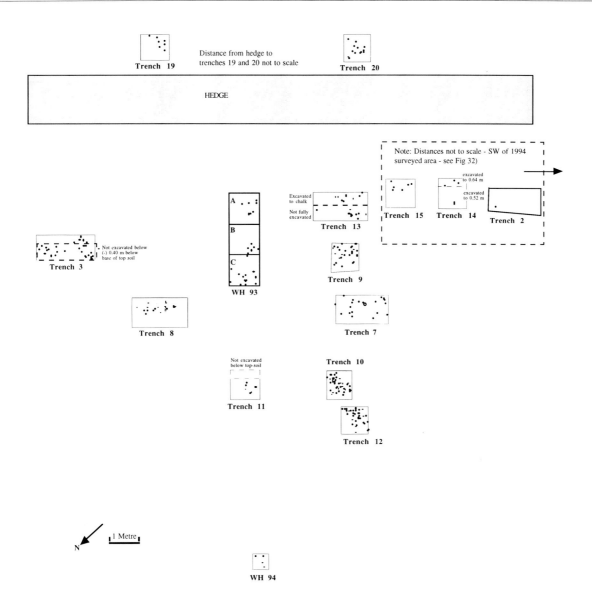

Figure 36 *Plan view of the distribution of the Wood Hill (1984/85, 1993 and 1994) Lower Palaeolithic artefacts: with no distinction between the depths at which the finds were made.*

given in some detail but the artefacts themselves are loosely defined, all the descriptions of these artefacts are, therefore, as originally catalogued by the finders. As yet, exact measurements are not available; determining the size difference between a small flake and a very small flake or, a flake and a thick flake must accordingly be subjective. Where, however, the site-archive records 'fragments' these may be interpreted as 'flake fragments'.

In the following summary (Table 1), I have listed the Wood Hill trenches in numerical order (see Figure 35 for their relative positions on Wood Hill) and added the suffix (L) to denote the larger trenches and (S) for the smaller to make the comparison

between the trenches somewhat easier. It should be noted however, that the type and number of artefacts shown here refers exclusively to those artefacts found *in situ* within the trenches during the 1984/85 excavation of Wood Hill, and does not include any of the surface-finds (e.g. artefacts from the top soil designated W.H.K-84-40).

Note: The Southern Rivers Palaeolithic Project (Report No. 2 1992–1993: 149–50) entry for Wood Hill appears to include only surface finds. The numbers and types of the Lower Palaeolithic artefacts listed there are therefore different to those shown here.

Table 1 *The distribution of Lower Palaeolithic artefacts in the Wood Hill trenches*

Trench size	L	L	L	L	S	S	S	S	L	S	S	S	S	Total
Trench nos.	T2	T3	T7	T8	T9	T10	T11	T12	T13	T14	T15	(T19	T20)	
Large flakes	–	2	–	2	4	2	–	–	4	1	–	–	–	15
Flakes	1	7	8	>4	7	5	2	7	8	–	1	2	8	>60
Small flakes	–	12	7	3	8	12	1	7	2	–	1	1	3	57
Very small flakes	–	1	1	-	9	3	-	7	2	3	-	-	2	28
Flake fragments	-	1	8	3	2	7	2	10	6	1	3	-	-	43
Blades	-	1	1	-	-	-	-	-	-	-	-	-	1	3
Small blades	-	4	-	-	-	-	-	-	-	-	-	-	-	4
Very small blade	-	1	-	-	-	-	-	-	-	-	-	-	-	1
Blade fragments	-	2	1	-	-	-	-	-	-	-	-	-	-	3
Cores	-	1	-	-	-	-	-	-	-	-	-	-	-	1
Cores fragments	-	-	2 grps	-	-	-	-	-	-	-	-	-	-	2 grps
Burnt flint	-	-	-	-	-	1	1	-	-	-	-	-	-	2
Totals	1	32	26	>8	30	30	6	31	22	5	5	3	14	>157

Discussion

It will be clear from the foregoing account that all the Lower Palaeolithic artefacts from the excavated trenches were found embedded in the deposits mapped as Clay-with-flints on the top of Wood Hill. As noted in the previous Section (4), recorded embedded find-sites are very rare. Consequently there are three features of the Wood Hill find-site that are highly important:

1. The fact that these artefacts exist at all – Wood Hill is today a small hill in a very exposed position. The deposits mapped as Clay-with-flints, which cap this hill, now form a small isolated area, much of which is covered by woodland (see Figures 34 and 35).
2. The excavations on Wood Hill, undertaken by the Dover Archaeological Group during 1984/85, were conducted with great care and attention to detail.
3. To date, no other fully comparable site exists.

Other embedded sites such as those discovered by Smith (1894) in the brickearth pits around Caddington appear to have been dug out long ago. Site A at Lower Kingswood, (Carpenter, 1966) was filled in with rubbish and other investigations in the Banstead area (Pemberton, 1971. Walls and Cotton, 1980) failed to locate Carpenter's Lower Palaeolithic floor. Although Todd (1932, 1934, 1935) found embedded artefacts on Folkington Hill, the presence of a Palaeolithic floor was not established there. Only Hackpen Hill remains relatively unchanged, but Kendall's (1916) Hackpen Hill excavations were limited to five small pits from which just nineteen artefacts were recovered – in contrast to the twenty one trenches dug by the Dover Archaeological Group during the 1984/85 Wood Hill investigations, with thirteen trenches producing at least one hundred and fifty seven excavated artefacts.

The 1984/85 Wood Hill excavations generated three important questions, the answers to which could not be found in the site archive:

1. Waste flakes were found in many sizes from very large to very small, but tiny flakes (<1cm) were not recovered. Was this because the 1984/85 excavators were not looking for them, or
2. was it because they were just not present in the deposit?
3. Are there any particular geological, geomorphological and/or archaeological relationships between strata and artefacts on Wood Hill, which the 13 trenches revealed? In other words, is there a distinct archaeological site (or more than one) present, or are we merely dealing with an amorphous scatter of artefacts?

As the artefacts and the deposits are inextricably linked, the answers to these specific questions could only be obtained by further excavations on Wood Hill. Information generated by such investigations would be pertinent not only to the Wood Hill site but might also provide data that could be widely applicable to Lower and Middle Palaeolithic occurrences in high-level areas mapped as Clay-with-flints. Therefore, this small hill in East Kent seemed a suitable area for further investigation and a fitting Case-study site and so, in the event, it proved to be.

Conclusion

The decision to use Wood Hill as the Case-study site was based on the results of my research, which suggested that:

1. The Lower and Middle Palaeolithic artefacts recovered from the Chalk Downlands capped with deposits mapped as Clay-with-flints, mostly as surface-finds but occasionally embedded within the deposit, represent an important and seriously neglected realm of British Lower and Middle Palaeolithic research (see General Introduction and Sections 3 and 4).

2. The deposits mapped as Clay-with-flints appear to have been subjected only to 'restricted change' (as defined in the General Introduction) since approximately the end of the Cromerian, a date at least as old as 500,000 yrs B.P. (see General Introduction and Explanatory Section 2).

3. Such deposits are widely found as a capping on the Chalk Downland plateaux and interfluves of southern England (see Explanatory Section 1 and 2)

4. The deposits mapped as Clay-with-flints include materials of differing ages, compositions and origins, with great variation existing within even small areas and between the different areas (see Explanatory Section 2).

5. The 1984/85 excavations of Wood Hill conducted by the Dover Archaeological Group had produced an important series of artefacts, and sufficient information to warrant further investigations of the site (this Section). The site was likely to yield information relevant to all of 1–4 above.

In the General Introduction, I suggested that it was necessary to employ rigorous modern scientific methods of investigation in order to understand the relationships between the Chalk Downlands of southern England, the superficial deposits mapped as Clay-with-flints which cap them, and the surviving presence of Lower and Palaeolithic artefacts on these same high-levels throughout both glacial and temperate periods.

The past research that has contributed to our understanding of the Chalk Downlands was reviewed in Explanatory Section 1 and that of the deposits mapped as Clay-with-flints in Explanatory Section 2. The Wood Hill Case-study, therefore, marks the first attempt using rigorous modern scientific methods to address certain fundamental questions and hypotheses (see General Introduction) posed by the surviving presence of Lower and Middle Palaeolithic artefacts on the hill-tops and plateaux capped with deposits mapped as Clay-with-flints on the Chalk Downlands of southern England.

To reiterate then; as a Lower Palaeolithic site, Wood Hill offered a prime opportunity to study one example within the range of variability observed in the deposits mapped as Clay-with-flints, in an archaeological context, to determine how geological processes have affected the archaeology and to obtain information at a level of detail not attempted before. The 1984/85 excavations had already produced a substantial number of Lower Palaeolithic artefacts, and this was useful in reducing data distortion by increasing the artefact sample size of the 1993 excavation, which was essentially a small, largely geologically/sedimentologically biased study. Indeed, the existing artefact sample from the 1984/85 excavations was sufficient to allow the concentration of resources of the 1993 excavation and 1994 investigations to be aimed at a greater understanding of the deposit mapped as Clay-with-flints, both in a local context, and for the purpose of placing the site within what is known about these deposits as they exist in southern England.

I cannot claim that this Case-study provides all the answers to the problems generated by the surviving presence of these high-level artefacts but I am confident that it affords new means of evaluating occurrences of Palaeolithic stone tools found in and on the deposits mapped as Clay-with-flints – evaluations which acknowledge the uniqueness of these deposits and their particular characteristics.

Section 6

The Case-study

Sub-section 6.1: Excavating a Palaeolithic site on deposits mapped as Clay-with-flints: Site methodology – excavation techniques; initial recording procedures and sampling strategy

Given that the only evidence normally available for high-level Palaeolithic sites, i.e. artefacts, have been subject to essentially geological and geomorphological processes over extremely long time-scales, the excavation of a Palaeolithic site on deposits mapped as Clay-with-flints requires a methodology that is very different in many respects to that in general use on other archaeological sites – whether Palaeolithic or later. In many ways the artefacts must be treated as integral components of the deposits in which they are found. An artefact is no more than a clast until we recognise it as such. As a very high resolution, three-dimensional reconstruction of the trench, and detailed recording of the deposits are required, I have developed this method of excavating and recording which is essentially designed from a geological, geomorphological and sedimentological perspectives.

Three paramount requirements therefore, distinguish the excavation of a Palaeolithic site on deposits mapped as Clay-with-flints: they are

– Extremely accurate and detailed recording of every natural clast and artefact (equal to or greater than 20mm) at every spit in the 'Control Area' (shown in Figure 38). This includes measurement of three dimensional orientations;
– Detailed recording of both the natural clasts and the artefacts at every spit in the trench as a whole;
– A precise, detailed and extensive sampling strategy of the deposits.

As such a high resolution is required there can be no 'short cuts'. It is therefore, impossible to over emphasise this need for attention to detail – even when using standard archaeological procedures.

Using electronic or basic (level and theodolite) surveying equipment and with reference to the Ordinance Survey (OS) national grid and datum (OD), standard (but very detailed) archaeological

excavation procedures are used to determine:

– The exact location of the proposed trench in relation to the general topography;
– The spit heights (5cm spits) within the trench (Figure 38);
– The accurate position of both artefacts and natural clasts within each spit;
– The geological, geomorphological, sedimentological and archaeological data within the trench throughout the excavation.

The major factor which determines the integrity of an excavation of a Palaeolithic site on deposits mapped as Clay-with-flints, and which is markedly different to other excavations whether at high or low-levels, is the use and attention given to the Control Area. The difference is both important and substantial, as measurements of the orientation (i.e. A-axis, Orientation of dip and Angle of dip) of *everything* in the Control Area, both artefacts and natural clasts, are recorded to afford an extremely high-level of detailed information that provides, *inter alia*, the data required for fabric analysis (fabric analysis is discussed in detail in Sub-section 6.2). Detailed fabric analysis is crucial, as it is the ONLY way to obtain mathematical data that is both repeatable and testable. This is necessary to determine geomorphologically, the *in-situ* (or otherwise) status of a Palaeolithic site on deposits mapped as Clay-with-flints and the types of movement associated with the process/es that operated in that specific high-level area during both temperate and periglacial periods.

The methodology set out here for the excavation and investigation of these high-level sites must be adhered to as a minimum, despite the fact that it is without doubt painstaking, time consuming and difficult work, particularly in adverse weather conditions. But without this crucial attention to detail, the research will be compromised and the integrity of these long neglected sites will be lost.

Adhering to the excavation methodology and the required investigations will produces data sets that can be used with confidence to identify *in-situ* Palaeolithic sites on deposits mapped as Clay-with-flints, by:

– Determining the nature of the deposits;
– Determining the processes that have acted upon the deposits over geological time;
– Facilitating the interpretation of the archaeological component within the deposits with references to past and present depositional processes whether naturally occurring or anthropogenic.

Within the context and framework of the Lower Palaeolithic Case-study site of Wood Hill the excavation methodology and the required investigation are now fully described and discussed.

The Case-study format

This Section (6), the Wood Hill Case-study, is divided into eleven Sub-sections. Examined and discussed in Sub-sections 6.1 to 6.6 are the relationships between the sedimentology, geology and geomorphology of the excavated areas and Wood Hill in general. Sub-sections 6.7 to 6.10 are devoted to the archaeology of the site. The results of these investigations are drawn together in Sub-section 6.11: Conclusion to the Case-study. The Sub-sections are as follows:

– Sub-section 6.1: Site methodology, initial recording procedures and sampling strategy.
– Sub-section 6.2: Fabric analysis, orientation data analysis and discussion.

– Sub-section 6.3: Particle size data analysis and discussion.
– Sub-section 6.4: Clay mineral analysis: a key to Palaeolithic sites?
– Sub-section 6.5: Particle shapes, lithological analysis – discussion and analyses.
– Sub-section 6.6: The resistivity survey.- Sub-section 6.7: Fossils, nodules and artefacts.
– Sub-section 6.8: Description and analysis of the Lower Palaeolithic artefacts recovered during the Wood Hill 1993 excavation and the Wood Hill 1994 resistivity survey.
– Sub-section 6.9: The Wood Hill Biface (WH9 3.F38).
– Sub-section 6.10: Burnt flint, dates and discussions.
– Sub-section 6.11: Conclusion to the Case-study, including three models:
  – The evolution of the Wood Hill site;
  – The Lower Palaeolithic occupation of this site;
  – Patterns of artefact distribution – a reduction sequence.

Setting a precedent: the excavation of the Lower Palaeolithic site at Wood Hill – site methodology, initial recording procedures and sampling strategy

The 1993 Wood Hill excavation began at the beginning of September and was originally scheduled to continue for approximately two weeks. However, very windy, very wet and cold weather became an established feature of the excavation. The team soon became experts at dealing with the many difficulties produced by these conditions, but at times on-site recording procedures were delayed and the cumula-

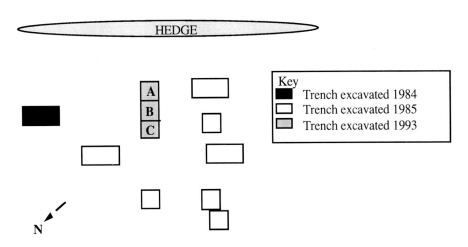

Figure 37 Diagram showing the relationship of trenches dug at Wood Hill, Kingsdown in 1984/85 to the 1993 excavation.

tive effect of these delays was to extend the excavation into the middle of October. In preparation for the 1993 excavation on Wood Hill, Keith Parfitt and Geoff Halliwell happily agreed to mark out the approximate position of a number of the trenches that they and other members of the Dover Archaeological Group had dug during 1984/85 (this was necessary as an area at the edge of the wood and the hedge on the top of Wood Hill, both of which had acted as marker points for the 1984/85 excavation, had subsequently been cut back). The trenches excavated in 1984/85 measured approximately 1m × 1m and 2m × 1m and were scattered across the hilltop (Figure 32 and Section 5). The 1993 excavation plan was to dig a single 3m × 1m trench which would be carefully placed between the 1984/85 scattered trenches (see Figure 37) paying special attention to recording both the geological deposits and the archaeology.

By excavating in this way it would be possible not only to address the questions set out in the 1993 excavation plan but also to answer some of the outstanding questions posed by the 1984/85 excavations.

Surveying the site – the basic survey

It is essential that the survey team chosen is equal to the various demands of these high-level investigations since there are particular difficulties associated with working in deposits mapped as Clay-with-flints. In wet weather the clay is a highly tenacious toffee-like deposit, conversely when dry, it resembles concrete. On site computer facilities are of great assistance during such surveying, allowing efficient use of the (often) short time and money available for these investigations. Before any excavation takes place a full detailed survey must be made of the hilltop/plateau – not just the immediate site-area under investigation. This is essential, as it is necessary to establish the site in its wider topographical context. This basic survey can be undertaken using for example, a simple level and theodolite or a more sophisticated co-axial EDM (electronic distance measurement) and a data logger. With reference to the Ordinance Survey (OS) national grid and datum (OD), standard archaeological procedures are used to determine accurate locations, both in plan and height. These data are fully recorded and the appropriate drawing produced for the site-archive.

The Auger survey

Using only a *small hand held auger* a survey is carried out along a line in such a way that a number of auger points coincide with specific survey points on the site grid. Results from the augering can then be used at a later date to check the results of the geophysical survey at these points. Augering is undertaken prior to the geophysical survey to determine:

– The edge of the deposits mapped as Clay-with-flints (i.e. the extent of the deposits in the area of interest) in relation to the Chalk;
– The nature of the Chalk (i.e. shattered or solid) and the depth of top soil, at the survey (grid) points at the edge of the deposits mapped as Clay-with-flints.
– The depth of the overburden (i.e. the Clay-with-flints deposits) at selected grid points across the site to provide data on – the nature the deposits mapped as Clay-with-flints and the Chalk at these grid points and the depth of top soil.

Augering, although necessary, *must be kept to the minimum*, as on Palaeolithic sites on deposits mapped as Clay-with-flints there is a very real danger of damaging the archaeology. It should therefore, be conducted with the utmost care, even to the extent of excavating an auger hole in 5cm. spits when an obstruction is encountered. Such procedures have, in the past, not only saved valuable Palaeolithic artefacts from destruction but has provided additional high quality detailed information that can be incorporated into the data sets (see Sub-section 6.8). Small soil samples including the clasts are collected during augering and consigned to light-fast bags for optically stimulated luminescence dating (OSL) as required.

The Geophysical survey

The integrated use of geophysical surveys, in conjunction with direct methods of investigation as part of as integrated site investigation strategy, has a proven track record in mapping solution features in the Chalk as well as determining the quality of the Chalk and depth of overburden in the area under investigation. The aim of the geophysical (tomographical) survey of a high-level Palaeolithic site is therefore to;

– locate the Chalk;
– map the shape of Chalk (i.e. map the solution feature/s);
– determine Chalk quality (i.e the presence or absence of shattered Chalk);
– determine the depth of the over burden (i.e. the depth of the deposits mapped as Clay-with-flints);
– measure the depth of top soil.

'Rapid ground cover can be achieved with a high degree of spatial resolution using electromagnetic ground conductivity mapping. Electrical resitivity profiles can produce electrical images of the near-surface revealing the lateral and vertical variations in overburden materials and rockhead weathering products. Careful analysis of the combined data sets can help to pinpoint the best locations for invasive inspection. In turn, the results from the direct observations can be used to refine the geophysical interpretation to produce an even clearer picture of the site' (Reynolds, 1997 Sht.5)

There are many different methods of geophysical exploration, several of which have been developed for applications that are totally unsuited for investigating high-level Palaeolithic sites on deposits mapped as Clay-with-flints. To date, the only really suitable methods are those outlined above (the resistivity (direct current) sounding method is slower but more detailed). The direct current method eliminates or reduces the problems of interference caused by radio/television and other communication masts/aerials and associated generators, all of which are often to be found at the same high-levels as the Palaeolithic site and lost or discarded parts of farm machinery, barbed wire, cables etc. In addition to being a 'well tried' method, the basic resistivity survey provides the necessary tomographical data and avoids problems in other seemingly appropriate methods such as ground penetrating radar (GPR) which cannot be used as,

'Even when depth penetration, reflectivity and resolution seem satisfactory, general environmental problems can prevent a GPS survey being successful. Radio transmitters are a potential source of interference and saturate receiver electronics. The presence of metal objects can also be disastrous (when these are not the survey targets). Reflections can come from objects off the side (sideswipe) in GPR surveys, just as in seismic surveys, and may be very strong if metallic reflections are involved. Features actually at the surface can produce strong sideswipe because of the ground-air interface if the ground conductivity is high' (Milsom, 1996: 137–138).

Seismic methods are also not appropriate as:

'A seismic wave transmits energy by vibration of rock particles. Low energy seismic waves can be regarded as elastic, leaving the rock mass unchanged by their passage, but rocks close to the seismic source may be shattered and permanently distorted' (*op. cit.*, 1996: 141).

Subsequent clast orientation investigations (see Fabric analysis Sub-section 6.2) on high-level Palaeolithic sites are therefore rendered useless as seismic methods produce clast re-alignment. The resistivity method works on the principle that;

'The resistivity of a rock is roughly equal to the resistivity of the pore fluids divided by the fractional porosity ... Graphite and most metallic sulphides conduct electricity fairly efficiently by the flow of electrons, but most rock forming minerals are very poor conductors. Ground currents are therefore mainly carried by ions in pore waters. Pore water is ionized to only a small extent and the electrical conductivity of pore water depends on the presence of dissolved salts, mainly sodium chloride. Clay minerals are ionically active and clays conduct well even if slightly moist' (*op. cit.*, 1996: 67).

As a guide the general resistivities (in ohm-metres) are:

- topsoil 50–100;
- clay 1–100;
- weathered bedrock 100–1000;
- limestone 500–10,000.

In areas mapped as Clay-with-flints the resistivity contrast between the surface layers and lower layers is usually good. The choice of electrode arrays must be restricted to either the Wenner or the Schlumberger. The Wenner array is acknowledged as the 'standard' array against which others are assessed, it is very widely used and there are many interpretational materials and computer packages available. However, an uncritical reliance on computer generated results is unsatisfactory as expert geological knowledge is required to interpret sounding information such as this.

The Wood Hill surveys

In accordance with the surveying principles and procedures set out above, before the Wood Hill 1993 excavation began a survey was made of the area using a simple level and theodolite ('dumpy-level'). During the excavation the 'dumpy' was also used for determining spit heights within the trench and for measuring the heights of both artefacts and natural clasts within each spit (see below and Figure 38). Details of the Wood Hill augering programme and geophysical survey are to be found in Sub-section 6.6. The Resistivity survey.

Excavation methodology

In order to determine the *in situ* (or otherwise) status of a Palaeolithic site, a detailed three-dimensional reconstruction of the trench and the deposits is required. To achieve this:

- The trench, which includes a 25cm wide 'Control Area' extending along the full length of the trench (as shown in Figure 38) is initially to be divided in 1m × 1m squares, and excavated in horizontal spits.
- All the spits are to be dug at 5cm vertical intervals throughout the trench, a depth that provides the level of detail required for the later three-dimensional reconstruction of the deposits.

The 25cm wide 'Control Area' extending the full length of the trench *must be excavated exclusively by trowel*. The resulting 5cm. vertically dug 'control spits' afford an extremely high level of detailed recording that provides, *inter alia,* the information needed for fabric analysis.

The Wood Hill 1993 Case-study excavation

Following the prescribed excavation methodology as set out above, the Wood Hill, 1993, 3m × 1m trench (including the control area) was divided into three 1m × 1m squares designated A, B and C, beginning at the south-east face (see Figure 38) with the control area of 25cm × 3m running along the south-west face and excavated in horizontal spits. All the spits were dug at 5cm vertical intervals throughout the trench, a depth that provides the level of detail required for the later three-dimensional reconstruction of the deposits. The 25cm wide × 3m long control area of the trench was excavated exclusively by trowel. The resulting 5cm vertically dug 'control spits' afforded the extremely high level of detailed recording that provided *inter alia* the information required for fabric analysis (see Sub-section 6.2).

Initial recording procedures: recording the deposits, artefacts and natural clasts (in the Control Area)

The recording system is subdivided into three major components:

1. Deposits;
2. Artefacts;
3. Natural clasts (i.e. all pebbles and flints not humanly struck);

Each reflecting the detailed data recovery strategy needed for the amount of information required.

The resultant data sets are fully recorded and the appropriate drawing produced (i.e. site plan; plans of context; stratigraphic sequence/section drawings).

Note: reference must always be made to the Munsell Color chart to identify and record the colour of both the geology and the artefacts.

Recording the deposits

Within each square and spit, individual units are planned and independently described. Following the standard practice developed by field workers in the earth sciences, the deposits are observed and recorded thus:

1. COLOUR: the colour of the deposits is to be determined by the use of the Munsell Color Chart. This not only identifies the dominant colour(s), but also any staining or mottling observed. Wet (not saturated) sediments are used.

2. TEXTURE: the relative proportion of clay, silt, sand and gravel in the deposit, for any component, equal to, or greater than, 10% of the sediment matrix.

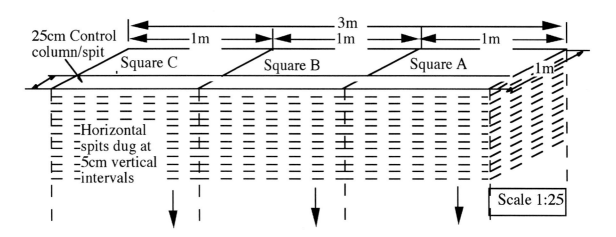

Figure 38 A simplified diagram of the Wood Hill 1993 excavation.

Wood Hill 1993 Section III
(NW face - SE facing)

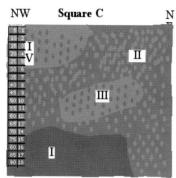

WH 93 SQ.C augered to 125 cms,
no Chalk found

Unit I: Similar to Unit 1 Section 1.
One homogeneous unit.
Colour: 7.5 YR 4/6 strong brown -
mottled manganese staining;
Texture: Sandy silty clay (20/30/50);
Inclusions: Occasional medium sub-
rounded to well-rounded gravels;
General description: Strong brown
sandy silty clay with moderate
manganese staining, with occasional
medium sub-rounded to well-rounded
gravel; compact.

Unit II: Similar to Unit 5 Section 2.
Colour: 7.5 YR 5/8 strong brown -
mottled 2.5 YR 5/6 light olive brown;
Texture: Sandy clayey silt (30/30/40);
Inclusions: Frequent medium rounded
to well-rounded gravels; very
occasional large (Chalk) flint nodules;
very occasional fine root traces;
General description: Strong brown
sandy clayey silt with frequent medium
rolled to well-rolled gravels; very
occasional large (Chalk) flint nodules;
very occasional fine root traces;
compact.

Unit III:
Colour: 2.5 Y 5/6 light olive brown -
occasional mottled 7.5 YR 5/8 strong
brown.
Texture: Sandy silty clay (20/30/50);
clast supported 55/60% gravel,
35/40% sandy silty clay.
Inclusions: Medium rounded to well-
rounded gravel.
General description: Light olive
brown sandy silty clay with medium
rounded to well rounded gravel.

Unit IV: Similar to Unit 4 Section 2.
Colour: 2.5 Y 5/6 light olive brown -
mottled 7.5 YR 5/8 strong brown,
moderate manganese staining
Texture: Sandy silty clay (20/30/50);
Inclusions: Occasional sandy silty
clayey gravel lenses (fine-medium sub-
angular to well-rounded gravels);
General description: Light olive brown
sandy silty clay with moderate
manganese staining occasional fine-
medium sub-rounded to well-rounded
gravels; very occasional gravel
(Bullhead) flint nodules; very occasional
fine root traces; Semi- compact to
compact.

Figure 41

Wood Hill 19 93 Section IV
(NE face - SW facing)

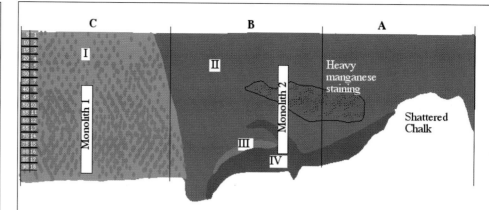

Unit I: Similar to Unit 5 Section 2.
Colour: 7.5 YR 5/8 strong brown - mottled 2.5 YR 5/6 light olive brown but with 7.5 YR 5/8 strong
brown mottling (increasng down the section);
Texture: Sandy clayey silt (30/30/40);
Inclusions: Moderate sub-angular to well-rounded fine to large gravels; very occasional large (Chalk)
flint nodules; very occasional fine root traces;
General description: Strong brown sandy clayey silt with moderate sub-angular to well-rounded fine to
large gravels; very occasional large (Chalk) flint nodules; very occasional fine root traces; compact.

Unit II: Similiar to Unit 1 Section 1,
 One homogeneous unit:
Colour: 7.5 YR 4/6 strong brown - mottled manganese staining;
Texture: Sandy silty clay (20/30/50);
Inclusions: Heavily stained manganese lenses; occasional medium sub-rounded to well-
rounded gravels, very occasional fine root traces;
General description: Strong brown sandy silty clay with moderate manganese staining,
with occasional medium sub-rounded to well-rounded gravel and very occasional fine
root traces; compact.

Unit III: (Lens);
Colour: 10 YR 5/8 yellowish brown;
Texture: Clayey sandy silt (30/30/40)
Inclusions: 3 rounded to well-rounded medium gravel pebbles;
General description: Yellowish brown clayey sandy silt with 3 rounded to well-rounded pebbles.

Unit IV: Similar to Unit 1Section 2 (also similar to Unit 1 Section 1)
One homogeneous unit.
Colour: 7.5 YR 4/6 strong brown, occasionally mottled 7.5 YR 5/8 strong brown;
Texture: Sandy silty clay (20/30/50);
Inclusions: Occasional medium sub-rounded to well-rounded gravels, very occasional fine root
traces;
General description: Strong brown sandy silty clay with moderate manganese staining, with
occasional medium sub-rounded to well-rounded gravel and very occasional fine root traces;
compact.

Figure 42

Wood Hill 1993 Section 1
(SE face - NW facing)

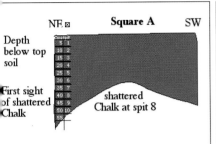

One homogeneous unit:
Colour: 7.5 YR 4/6 strong brown - mottled manganese staining;
Texture: Sandy silty clay (20/30/50);
Inclusions: Occasional medium sub-rounded to well-rounded gravels; very occasional fine root traces;
General description: Strong brown sandy silty clay with moderate manganese staining, with occasional medium sub-rounded to well-rounded gravel and very occasional fine root traces; compact.

Figure 39

Wood Hill 1993 Section II
(SW face - NE facing)

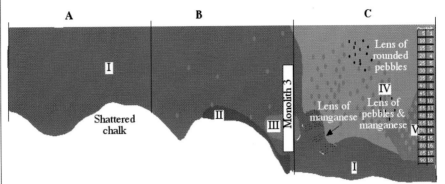

Unit I: One homogeneous unit (similar to Section 1) except:
Colour: 7.5 YR 4/6 strong brown, occasionally mottled 7.5 YR 5/8 strong brown; compact.
Texture: Sandy silty clay (20/30/50);
Inclusions: Occasional medium sub-rounded to well-rounded gravels, very occasional fine root traces;
General description: Strong brown sandy silty clay with moderate manganese staining, with occasional medium sub-rounded to well-rounded gravel and very occasional fine root traces; compact.

Unit II:
Colour: 10 YR 2/2 very dark brown;
Texture: Silty sand (40/60);
Inclusions: Very occasional very fine root traces;
General description: Very dark brown silty clay with very occasional very fine root traces; compact.

Unit III (Lens)
Colour: 7.5 YR 5/8 strong brown with very occasional manganese staining;
Texture: Clayey silty sand (30/30/40);
Inclusions: None;
General description: Strong brown clayey silty sand with very occasional manganese staining; compact.

Unit IV:
Colour: 2.5 Y 5/6 light olive brown - mottled 7.5 YR 5/8 strong brown, moderate manganese staining
Texture: Sandy silty clay (20/30/50);
Inclusions: Occasional sandy silty clayey gravel lenses (fine-medium sub-angular to well-rounded gravels);
General description: Light olive brown sandy silty clay with moderate manganese staining occasional fine-medium sub-rounded to well-rounded gravels; very occasional gravel (Bullhead) flint nodules; very occasional fine root traces; Semi- compact to compact.

Unit V:
Colour: 7.5 YR 5/8 strong brown - mottled 2.5 YR 5/6 light olive brown;
Texture: Sandy clayey silt (30/30/40);
Inclusions: Frequent medium rounded to well-rounded gravels; very occasional large (Chalk) flint nodules; very occasional fine root traces;
General description: Strong brown sandy clayey silt with frequent medium rolled to well-rolled gravels; very occasional large (Chalk) flint nodules; very occasional fine root traces; compact.

Figure 40

Munsell Color chart equivalents

2.5. Y 5/6 light olive brown

7.5 YR 4/6 strong brown

7.5 YR 5/8 strong brown

10 YR 5/8 yellowish brown

10 YR 2/2 very dark brown

Division in the deposits clear to within 0.05m

3. INCLUSIONS: anything found within the sediment matrix that was not recorded under the textural section. This includes materials that make up less than 10% of the matrix and features such as manganese staining or roots.

4. GENERAL DESCRIPTION: here, a description is given of the information provided in the above three categories. It also provides an opportunity to record observations and additional data which does not fit easily into the other three categorises.

Soil profiles of the Wood Hill 1993 trench

The four soil profiles of the Wood Hill 1993 trench are summarised as follows (see Figures 39; 40; 41; 42; for trench section diagrams):

SECTION 1: SE face (Figure 39). Section description – One homogeneous unit:
Colour: 7.5 YR 4/6 strong brown – mottled manganese staining;
Texture: Sandy silty clay (20/30/50);
Inclusions: Occasional medium sub-rounded to well-rounded gravels; very occasional fine root traces;
General description: Strong brown sandy silty clay with moderate manganese staining, with occasional medium sub-rounded to well-rounded gravel and very occasional fine root traces; compact.

SECTION 2: SW face (Figure 40). Section description – Divisions in the deposits clear to within 0.05mm.
UNIT 1: One homogeneous unit (similar to Section 1) except:
Colour: 7.5 YR 4/6 strong brown, occasionally mottled 7.5 YR 5/8 strong brown; compact.
Texture: Sandy silty clay (20/30/50);
Inclusions: Occasional medium sub-rounded to well-rounded gravels, very occasional fine root traces;
General description: Strong brown sandy silty clay with moderate manganese staining, with occasional medium sub-rounded to well-rounded gravel and very occasional fine root traces; compact.

UNIT 2:
Colour: 10 YR 2/2 very dark brown;
Texture: Silty sand (40/60);
Inclusions: Very occasional very fine root traces;
General description: Very dark brown silty clay with very occasional very fine root traces; compact.

UNIT 3: (Lens).
Colour: 7.5 YR 5/8 strong brown with very occasional manganese staining;
Texture: Clayey silty sand (30/30/40);
Inclusions: None;
General description: Strong brown clayey silty sand with very occasional manganese staining; compact.

UNIT 4:
Colour: 2.5 Y 5/6 light olive brown – mottled 7.5 YR 5/8 strong brown, moderate manganese staining
Texture: Sandy silty clay (20/30/50);
Inclusions: Occasional sandy silty clayey gravel lenses (fine-medium sub-angular to well-rounded gravels);
General description: Light olive brown sandy silty clay with moderate manganese staining occasional fine-medium sub-

rounded to well-rounded gravels; very occasional gravel (Bullhead) flint nodules; very occasional fine root traces; Semi-compact to compact.

UNIT 5:
Colour: 7.5 YR 5/8 strong brown – mottled 2.5 YR 5/6 light olive brown;
Texture: Sandy clayey silt (30/30/40);
Inclusions: Frequent medium rounded to well-rounded gravels; very occasional large (Chalk) flint nodules; very occasional fine root traces;
General description: Strong brown sandy clayey silt with frequent medium rolled to well-rolled gravels; very occasional large (Chalk) flint nodules; very occasional fine root traces; compact.

SECTION 3: NW face (Figure 41).
Section description:
UNIT 1: Similar to Unit 1 Section 1.
One homogeneous unit.
Colour: 7.5 YR 4/6 strong brown – mottled manganese staining;
Texture: Sandy silty clay (20/30/50);
Inclusions: Occasional medium sub-rounded to well-rounded gravels;
General description: Strong brown sandy silty clay with moderate manganese staining, with occasional medium sub-rounded to well-rounded gravel; compact.

UNIT 2: Similar to Unit 5 Section 2.
Colour: 7.5 YR 5/8 strong brown – mottled 2.5 YR 5/6 light olive brown;
Texture: Sandy clayey silt (30/30/40);
Inclusions: Frequent medium rounded to well-rounded gravels; very occasional large (Chalk) flint nodules; very occasional fine root traces;
General description: Strong brown sandy clayey silt with frequent medium rolled to well-rolled gravels; very occasional large (Chalk) flint nodules; very occasional fine root traces; compact.

UNIT 3:
Colour: 2.5 Y 5/6 light olive brown – occasional mottled 7.5 YR 5/8 strong brown.
Texture: Sandy silty clay (20/30/50); clast supported 55/60% gravel, 35/40% sandy silty clay.
Inclusions: Medium rounded to well-rounded gravel.
General description: Light olive brown sandy silty clay with medium rounded to well rounded gravel.

UNIT 4: Similar to Unit 4 Section 2.
Colour: 2.5 Y 5/6 light olive brown – mottled 7.5 YR 5/8 strong brown, moderate manganese staining
Texture: Sandy silty clay (20/30/50);
Inclusions: Occasional sandy silty clayey gravel lenses (fine-medium sub-angular to well-rounded gravels);
General description: Light olive brown sandy silty clay with moderate manganese staining occasional fine-medium sub-rounded to well-rounded gravels; very occasional gravel (Bullhead) flint nodules; very occasional fine root traces; Semi-compact to compact.

SECTION 4: NE face (Figure 42).
Section description.
UNIT 1: Similar to Unit 5 Section 2.
Colour: 7.5 YR 5/8 strong brown – mottled 2.5 YR 5/6 light olive brown but with 7.5 YR 5/8 strong brown mottling (increasing down the section);
Texture: Sandy clayey silt (30/30/40);
Inclusions: Moderate sub-angular to well-rounded fine to large gravels; very occasional large (Chalk) flint nodules; very occasional fine root traces;

General description: Strong brown sandy clayey silt with moderate sub-angular to well-rounded fine to large gravels; very occasional large (Chalk) flint nodules; very occasional fine root traces; compact.

UNIT 2: Similar to Unit 1 Section 1,
 One homogeneous unit:
Colour: 7.5 YR 4/6 strong brown – mottled manganese staining;
Texture: Sandy silty clay (20/30/50);
Inclusions: Heavily stained manganese lenses; occasional medium sub-rounded to well-rounded gravels, very occasional fine root traces;
General description: Strong brown sandy silty clay with moderate manganese staining, with occasional medium sub-rounded to well-rounded gravel and very occasional fine root traces; compact.

UNIT 3: (Lens).
Colour: 10 YR 5/8 yellowish brown;
Texture: Clayey sandy silt (30/30/40)
Inclusions: 3 rounded to well-rounded medium gravel pebbles;
General description: Yellowish brown clayey sandy silt with 3 rounded to well-rounded pebbles.

UNIT 4: Similar to Unit 1Section 2 (also similar to Unit 1 Section 1)
One homogeneous unit.
Colour: 7.5 YR 4/6 strong brown, occasionally mottled 7.5 YR 5/8 strong brown;
Texture: Sandy silty clay (20/30/50);
Inclusions: Occasional medium sub-rounded to well-rounded gravels, very occasional fine root traces;
General description: Strong brown sandy silty clay with moderate manganese staining, with occasional medium sub-rounded to well-rounded gravel and very occasional fine root traces; compact.

Recording artefacts and natural clasts

Within each 'control spit' (see Figure 38) the position of both the artefacts and the natural clasts with a length equal to or greater than *20mm* are to be recorded in three-dimensions. Outside the control area, only the artefacts (measuring 20mm or more) are recorded in three-dimensional detail. It is necessary to record both natural clasts and artefacts in the control area since comparative data on their occurrence is needed. Artefacts, fossils and important geological material, measuring less than 20mm, recovered by the subsequent sieving of the deposits are to be recorded by spit and/or unit number.

Artefacts are as much a part of the sediment matrix as the rest of the deposit components. If only the artefacts were recorded, there would be problems and inaccuracies when attempting the integration of the archaeological data with those of the natural sedimentary environment. Recording only the artefacts on sites on deposits mapped as Clay-with-flints might possibly be acceptable if the depositional and post-depositional processes of these sediments, in any one place, were fully understood, but this is not the case. This system of recording therefore makes it possible to clarify the relationships

of the artefacts to the containing sediments.

The recorded details required for all artefacts with a length equal to or greater than 20mm are as follows. (Note: a compass clinometer is used to provide the appropriate information).

1. Artefact number;
2. Square and Spit number;
3. Location, given as Eastings, then Northings (both to artefact centre);
4. Height (below datum line);
5. Orientation of the a-axis, in relation to north (see Figure 43);
6. Orientation of dip (which in this study is taken at the maximum angle of dip, not just the b-axis), in relation to horizontal (see Figure 43).
7. Angle of dip, in relation to horizontal (see Figure 43);
8. Dorsal or ventral surface upwards;
9. Comments.

The recording of the artefact's number, square and spit location and height within the spit needs no explanation. The exact location of the artefact within the site is provided by measuring from the centre point, to the nearest millimetre, the Eastings and the Northings coupled with the height data. Such spatial data can be used, for example to assess artefact clusters. Measuring the orientation of the a-axis, the orientation of the dip and the angle of dip of each artefact (see Figure 43) provides data on the precise positioning of each artefact at its location within the deposits. This generates data for fabric analysis (see Sub-section 6.2) that could show, for example, whether preferential orientations existed, and thus provide information which may help to isolate depositional and post-depositional processes.

Note: the measurements of height, position and orientation are obviously different, but given difficult on-site conditions and inexperienced workers, misunderstanding and mistakes can easily occur. *Care must be taken therefore, to ensure that the procedure for measuring and recording the orientation of the artefacts and clasts in the Control Spits, is not confused with the general recording procedure for measuring the height and position of the artefacts and clasts within the trench per se at each spit.*

Whether a particular artefact lies dorsal or ventral side up, may be of interest when the shapes of the artefacts are considered generally, in relation to their orientations and angles of dip. Additional information relating to the artefacts is added under 'Comments', for example, physical condition and the presence or absence of cortex. If artefacts are seen as components in a sedimentary system, then once placed in a sedimentary system, they are subject to, and will act in a manner reflective of, its depositional and post-depositional environment. The procedure

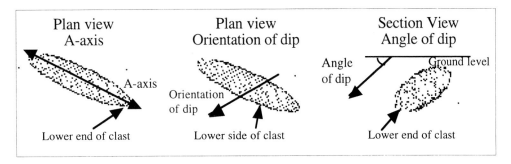

Figure 43 *Diagram showing A-axis, Orientation of dip and Angle of dip.*

and isolation of variables is the same for both natural clasts and artefacts, as a similar and compatible data-set is sought for both categories.

Recording natural clasts (in the control area) measuring 20mm or more

All the natural clasts within the control area with a length equal to or greater than 20mm are to be recorded. The procedure is similar to that applied to the artefacts but with minor alterations. These take into account differences between natural clasts and artefacts, for example the roundness of a pebble and the lack of 'dorsal orientation' faces. A compass clinometer is used to provide the appropriate details. The variables recorded are:

1. Natural clast number;
2. Square and Spit number;
3. Location, given as Eastings, then Northings (both to clast centre);
4. Height (below datum line)
5. Orientation of a-axis in relation to north (Figure 43);
6. Orientation of dip in relation to north (which in this study is taken at the maximum angle of dip not just the b-axis (Figure 43));
7. Angle of dip in relation to horizontal (Figure 43);
8. Angularity;
9. Comments.

The only real difference between recording natural clasts and artefacts is that the natural clasts are often rounded. However, locating the angle of dip does not present too great a problem, for as can be seen from Figure 43, the a-axis orientation would be the same as the orientation of dip only if the clast's dip was along its longest axis. Angularity of the clasts is recorded using Power's visual scale (1982), i.e. very angular through to well rounded. The comments section is to be used by the excavation team to

distinguish between the several types of flint present, for example:

– Tertiary pebbles: often predominantly black, brown and red well-rounded clasts;
– Bullhead flint: having an orange-brown rind directly under a greenish cortex;
– Tabular flint: formed in broad flat (thin) strata;
– Nodular (Chalk) flint: derived from the underlying Chalk.

Recording the different types of flint present will help in the identification of the remnant beds from which the Clay-with-flints deposits were derived (at Wood Hill, for example Bullhead flint was found, see Explanatory Section 2 and Sub-section 6.5). In addition, it contributes to our understanding of the lithic procurement strategy of Palaeolithic people (see Sub-sections 6.7 and 6.11 – the lithic procurement of the Lower Palaeolithic peoples on Wood Hill). The procedure and isolation of variables is the same for both natural clasts and artefacts, as a similar and compatible data-set is sought for both categories.

Sampling strategy

It is essential that the sampling strategy for Palaeolithic excavations on deposits mapped as Clay-with-flints that includes as many variables as might become necessary. Often little is known in advance about the actual nature of the specific deposits mapped as Clay-with-flints in the site area and the processes that have operated in that area over geological time and which are affecting them today. With due consideration for the time and resources available, future investigations, and the need to encompass as many analytical techniques as possible, the sampling strategy is aimed to achieve:

– The removal of small (circa 2–3kg) samples from individual units identified within the squares, at the 5cm spit intervals. These samples would be representative of small areas that, for one reason or another, were different to the main body of the deposits and would be suitable for a variety of techniques requiring only small sub-samples. For example, particle size analysis of distinctive area; textural analysis of sand-size particles; clay mineral analysis and heavy mineral analysis and chemical analysis (see Wood Hill analyses Sub-sections 6.3; 6.4; 6.5).

– The sampling of the squares at 5cm spit intervals by taking gross bulk samples (15–20kg). These would be used for the analysis of particle sizes; the shape and texture on both sand and gravel size particles; clay mineral analysis, and heavy mineral and chemical analysis (see Wood Hill analyses Sub-sections 6.3; 6.4; 6.5).

– The extraction of selected monolith samples from the sections to make thin-sections for analysis to provide (where funds/time allow) additional information not forthcoming from the unit and bulk, for example, soil micromorphology and magnetic susceptibility. If however, constraints on time and funds prevented the immediate use of micromorphological analysis, thin-sections may still be produced from the monolith/s and this form of analysis pursued at a later date.

There are many investigations which could be undertaken that are both appropriate and desirable for this research, though most are very time consuming and expensive. However, corroboration of results from a number of different methods of analysis is vital, if interpretations are to be made with confidence. It must be understood therefore, that the investigations set out here are the *absolute minimum* required for the excavation/investigation of a Palaeolithic site on deposits mapped as Clay-with-flints and that these investigations have been selected to complement each other, with no one method determining the outcome of the research. The chosen investigations which can realistically be undertaken and will certainly produce useful results, are as follows:

– Fabric analysis: orientation data (see Sub-section 6.2).
– Particle size analysis (see Sub-section 6.3).
– Clay mineral analysis (see Sub-section 6.4).
– Particle shapes, lithological analysis (see Sub-section 6.5).
– Resistivity and auger survey of the site (see Sub-section 6.6).
– Burnt flint analysis (see Sub-section 6.10)
– Pollen analysis (see Sub-section 6.10).

Because so many mechanical, chemical and biological weathering processes have acted simultaneously on the archaeological material and natural clasts within the deposit, wherever applicable the same analytical techniques are carried out on both artefacts and natural clasts. The application of each technique to solving particular archaeological, geological and geomorphological problems, its limitations and its specific application to the deposits mapped as Clay-with-flints with particular reference to Wood Hill are now considered in the various Sub-sections of this Case-study.

Sub-section 6.2: Fabric analysis, (orientation data) analysis and discussion

In the General Introduction, I set out certain fundamental questions and hypotheses aimed at understanding the relationships between the Chalk Downlands of southern England, the deposits mapped as Clay-with-flints which cap them, and the presence of Lower and Middle Palaeolithic artefacts on these same high-levels which have evidently survived throughout both glacial and temperate periods. The two questions and one hypothesis selected for particular consideration in this Case-study were discussed in detail in the General Introduction.

Processes

Climatic changes over hundreds of thousands of years have generated various processes of erosion and deposition. The main processes involved and the resulting movement of particles within soils and unconsolidated deposits can be summarised as follows. Freeze/thaw processes in cold environments produce movement within the soils and unconsolidated deposits such as frost wedging, which breaks up material, producing angular fragments of all sizes and frost heave, frost thrusting and needle ice, which generate vertical movements of particles (both up and down) within deposits, generally the stones moving upward and fines downwards; 'ejection of stones from fines by un-freezing is commonly accepted' (Washbourne, 1973: 66). The upward movement is also more rapid in wetter soils and those with sparse vegetation cover. Elongated or tabular stones become orientated so that they stand on end or on edge and large stones are heaved more rapidly than small stones (Catt 1986: 70). Other processes associated with frost action can cause upward or downward mass displacement (for example, cryoturbation and involutions). These are thought to be due to moisture-controlled changes in the intergranular pressure and cryostatic pressure (confined freezing usually in a closed system; Washbourne 1973). As previously discussed in Sub-section: 6.2 (Fabric analysis and orientation data analysis) the vertical alignment of clasts in a matrix is often regarded as the result of freeze/thaw processes. However, it must be noted that freeze/thaw processes are not alone in producing this effect. Vibrations penetrating the ground, whether caused by animals or humans, can also produce vertical clasts.Water percolating through a deposit has the effect of moving finer particles downwards. In Downland areas, 'solution' is an additional process generated by water passing through and dissolving the porous Chalk. The insoluble residues (which include, for example, tabular and nodular flint) remain and then become part of the Clay-with-flints deposits. In addition to these vertical movements within the deposit, there are lateral movements across deposits of material generated by processes such as gelifluction, frost creep and solifluction in predominately cold environments and, as the climate ameliorated, processes associated with mass movements such as mudflows (rapid flow), slower flows such as hill-wash, which may produce rilling and gullying and imperceptible flows such as soil creep. Within soils and unconsolidated deposits, bioturbation in the form of burrowing fauna and root activity, for example, effectively moves particles around (see Sub-Section 6.3). Wind action can either remove the finer material from the surface, leaving the larger material behind and thereby producing a 'lag deposit', or it can introduce material into the area in the form of aeolian deposits, for example, loess (predominantly coarse silt), and/or coversands (predominantly fine sand). Wind-blown materials are discussed in detail in Sub-section 6.5. The extent to which a deposit is affected by the processes outlined is governed by many variables: for example, the basic components of the deposits (i.e. particle size distribution, chemical and mineral composition); the amount of moisture at any one time in the deposit

(this can vary along contour lines); the depth of the deposit and the local effects such as micro-climates generated by the topography of the area and the aspect. Every time a process (however small) operates on a deposit, it leaves a feature; over time an individual feature associated with any particular process may become blurred, overwritten or obliterated by subsequent occurrences.

Fabric data and problem solving

By analysing the a-axis, orientation of dip and angle of dip of both natural clasts and artefacts (e.g. as recorded during the Wood Hill 1993 excavation), data is generated that provides clues to the identification of processes that had operated on the high-levels during both temperate and glacial periods in the Middle and Upper Pleistocene. As the deposits mapped as Clay-with-flints lay beyond the Anglian glacial maxima, they have been subject only to restricted change since at least the Cromerian (500,000 yrs. B.P.). It is possible, therefore immediately to eliminate a number of processes (for example, glacial outwash) when analysing this orientation data. However, over geological time, freeze/thaw processes (in which material is moved vertically up and down in the deposit – for example, frost heave) may well have modified the lateral features produced by such processes as solifluction and soil creep, thereby producing orientations that read as essentially random. The difficulty, then, is to isolate now, from any 'background noise' of freeze/thaw vertical movements and bioturbation, true stratigraphic features associated with lateral movements.

As a primary aim of this research is to understand the relationship between the deposits mapped as Clay-with-flints and the Lower and Middle Palaeolithic artefacts found on and in them, a cautious but open approach must be adopted when interpreting both the orientations and angle of dip data (derived from the Wood Hill 1993 excavation). I have, therefore, wherever possible and appropriate (as can be seen from the 1993 Wood Hill excavation data), employed various statistical analyses on the raw data in an attempt to 'draw out' the maximum information, being however always mindful of the limitations of such statistical analyses. Orientation diagrams were produced using absolute (rather than percentage) values, in order to show comparative numbers of clasts and artefacts as well as their relative orientations.

The results from the 1994 Wood Hill Resistivity survey (Sub-section 6.6) show that the deposits mapped as Clay-with-flints on Wood Hill are contained in a 'basin like' solution feature within the Upper Chalk. Solution features, as we shall see, play a very important role in the retention of Palaeolithic artefacts on high-level site. It can be clearly seen from the section drawings produced during the 1993 excavation (see Figures 39, 40,41,42) that the Clay-with-flints deposits in both squares A and B are very similar. However, the deposits mapped as Clay-with-flints in square C are somewhat different, as they exhibit a proportional increase in the silt and sand fraction (see Sub-section 6.3). Furthermore, the area of square C appears to represent an infill in the 'basin' feature within the Clay-with-flints deposit itself. All these points need to be fully taken into account when any interpretation of the orientation data is proffered.

Fabric analysis

'The term 'fabric' is generally used to refer to the orientation (location or position relative to the points of the compass and the line or direction followed in the course of a trend, movement, or development) of particles in a sediment; it is therefore an intrinsic property of every deposit.' (Gale and Hoare 1991)

One of the most important considerations is the degree and type of movement (or lack of movement) of, and within, the deposit. It is for this reason especially that such detailed recordings are made of both artefacts and natural clasts to provide data needed for fabric analysis.(see the Wood Hill 1993 excavation Sub-section 6.1). Fabric is normally determined by measuring the declination (a sloping or bending downwards) and inclination (a degree of deviation from a horizontal or vertical) of the a-axis of elongated clasts. Unlithified, poorly-sorted sediments, such as Clay-with-flints (*sensu lato*), that consist of gravel-sized clasts set in a muddy matrix, are given the non-genetic name of 'diamicton'; such material may form in a variety of environments. Diamictons can resemble each other superficially, but it may be possible to determine their true origins by detailed study of their fabric and any other associated features (including deformational features).

A suitable sample size

The methods employed for the collection of data for fabric analysis during the 1993 excavation of Wood Hill, followed the recommendations set out by Bridgland (1986), Graham (1991), and Gale and Hoare (1991). It is essential that sufficient material (of the correct size) is collected to yield enough clasts for a statistically valid analysis. There was of course no real way of knowing the actual composition of the deposits in the Wood Hill 1993, 3 m × 1m trench before excavation. However, my previous research had suggested that it would be possible to formulate

the required level of resolution for a detailed study. The decision to record (and save for further investigations) all the natural clasts equal to, or greater than, 20mm, in each 5cms 'control spit' (the control area being 25cms wide × 3m long) and all the artefacts (measuring 20mm or more), from any part of the trench, reflected an attempt at a high level of data recovery for a detailed three-dimensional reconstruction at a later date (as discussed in Section 6.1).

A minimum number of clasts have to be measured, in order to be certain that the sample reflected the population from which it was drawn. Normally (in the study of Tills, for example), the larger the number of clasts measured, the greater the risk of moving from one population to another. This, however, does not apply to the clasts sampled from high-level sites such as Wood Hill. The number of clasts examined in various studies of diamicton macrofabrics are given in Gale and Hoare (1991: 136). These range from 25 (Domack and Lawson 1985: 578–9; Clark and Hansel 1989: 205) to 800 (Holmes 1941: 1308), although 50–100 clasts are most commonly measured. Holmes (1941: 1308) and King (1966: 75) considered that a sample of fifty clasts gave valid results, whilst McGowan and Derbyshire (1974: 229) regarded twenty-five as the minimum acceptable sample size on (unspecified) statistical grounds. Most of these studies are of Tills, and none was conducted on deposits mapped as Clay-with-flints. As the recommended number of clasts for fabric analysis of diamicton macrofabrics is so varied, I consider that the fabric analysis of clasts recovered from high-level sites such as Wood Hill is valid.

Recording the Wood Hill data

As the full data recording procedures for the Wood Hill 1993 excavation were discussed in detail in Sub-section 6.1; it is sufficient to note here that small artefacts, fossils and concretions measuring less than 20mm recovered during the excavation were recorded by Square and Spit only. Very small artefacts (flakes and flake fragments), very small fossils and minerals (quartz grains for example) were retrieved only after the sieving of sediment samples for particle-size analysis (see Sub-sections 6.2, 6.5 and 6.7). At the end of the 1993 excavation on Wood Hill a total of 26 artefacts plus 1,522 natural clasts, equal to (or greater than) 20mm in both cases, had been recovered *in situ*.

Data analysis – orientation of clasts

The orientation of particles in a sediment can give indications of origin and subsequent processes (Gale and Hoare, 1991: 125; Graham, 1991: 37). As we saw in Sub-section 6.1; all natural clasts (in the control area) and all artefacts (wherever they occurred in the trench), measuring at least 20mm (along the a-axis), are assessed to determine the orientation of the a-axis, the orientation of dip (at maximum angle of dip) and the angle of dip. It can be seen from Figure 43, that the a-axis orientation would be the same as the orientation of dip only if the clast's dip was along its longest axis. Similarly, if the clast's dip were at right angles to its longest axis, then the a-axis and orientation of dip would be 90° apart.

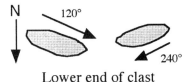

Lower end of clast

Figure 44 Orientation of Dip

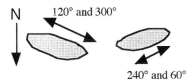

Figure 45 A-axis

Correction to Grid North

As the orientation data is recorded on site in relation to magnetic North, the following adjustments are needed to correct to Grid North. On Wood Hill for example, magnetic North at the centre of the relevant map sheet was 7.5° W of Grid North. This magnetic variation was measured in 1979 and the annual rate of change in magnetic variation is 0.5° E every three years. Over the 14 years between 1979 and 1993 the difference would have reduced by 2.5° giving an adjustment of 5° (7.5° – 2.5°). Thus 5° was subtracted from each measurement to calculate orientations in respect of Grid North. By correcting to Grid North, direct comparisons can be made with a variety of data. No correction is necessary for angle of dip, as it is inclinational not directional.

Data analysis methodology

The method for analysing fabric data is a two step process:

1. The field data for each clast and artefact, including corrected orientation data and dip data, is entered into a database for subsequent analysis and to produce statistics and charts for a-axis orientation, orientation of dip and angle of dip.
2. The data for each angle (a-axis, orientation of dip and angle of dip), for each square in each spit, is then input to a software package, Oriana (Kovach 1994) which assists in the analysis of circular data and drawing of Rose diagrams (Figures 49, 50). The results of the Oriana data are calculated and analysed for each spit within each square. The summarised results for the Wood Hill 1993 squares grouped by statistical similarity are shown at Figures 49, 50 and 51.

Rose Diagrams

A-axis and orientation of dip are both directional, with values between 0° and 360°. Their circular nature means that normal linear statistical techniques (e.g. histograms, mean etc) do not apply as, for example, the value 360° is in fact equal to the value 0°. The values in degrees measure the distance between orientations, but not the relative 'size' (e.g. where, in linear numbers, 100 would not just be different from 60 by 40 points but would also be 40 points greater). The values are circular and a set of statistical techniques known as circular statistics must be employed. Rose Diagrams show the frequency of circular items at equal degree intervals (e.g. 0° to 9°, 10° to 19° etc), in the same way that a histogram would achieve for linear data. In Rose Diagrams, the area, rather than the radius, should be proportional to the class frequency. Nemec (1988) and Gale and Hoare (1991) give a number of very useful examples from the many published circular histograms which are in fact drawn incorrectly, with the radius proportional to frequency. This pitfall is avoided by specifying the 'area based' rose diagram option in Oriana.

The methods used to derive circular statistics are as recommended by Kovach, (1994); Gale and Hoare, (1991: 125–146); Graham, (1988: 45) and Lindholm, (1987: 47–50). For orientation of dip (measured here at the maximum angle of dip not just the b-axis) the clast angle is measured as 'facing' the dip end and is 'single ended' (Figure 44). The orientation, therefore, is towards the lower end of the clast and can be measured over a full 360°.

The measurement of a-axis, however, is double ended as there is a measurement of declination with no sense of inclination (Figure 45). For double ended orientations the rose diagram is drawn as symmetrical with the measurements converted to fall within a 180° range (by subtracting 180° from all measurements over 180° and adding 180° to all measurements under 180° (Gale & Hoare 1991: 138).

For double ended measurements, the calculation of the vector mean and dispersion is calculated with the figures converted to a 180° degree range.[2] For single ended (i.e. orientation of dip) with phi representing the individual orientations, the statistics are calculate as follows:

> V as the sum of cos phi values, W as the sum of sin phi values
> The vector mean is the arctan (in degrees) of W/V
> R, the magnitude of the resultant vector is the square root of (V*V+W*W)
> L, the percentage magnitude of the resultant vector, is (R/n)*100 where n is the no of items.

For double ended (i.e. a-axis) with phi representing the individual orientations, the distribution will have two modes of equal strength and opposite direction. In this instance the value of the angle phi must be doubled, giving the formula:

> V as the sum of cos 2 phi values, W as the sum of sin 2 phi values
> The vector mean is the 1/2 arctan (in degrees) of W/V
> R, the magnitude of the resultant vector is the square root of (V*V-W*W)
> L, the percentage magnitude of the resultant vector, is (R/n)*100 where n is the no of items.

Many of the statistical parameters used in circular statistics are based on the mean vector. A group of orientations (or individual vectors) have a mean vector that can be calculated by combining each of the individual vectors. The mean vector has two properties; its direction (the mean angle) and its length (often referred to using the letter r). The lengths range from 0 to 1; where a larger number indicates that the observations are clustered more closely around the mean than lower numbers. The mean vector is an expression of preferred orientation (similar to the mean of a linear data series) whilst the vector magnitude is a sensitive measure of dispersion around the mean. A high value for vector magnitude means that the orientations varied greatly.

'Concentration' is a parameter specific to the circular distribution and measures the departure of the distribution from a perfect circle (or a uniform distribution). It is related to the length of the mean

vector. The circular variance and circular standard deviation are equivalent to their common counterparts, but are calculated in a very different way. Variance was calculated from the length of the mean vector; standard deviation was then derived from this. The standard error of the mean was also calculated based on the length of the mean vector (r). It again assumes that the data adheres to the circular normal distribution. The 95% and 99% confidence intervals are based on the standard error. When the standard error is calculated, a check is made by Oriana of the concentration for the sample as well as the sample size.

Significance tests

There are several problems with tests of significance for circular distributions. The most obvious significance test for comparing a distribution with an expected random distribution is Chi squared. The method is to group the readings into equal sectors (e.g. 0°–19°, 20° to 29° etc) then compare their actual frequencies with predicted frequencies calculated by n (number of readings) divided by k (number of sectors). Chi squared is useful as it is non-parametric and suitable for non-normal circular distributions with one mode. It is less useful if there is more than one strong mode. A particular danger in circular distributions is the choice of origin point as this will change the number of items in each sector. If, for example, there were 12 items with an orientation of 40 then a sector of 35 to 44 would include them but 30 to 39 would not. Ballantyne and Cornish (1979: 773) showed that the level of significance in data sets could be entirely due to the choice of point of origin. Woodcock and Naylor (1983) also suggest that Chi squared is biased and shows more significant distributions than other tests. The fact that most studies use a point of origin of 0° or 1° is arbitrary and calls into question the validity of the significance found. They suggest that Chi squared should be avoided and an alternative such as Ajne's An statistic should be used. This is not sensitive to a particular point of origin, does not require conformance to a circular normal distribution and can be used for declination and inclination. Its main disadvantage is that it may show polymodal distributions as not significantly different from uniform. Gale and Hoare suggest that

---

[2] It is important that the signs of the trigonometric functions are accurate (Lindholm 1987:48). If the tangent is negative and in the second quadrant then the azimuth (e.g. -74°) is plotted counter clockwise from zero at the bottom of the circle giving 106°. In the second segment add 180, in the third segment also add 180, in the fourth segment add 270°. For double ended measurements the orientation of the clasts is represented by the angle and its complement (180° opposite).

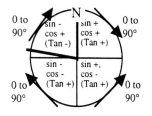

Kolmogorov Smirnov should therefore be used where possible (*op. cit.* 1991: 141).

As the analysis of significance of circular distributions is a complex and contentious subject, I recommend the use of accepted relatively simple methods that are supported by available software package. The Rayleigh test, for example, is a simple method of testing whether a set of data possesses a distribution of orientation that is significantly different from normal. A probability less than the chosen significance level of 0.05 indicates that the data are not distributed uniformly and that they show evidence of a preferred direction (Graham 1988: 45, Lindholm 1987: 47). For the Wood Hill Case-study, the results were calculated using Oriana to provide detailed rose diagrams for each spit within each square, summaries of which are shown in Figure 49 and Figure 50. Chi squared tests were used to analyse the differences between groups of spits where there appeared to be overall differences. The grouped spits were also analysed using the Kolmogorov-Smirnov Test and the following tests utilised with the results incorporated into the conclusions.

Watson's F-test

Watson's F-test compares two selected samples to determine if their mean angles differ significantly. The F-test basically proceeds by comparing the lengths of the mean vectors for each sample with that for the pooled data of the two samples. The resulting F statistic is the same as Fisher's variance ratio statistic which is commonly used in linear statistics, including analysis of variance. The p value printed for each test is the probability associated with the null hypothesis that the two mean angles are equal. If this probability is less than the chosen significance level of 0.05 then the null hypothesis can be rejected in favour of the hypothesis that the two means are different. This test assumes that the two samples are independent and drawn at random from a population with a circular (von Mises) distribution.

Chi-squared test

Oriana can perform Pairwise Chi-squared tests between any two selected samples and determines whether the two samples differ significantly from each other in some way. The p value printed for each test is the probability associated with the null hypothesis that the two samples are drawn from the same population. If this probability is less than the chosen significance level of 0.05, then the null hypothesis can be rejected in favour of the hypothesis that the two samples are from different populations

that differ in some way. The difference may be in the distribution, mean direction, or other parameter. Further investigation is then needed to determine the nature of difference between the two samples.

Angle of dip

The angle of dip is not a circular measure as inclination can only range from 0° to 90° where 90° is greater than 0°. Thus normal linear statistical measures can be employed. One way of illustrating inclination is to use stereographic diagrams, which show both declination and inclination on one diagram (Gale and Hoare 1991:139). It is felt however, that the separation of inclination and declination gives a clearer picture, so histograms should be drawn. Mean and standard deviations were calculated for the Wood Hill data showing most means around 30° but with high standard deviations (Figure 51).

Final presentation

The rose diagrams and relevant statistics for all spits are calculated for each of a-axis, orientation of dip and angle of dip for comparison (Figure 46; 47 and 48). These diagrams also include rose diagrams and statistics for the artefacts. One of the advantages of this diagrammatic method is that it allows immediate visual comparisons. For example, Wood Hill data for square C4 was rechecked as it seemed to contain a high number of clasts relative to the surrounding spits (the control area in square C 4 in fact contained a small pebble lens).

Orientations and angles of dip

As rose diagrams were produced from the Wood Hill 1993 Control area orientation data for both clasts and artefacts in each individual spit and square (see Figures 46; 47; 48), the orientations and the angle of dip for both natural clasts and (where they occurred) artefacts is available for spits 1 to 13 inclusive and spit 16. The absence of this type of data for all squares in spits 14, 15, 17, and 18 and a number of individual squares in other spits was directly related to the sampling size adopted for the excavation, as the recording of the orientations and angle of dip was restricted to natural clasts and artefacts equal to, or greater than 20mm (see Sub-section 6.1).

Note: Changing the sampling size to recording the orientations and angle of dip of clasts and artefacts measuring less than 20mm is not normally a viable proposition, as it can be difficult to measure these small clasts/artefacts – a situation exacerbated by adverse on-site weather condition.

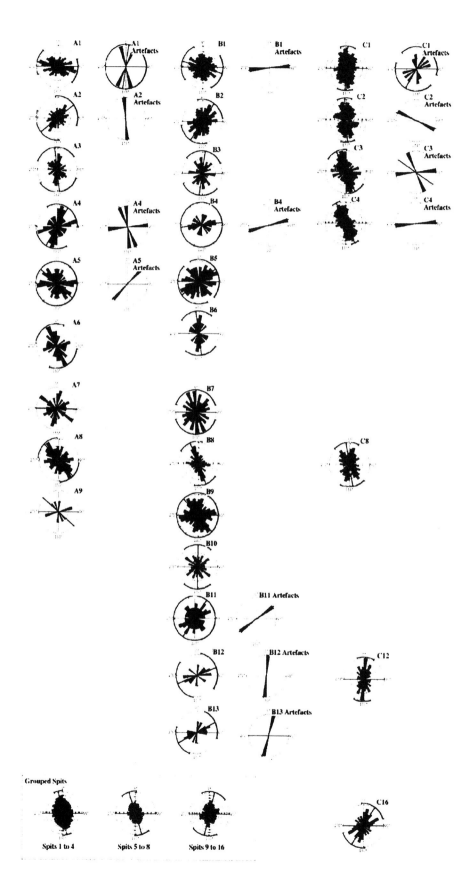

Figure 46 *A-axis rose diagrams for each square and spit.*

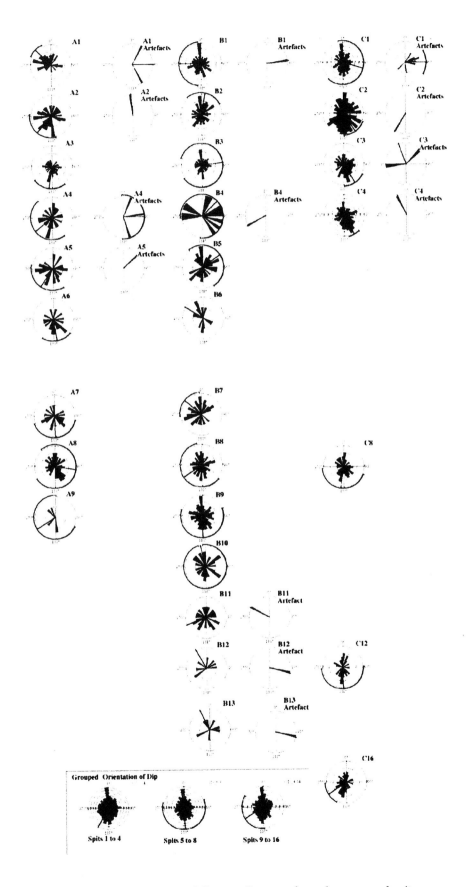

Figure 47 Orientation of dip rose diagrams for each square and spit.

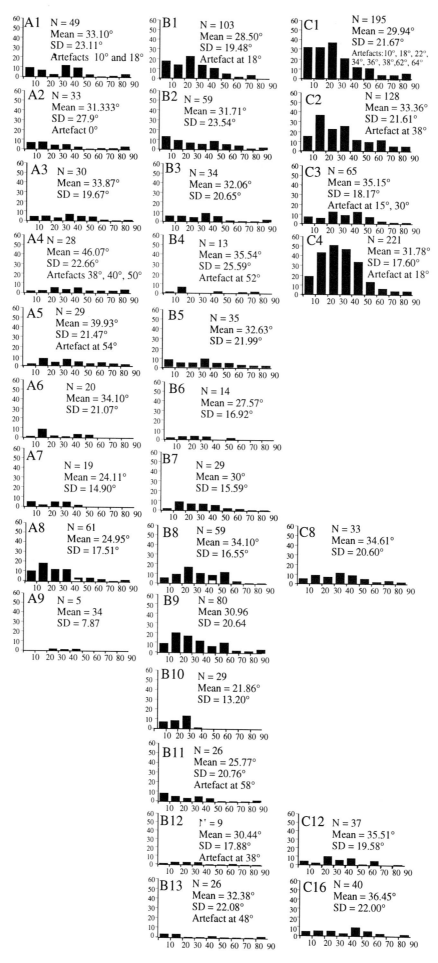

Figure 48 Angle of dip histograms for each square and spit.

A Axis - Grouped spits 1 to 4, 5 to 8, 9 to 16

Spits 1 to 4
(excluding C4)

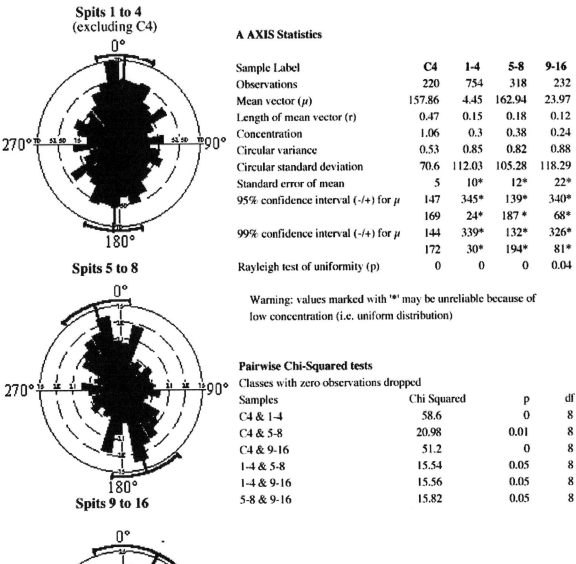

A AXIS Statistics

Sample Label	C4	1-4	5-8	9-16
Observations	220	754	318	232
Mean vector (μ)	157.86	4.45	162.94	23.97
Length of mean vector (r)	0.47	0.15	0.18	0.12
Concentration	1.06	0.3	0.38	0.24
Circular variance	0.53	0.85	0.82	0.88
Circular standard deviation	70.6	112.03	105.28	118.29
Standard error of mean	5	10*	12*	22*
95% confidence interval (-/+) for μ	147	345*	139*	340*
	169	24*	187 *	68*
99% confidence interval (-/+) for μ	144	339*	132*	326*
	172	30*	194*	81*
Rayleigh test of uniformity (p)	0	0	0	0.04

Warning: values marked with '*' may be unreliable because of low concentration (i.e. uniform distribution)

Spits 5 to 8

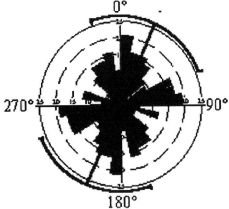

Pairwise Chi-Squared tests
Classes with zero observations dropped

Samples	Chi Squared	p	df
C4 & 1-4	58.6	0	8
C4 & 5-8	20.98	0.01	8
C4 & 9-16	51.2	0	8
1-4 & 5-8	15.54	0.05	8
1-4 & 9-16	15.56	0.05	8
5-8 & 9-16	15.82	0.05	8

Spits 9 to 16

Figure 49 Grouped clasts' a-axis: rose diagrams, circular statistics and pairwise chi-squared tests.

Orientation of Dip - Grouped spits 1 to 4, 5 to 8, 9 to 16

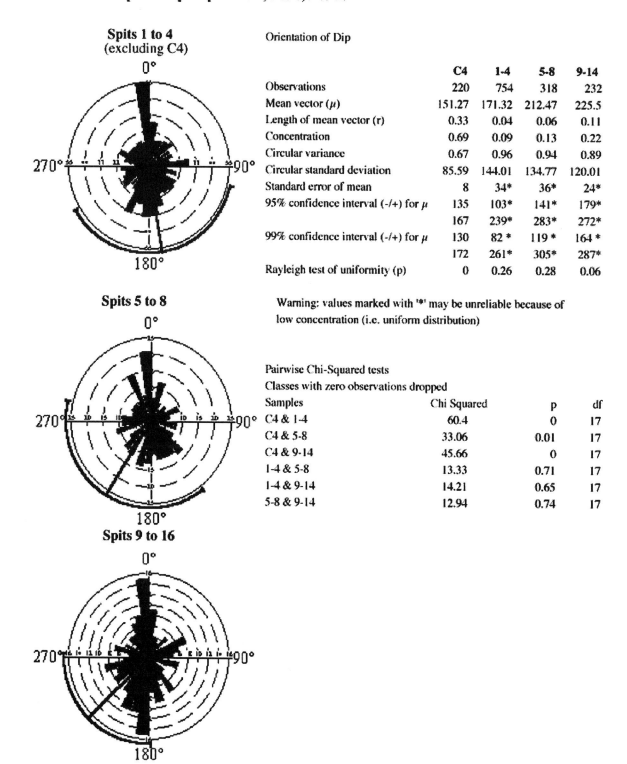

Orientation of Dip

	C4	1-4	5-8	9-14
Observations	220	754	318	232
Mean vector (μ)	151.27	171.32	212.47	225.5
Length of mean vector (r)	0.33	0.04	0.06	0.11
Concentration	0.69	0.09	0.13	0.22
Circular variance	0.67	0.96	0.94	0.89
Circular standard deviation	85.59	144.01	134.77	120.01
Standard error of mean	8	34*	36*	24*
95% confidence interval (-/+) for μ	135	103*	141*	179*
	167	239*	283*	272*
99% confidence interval (-/+) for μ	130	82 *	119 *	164 *
	172	261*	305*	287*
Rayleigh test of uniformity (p)	0	0.26	0.28	0.06

Warning: values marked with '*' may be unreliable because of
low concentration (i.e. uniform distribution)

Pairwise Chi-Squared tests
Classes with zero observations dropped

Samples	Chi Squared	p	df
C4 & 1-4	60.4	0	17
C4 & 5-8	33.06	0.01	17
C4 & 9-14	45.66	0	17
1-4 & 5-8	13.33	0.71	17
1-4 & 9-14	14.21	0.65	17
5-8 & 9-14	12.94	0.74	17

Figure 50 *Grouped clasts' orientation of dip: rose diagrams, circular statistics and pairwise chi-squared tests.*

Statistical investigations – Pairwise Chi-Square analysis of grouped spits

A straight-forward comparison of the Wood Hill orientation of clasts' a-axis as shown on the individual rose diagrams, suggested a number of interesting changes in direction. To confirm the validity of these observations, Pairwise Chi-squared tests were carried out on particular groups of data (data distortions were avoided by returning to the raw data and by including and excluding C4, which contained a small pebble lens). The artefacts were not included in the Pairwise Chi-square tests as the sample size is too small to give accurate results, however the relevant data is included and shown separately on the individual rose diagrams (Figures 46; 47). The spits were grouped thus:

– Spits 1 to 5 (in which Lower Palaeolithic artefacts were found);
– Spits 6 to 9;
– Spits 10 to 16 (Lower Palaeolithic artefacts were found in spits 11,12 and 13).

As the Pairwise Chi-squared test on the grouped a-axis data confirmed the changes that I had noted previously (see Figure 49) the same test was carried out on the orientation of dip data (see Figure 50) and the angle of dip data (see Figure 51).

Pairwise Chi-squared test – Orientation of a-axis

Changes in the direction of the orientation of the clasts' a-axis in the grouped spits are clearly seen in (see Figure 49) and are summarised as follows:

– Spits 1 to 5 differ from spits 6 to 9;
– Spits 6 to 9 differ from spits 10 to 16.
– Spits 10 to 16 are different to 6 to 9 but similar to spits 1 to 5.
– Spits 1 to 5 exhibit a bimodal population whereas;
– Spits 6 to 9 and spits 10 to 16 show polymodal populations.

'A random or polymodal distribution [as in spits 6 to 9 and 10 to 16] of clast a-axis declinations in sediment flow and debris flow may indicate either a short distance of transport, or a high flow strength and/or viscosity' (internal resistance to flow) (Nemec and Steel 1984: 13).

'Well-developed modes [as in spits 1 to 5] may indicate that clasts have been able to move with respect to each other and that they have adopted positions that are related to forces imposed by the flow mechanism' (Harms *et al.* 1982: 6.3).

– Spits 1 to 5; preferred orientation NNE–SSW (mean vector around 4 degrees);

– Spits 6 to 9; are orientated NW–SE (mean vector around 160 degrees);
– Spits 10 to 16; are orientated NE–SW (mean vector around 29 degrees).

Pairwise Chi-squared test – Orientation of dip

The orientation of dip, between the grouped spits, is statistically less different (see Figure 50). There is a general mode at around 350 degrees which is strongest in spits 1 to 5 and weakest in spits 10 to 16 with spits 10 to 16 also displaying a second mode at around 180 degrees.

– Spits 1 to 5; are orientated SSE (mean vector 171.21 degrees, strong mode at 350 degrees);
– Spits 6 to 9; are orientated SSW (mean vector 207.38 degrees, mode at 350 degrees);
– Spits 10 to 16; are orientated SW (mean vector 240.51 degrees, weak mode at 350 degrees + second mode around 180 degrees).

'Gravel clast inclinations in sediment flow and debris flow deposits are generally shallow. Imbrication of the a- or b- axes is a common feature (Harms *et al.* 1982: 6.4; Nemec and Steel 1984: 13), 'although inclination may bear no relationship to the direction of flow' (Gale and Hoare 1991: 130).

Pairwise Chi-squared test – Angle of dip

The results of the Chi-squared test on the angle of dip data (see Figure 51) show that:

– Spits 1 to 5; have a mean vector of 35.52 degrees;
– Spits 6 to 9; have a mean vector of 30.45 degrees;
– Spits 10 to 16; have a mean vector of 30.24 degrees.

A Pairwise Chi-squared comparison of the grouped spits shows that:

– Spits 1 to 5 and 6 to 9 have a Chi-squared value of 19.12 which, with 8 degrees of freedom, indicates that there is a difference between the populations.
– Spits 6 to 9 and 10 to 16 have a Chi-squared value of 19.81 which, with 8 degrees of freedom indicates that there is a difference between the populations.
– Spits 1 to 5 and 10 to 16 have a Chi-squared value of 10.80 which, with 8 degrees of freedom indicates that there is no difference between the populations.

From the diagram (Figure 51) it can be seen that in each grouping, there are a small number of clasts with a recorded angle of around 90 degrees (i.e. clasts positioned vertically in the deposit).

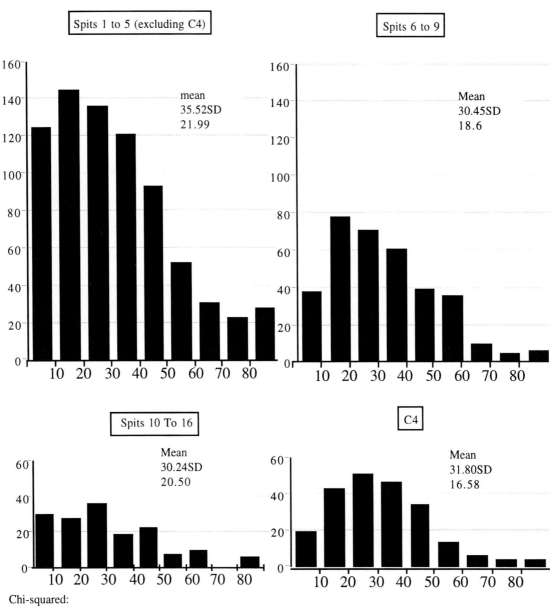

Chi-squared:
comparing 1 - 5 and 6 - 9. Chi-squared = 19.12, df = 8 therefore there is a difference between the populations
comparing 6 - 9 and 10 - 16. Chi-squared = 19.81, df = 8 therefore there is a difference between the populations
comparing 1 - 5 and 10 - 16. Chi-squared = 10.80, df = 8 therefore there is no difference between the populations

Figure 51 *Grouped clasts' angle of dip: Histograms and pair-wise chi-squared tests.*

'Clasts may be aligned vertical/near-vertical in a deposit as a result of freeze/thaw processes (Washbourne 1973: 66) also those materials having a low original water content may contain a small number of near-vertical clasts resulting from collisions' (Lawson 1979a: 71; 1979b: 639–40).

Conclusion

Data interpretations are often governed by expectations, and this is certainly the case with those applied by others to the deposits mapped as Clay-with-flints, the processes affecting these deposits and the artefacts associated with them. With this in mind, I have sought the opinions and advice of many specialists in such fields as geology, geomorphology, sedimentology, statistics and archaeology. Although the interpretations and suggestions have (as one would expect) often been at variance, this has not been detrimental to this study; rather it served to stress its importance and the need for further research. A prerequisite of this research is that a number of preconceived ideas, which relate to the deposits mapped as Clay-with-flints and the associated artefacts, be challenged or at least held in abeyance. If not, our understanding of the deposits and associated artefacts will advance no further forward. However, this study is, as I have previously stressed, not the definitive answer but rather a springboard to launch further enquiries.

This analysis of the orientation of the a-axis, orientation of dip and the angle of dip of the natural clasts and artefacts as recorded during the 1993 excavation of the Lower Palaeolithic site at Wood Hill clearly demonstrates that:

1. The deposits mapped as Clay-with-flints in the excavated area of Wood Hill form a coherent sequence, not a cryoturbated mix and jumble. The three sequences identified by the orientation of the a-axis of the natural clasts are as follows: Spits 1 to 4/5; 5/6 to 8 /9; 9/10 to 16 (spit 16 marks the maximum depth of recorded orientation data). Lower Palaeolithic artefacts were found in spits 1 to 5 and in spits 11, 12 and 13.

2. The analysis of orientation of dip data shows that the natural clasts in the deposits are aligned predominantly parallel to flow but exhibit two modes (see Figure 50). The orientation of clasts moving forward very slowly may show two patterns (modes) as a proportion of the clasts can be orientated backwards in the opposite direction to the (downslope) movement. This movement which is associated with cold plastic surfaces is very slow indeed (almost imperceptible) and is perhaps best described as an 'ooze'. The clasts can be moved on the surface or move within the top (shallow layer of the deposit).

3. An orientation pattern such as this could not be produced by cryoturbation or a random mixing of the deposits. Therefore, soil creep seems the most likely process.

4. The interpolation of the deposit's shape (see Sub-section 6.3.) appears to reflect the pattern of the surface of underlying Chalk, as the surface of the Chalk in square A and part of square B can be seen as small solution hollows. The stratigraphic 'highs' in square B would have the effect of moving the materials gently either side, which is indeed the case in the top spits, 1 to 10, whereas;

5. In spits 11 to 17 (now square B and square C only, square A having reached Chalk at spit 10) the effect of the Chalk underlying the deposits (but now at a much greater depth) is a tendency to move the clasts in the direction of B (i.e. away from C).

6. The patterns of orientation of the natural clasts in the grouped spits strongly suggest an input of deposits (by soil creep perhaps?). Some of the material however, may have moved down from one spit to another as the change in direction of the a-axis orientations (between the grouped spits) is somewhat limited. A difficulty with the Wood Hill data is that the direction of flow over time may be constant, that is, because the movement of materials occurs within the same range of degrees, the number of actual occurrences may not be reflected in the data. The measurements may suggest one large sluggish movement of material, when in fact there may have been many small gentle inputs over a long/ short period of time. It is important to note that, before final conclusions can be reached the data derived from the fabric analysis *must be combined* with the results of the other investigations.

7. The Lower Palaeolithic artefacts were found in the uppermost part of the trench, predominantly in spits 1 to 5 and again in spits 11, 12 and 13. This pattern of artefact distribution is not confined to those artefacts recovered during the 1993 excavation of Wood Hill but it is also reflected in the finds from the trenches which were dug in 1984/85 and also from the auger pit dug during 1994 (see Figure 38 and detailed discussion in Sub-section 6.11).

8. The overall patterns of movement as deduced from the analysis of the orientation of the a-axis, orientation of dip and angle of dip of both natural clasts and artefacts, strongly suggests at least two separate occurrences of Lower Palaeolithic artefacts in this particular area of Wood Hill.

Sub-section 6.3: Particle-size analysis and discussion

The size of the component particles, and the way in which they are distributed within a deposit, are among the basic physical properties of geological materials. Particles in regolith materials (the layer of unconsolidated (non-cemented) weathered material including rock fragments, mineral grains and all other superficial deposits, that rest on unaltered, solid bedrock) can range in size from boulders measuring several metres to the finest clay fraction measuring less than one micrometre.

Many workers suggest that it is essential to determine the parameters of a deposit in any attempt to characterise fully the lithology of unconsolidated geological material, but that particle-size distribution alone is usually inadequate as a means of determining the environment of deposition of a sediment and needs to be used in conjunction with the results from other analyses, such as fabric analysis; lithological analysis and mineral analysis. (Griffiths, 1967; Catt and Weir, 1976: 77; McManus, 1991: 63; Gale and Hoare, 1991: 56, 74).

Particle size definitions

The definitions used for the bounding of particle sizes are not uniform, although there is fairly general agreement on the terms to be applied to sediment particles of various sizes. Particles are variously referred to as boulders, cobbles, pebbles, granules, gravels, sand, silt and clay. McManus provides the following concise explanation:

> 'Most workers take values based on the Udden-Wentworth (1922) scale which is a ratio scale in which the grade boundaries differ by a factor of 2. One grade coarser is twice the size of its predecessor and one grade finer is half the size. The grade boundaries are established at 4, 2, 1, 0.5 and 0.25mm etc. Even with agreement on the form of the scale and grade boundaries in the coarser ranges, different authors still place the silt-clay boundary variously at 2um (Briggs, 1977; Friedman and Sanders, 1978), which is a size commonly used by soil scientists, or at 4 um, as in the original Udden-Wentworth system (Tanner, 1969; Pettijohn, 1975) as is more normal amongst geological sedimentologists' (*op cit.* 1991: 73).

Source control on particle-size distribution

Sedimentary deposits, such as the deposits mapped as Clay-with-flints, are often formed from a variety of processes acting upon different bodies of different material over a variable time scale (see Explanatory Section 2). Analysis of particle-size data requires a number of factors to be taken into consideration such as weathering; pedogenesis; the processes of erosion, transport, deposition and (perhaps most importantly) the source or sources of the original material from which the deposit was derived. The parent rock from which later sediments are derived controls the distribution of particle-size within the sediments. This is known as the source control. For example, if the parent material contained only a small percentage of sand, then sand would not be expected to exhibit a high percentage in the derived sediments (Briggs and Griffin 1986). At Wood Hill for example, the source control of the deposit mapped as Clay-with-flints appears at this stage of the research to be a remnant Tertiary bed, possibly Thanet Beds (see Sub-section 6.5), since the superficial deposits at Wood Hill contain Bullhead flint. Source control may be significant in this study. If a narrow range of particle size existed in the source material, this will limit the distribution of particle sizes in the present deposit, thereby reflecting the simple unavailability of a range of particle sizes rather than the actual 'sorting' processes of deposition.

Weathering processes and particle sizes

Weathering processes have a number of effects on particle-size distribution. They break down particles, reducing the overall size of the material, and modifying the distribution of the sizes. Particles may then be redistributed within a sequence, by either sorting or homogenising processes. For example, fracturing processes such as frost action and desiccation may allow particles to move down fractures in the deposit. The effect of this may be the mixing of material from different levels within the sequence. Clasts may also be moved through the regolith by changes in the volume as it expands and contracts in response to freeze/thaw activity, wetting/drying cycles and stress release (Washbourne, 1973: 65–81; Selby 1982: 17; Catt, 1986: 70; Gale and Hoare, 1991: 67; Ballantyne and Harris, 1994). Chemical and biochemical weathering processes may also cause notable changes in the original chemical composition of a material.

Many processes of pedogenesis (natural soil formation) are identical to those of weathering and have the same consequences for the particle-size distribution of materials (Gale and Hoare 1991:68; Avery 1980: 30). One aspect of pedogenesis that is particularly important to the study of the Clay-with-flints deposits is the process of lessivage (clay shift or translocation) which has the greatest impact on the soil texture. This process results in the clay enrichment of B horizons (for a detailed explanation of soil horizons the reader is directed to Catt, 1995: 59–66). Avery suggests, in extreme cases, paleo-argillic B horizons may contain up to 30% illuvial clay (*op cit.* 1980: 31).

> 'The extent to which clay illuviation has occurred in any soil profile depends on the nature of the soil parent material and past climatic conditions. It is favoured by seasonally dry climate, a well developed system of macrovoids such as those formed by the dissolution of carbonate clasts, low concentration of cementing and flocculating agents (e.g. carbonates, soluble organic matter, sesqui-oxides, exchangeable Al, Ca, Mg.)' (Catt 1986: 174).

As the clay is carried downwards by the process of illuviation, it is redeposited where the sub-soil is dry. Capillary action has the effect of drawing water from the non-capillary voids into the capillary voids and in the process the clay is 'filtered' out. However, the clay may also be redeposited where a less permeable horizon causes a decrease in downward illuviation rates.

> 'The continued deposition of clay in non-capillary voids may eventually impede drainage of the soil and cause gleying in or above the clay enriched horizons, but this point may never be reached in soils subject to periodic cryoturbation or other subsoil disturbances, which create new voids' (*op. cit.*: 175).

Note: Gleying was observed in the Wood Hill 1993 trench, as the soil in many of the pebbled areas was mottled predominantly grey (and to a lesser degree rust coloured).

Bioturbation

The disruption of unconsolidated sediments by bioturbation can be divided into two groups; those effected by man and those produced by plants and animals. Bioturbation is vigorous close to the surface of the soil and in favourable conditions it will extend to a much greater depth, reaching down several metres in some cases. Only during the warmer periods of the Quaternary was bioturbation common in the present temperate regions of the world. As both large and small organisms inhabiting the soil are therefore responsible for the breakdown of dead plant material and its eventual incorporation into the upper layers of the mineral material, bioturbation works on two scales. The localised macro-morphological effects produced by the larger burrowing

animals, (moles, rabbits, foxes, etc.), whose activities are also implicated in the downslope movement of all types of soil, and the actions of the far more numerous soil mesofauna (earthworms, insects, myriapods etc.) which by contrast, are continuous, comprehensive and homogenising (Catt, 1986: 100). The importance of earthworms in the process of bioturbation and their archaeological significance was expounded by Atkinson (1957: 219–33). Earthworms of all species live in burrows, which are formed by the ingestion of earth, the pointed front segments of the body being inserted and expanded in the interstices of the soil. After digestion, the ejected soil is either voided in empty spaces below ground level, or on the surface as worm-casts, or is used to line the walls of the burrow, particularly where it passes through coarse or angular material.

The major factor governing worm activity is the soil type. Clay-with-flints deposits are acid (in contrast to many soils in the Lowland Zone, which are neutral or alkaline). Atkinson noted that on acid soils, 'the worm populations are generally smaller and contain a narrower range of species, from which the casting and deep-burrowing types are often largely missing.' (*op. cit.* 1957: 221). The casting and deep-burrowing species are the very ones which cause the most soil disruption and by association potential disturbance of Palaeolithic sites. Cultivation generally improves acid soils and thereby increases the worm population. Given the right conditions, objects (e.g. Palaeolithic artefacts) will continue to fall to the maximum depth of worm activity (about 6 ft). Below the top 6–8 in. of soil in which the majority of worms normally live, objects will sink with increasing slowness, at only a tenth or a hundredth of the rate in the upper layer, since there will be less active proportions of worms, and less subsidence of empty burrows (*op. cit.* 1957: 222).

However, in areas mapped as Clay-with-flints, modern farming methods (and indeed the older methods to a lesser degree) have produced an increasingly hostile surface environment for earthworms as the flints and pebbles in the surface layer of the acid soil are regularly shattered. This is a process that continually increases the number of clasts and their angularity. The situation is exacerbated by the freeze/thaw process, which effectively breaks up the existing flints and pebbles to produce a further increase in the number of shattered angular clasts. Atkinson states,

> 'While they [earthworms] will burrow in material which contains a high proportion of stones and rubble, they will not normally penetrate pure rubble, gravel or other coarse and angular material in the absence of admixed earth; and less still the natural subsoil' (*ibid.*)

Clearly, the acid Clay-with-flints deposits do not appear to provide an environment conducive to earthworms. The worm populations are likely to be smaller and contain a narrower range of species. Furthermore, this range of species is unlikely to include the casting and deep-burrowing species association with extensive and deeply disruptive soil disturbances and as such contributes to the restricted change of the deposits and the retention, *in situ,* of Palaeolithic artefacts.

Depth functions

The deposits mapped as Clay-with-flints often show characteristic changes (which are best seen in thin sections) of composition in relation to depth below the ground surface. These result from soil development processes, for example clay illuviation; decalcification and redeposition of carbonates in subsoil horizons; incorporation of organic matter; weathering of clay and other minerals and the mobilisation and subsoil reprecipitation of iron, alumina, and humus (podzolization). (Catt 1986: 182).

Interpretations using particle-size data

Data on the particle-size distribution of geological materials can be used to characterise the distributions of materials numerically and then to relate these results to the environment in which the materials were formed. However, several complicating factors present themselves when attempts are made to use particle-size analyses to detect the depositional environments of ancient sediments. Many sediments are actually a combination of two or more different grain size populations of different origins. This may reflect the mixing of sediments of different environments or the presence of several populations in one sample. It may also reflect the action of different physical processes (Griffiths 1967: 86; Selly 1982: 19). The way in which sediments are laid down, the particular mechanisms involved and distinctive particle-size distributions, have been the subject of much study over many years. Many attempts have been made to establish what particle-size characteristics are indicative of which sedimentary environments, but many different processes are involved and there is considerable overlap between characteristics of sediments from different environments. However, Gale and Hoare (1991: 8) note it is generally agreed that despite the many complicating factors, it is possible to make some generalisations in respect of particular mechanisms from the particle-size distribution of clastic sediments.

Throughout the Quaternary therefore, a period of around two million years, temperature differences have been superimposed on changes in the type and rate of soil development associated with fluctuating rainfall. As the increases in both temperature and rainfall were often synchronous, pedogenesis was accelerated during temperate periods. During glacial periods the synchronous decrease in temperature and rainfall effectively restricted weathering and soil development (Morrison 1978). The processes of soil formation are many and varied and include:

> 'the physical disruption of rock and mineral particles; disturbance by frost action; desiccation; root penetration, tree fall and animal burrowing; chemical weathering (hydrolysis, oxidation, carbonation); incorporation of organic decomposition products; reduction of iron compounds (gleying); leaching of soluble weathering products; accumulation of insoluble residues; downward movement (illuviation) of solid particles' (Catt 1986b: 166).

Over time, a succession of layers (horizons) form, which are approximately parallel to the ground surface; often these horizons are unconformable with bedding or other structures in the rock. It is generally agreed that not all soil forming processes operate at the same rate. Some are more rapid than others. Also, the production of recognisable soil horizons usually requires the continuity of one or more processes for a period of at least a thousand years.

Palaeolithic high-level sites will have been subjected to physical, chemical and biological weathering processes before, during and after Palaeolithic occupation of the area. Data derived from particle-size analysis of the sediment samples collected during an excavation will contribute towards an understanding of the processes that have operated on that particular high-level site over geological time.

Sampling procedures for particle-size analysis – with special reference to Wood Hill

As previously described in detail (see Sampling strategy Sub-section 6.1) both bulk and unit sediment samples are to be collected from each of the horizontal spits which are dug at 5cm vertical interval throughout the trench.

During the 1993 excavation of Wood Hill, samples of the sediments were collected from each of the 18 horizontal spits dug at 5cm vertical intervals throughout the trench (see Figure 38). Bulk samples and unit samples of the deposits mapped as Clay-with-flints were collected for analysis. Bulk samples are large samples (15–20kg) of the deposit most characteristic of each spit. Unit samples are samples taken from smaller areas within the spit which for one reason or another, differed (for example, in colour or texture) from the main body of the sediments.

In total, 41 sediment samples for particle size analysis were selected from the deposits mapped as Clay-with flints taken from the Wood Hill 1993 trench. Restrictions on both time and money prevented the sieving of the low-level, potentially less important, B13, B16 and C16 bulk samples (these are available to be sieved at a later date). To avoid possible data distortions, the samples were sieved by three different establishments with a number of duplicate samples being distributed between the three different batches, so that the resulting particle size analysis of these duplicates could be compared, one against the other. All samples were sieved to British Standard 1377: part 2.1990, test 9.2 (Wet sieving) and British Standard 1377: part 2. 1990 test 9.5 (Hydrometer sedimentation) in order to determine the percentage ratios of the clay, silt, sand, gravel and cobbles (referred to as the fractions or particles of the deposit). The sieved residues were retained as separate units for further analyses. Laser analysis of the Wood Hill 1993 sediments was not available. It is perhaps both quicker and could possibly be more accurate but sieving to obtain debitage, small fossils and quartz grains etc. would still be needed.

Particle size analysis

The analysis of particle sizes is normally presented on a logarithmic scale, where each successive size fraction covers twice the size range of the previous one. This system was extended by Krumbein (1934) who proposed the Phi scale where for each phi unit increase in scale the corresponding size in millimetres is halved. There are two major disadvantages of using Phi: firstly, other related disciplines (engineering geology etc) do not use the system and secondly, the underlying assumption that particle sizes follow a normal distribution is open to question. However, as Palaeolithic archaeological projects have in the past used Phi, this form of measurement was included so that comparisons could potentially be explored.

Statistical analysis

There are two types of statistics that can be used to analyse particle size distributions. The first, graphical statistics, uses data taken directly from the graphs at certain percentage points. The second, moment statistics, uses all the data and is more accurate and representative, but can only be used if data are available for the whole sample, i.e. if all grain sizes present lie within the defined grain size limits (a total of less than 1% undefined is acceptable). In the case of Wood Hill 1993 sediments over 40% of the sample are less than +10 Phi, so we do not have a complete picture and have therefore used the graphical method. From the relevant Phi values at the given percentage points, the mean, standard deviation, skewness and kurtosis were calculated (see Gale and Hoare, 1991 for formulae). Graphic statistics were produced as shown below (Table 2).

As expected from a site on deposits mapped as Clay-with-flints, the Wood Hill 1993 results show a high proportion of clays, giving a positive skew towards fine particle size and a low overall standard deviation. Bivariate analyses charts (where, for example, mean is charted against standard deviation) were produced on the graphic statistics above, in order to identify any distinct process diagnostic groupings (see McManus 1988:80). There were no clear groupings except between standard deviation

Table 2 Graphic Statistics

	A1	A2	A3	A4	A5	A6	A7	A8	A9	A10					
Mean	7.7	7.6	7.5	4.9	8.3	6.2	8.3	8.3	8.6	8.8					
SD	-3.5	-3.8	-3.7	-6.0	-2.4	-5.2	-2.1	-1.9	-1.8	-3.3					
Skewness	0.8	0.8	0.7	0.9	1.0	0.9	1.0	0.5	1.0	1.0					
Kurtosis	1.1	1.2	1.1	1.1	0.9	1.2	0.5	0.8	0.9	2.5					

	B1	B2	B3	B4	B5	B6	B7	B8	B9	B10	B11	B12	B14	B15	B17
Mean	8.2	8.0	4.3	8.6	7.4	8.0	8.2	8.0	7.5	5.6	4.7	6.5	7.0	6.7	5.3
SD	-2.7	-3.6	-5.8	-2.2	-3.4	-2.8	-2.5	-2.7	-3.2	-5.4	-5.5	-4.6	-4.2	-4.0	-5.7
Skewness	1.0	0.9	0.6	1.0	0.6	0.7	0.9	0.6	0.6	1.0	0.6	0.8	0.8	0.4	1.0
Kurtosis	0.7	1.3	0.5	1.0	0.9	1.1	0.7	1.2	0.9	1.0	1.0	1.1	1.1	1.1	1.2

	C1	C2	C3	C4	C5	C6	C7	C8	C9	C10	C11	C12	C13	C14	C15	C17
Mean	5.1	7.7	4.3	7.7	3.6	6.8	3.7	4.9	4.6	4.0	4.8	4.5	4.0	4.7	7.0	5.7
SD	-5.1	-3.9	-5.5	-3.8	-5.8	-4.0	-5.7	-5.5	-5.4	-5.8	-5.5	-5.5	-5.7	-5.4	-3.9	-5.5
Skewness	0.6	1.0	0.5	1.0	0.3	0.5	0.3	0.6	0.6	0.5	0.6	0.5	0.4	0.4	0.6	0.9
Kurtosis	0.9	1.1	0.5	1.0	0.4	1.0	0.4	1.0	0.8	0.5	1.0	0.9	0.7	1.1	1.1	1.3

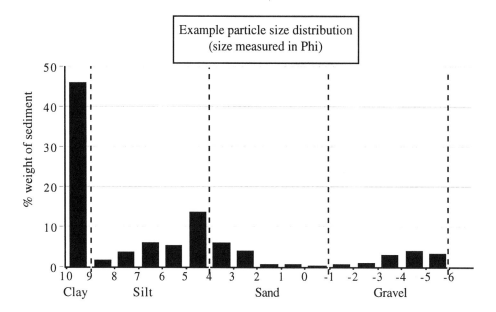

Figure 52 *Example particle size distribution (Square A spit 2) showing three sub distributions in one sediment sample.*

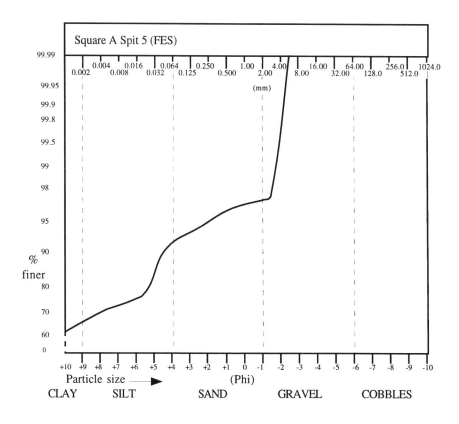

Figure 53 *Typical cumulative frequency curve showing three distributions. (Square A spit 5).*

(SD) and mean, where the C squares in general showed a larger mean and standard deviation reflecting their higher gravel content. Square A had significant differences in mean (smaller), and kurtosis (much more leptokurtic) reflecting its much higher proportion of clay and higher concentration around the mean.

Spencer (1963) makes a compelling argument that most distributions seem to be composed of three or less separate normal distributions (see Figure 52). Combining the data for these can create false measures of mean, dispersion and skewness. If the two curves are well separated, then their bimodal nature is obvious, but if they are separated by only, say, 2 standard deviations then the combined distribution loses its bimodal character and develops marked kurtosis. He therefore postulates that most sediments can be separated into:

- Gravel (median -3.5phi to 2phi , SD 1phi to 2phi)
- Sand (median 1.5phi to 1phi SD .4phi to 1phi)
- Clay (median 7phi to 9phi SD 2phi to 3phi)

The mean of two distributions will lie closer to the more dominant parent. In this case, a measure of overall dispersion (SD), instead of measuring sorting, will actually measure mixing between the two distributions. The effects of true sorting where, for example, all units smaller than 4phi were lost, would be shown by the truncation of the separate distributions. Dispersion shows mixing and will only show sorting if the original populations have been mixed in equal proportions.

In the Wood Hill 1993 samples, cumulative frequency distribution curves (plotted on probability scales e.g. Figure 53) showed three distributions, but these samples had a silt, rather than a sand, sub-distribution. Square A, spit 5, (Figure 53) for example, had a clay mode, a silt mode and a gravel mode. The fact that, in this case, over 60% of the sediment is clay with a size less than 10phi means the shape and nature of the clay sub distribution is difficult to analyse (as the clay fractions were not determined by laser analysis). From the cumulative frequency curve for each square it could be seen that most of the distributions in the Wood Hill deposit have a very large clay fraction, a smaller silt fraction, very little sand and a relatively small gravel fraction, particularly of clasts equal to or greater than 20mm.

Investigating and interpreting – the Wood Hill 1993 particle size analysis data

The area of the Wood Hill 1993 trench, designated squares A and B, forms an edge of the solution hollow (see Figures: 39; 40; 41; 42, section drawings of the trench and Sub-section 6.6). Results of the particle size analysis confirmed the similarities noted in the on-site observations of the deposits in these squares (A and B – down to where shattered Chalk appears in spit 11 square A). Square C, the area which appears to represent the infill of the solution hollow, is, however, somewhat different from both square A and B, as the relative proportions of coarse silt and fine sand are greater throughout this part of the trench

During the Wood Hill 1993 excavation it rained very heavily indeed for several weeks, it therefore became necessary to dig (on the morning of Friday 1 October) a sump pit just outside the trench in the Square C area, to divert water away from trench. The sump digging revealed what appeared to be an

extension of the Brickearth type deposits which had been observed in the Square C (brickearth, as previously noted, can be either waterlain or windblown). Although there is no record as such of brickearth being found in the 1984/85 trenches, the section drawings and descriptions in the site-archive suggest that brickearth may well have been present. The relevance of the brickearth and general questions regarding the formation of the Clay-with-flints were put to Prof. John Catt who had arrived on site that afternoon. John remarked that the brickearth which had been uncovered in the sump pit on Wood Hill and which seemed to be incorporated into Square C, is very similar to that found at Caddington, Gaddesden Row and Kensworth (all sites explored by W.G. Smith, see Section 4). He also echoed the suggestion then put forward by Dr. Martin Bell (also present) that the sands-brickearth could be sampled by optical stimulated luminescence dating (OSL), and the relationship between Squares A, B, and C could be determined or suggested by mineralogy and micromorphology. The value in analysing the top soil particle size breakdown (i.e. what does it contain and in what proportions) was discussed. The 'actual' top soil above the Wood Hill deposits mapped as Clay-with-flints is very much more silty; – the clay content may represent 30% of the overall particle size fraction. This would suggest that the deposits mapped as Clay-with-flints in this area were at one time overlain with deposit/s that are now missing.

A Scanning Electron Microscope analysis was conducted on a number of the Wood Hill 1993 samples of coarse silt/fine sand and quartz grains, in order to test for the presence of windblown materials, the results and implications of these investigations are discussed in Sub-section 6.5.

Particle size distribution and identifiable stratigraphy

In order to investigate the differing proportions of the sediments, a summary histogram (Figure 54) was produced showing the relative proportions of clay, coarse silt and fine sand and gravel in each excavated square (dug as horizontal spits at 5cm vertical sections). Having produced, and studied the histogram (Figure 54) it was clear that if the C squares in the top spits were aligned one spit lower to the A squares in the top spits (i.e. C2 to A3) an interesting pattern in the relative distribution of the particles appeared. Further investigations were therefore necessary.

Unlike excavations in which spits are dug parallel to the known boundaries of the strata, the Wood Hill 1993 spits were dug at measured, horizontal and vertical intervals which cut through the soil without

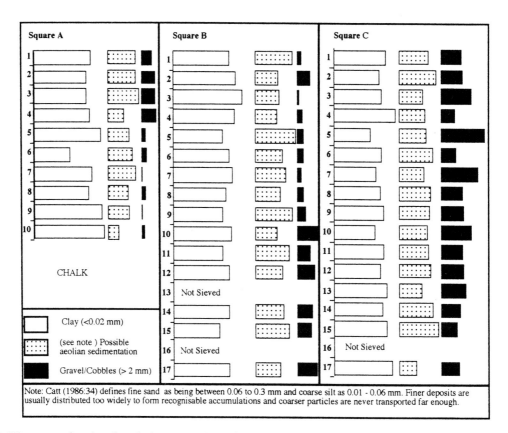

Figure 54 *Histogram showing the relative proportions of clay, coarse silt and fine sand and gravel in each excavated square.*

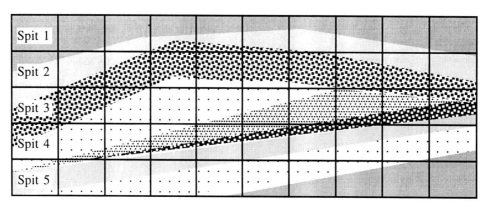

Figure 55 *Example of horizontal spits dug at vertical intervals cutting across stratified buried landsurfaces which slope or are very irregular.*

special reference to the form of any underlying stratigraphy. In a large excavation, this procedure may present few problems when subsequently the data is interpreted, however in a small trench this may not always be so. If the angle at which the spits are cut, i.e. horizontal or vertical, accurately mirrors the visible stratigraphy in the restricted space all is well, but this might not be the case, as horizontal spits dug at vertical intervals could cut across stratified buried landsurfaces which slope or are very irregular (see Figure 55).

If, as in the case of Clay-with-flints deposits, stratigraphy is predominately identified by particle-

size analysis and fabric data, this fact requires careful consideration. Samples taken along a spit and analysed without bearing this in mind may result in misleading or erroneous interpretations of the data – interpretations that might suggest that the site is not stratified but is a mixed deposit.

As previously noted, a pattern can be detected if the C squares in the top spits are aligned one spit lower to the A squares in the top spits (i.e. C2 to A3). Consequently, the relative percentages of clay, coarse silt/fine sand and gravel were analysed to indicate similarities across the squares. In the first instance, the patterns of increases and decreases in

Table 3 *Calculation to identify relative levels with most similar percentages of clay (C) and coarse silt/fine sand (S) between each of the squares.*

FRACTIONS - CLAY=C, COARSE SILT/FINE SAND = S

SPIT	AC	AS	BC	BS	CC	CS
1	52	10	52	22	47	10
2	47	10	57	6	41	26
3	48	20	63	16	43	15
4	51	5	56	5	56	12
5	61	8	45	22	32	12
6	33	8	52	9	43	22
7	53	15	55	14	38	10
8	50	3	48	10	42	18
9	62	7	45	6	45	12
10	64	1	53	5	37	17
11	Chalk		45	30	45	17
12			51	10	42	16
13			-	-	48	12
14			52	10	44	23
15			42	18	48	20
16			-	-	-	-
17			51	20	53	10

CALCULATIONS

Subtract x from y	A1-C1 C	A1-C1 S	A2-C1 C	A2-C1 S	A1-C2 C	A1-C2 S	B1-C1 C	B1-C1 S	B2-C1 C	B2-C1 S	B1-C2 C	B1-C2 S	A1-B1 C	A1-B1 S	A2-B1 C	A2-B1 S	A1-B2 C	A1-B2 S	A3-B1 C	A3-B1 S
1	5	0	0	0	11	16	5	12	10	4	11	4	0	12	5	12	5	4	4	2
2	6	16	7	6	4	5	16	20	22	10	14	9	10	4	9	14	16	6	6	1
3	5	5	8	10	8	8	20	1	13	10	7	4	15	4	12	11	8	15	2	8
4	5	7	5	4	19	7	0	7	11	10	24	7	5	0	5	3	6	17	23	3
5	29	4	1	4	18	14	13	10	20	3	2	0	16	14	12	14	9	1	8	7
6	10	14	10	7	5	2	9	13	12	8	14	1	19	1	1	6	22	6	2	6
7	15	5	12	7	11	3	17	4	10	0	13	4	2	1	5	11	5	5	7	7
8	8	15	20	11	5	9	6	8	3	12	3	2	2	7	14	3	5	3	16	9
9	17	5	19	11	25	10	0	6	8	7	8	11	17	1	19	5	9	2	-	-
10	No spits below 9 for square A						16	12	8	13	8	12	No spits below 9 for square A							
11	(Shattered Chalk from here)						0	13	6	7	3	14	(Shattered Chalk from here)							
12							9	6	-	-	3	2								
13							-	-	4	2	-	-								
14							8	13	2	5	4	10								
15							6	2	-	-	-	-								
16							-	-	-	-	-	-								
17							2	10	-	-	-	-								
Total	100	71	82	60	106	74	86	81	109	64	96	42	86	44	82	79	85	59	68	43
Clay + silt		171		142		180		167		173		138		130		161		144		111
Mean:1-9	11	8	9	7	12	8	10	9	12	7	11	5	10	5	9	9	9	7	8	5
Mean:C+S		19		**16**		20		19		19		**15**		14		18		16		**14**
Mean10+17							7	9	5	7	4	10								
Mean:C+S								16		**12**		14								

percentages between spits indicated that the A squares showed a similar pattern to the C squares but one spit lower.

In order to test whether the squares showed similarities in particle size distributions, to each other but at different spit levels, the following method was developed to derive a single comparative figure for each combination of spits within squares compared to spits at different levels in other squares. The lowest value produced by the following method represents the most similar combination of spit levels across squares. In order to calculate this comparison number, a spreadsheet was used to subtract the relative particle size percentages for a particular square in a particular spit from: (a) the relative percentages in the same spit in a different square and (b) a different spit in a different square. For example, the percentage of clay in square A, spit 1 (A1) was subtracted from the percentage of clay in square B, spit 1 (B1). The same calculations were carried out between all the spits in all the squares and an average of all the absolute (i.e. with the positive or negative sign ignored) values was produced. A data distortion was avoided by excluding Spit 10 Square A from the calculations as this spit lay immediately above the Chalk and had, therefore, a greatly increased proportion (97%) of the clay and fine silt fraction. The calculations were also carried out for the coarse silt/fine sand fractions. The overall averages for both the clay and coarse silt/fine sand fractions (gravel being the remainder) were added to give the final total for subsequent comparison (see Table 3 above).

This exercise was repeated comparing squares which were one and two spits above and below the original (for example, A3 was compared with B1, B2, B4 and B5). The same calculations (as above) were then carried out between squares A and B, B and C and A and C. In each case, the lowest value showed the relationship with the most similar percentages of clay and coarse silt/fine sand. Thus, for spits 1 to 10 (excluding A10), each A square relates most closely to a B square which is two spits higher and a C square which is one spit higher. This relationship was checked and confirmed as the figures for B and C showed the same relationship as predicted from the calculations for A and C and A and B. This confirmed the original interpretation of Figure 54. For spits 11 to 17, only B and C data were available, as the square A spits had reached Chalk. From spit 11 there is a change in the relationship between the B and C squares. The B squares now related to the C squares one spit higher. Using this data, it was possible to interpolate the shape of the deposits, which is shown as the thicker black lines on Figure 56. As the horizontal spits were dug at 5cm vertical intervals across the 3m × 1m trench and each square/spit sampled separately, data distortions were reduced, nevertheless, built in errors may well occur. Any decrease in particular percentages, however small, would in theory flatten the interpolated shape of the deposit at any one point, conversely any particular percentage increase could increase the interpolated angles.

At the beginning of this particle size analysis I became aware of what appeared to be a corres-

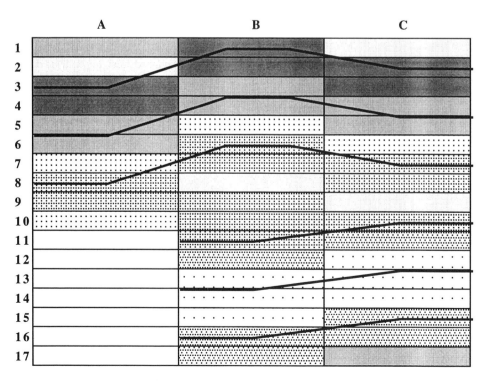

Figure 56 Staggered spits showing interpolation of the shape of the deposit.

ponding stratification of an increase and decrease of the coarse silt and fine sand fractions within squares A and B, particularly at spits 6 to 10 (A10, as noted above, having an extremely high proportion). However, the increase and decrease in the coarse silt and fine sand fraction in square C at these spits (6 to 10) was a 'mirror image' of the pattern found in both A and B. This effect is eliminated if the square and spits are 'staggered' as described above (Figure 56). When viewed level by level the coarse silt and fine sand fractions exhibit a regularity in the stratigraphic pattern of increases and decreases (Figure 57).

However, the clay fraction which also displays increases and decreases across levels (not necessarily in the same sequence as the coarse silt and fine sand), appears to be of a more random nature. The statistical methods employed in this analysis had proved entirely adequate, but if further statistical analysis were to be undertaken a different approach was required.

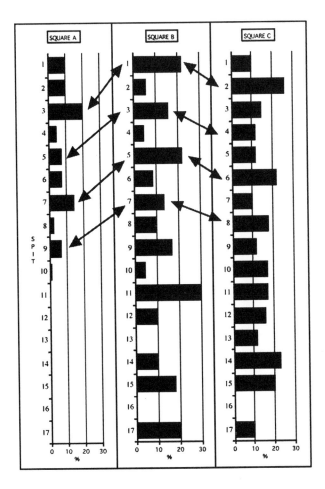

Figure 57 Diagram showing regularity in the stratigraphic pattern of increases and decreases of the coarse silt and fine sand fractions when displayed with staggered spit adjustment.

Closed data, induced correlations and non-parametric tests

There is an inherent, but often ignored, problem in applying closed statistical techniques (see below), where the distribution of total population cannot be fully determined. For particle size analysis, it will always be impossible to distinguish between populations below a certain size (e.g. particle sizes below +10 phi). Since the fractions are expressed as percentages of the whole sample, this form of closed data (where the data are expressed as proportions of a whole rather than absolute numbers) cannot be statistically analysed by normal parametric methods. However, since in petrology and many other fields of geology it is impossible to escape dealing with closed data, various procedures have been developed to detect real bivariate relationships. The problem in bivariate statistics is that the values of any two variables are not, in principle, independent: regardless of the underlying geological process, 'the value of one variable will automatically tend to affect the values of the other variable' (Swan and Sandilands 1995: 155–156).

The use of non-parametric tests based on the ranks of percentages are therefore appropriate. Non-parametric tests do not rely on absolute values for data but use ordinal scales, or ranks. This overcomes the impossibility of using percentages to calculate parametric statistics, such as the arithmetic mean, in order to explore correlations (pers. comms, Dr. M. Cortina, Statistical Department, University of Oxford). Spearman's Rank Correlation is the most common method of establishing correlations of ranks. Swan and Sandilands (1995) suggest that this method, used in geology, is as accurate as the parametric correlation methods.

> 'It is unusual for Pearson's [parametric method] to provide a statistical result superior to Spearman's' (*op. cit.* 1995: 191).

In this instance, the recommended variation (of the Spearman method) is that proposed by Lehmann (1975: 290–7, 433), which tests the hypothesis of no change in a variable against the alternative of an upward or downward trend. The trends for the clay, coarse silt/fine sand and gravel fractions were investigated in each of the relevant spit groupings (as identified in the fabric analysis see Sub-section 6.2) and then for all individual spits. Both the Spearman and Lehmann methods were used and provided comparable results indicating the following trends (Table 4).

It can be seen that there is a downwards trend of clay for all the grouped spits in squares A and C. For example, within squares A6 to A10, there is an internal downward trend for clay. The deposit, from

Table 4 *Particle size correlations – percentages of fractions significantly trending upwards or downwards.*

PARTICLE SIZE RANK CORRELATIONS
(Percentages of clay etc trending upward or downward)

CLAY

A			B			C		
A3 to 5	DOWN		B 1-3	DOWN		C 2-4	DOWN	
A6 to 10	DOWN		B 4-8	NT		C 5-9	DOWN	
			B 9-	NT		C 10-	DOWN	
All spits	DOWN		All spits	UP		All spits	DOWN	

COARSE SILT/FINE SA

A			B			C		
A3 to 5	NT		B 1-3	NT		C 2-4	UP	
A6 to 10	NT		B 4-8	NT		C 5-9	NT	
			B 9-	DOWN		C 10-	NT	
All spits	NT		All spits	NT		All spits	NT	

GRAVEL

A			B			C		
A3 to 5	NT		B 1-3	NT		C 2-4	NT	
A6 to 10	NT		B 4-8	NT		C 5-9	NT	
			B 9-	NT		C 10-	UP	
All spits	UP		All spits	DOWN		All spits	NT	

NT = no trend

top to bottom in squares A and C, has a downward trend for clay. Square B initially appears to show a different situation, with an upward trend for clay over all spits, despite having the expected downward trend in spits 1 to 3. This illustrates the need to consider the underlying deposit when interpreting statistical results. The lower spits in square B have relatively high levels of gravel, which means, as the results are in percentages, that there has to be less clay and/or silt/sand. Looking at the data in more detail, it is clear that there is no upward trend in B. There is simply less clay in the lower 8 spits than in the upper 8 spits – probably due to the increase in the gravel fraction. This is supported by the lack of trending in the lower B spits for clay and the overall, and misleading, trend downwards for gravel in B which again represents not so much a real trend as an increase in all the lower spits compared to the upper. The other particle size fractions generally show no trends upwards or downwards except for a downward trend in silt/sand in spits 9 to 17 for B and an upward trend for gravel in the A spits (which again represents a higher gravel content in the lower spits).

The 'Staggered' Square format

Having first established the relative association of both squares and spits within the Wood Hill 1993

deposits (as shown in Figure 54) and thereby reducing the effects of the artificial divisions (an unavoidable and necessary component of any excavation (Figure 55), the next stage was to plot out the percentages of the clay, coarse silt /fine sand and gravel accordingly (see Table 5 below).

In the analysis that follows, the significance of the percentage increases and decreases of clay and course silt/fine sand fractions are considered at each level, whereas the gravel fraction is only discussed when and where changes of significance occur. With the artificial divisions removed, it was now possible to determine various patterns. (Note, square A (as shown in Table 5) is used to determine the level numbers according to the 'staggered' square format).

– If reference is made to both the particle size data for square A1 in Table 5 and to the orientation data for square A1, the percentage of clay in the 'isolated' square A1 (as shown in Figure 54) could be seen as evidence of an increase in the clay fraction (clay illuviation) derived from a once overlying deposit and the impeded downward illuviation of the clay. The percentage of coarse silt/fine sand (i.e. 10%) recorded for square A1 is the same as that for level 2.

– In level 2 (A2 and C1 are either side of B1, the stratigraphic high which is therefore not included in this group) the percentage of clay decreases if compared with square A1.

Table 5 Percentages of the clay, coarse silt /fine sand and gravel (gravel further analysed into fine, medium, coarse).

Clay %					
		A		**B**	**C**
Level		%		%	%
1	A1	52			
2	A2	47			C1 47
3	A3	48	B1	52	C2 41
4	A4	51	B2	57	C3 43
5	A5	61	B3	63	C4 56
6	A6	33	B4	56	C5 32
7	A7	53	B5	45	C6 43
8	A8	50	B6	52	C7 38
9	A9	62	B7	55	C8 42
10	A10	64	B8	48	C9 45
11			B9	45	C10 37
12			B10	53	C11 45
13			B11	45	C12 42
14			B12	51	C13 48
15			B13	no data	C14 44
16			B14	52	C15 48
17			B15	42	C16 no data
18			B16	no data	C17 53
19			B17	51	

Coarse silt/fine sand %					
		A		**B**	**C**
Level		%		%	%
1	A1	10			
2	A2	10			C1 10
3	A3	20	B1	22	C2 26
4	A4	5	B2	6	C3 15
5	A5	8	B3	16	C4 12
6	A6	8	B4	5	C5 12
7	A7	15	B5	22	C6 22
8	A8	3	B6	9	C7 10
9	A9	7	B7	14	C8 18
10	A10	1	B8	10	C9 12
11			B9	6	C10 17
12			B10	5	C11 17
13			B11	30	C12 16
14			B12	10	C13 12
15			B13	no data	C14 23
16			B14	10	C15 20
17			B15	18	C16 no data
18			B16	no data	C17 10
19			B17	20	

Gravel %					
		A		**B**	**C**
Level		%		%	%
1	A1	9			
2	A2	12			C1 18
3	A3	12	B1	2	C2 19
4	A4	13	B2	11	C3 27
5	A5	3	B3	1	C4 12
6	A6	4	B4	4	C5 39
7	A7	1	B5	5	C6 13
8	A8	3	B6	5	C7 33
9	A9	1	B7	2	C8 19
10	A10	2	B8	5	C9 20
11			B9	6	C10 27
12			B10	18	C11 19
13			B11	11	C12 20
14			B12	15	C13 22
15			B13	no data	C14 17
16			B14	13	C15 14
17			B15	12	C16 no data
18			B16	no data	C17 16
19			B17	17	

Gravel % Breakdown

		A				**B**				**C**		
		F	M	C		F	M	C		F	M	C
1	A1	2	7									
2	A2	2	6	4					C1	4	14	0
3	A3	2	10	0	B1	2	0	0	C2	5	14	0
4	A4	1	6	16	B2	1	6	4	C3	3	19	5
5	A5	2.6	0	0	B3	1	0	0	C4	2	10	0
6	A6	0	2	14	B4	1	2	1	C5	3	25	11
7	A7	1	0	0	B5	5	0	0	C6	2	7	4
8	A8	0	0	3	B6	0	3	2	C7	1	23	9
9	A9	1	0	0	B7	2.5	0	0	C8	2	7	10
10	A10	0	0	8	B8	1	1	3	C9	1	19	0
11					B9	6.2	0	0	C10	2	15	10
12					B10	2	12	4	C11	2	11	6
13					B11	2	9	0	C12	2	10	8
14					B12	1	8	6	C13	2	20	0
15					B13	no data			C14	2	14	1
16					B14	1	8	4	C15	2	12	0
17					B15	2	4	6	C16	no data		
18					B16	no data			C17	2	7	7
19					B17	1	16	0				

F = Fine (>2mm, <6.3mm)
M = Medium (>6.4mm, <20mm)
C = Coarse and greater (>20mm)

– From level 3, there is a general clay percentage increase, a pattern which continues down through level 4 to level 5. There is also a substantial increase in coarse silt /fine sand input in level 3. The percentage of coarse silt/fine sand then follows a similar pattern to that of the clay down to level 5, although the percentage increase at level 5 is generally modest compared to that in level 3.

– Relatively consistent percentages in the gravel fraction are exhibited down to level 4. At level 4 the gravel fraction shows a change: there is a percentage increase in all three squares, notably in the coarse gravel size (see Table 5).

- At level 5 the downward rate of the clay illuviation appears to be decreased (by a less permeable horizon, perhaps) as the percentage of illuviated clay exhibits a substantial increase to that which in found in level 6. A change in the a-axis orientation of the clasts in levels 5/6 to 8/9 in relation to levels 1 to 4/5 and 9/10 to 17 (see Subsection 6.2) suggests an input of material between levels 5/6 to 8/9. This may have produced a horizon, which could then account for the build-up of the clay in level 5.
- The clay in level 6 shows a percentage decrease from that of level 5.
- The amount of coarse silt/fine sand is the same in level 6 as it is in level 5 for both square A (6) and square C (5), but there is a decrease in square B (4).
- By contrast, the gravel fraction in level 6 shows a percentage increase, particularly in squares A and C, with C showing the highest (25%) recorded percentage of medium gravel (>6.4mm – <20mm) in this analysis.
- At level 7 the percentage of clay is generally increased by comparison to that found in level 6 (although it is somewhat reduced in square B. This may be a statistical problem associated with the percentage of gravel in the sieved sample (which may also be operating in B9).
- An additional change occurring in level 7 is an increased percentage of coarse silt/fine sand. This strongly suggests another horizon, the percentage increase in this level is as substantial as that seen in level 3.
- From level 7 downwards, the square A gravel fraction is greatly reduced. This decrease is not reflected in square B or C. In fact the percentage of medium gravel is increased in C to 23%.
- In level 8 the percentage of clay once again decreases, although there is an increase in B (6).
- At level 8 the percentage of coarse silt/fine sand also decreases.
- Both level 9 and level 10 show corresponding gradual downward increases in the clay percentage. In square A level 10, where the Clay-with-flints meets the shattered Chalk, the percentage of illuviated clay is predictably high, whereas the clay percentage in square B shows a reduction; however, at this level the relationship between the squares starts to change (refer to Figure 54).
- Although the percentage of coarse silt /fine sand increases in level 9 (relative to level 8) it decreases in level 10 (unlike the clay fraction).
- Below level 10 (i.e. between levels 11 and 17, where the excavated area was reduced to squares B and C), the clay fraction exhibits a consistently alternating stratigraphic pattern of increases and

decreases. Notable percentage increases in the clay and coarse silt/fine sand and gravel, in the individual squares are as follows:
- Level 11: increase percentage of coarse silt/fine sand; percentage increase in gravel;
- Level 12: increase in the clay percentage; (C11) the same increase percentage of coarse silt/fine sand as in level 11 (C10); (B10) percentage increase in gravel;
- Level 13: increase percentage of coarse silt/fine sand; a value of 30% makes this the largest recorded percentage of coarse silt/fine sand in any square in the trench;
- Level 14: increase in the clay percentage; (C13) a percentage increase in medium gravel;
- Level 15: increase percentage of coarse silt/fine sand;
- Level 16: increase in the clay percentage; (C15) increased percentage of coarse silt/fine sand;
- Level 17: increased percentage of coarse silt/fine sand;
- Level 18: increase in the clay percentage;
- Level 19: increase in the clay percentage; (B17) increased percentage of coarse silt/fine sand.

Summarised results of the Wood Hill 1993 particle size analyses

A summary of the clay fraction analysis, using the 'staggered' square format, suggests:

- The remains of an illuvial horizon in square A1;
- An illuvial horizon at level 5;
- A possible horizon at level 7;
- An illuvial horizon in levels 9/10;

A summary of the coarse silt/fine sand analysis, using the 'staggered' square format suggests:

- A major input centred in level 3;
- A major input centred in level 7;
- A major input confined to level 13 (B11).

A summary of the gravel analysis, using the 'staggered' square format suggests that;

- Throughout all levels, square C consistently contains a larger amount of medium and coarse gravel than either square A or square B;
- There is a general substantial increase in gravel in level 4;
- There is a general increase in gravel in level 6;
- Between levels 11 and 19 the proportions of gravel (all sizes) in both square B and square C is constant, although proportionally there is more gravel in C.

Only one modern root system was found during the 1993 excavation of the Wood Hill site. This was confined to spit 3. If the relevant squares (A3, B3, C3) are plotted out in the 'staggered square' format, the roots may have modified the particle size distribution in: square A in level 3; square C in level 4; square B in level 5. There is no conclusive evidence to this effect. However, there is a slight percentage increase in fines (clay, coarse silt/fine sand) in these areas though this is not at variance with the overall pattern at these levels. Interestingly, (refer to Subsection 6.2) very few worms indeed or other insects were found in the trench (although the soil was damp). Their activity, as observed, was minimal and confined almost exclusively to the top soil. No worm activity was observed below spit 2. (Note: as bioturbation data is not recorded in the 1984/85 site-archive comparisons cannot be made between the various trenches dug then, and the 1993 and 1994 excavations).

In conclusion, identifiable changes in the sequence at the Wood Hill 1993 site – as derived from the particle size analysis and set out in the 'staggered' square format are as follows:

– Level 1: illuvial horizon (clay);
– Level 3: input of coarse silt / fine sand;
– Level 4: increase in gravel;
– Level 5: illuvial horizon (clay);
– Level 6: increase in gravel;
– Level 7: input of coarse silt/fine sand and illuvial horizon (clay);
– Level 9: illuvial horizon (clay);
– Level 10: illuvial horizon (clay);
– Level 13: input of coarse silt/fine sand;
Below level 13 the data was inconclusive.

Sub-section 6.4: Clay mineral analysis – a key to Palaeolithic sites?

In the General Introduction, three questions were set out which require answers. The focus of question (c) is that as the deposits mapped as Clay-with-flints include materials of different ages, composition and origins with great variation existing within (even small) areas and between different areas, there may be a correlation between particular facies of deposits mapped as Clay-with-flints and the occurrence of Palaeolithic artefacts. Although extensive in depth investigations to provide answers to question (c) have not (to date) been included in my research, I have nevertheless uncovered two factors, each of which, operating separately or together in any particular area of deposits mapped as Clay-with-flints, may possibly greatly affect the amount and type of change in that area. The first factor is the specific clay mineral type which dominates the deposits (in any particular area), the second is the overall percentage of silt in any particular deposit mapped as Clay-with-flints.

'The mineralogy of the fines can influence the freezing process with respect to migration of water and heaving. Clays with expandable structure are liable to hold more water, but the water is generally relatively immobile compared with non-expandable clays. Consequently, strong frost heaving is more likely to be associated with

kaolinite than bentonite or montmorillonite' ... and ... 'Silt is particularly prone to heaving, since it permits relatively easy migration of moisture during freezing and in open systems this factor favours a greater ice content in silt than in clay (other conditions remaining equal)... Salts such as NaC^l and CaC^{l2} influence freezing by depressing the freezing point significantly but other additives may be more effective in reducing the frost susceptibility of soils' (Washbourne, 1973: 56–57).

Clay minerals – and Chalk Downlands

A possible link between the occurrence of specific clay minerals, particular facies of deposits mapped as Clay-with-flints and the retention of Lower Palaeolithic artefacts on the high-levels in these areas, comes from a paper by Mortimore (1986, given at the Fourth International Flint Symposium), in which he states:

'A curious feature in much of the Chalk of Sussex is the clay mineral species distribution which must reflect sedimentation patterns and may have a bearing on the chalk and flint diagenesis. Weir and Catt (1965) analysed samples in the Arun Gap and found that montmorillonite predominated;

however analyses of the Chalk at Lewes and Seaford Head (Mortimore 1979) found no montmorillonite, only illite with rare kaolinite' *(op. cit.* 1986: 34) – see also Figure 58.

The question therefore is; has this change in the clay minerals in the Chalk been determined by the overlying deposits mapped as Clay-with-flints through clay illuviation and solution or, conversely, could the proportions of specific clay minerals in the overlying deposits be affected by the dissolution of the underlying Chalk through the incorporation of the insoluble chalk residues into the overlying deposits, or both ? Mortimore does not provide us with an answer.

Silt content – and stability

Silt is widely distributed across the Chalk Downlands of southern England. Its presence in any particular area mapped as Clay-with-flints is therefore to be expected. However, in deposits where there is an increased percentage of silt there is, as previously noted, a corresponding increase in freeze/thaw activity. As both silt and specific clay minerals have the capacity to effectively increase the amount of water retained in the deposits, (thereby increasing the propensity for freeze/thaw activity in that particular area), then if both factors (for example high silt and kaolinite) are operating individually, or more importantly together, in any one area, they may be instrumental in amplifying destabilising effects on the deposits mapped as Clay-with-flints and therefore, by association, on the Palaeolithic artefacts. The results of any previous investigations in these specific areas could have enforced the view that deposits mapped as Clay-with-flints are so cryoturbated that

any associated archaeology is of limited value. The need for further research is clear, for if predominantly montmorillonite areas (and other clay minerals with similar properties) with, or indeed without, a low silt percentage can be linked to high occurrences of Palaeolithic artefacts, another benchmark in the search for *in situ* Palaeolithic sites on the deposits mapped as Clay-with-flints may have been found.

Clay mineral analysis of the Wood Hill 1993 samples

To identify the type of clay minerals in the Wood Hill Clay-with-flints deposits, sediment samples collected during the 1993 excavation were analysed by X-ray diffraction (XRD) at the Department of Earth Science, University of Oxford. XRD provides the most efficient means of determining the clay minerals in for example, mudrocks, sandstones and limestones and therefore in deposits mapped as Clay-with-flints. Two samples were processed, one from the top of the trench WH93 B3 unit 3 (spit 3 square B) and one from the lower part of the trench WH93 B11 unit 1 (spit 11 square B) (see Figure 54) The results of the XRD are as follows:

– WH93 B3 unit 3:   Montmorillonite;
                    Quartz;
                    Feldspar;
                    Chlorite (possibly).

– WH93 B11 unit 1: Montmorillonite (2 variations
   possibly);

                    Quartz;
                    Hydrobiotite (possibly).

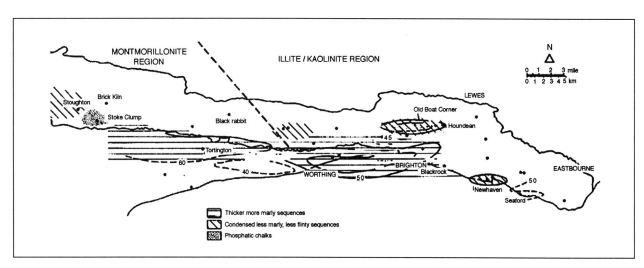

Figure 58 Examples of predominantly montmorillonite and illite/kaolinite regions. After Mortimore (1986)

Conclusion

The XRD sample size, although very small indeed, produced useful results. Montmorillonite is the dominant clay mineral throughout the trench; the silt fraction is small (see Sub-section 6.3); there is no evidence of cryoturbation in the trench (see Sub-section 6.2); embedded Lower Palaeolithic artefacts were recovered *in situ* (see Sub-section 6.8). All of which would indicates that Wood Hill has been subjected to only restricted change during the past hundreds of thousands of years. The results appear to tentatively support the theory that an analysis of both the clay mineral type and silt content in any one area may indeed provide an additional benchmark in the search for *in situ* Palaeolithic sites.

Sub-section 6.5: Lithological analysis, particle shapes and surface textures – discussion and analyses

As previously noted in Section 5, there are no geological memoirs or soil studies which include the Wood Hill, Kingsdown area of East Kent. Consequently, the only source of geological information available for this specific area is that which is shown on the British Geological Survey map Sheet 290. The additional information set out below is therefore directly derived from this research.

The Clay-with-flints deposits on Wood Hill conform to Whitaker's (1861) original description of Clay-with-flints (see Explanatory Section 2): a uniform reddish brown, often black-stained clay containing unworn flint nodules, which form a thin layer resting directly on irregular Chalk surfaces, and often underlying thicker and more heterogeneous drift deposits (grouped as Brickearth by Whitaker). The Wood Hill deposits mapped as Clay-with-flints also conform to Loveday's (1962) definition of Clay-with-flints *sensu stricto* and *sensu lato* (see Explanatory Section 2).

Deposits mapped as Clay-with-flints are included in the 'Luvic Brown Soils' and are classified as paleo-argillic and stagnogleyic chromoluvic B horizons which are characterised by strong brown to red colours and mottled horizons. According to Catt (1986: 197–8), typical paleo-argillic brown earths were formed in temperate periods in grasslands areas and in areas of deciduous forest on base-rich parent materials. Decalcification, oxidative mineral weathering, leaching and some pedoturbation (animal burrowing and treefalls) led typically to the development of brown earths. These brown earths were very often modified by vertical movements of clay particles (clay illuviation), to form argillic brown earths, and the formation of haematite to produce reddish colours (rubefication) as in paleo-argillic brown earths. In areas where the parent materials were less permeable (e.g. clay-rich) there was less weathering, clay illuviation, and rubefication because the throughflow of water (leaching) and air was greatly diminished. In fairly warm areas, seasonally anaerobic conditions led to partial reduction of iron compounds and the development of grey and brown (or reddish) mottled pseudogleys. Acidic stagnogleys with mor or peaty surface horizons over grey iron-depleted Age horizons were formed in cooler, wetter climates, where an unconfined groundwater body supported by a small impermeable unit (a perched water table) persisted for much of the year.

The Clay-with-flints soils are classified and mapped according to the relative heights at which they are found, for example the Batcombe, Winchester and Casten series (see Explanatory Section 2); the Wood Hill deposits may be belong to the Winchester series (John Catt, pers. comms.) The Winchester series is classified as a typical paleo-argillic brown earth, which is described as extremely stony, with reddish brown clay sub-soil resting on an irregular Chalk surface. Munsell Color Chart values for the deposits mapped as Clay-with-flint in the 1993 trench are: squares A and B: 7.5 YR 4/6 (strong brown); 7.5 YR 5/8 (strong brown); 10 YR 2/2 (very dark brown) and for square C: 10 YR 5/8 (yellowish brown); 2.5 Y 5/6 (light olive brown). Typically red soils in southern England are about 5 YR 4/4 (reddish brown). The range of soil colours observed in the Wood Hill (1993) trench does not correspond particularly well to the Munsell Colors given for the Winchester series. This may be due, in part, to the depth of excavation, which was restricted to 0.90m below top-soil in square A and part of square B and augured down to 1.25m in square C without the Chalk being found (Figures 39, 40, 41, 42). The observed Clay-with-flints deposits were less red and dark mottling was very much in evidence, also the deposit is not extremely stony, when contrasted with other areas of deposits mapped as Clay-with-flints.

In Explanatory Section 2 it was noted that the identification of the particular type of Clay-with-flints deposit (i.e. *sensu stricto* or *sensu lato*) in a specific area is based predominantly on the colour of the deposit itself and any associated mottling along with the clay/silt/sand percentage content of the deposit and the percentage/condition of the flint nodules and other stones. As I have previously stated, the Clay-with-flints deposits are not all derived from the same type of basal Palaeogene (remnant) beds, therefore much variation in both colour of the deposit and stone content should be expected. It is clear from the few studies that have been undertaken (in particular those in which the Munsell Color chart was used), that the particular colours/hues associated with both Clay-with-flints *sensu stricto* and *sensu lato* in different areas, do indeed differ (see Pepper's (1968) observations, for example).

However, a problem now presents itself. The colour/hue values (based on the Munsell Color chart) for the Clay-with-flints deposits, which were obtained from relatively few studies conducted in a restricted number of areas, have effectively become the 'bench marks' for *all* the Clay-with-flints *sensu stricto* and *sensu lato* deposits in southern England. Clearly, there is need for further research, as the Palaeogene basal beds from which these deposits are derived are not the same, in addition the aspect and height at which these deposit are found varies. These are all factors which have modified the processes which in turn have produced the colour of the Clay-with-flints deposits we see today. Furthermore, as the colour of a deposit is a reflection of the processes that have acted upon it, it is possible that certain Clay-with-flints deposits exhibit a particular range of colour values/hues which reflect specific conditions which could be linked to the surviving presence of Lower and Middle Palaeolithic artefacts in those areas (for example, Clay-with-flints with associated artefacts, held in solution features, see Sub-sections 6.6 and 6.11). I have therefore included in this Sub-section, details of soil profiles for the benefit of those who may need them for further research.

It would have been of some interest at this stage of the discussion to compare and contrast the deposits found on Wood Hill with other analysed deposits mapped as Clay-with-flints in East Kent and elsewhere. Unfortunately, the Smart, Bisson and Wors-sam (1975) memoir does not include the Wood Hill, Kingsdown area which is covered by the geological map Sheet 290 (see Section 6 for details of other Kent memoirs). Furthermore, although deposits mapped as Clay-with-flints and Brickearths found in other areas of East Kent are sometimes described in detail by those authors, the Munsell Color Chart was not used, thereby making many of these descriptions too inexact for this study.

Avery (1990) quotes two profiles, neither of which is directly applicable (if the Wood Hill deposits do indeed belong to the Winchester series). Profile 74 (Cope, 1976) comes from Wiltshire and is classified as Carstens series, the other (profile 76, Avery *et al.*, 1959; Avery, 1964; Ragg and Clayden, 1973) comes from Buckinghamshire and belongs to the Batcombe series. The only profiles of Winchester series I have located (to date) are to be found in Fordham and Green (1980: 93–95), Soils of Kent (profile by Jarvis *et al.* (1979) from Broad Downs, Wye, Kent (a convex escarpment crest) and the three profiles described by Hodgson, Catt and Weir (1967) from West Sussex namely Perry Hill, Jack Upperton's Gibbet and Blackpatch Hill. Only one face of each trench is shown in these profiles and all three profiles have inclusions that resemble weathered Reading Beds (not basal Thanet Beds as at Wood Hill). The Perry Hill profile is somewhat similar to the south-east face of the Wood Hill 1993 trench. To date this is the only recorded profile I have found which resembles the Wood Hill deposits. It is also interesting to note that (with the exception of Wood Hill) no archaeological finds appear to be associated with any of these analysed profiles, but then, the identification of Palaeolithic waste flakes in Clay-with-flints deposits is not always easy even for the trained archaeologist!

The deposits mapped as Clay-with-flints at Wood Hill contain Bullhead flints. Although Tertiary pebbles, Nodular flints and Tabular flints are common components of Clay-with-flints deposits throughout the Chalk Downlands of southern England, Bullhead flint is not. There is only one recorded primary source of Bullhead flint (in southern England), namely the Bullhead Bed which originally formed the basal layer of the (Palaeogene) Thanet Beds. The Thanet Beds being the oldest of the Palaeogene Beds, were sometimes overburdened by other Beds. It is therefore possible to find Bullhead flints at the base of the Woolwich and Reading Beds. As tectonic activities lifted and folded the Chalk of southern England, the Downlands were formed. Superficial deposits, which had once formed part of the various Beds at low levels, became isolated on what are now the higher plateaux and interfluves of the Chalk outcrop. As discussed in Explanatory Section 2, deposits mapped as Clay-with-flints are generally regarded as being derived from almost undisturbed Palaeogene formations mainly Reading and Woolwich Beds, sometimes Blackheath Beds, although on the North Downs in Surrey there is a thin representation of the Thanet Beds. If the presence of the Bullhead flints is indeed indicative of the Bullhead Bed (the basal layer of the Thanet Beds), it would seem therefore that the Clay-with-flints deposits to be found on Wood Hill are derived certainly from remnant Bullhead Bed and possibly also from the overlying Thanet Beds. The sequence I propose for the development of the Clay-with-flints deposits on Wood Hill is:

1. Following the formation of the Chalk during the Cretaceous period, the area was overlain by Thanet Beds including the Bullhead Layer at their base.
2. The area was subsequently uplifted and tilted.
3. Throughout the Tertiary and Quaternary periods, the Palaeogene Thanet Beds covering the uplifted sub-Tertiary marine erosion surface, and the underlying Chalk, were subject to subaerial weathering processes associated with both temperate and periglacial environments.
4. The deposits mapped as Clay-with-flints now to be found on Wood Hill seem, therefore, to be derived from remnant Palaeogene Thanet Beds with their basal Bullhead Bed layer, combined with the residues left after the dissolution of some of the underlying Chalk and the inclusion of aeolian and water-lain deposits.

To determine with certainty the remnant Tertiary Beds, from which the Wood Hill superficial deposits are derived, would require detailed measurement and analysis of the gravel-size fraction to include flints (in additional to that described in this Sub-section), quartz, chert and quartzite plus heavy mineral analysis of selected samples and micro-morphological investigations of thin-sections. These additional investigations could not be incorporated into the 1993 and 1994 research. However, as all the clasts from the Wood Hill 1993 control area have been retained, it would be possible to use these in future work to plot the colour of a pebble (e.g. black, brown or red) and therefore the flint type, against its angularity, to provide information which may relate to the effects of weathering processes on different coloured flints (i.e. different flint types). This, in turn, could provide a body of comparative data for study of other areas mapped as Clay-with-flints, as the pebble colours appear to vary proportionally.

Surface texture analysis of gravel-grade particles

There are two aspects of gravel surface texture; degree of dullness or polish, and surface markings, of which there are many. Surface markings are produced by processes of erosion, transport and deposition, with certain features widely regarded as diagnostic of particular environments. In any given environment, the effect of a process may not be equally reflected on all the clasts as the lithology and texture of a clast will strongly control the presence and preservation of the surface markings. Much of the study of surfaces textures has been focused on sand grains and

> 'few attempts have been made to study the surface of larger particles. As a result, no comparable body of information on the surface texture of gravels exists and little effort has been made to treat gravel surface textures in anything but a qualitative manner' (Gale and Hoare, 1991: 106).

Although the surface texture analysis of the gravel-size fraction is not (to date) a viable option, much can be learnt from the study of both the coarse silt and fine sand-size fractions as these fractions can be regarded as key components in the systems of deposition and erosion. Information derived from the analysis of the Wood Hill coarse silt and fine sand-size fractions is discussed later in this Sub-section (see scanning electron microscope (SEM) analysis).

Particle shapes

Many detailed studies have been undertaken, to determine the effects of particular processes on the larger particles, the gravels, in an effort to identify what processes give rise to which shapes and whether these shapes are sufficiently distinctive to be diagnostic of such processes. A few examples are listed here. River and beach gravels have been studied by Dobkins and Folk (1970), Stratten (1974) and Gale (1990), while work was done on glacial transport of gravels by Boulton (1978) and Dowdeswell *et al.* (1985: 700).

Difficulties may arise when analysing a sediment, if there exist distinctive particle shapes that have been inherited from pre-existing sediments (as in the case of the Tertiary pebbles in the deposits mapped as Clay-with-flints), or a particular rock type that produces a characteristic shape. Bridgland (1986: 29) suggests that problems can be minimised if the analyses are specific to particular lithological types, provided that these do not vary greatly. He then adds a note that is particularly relevant to this study, as it suggests that flints found on and in the deposits mapped as Clay-with-flints have reached their present form with less movement than would generally have been expected:

'it must be recorded that flint, probably the most frequently used lithology for studies of this type in southern England, appears to be much more readily rounded when already weathered or deeply patinated. This means that a higher roundness coefficient may reflect a higher proportion of weathered material rather than a longer transport history or a more effective rounding agent' (*ibid.*).

The Wood Hill 1993 excavated flints - summary of the number and type

As detailed analysis of particle morphology is very time-consuming, the number of investigations which could reasonably be undertaken on the Wood Hill 1993 materials was limited. The lithological analysis of the gravel-size fraction (particles equal to or greater than 20mm) was therefore restricted to recording the excavated flint types and angularity. In accordance with the excavation methodology (Sub-section 6.1); the lithology and angularity of 1,522 natural clasts (flints) from the control spits were recorded on site (lithological information derived from sieving of the bulk and unit samples are discussed separately in this Sub-section (see Sub-section 6.8 for lithological details of the artefacts). A summary of the lithological analysis data – number and type of flints from the control spits/squares measuring 20mm or more is given below (Table 6).

Interestingly, no nodular flints (measuring 20mm or more) were found below spit 12. However, a number of very large Chalk flint nodules (of varying sizes but generally measuring around >24cms × >24cms × >9cms), having Munsell Color values of 2.5YR 8/1(white), 2.5YR 8/2 (pale yellow) and 10YR 8/4 (very pale brown) were found within the top spits and around spits 10, 11 and 12. A very large nodule was found in spit 1 square C, embedded in the side of the trench. This nodule had fractured *in situ*. The fractured surfaces were heavily patinated and all pieces could be conjoined. The significance of these large Chalk flint nodules is discussed in Sub-Section 6.7. Fossils, Nodules and Artefacts. Post-excavation cleaning and detail examination revealed that:

- None of the Bullhead flint nodules (which are long and thin) measures more than 90cms. Most are undamaged and exhibit 100% cortex, but where they were broken in antiquity the damaged area is heavily patinated.
- Many of these Bullhead nodules exhibit black staining over the greenish cortex. The very small number of Chalk flint nodules recovered from the Clay-with-flints deposits are small and invariably stained black, in a similar manner to the Bullhead nodules. Many of the Tabular flints are also stained black.
- Frost-plucked flint and thermal fracturing is

Table 6 The number and type of flints from the control spits/squares measuring 20mm or more.

Squares	Nodular			Nod.frags.			Bullhead			Tabular			Tertiary pebbles		
	A	B	C	A	B	C	A	B	C	A	B	C	A	B	C
Spit 1.	0	0	0	3	4*	9	8	7	12	4	3	12	31	81	154
Spit 2.	0	2*	1	3*	1	5*	9	10	10	1	3	10	19	43	139
Spit 3.	1	1*	0	0	2	4	11	13	4	3	2	1	14	17	54
Spit 4.	1*	1*	1	1	0	2	7	3	24	0	2	6	19	5	184
Spit 5.	0	1*	<	1	0	<	4	6	<	3	2	<	21	20	<
Spit 6.	1*	2*	<	0	2*	<	6	7	<	0	1	<	13	2	<
Spit 7.	3*	1*	<	1	0	<	8	11	<	1	2	<	10	12	<
Spit 8.	2*	1*	3*	0	0	1	4	12	10	4	2	6	48	45	29
Spit 9.	2*	1*	0	0	6*	<	0	17	<	0	3	<	2	60	<
Spit 10.	<	2*	<	<	2*	<	<	3	<	<	4	<	<	12	<
Spit 11.	Ck.	3*	<	Ck. 0		<	Ck. 2		<	Ck.2		<	Ck. 14		<
Spit 12.	Ck.	1*	0	Ck. 0		2	Ck. 2		5	Ck.1		2	Ck. 5		29
Spit 13.	Ck.	0	<	Ck. 0		<	Ck. 0		<	Ck.3		<	Ck. 5		<
Spit 14.	Ck.	<	<	Ck	<	<	Ck.	<	<	Ck.<		<	Ck.	<	<
Spit 15.	Ck	<	<	Ck.	<	<	Ck.	<	<	Ck.<		<	Ck.	<	<
Spit 16.	(Ck.	<	1	Ck.	<	1	Ck.	<	3	Ck.	<	2	Ck.	<	31)

present; a few pot lid flints were found in C2, but there is little evidence of frost plucking on the pebbles. Also a comparatively small number of pebbles are broken.

– In many cases the surfaces of the Bullhead and Chalk flint nodules are weathered (see Subsection 6.8 for definition).

– Very few Chalk particles were found either during the excavation or later in the sieved deposits.

Loess, coversands and brickearths – analysis of the Wood Hill sediments

One of the key questions addressed in the General Introduction to this research was, 'How could Palaeolithic artefacts become incorporated into, and/ or remain on the surface of the deposits mapped as Clay-with-flints over many hundreds of thousands of years?'. In order for these artefacts to be retained in place it would necessary for them to 'be sealed' in on the Palaeolithic landsurface.

Four processes, the effects of which could effectively; retain, cover and 'seal in' the artefacts are:

– the formation of solution features and tree-throw hollows (see Explanatory Section 1; Section 4; Sub-sections 6.6 and 6.11);

– worm activity (see Sub-sections 6.3; 6.6 and 6.11);

– soil creep (see Sub-sections 6.2; 6.6 and 6.11) and

– the accumulation of windblown (aeolian) deposits (the subject of the next discussion), for example

loess/coversands and brickearths, not all of which are windblown (see also Sub-sections 6.6 and 6.11).

As coarse silt and fine sand-size fractions can therefore be regarded as key components in the system of deposition and erosion an analysis was made of the Wood Hill 1993 fractions.

Aeolian deposits in southern England

There is considerable evidence for the existence on the Downlands of southern England (Figure 59) of aeolian (windblown) materials such as Loess, Coversands and Brickearths though not all the Brickearth sediments are in fact windblown, often the main transportive agent is thought to be solifluction. The association between deposits mapped as Clay-with-flints and Brickearths is discussed in Explanatory Sections 1 and 2, and Section 4.

A Late Devensian age has been assigned to much of the loess in England and Wales, but isolated deposits of undoubted pre-Devensian loess occur at several archaeological sites in south-east England (Catt, 1978: 16). There are examples of wind-blown deposits in the Thames Valley (Chartres, 1980, 1984; Bridgland, 1994); at Bobbitshole, Ipswich (West, 1958); and at Barham in the Gipping Valley, Suffolk (Rose and Allen, 1971). In many localities in the Weald (Kent) there occur deposits of buff structureless loam or silts. In lithology and mode of occur-

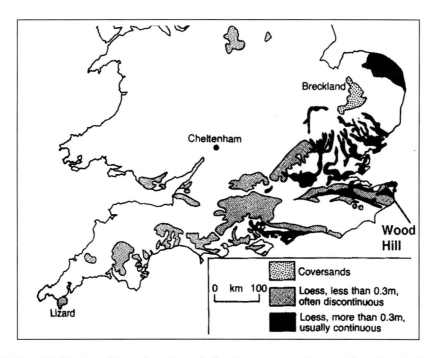

Figure 59 *The distribution of loess deposits and of aeolian coversands in southern England and Wales. After Catt (1977) and Goudie (1993) with modifications.*

rence, a number of these evidently wind-blown deposits closely resemble the loess deposits of northern Europe (Gallois and Edmunds, 1965: 62). Wind-blown deposits have also been found in East Kent. Murton records that the 'Head Brickearth' on the Isle of Thanet 'is probably of polygenetic origin, including primary loess, loess redeposited by hill-wash and solifluction, and degraded silty Thanet Beds'(*op. cit.* 1988: 21, 26, 30). Studies of the deposits at Pegwell Bay (Isle of Thanet) show that there exists in this area a <4m thick layer of loess, the basal layer of which shows faint stratification (Murton *et. al* 1988: 36). While in the Ashford area of Kent, loess is to be found on gently inclined slopes that face east rather than west. The deposition of loess on these slopes during the Late Devensian occurred as predominantly easterly winds blew the loess westwards directly across the country from the source area in the North Sea basin (Catt: 1978).

SEM analysis of the Wood Hill 1993 sediments

Particle-size analysis of sediment samples can determine the presence of wind-blown materials, since wind-blown deposits are confined to the coarse silt (0.01 to 0.06mm) and fine sand (0.06 to 0.3mm) fractions. Finer deposits are usually distributed too widely to form recognisable accumulations and coarser particles are not transported far enough to form recognisable deposits (*op. cit.* 1986: 34–5; 1995: 59–68). However, the most effective means of identifying wind-blown material in sediments (and in particular individual grains) is by the use of the scanning electron microscope (SEM). The identification of wind-blown material in the form of loess or coversands in the sediment samples from the Wood Hill 1993 trench had the potential to be a most useful addition to this research. As the SEM facilities available were very restricted, selecting the appropriate samples to be scanned was somewhat problematical. I decided to concentrate mainly on the quartz grains in the samples, whilst retaining the option to analyse the coarse-silt fraction later should the opportunity arise. The investigations were conducted in two stages.

SEM analysis: Stage one

In the first stage, 5 sediment samples of the coarse silt/fine sand fraction were selected. Three samples came from the uppermost spits of the trench, namely A1, B1 and C1, artefacts having been recovered from all three squares at this level. A further two sediment samples, C10 and B11, came from lower down in the trench. The B11 sample was taken from a spit close to

the one in which the Lower Palaeolithic handaxe had been found (see Sub-section 6.11). Initial particle-size investigations suggested that spits C10 and B11 contained a silt loam. A sixth sample came from the 'sump', which had been dug just outside the (1993) trench. A general scan of each sample was carried out (by Mr. C.R. Fagg, Department of Earth Sciences, University of Oxford) at ×45 magnification and on the basis of this, particular grains were selected for further enlargement (at either; ×55, ×60, ×300, ×350, ×370 or ×750).

SEM analysis: Stage two

Stage two of these investigations involved the detailed SEM analysis of 5 quartz grains and a general analysis of samples of the fine-sand fraction from the corresponding spits (many more quartz grains were available for analysis, but there were restriction on the number that could be processed in the allotted time available). The grains came from spits where there was an increase in the silt fraction. A predominance of samples came from Square C as this is in many ways different to both Square A and Square B. The overall conclusions reached by Dr. P.A. Bull (School of Geography, University of Oxford) after SEM analysis of the fine-sand sediments samples and the quartz grains from the Wood Hill 1993 trench, can be summarised as follows:

- rounded grains hit by rounded grains;
- all from similar source rock;
- large grain size (500 um) = high impact;
- Herzmian fractures;
- upturned plates visible;
- all the grains previously derived from the same place;
- suggested mode of deposition on Wood Hill = Storm emplacement (wind-blown).

Therefore:

1. All the quartz grains have a common origin (as there is neither contamination of the quartz nor other types of quartz).
2. The source from which the sand-fraction is derived cannot be too far away, as the grains are very large (500 microns).
3. The source rock may not be marine (sands); if it is not, it must be a rounded grain mature sandstone.

With such homogeneity of the sand fraction, it was not possible to interpret how many episodes of storm emplacements were involved (it could conceivably be only one, but it might be many). As one possible source rock may be quartzite sandstone (quartz sandstone with quartzite cement); it may be useful to search for this, and also to look for micro fossils in the samples. However, it is conceivable that the Wood Hill sand fraction has the same origin as the Goodwin Sands which now lie out to sea close to Oldstairs Bay (see Figure 31).

Conclusion

The intention of the SEM investigations of the coarse-silt and fine sand fractions from Wood Hill was principally to search for wind-blown material. Although aeolian deposits in the form of loess, brickearth and coversands have been recorded in East Kent, evidence of the presence of such deposits within the 1993 trench was needed to add to the body of information being amassed for this research – data which might explain the surviving presence of Lower Palaeolithic artefacts on this hilltop in particular, and Clay-with-flints capped areas in general. As previously noted in Sub-section 6.3, Catt observed that the brickearth which had been uncovered in the sump pit on Wood Hill and which seemed to be incorporated into Square C, was very similar to that found at Caddington, Gaddesden Row and Kensworth (see Section 4). The results of these investigations confirm that wind-blown material is indeed present in the Wood Hill deposits mapped as Clay-with-flints. The role of wind-blown deposits in preserving *in situ* the Wood Hill Lower Palaeolithic artefacts is discussed in Sub-section 6.11.

Sub-section 6.6: The Resistivity survey, augering programme and subsurface hollows

As Palaeolithic peoples manufactured their stone tools on the Clay-with-flints capped hilltops and plateaux, the working debris, and doubtless some of the implements too, fell onto the ground. Initially these artefacts may have been retained on the landsurface by the presence of vegetation. However, both short term and long term changes in the climate altered the nature of the processes of erosion and deposition on these landsurfaces. It may well be that the 'preservation potential' of a Palaeolithic assemblage in an *in situ* context, in any one place on the deposits mapped as Clay-with-flints, is directly related to a particular topographical feature of that specific high-level area, combined with particular climatic conditions operating at the time the artefacts were manufactured, as it would seem that the quicker an assemblage could become retained and 'sealed in', by whatever means, the greater chance of its survival as a discrete entity. The role that the climate, bioturbation and the surface and subsurface topography all play in the retention of Palaeolithic artefacts on the highest hill-tops and plateaux is now considered.

Climate

In arid environments (whether cold or hot) wind-blown materials (either locally derived or from further afield) falling onto the artefacts may have helped to retain them in their original position of deposition, the depth of wind-blown covering perhaps increasing over time in both cold and warm arid environments. In cold periods, whether seasonal or periglacial, artefacts falling onto the ground could become frozen onto the surface. However, material on slopes as low as 1° could be removed by gelifluction and nivation. During cold and wet and warm and wet conditions, any wind-blown covering may also be removed or reduced in depth by creep (soil or frost), surface runoff (rilling) and processes associated with mass movements, such as solifluction. Clearly, the movement of soil material across an area could either 'seal in' or remove the artefacts, but this would depend on the particular topography of the immediate area (see Explanatory Section 1. hill-slope processes; Sub-section 6.3 soil creep and Sub-section 6.5 wind-blown deposits).

Bioturbation – reworking of the surface layer

'Material deposited on the surface of a field, even if not soluble by rain, will gradually disappear and after a lapse of several years will be found, still as an integral layer, at some distance below the surface' (Atkinson, 1957).

Palaeolithic artefacts, no less than other material, lying on the surface of a ploughed field gradually sink below it when the field is put to grass. Discussed in detail in Sub-section 6.3 is Atkinson's (*ibid*) suggestion that this processes is entirely due to the action of worms which bring soil, as worm casts, to accumulate on the surface and also produce local soil subsidence due to collapsing disused burrows. Objects lying on the surface will gradually sink below it while the absolute level of the surface remains unchanged. The amount and depth of soil disruption is governed by various factors, namely the soil type, the depth of soil at the particular point, the agricultural history of the immediate area, the number of species of worm present and the actual number of worms in the specific area. However, as previously discussed (Sub-section 6.3) the coarse acid Clay-with-flints deposits containing many angular clasts do not appear to provide an environment conducive to earthworms, in particular the casting and deep-burrowing species – the ones that cause the most soil disruption. The amount of disruption to Palaeolithic sites on deposits mapped as Clay-with-flints by worm activity is therefore limited.

Subsoil hollows

The optimum topographical feature for the retention, at any particular point of the deposits mapped as Clay-with-flints and therefore, by implication, Palaeolithic artefacts in these areas, is one that resembles a 'basin-like' hollow depression or a 'shaft' in the underlying Chalk. These important subsoil features now considered can be produced by two very different processes; mechanical in the case of tree-throw hollows and (as previously discussed in Explanatory Section 1) the chemical process of solution which effects a change on the Clay-with-flints/Chalk interface to create solution hollows in the Chalk bedrock itself in areas where there is a local increase in the rate of carbonation resulting from enhanced drainage. Solution features are a common occurrence in Chalk Downland areas, and are referred to variously as solution-hollows, dolines, pipes, swallow-holes and sink-holes.

Tree-throw subsoil hollows

Fallen trees, in Palaeolithic times, may have been an important resource for both animals and people. Tree-throw hollows may well have afford a suitable place for the Palaeolithic people to manufacture stone tools and in areas where the Clay-with-flints subsoil overlying the Chalk was deep and relatively impermeable there would be a natural tendency for rainwater to 'puddle' in these small hollows thereby creating freshwater 'ponds'. A source of fresh water on at a high level on a hilltop or plateau would have

been welcomed by both animals and people. For animals, a felled tree could also yield an easy access to leaves (and possibly fruit) and in turn, the animals visiting the hollow, could become a food source for the people. In addition to being an important source of fresh water and food, the tree itself would have supplied fuel for fires and wood for shelters for the people. Tree-throw hollows in thin soils on the Chalk may not have provided water but they may well have been a source of knappable flint – the flint being exposed when the tree roots where ripped out of the underlying Chalk as the tree toppled over.

In such a wind lashed island as Britain, trees have always been vulnerable to felling by storms. The number of pits produced by fallen trees over geological time must, therefore, be considerable and the effect on the landsurface, not insignificant. Stephens (1956) has shown that where trees topple over, they often throw-up soil into hummocks, a surface morphology that would have lasted for around 500 years. Also, Veneman *et al.* (1984) and Schaetzl (1990) noted that the subsoil hollows became focal points for the drainage of precipitation (see Bell, 1977; 1992 for examples of Downland tree-throw subsoil hollows). Macphail (1992: 205) suggests that over time, soils from the different horizons fall back into the hollows and if subsoils were unstable they slacked under rainfall impact and were washed into any soil fissures. The width and depth of the subsoil hollow produced by a fallen tree, is determined by a number of factors, i.e. the size of its rootball, which in turn will depend on the age and species of tree and the depth and type of soil in which it was growing. Generally however, fallen trees on thin soils overlying the Chalk produce hollows that are wide but comparatively shallow. Where there is an increase in the soil depth overlying the Chalk, there may be a relative increase in the depth of the subsoil hollows. Catt (1986: 103) states

> 'the sub-soil hollows left by fallen trees (tree-holes) and their larger roots are often difficult to distinguish from involution but the fossil content of the infilling materials may provide useful clues; for example, tree holes may contain typical woodland molluscs or beetles'.

However, on deposits mapped as Clay-with-flints it is possible that such ancient fauna would be lost by decalcification.

Solution features and in situ Palaeolithic sites

Many of the solution features which contain deposits mapped as Clay-with-flints and associated Palaeolithic artefacts, were undoubtedly in existence before these same artefacts were manufactured and deposited on the Palaeolithic landsurface. This is not to say that solution features did not subsequently deepen or that solution features did not continue to form after the deposition of Palaeolithic artefacts on hill-top landsurfaces, but rather that they could have existed on these high-levels at any time. The practical effect of these features in many areas may have been to create depressions in a ground surface otherwise level to a greater or lesser degree. Small depressions, whether produced by solution or as previously noted tree-throw, could effectively contain localised knapping waste, whereas large depressions could no doubt have provided something more akin to an occupation area where knapping and tool use took place. An important feature in human survival strategy is the close proximity of fresh water. In a similar way that the mechanical process of tree-throw facilitates the 'ponding' of water in small hollows, the chemical process of solution produces the hollows which in the given circumstances will also 'pond'. The existence of modern natural high-level pools and ponds in depressions near the Lower Palaeolithic sites in the Caddington area was noted by Smith (1894), and the ability of depressions in Clay-with-flints deposits to retain water near the Lower Palaeolithic site on Hackpen Hill was also seen by Kendall (1916) (see Section 4 and Sub-section 6.11). During fieldwork in various counties in southern England, I too have observed the tendency for hollows in the deposits mapped as Clay-with-flints to retain water for various lengths of time, most

notably perhaps are the two large permanent high-level ponds on Hackpen Hill, Wiltshire – one of which is the 'Glory Ann pond' the other somewhat smaller, is now a lilly pond.

As I am of the firm opinion that there is a link between the retention of Palaeolithic artefacts on hilltops and plateaux capped with deposits mapped as Clay-with-flints and the presence of hollows, I decided to put this theory to the test by conducting both a Resistivity Survey and augering programme (refer to Sub-section 6.1) of Wood Hill in August 1994. Included in the surveyed area (Field 2, see Figure 60) were the locations of the trenches dug by the Dover Archaeological Group in 1984/1985 and that of the trench which I had excavated in 1993.

Methodology – basic survey; auger survey; resistivity survey

The Resistivity Survey proper was preceded by a detailed survey (plane table surveying using a micro optic alidade) of the area under investigation (see procedures in Sub-section 6.1). As shown in Figure 61, the survey was carried out at 4m grid intervals with the rows labelled from 8 to 1 downhill and columns Y to N (across the site). An extra run was taken at 2m from the first point (labelled as row 7.5) to pass through the 1993 trench. The conversion to height above OD was achieved by using the 1993 survey calculation of 63.189 (at the fixed point nail height).

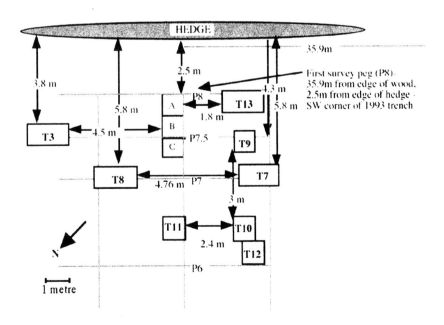

Figure 60 *Diagram showing relationships between the Wood Hill 1993 trench and the 1984/85 excavations in the area surveyed in 1994.*

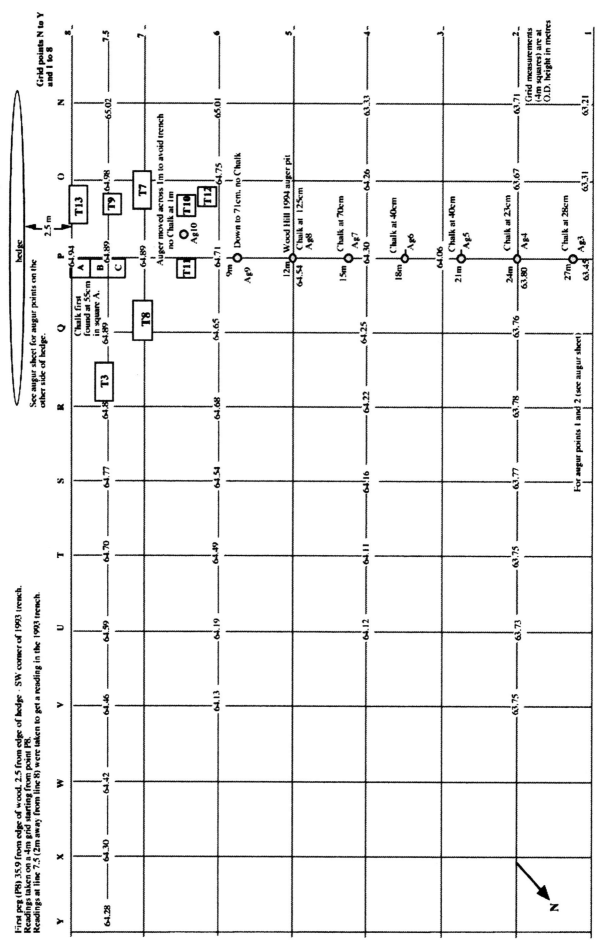

Figure 61 Diagram showing the Wood Hill 1994 Survey Grid.

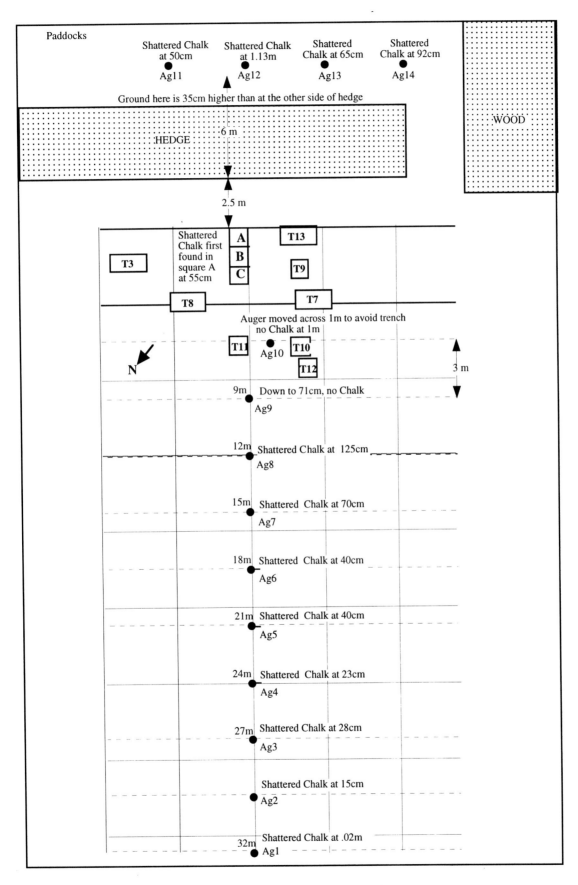

Figure 62 Wood Hill 1994 auger points.

The auger survey

Prior to the resistivity survey, an auger survey was conducted in accordance with the recommendations set out in Sub-section 6.1. Augering on high-level Palaeolithic sites must be undertaken with the greatest of care, for as previously noted in Sub-section 6.1 there is a very real danger of damaging the archaeology. The augering was carried out along the line 'P' at 3m intervals (see Figure 62 and Figure 63) so that auger points P2 and P5 coincide with the resistivity survey points (results from the augering could then be used at a later date to check these points (P2 and P5) and confirm the results of the resistivity Survey). Three auger points were also plotted out in Field 9 (behind the hedge, see Figure 62) in an attempt to locate the Chalk and to provide data on: the depth of top soil, the Clay-with-flints deposits and the nature of the Chalk at these points. Soil samples were collected during augering and consigned to light-fast bags for Thermoluminescence Dating if the opportunity should arise.

The Resistivity survey

It was essential that the resistivity Survey team should be equal to the various demands of the investigations since there are, as previously noted, a number of difficulties associated with working on deposits mapped as Clay-with-flints. A key member of the survey team was Dr. Ian Slipper (University of Greenwich), who has made a special study of the Chalk in East Kent. On-site computer facilities were set-up by two members of the team; these were of great assistance during the surveying, allowing efficient use of the short time available for these investigations. The aims of the Wood Hill 1994 geophysical (tomographical) survey of the 1993 and 1984/85 excavated trenches area, were to

- Locate the Chalk;
- Map the shape of Chalk (i.e. map any solution feature/s);
- Determine Chalk quality (i.e presence or absence of shattered Chalk);
- Determine the depth of the over burden (i.e. the depth of the deposits mapped as Clay-with-flints);
- Measure the depth of top soil.

Resistivity survey – results and analysis

Twenty-four soundings (see Figure 61) were taken at: P1, P2, P3, P4, P5, P6, P7, P8, S4, S6, S7.5, R 4, R6, R7.5, Q4, Q6, Q7.5, O4, O6, O7.5, N4, N6, N7.5. Nearly all of these gave results that could be usefully analysed. The readings at P7 and P7.5 were affected by the recent (1993) excavation, which was to be expected. N7.5 could not be analysed by computer but did nevertheless yield a graphical solution.

Interpreting the subsurface model

The graphs were examined and estimate readings were put into analysis routines which produce models (together with % relative error). The values of the resistivity and thickness were manually adjusted until the errors were around 1 or 2%. Sometimes it was not possible to get the errors down to an acceptable level, so the best compromise between positive and negative errors was chosen. Expert geological knowledge is required to interpret sounding information such as this. An uncritical reliance on computer generated results is unsatisfactory as there are often various solutions to these kinds of data.

The computer report on the model

The data considered were: the spacing; the resistivity transform of the fitted apparent resistivity; the computed resistivity transform from the model parameters; and the percent error between the computed curve and the computed model curve.

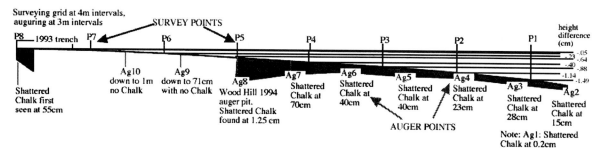

***Figure 63** Wood Hill profile showing 1994 auger points at 3m intervals and 1994 survey points at 4m intervals (all depths approximate ±5cm).*

This last set of data is the one which directs the interpretation procedure, and was the one to check for dubious results.

Results and interpretations

Next a graphical representation of the subsurface layer was produced. All the data were then collated. The subsurface layer model information was combined with the plane table survey to produce heights OD for the various layers. These data were then used to construct four sections: three are orientated NE-SW and are labelled as 7.5, 6 and 4 (see Figure 64). The fourth is orientated NW-SE and is labelled P8–P1 (Figure 65). The resistivity contrast between the surface layers and lower layer was good, so the line could be drawn with confidence.

– Chalk usually gives a resistivity of about 140 ohm-metres, but the survey area at Wood Hill is seen here to vary between 101 to 700 ohm-metres.
– Shattered Chalk will give slightly lower results and is possibly represented by values of 40 to 90 ohm-metres.
– The principal soil layer shows values between 10 and 30 ohm-metres, except for some very low surface layer values which may indicate increased clay content or increased moisture content (a considerable amount of rain fell while the resistivity survey was in progress).

The heights OD for the high resistivity layer, interpreted as solid Chalk, were plotted to give a contour map (see Figure 66). There is no consistent spatial variation in the resistivity of the Chalk. The map shows two high areas of Chalk trending E-W with a low trough between also trending E-W. This is consistent with the type of Chalk palaeokarst known as 'rock-ridges'.

Analysis

By comparing the Wood Hill survey plan of Field 2 (Figure 61), which shows, in addition to the survey grid, the position of the trenches excavated in 1984/85 and 1993, with the results of the resistivity soundings and the section diagrams constructed by Ian Slipper from these resistivity soundings (Figures, 64, 65, 66) it is clear that the Lower Palaeolithic site at Wood Hill is indeed contained in a 'basin-like' solution hollow (Figure 67).

The survey grid points in Field 2 (see Figure 61) were set out as follows: grid points ('up slope') numbered 1 to 8; grid points across the hill labelled N to Y. Both the 1984/85 and 1993 excavated areas in Field 2 are contained in the area plotted as grid points O, P, Q, R (across the hill) and 8, 7.5, 7, 6 (going 'down slope').

1. The solution hollow extends across Wood Hill between grid points N and S, a distance of approximately 20m, and downslope from grid points N8 to S8 through to N4 to S4, a total length of approximately 16m.
2. The deposits mapped as Clay-with-flints in the solution hollow appear to be thickest around the area:
   – at P7.5 Chalk was found at >1.50 m. this point corresponds to the 1993 trench. Augering carried out in Square C of the trench to a depth of 1.25m failed to locate the Chalk.
   – at survey point Q 7.5 (approximately >1.48 m).

The deposits then become progressively thinner for example:
   – at P6 (approximately >1.17 m);
   – at O7.5 (approximately 0.88 m);
   – at Q6 (approximately 0.88 m);

A thickness of 1.25 m was recorded for the deposits at auger point 8 in the P5 area (see Figure 67).

3. Between grid points P4 and S4 the solution hollow becomes very shallow. Where the Chalk outcrops at the surface around P4 it is covered with a thin layer of top soil which measured 11cm. in depth.

Restrictions on both time and funds meant that it was not possible to take the resistivity survey beyond grid points N and S or into Field 9. However, other small solution features are known to exist in Field 2 on Wood Hill, as in the case of Trench 2 (see Figure 32). Also, the varying depth of deposit recorded during the 1984/85 excavations in Field 9 strongly suggest that a solution hollow/s is present here (see Figure 32). The Lower Palaeolithic artefacts found in Field 9 may therefore have been contained in a similar solution feature as that in Field 2. As previously noted, shattered Chalk was recorded at 7 points:

-P8:	Layer 2;	1.6 tk;	1.86 dp (OD.63.08).
-R7.5:	Layer 2;	1.7 tk;	1.89 dp (OD.62.95)
-S7.5:	Layer 3;	1.04 tk;	1.39 dp (OD.63.38)
-O6:	Layer 2;	1.2 tk;	1.3 dp (OD.63.45)
-N4:	Layer 2;	0.87 tk;	1.032 dp (OD.62.30)
-P2:	Layer 2;	0.28 tk;	0.47 dp (OD.63.33)
-P1:	Layer 1;	0.29 tk;	0.29 dp (OD.63.16)

Discussion

The resistivity survey of Wood Hill (Field 2 between grid points N and S) combined with augering in both Field 2 and Field 9 and records from the site-archives of both the 1984/85 and 1993 excavations have

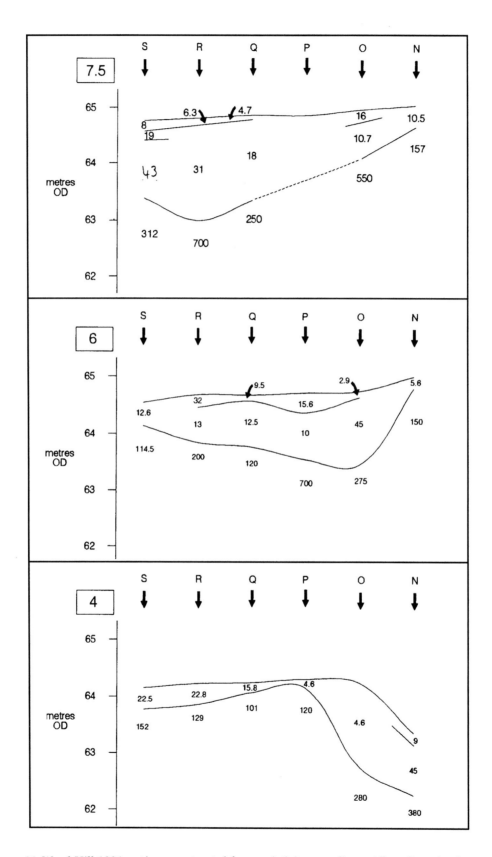

Figure 64 *Wood Hill 1994 sections constructed from resistivity soundings. All readings in ohm-metres.*
After Slipper (1994)

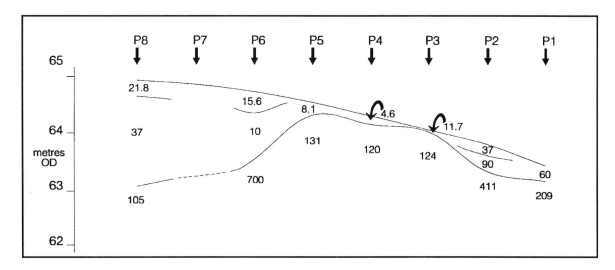

Figure 65 *Wood Hill 1994 section constructed from resistivity sounding. All readings are in ohm-metres. After Slipper (1994).*

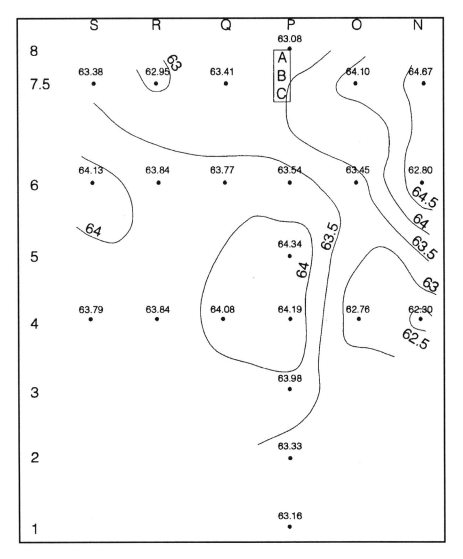

Figure 66 *Wood Hill 1994 contour map of surface of high resistivity layer. All contours are in heights OD. After Slipper (1994).*

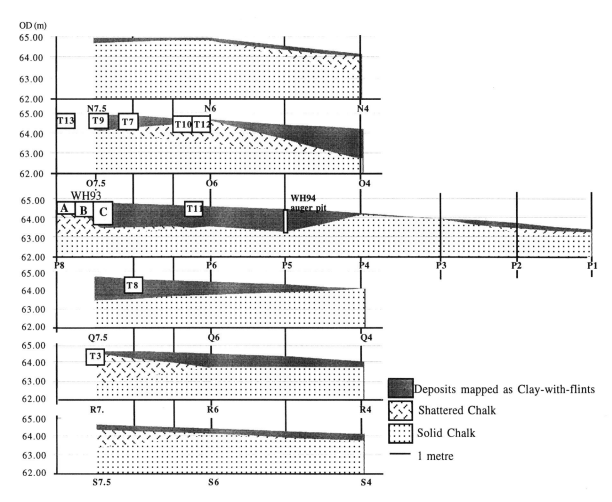

Figure 67 *Diagram of sections across Wood Hill constructed from the 1994 resistivity data: showing the solution hollow(s) and associated 1984/85 and 1993 Wood Hill trenches.*

revealed both the presence of solution hollows and of frost shattered Chalk. In addition, a small area of frost shattered Chalk can be seen exposed within the National Trust owned wood on top of Wood Hill. This may be another natural hollow; however, it is also known to have been the site of gun-flint manufacture during the Napoleonic wars (gun flints can still be found here). Animal activities in the wood have also revealed the presence of frost shattered Chalk.

There is, according to Williams (1986: 161), no direct way of dating the frost shattered Chalk, but its widespread preservation as a fairly continuous layer (on the South Downs for example see Explanatory Section 1) suggests that it developed mainly towards the end of the Devensian and 'because the shattered zone is so extensively preserved, there can have been very little change in the general form of the land surface of the Downs during the Post-glacial'. However, as the Devensian was just one of many glacial periods it is, as Williams suggests, likely that frost shattered Chalk was formed in the earlier parts

of the Devensian and in previous periglacial periods but that any frost shattered Chalk exposed to erosional processes was sludged away downslope before the end of the Devensian (*ibid.*). Evidence for the restricted erosion of Wood Hill since at least the late Devensian can be substantiated by the presence of frost shattered Chalk on the hill, particularly as frost shattered Chalk is also to be found *in situ* on the slopes.

Although, as we have seen, most shattering is thought to have occurred towards the end of the Devensian, there is no reason to preclude the possibility that frost shattered Chalk formed on Wood Hill during previous periglacial periods. Ascertaining the exact processes by which solution features were formed on Wood Hill was beyond the scope of this research. However, in an attempt to solve a number of problems generated by this research, I have sought a meeting with various people. During one discussion it was suggested that I should try to extrapolate from any data available today the rate of solution of the Chalk to reconstruct the topography as it was around 300,000 to 250,000 years ago and then to 'plot out' the relative position of the Lower Palaeolithic artefacts found on Wood Hill. I was not convinced that this line of investigation would be greatly useful, as there was no means of knowing all the variables that would be needed to be taken into account in order to produce solid data. R.B.G. Williams, who has studied solution features on the South Down (see Explanatory section 1) had applied this method of reasoning to the Chalk Downlands, and had calculated a solution rate of between 65mm to 61mm per 1000 yrs, depending on where the measurements where taken. The solution rate was obtained by first taking the figures for the annual rainfall, then reducing these figures by 50% to allow for evaporation and transpiration and then measuring the amounts of calcium carbonate present in wells and spring water. Williams (pers. comm) confirmed my view that this was not a feasible line of investigation for this research, as this rate would produce a landscape that is both disproportionate and much higher than that we see today.

Conclusion

The aims of the resistivity survey of Wood Hill, Field 2 were:

1. To locate and determine the nature of the Chalk beneath the deposits mapped as Clay-with-flints (the overburden).
2. To measure the depth of this overburden.
3. To identify any solution features in Field 2, particularly features associated with the site of the 1984/85 and 1993 excavations.

The investment of both time and money in the resistivity survey of Wood Hill during 1994 was amply rewarded, as all the stated aims (and more, see Sub-section 6.8) were achieved. The results of the resistivity survey strongly suggests that the main solution hollow on Wood Hill may well have been in existence before the arrival of the Lower Palaeolithic peoples, a conclusion supported by the results of both the Fabric analysis (Sub-section 6.2) and the Particle-size analysis (Sub-section 6.3). Discussed later in Sub-section 6.11 are the three 'models' designed to explain the relationships between the solution features; the frost shattered Chalk and the Lower Palaeolithic artefacts on Wood Hill.

Sub-section 6.7: Fossils, nodules and artefacts

A total of 41 sediment samples taken from the Wood Hill 1993 trench were collected from 18 horizontal spits dug at 5cms vertical intervals throughout the trench, in accordance with sampling strategy described in Sub-section 6.1. The sediment samples were sieved in order to determine the percentage ratios of the clay, silt, sand, gravel and cobbles. These are commonly referred to as the 'fractions' of a deposit (see Sub-section 6.3). The fractions were retained as separate units. Careful examination of these fractions revealed the presence of a few fossil belemnite fragments, two complete echinoids and many very small fossil fragments which may be plants, concretions (whether of mineral and/or organic origin), also many artefacts within the size range of >20mm to less than 4mm of the type one would expect to find associated with a Lower Palaeolithic working site.

Artefact and fossil distributions

The results of the fabric analysis (see Sub-section 6.2) confirm that the deposits mapped as Clay-with-flints

in the excavated area of Wood Hill form a coherent sequence – not a cryoturbated mix and jumble. The identified sequence, shown as grouped spits, is as follows:

– Spits 1 to 4/5;
– Spits 5/6 to 8/9;
– Spits 9/10 to 16, spit 16 marks the maximum depth of recorded orientation data.

All the larger (>20mm) Lower Palaeolithic artefacts from the excavation were confined to spits 1 to 5 and spits 11 to 13.This pattern of artefact distribution throughout the 1993 trench is also reflected in the pattern of artefact recovery during subsequent augering of the site in 1994 (see Sub-section 6.8) and also applies to the excavations conducted by Halliwell and Parfitt 1984/85 (see Section 5 and Sub-section 6.11). The distribution pattern of the artefacts within the trench does not, therefore, appear to be random. It has already been noted that the larger excavated artefacts were found in spits 1 to 5 and 11 to 13 and the small artefacts recovered from the sieved residues seem to follow a similar distribution pattern:

- Between spits 1 and 6 the artefacts, range in size from >20mm to less than 1mm.
- In spits 7 and 8 all the flake fragments measure around 5mm or less.
- A marked change is centred in both square B spit 9 and in square C spit 10, when once again, a wide range of sizes are present, with flake fragments measuring around 15mm to < 2mm. At spit 10 and below, the flakes are again very small, with one exception: a flake measuring 10mm was found in spit 15, square B.

The fossils and fossil fragments from Wood Hill, predominately Cretaceous belemnites, echinoids and fossil fragments, appear to be siliceous, that is they have undergone processes which have changed their more delicate original calcareous composition (a structure containing calcium carbonate, ($CaCO_3$) into a more robust one composed of silica (SiO_2). Other 'finds' in the deposit include nodules of iron and unidentified concretions. All the fossils and fossil fragments have been degraded by the action of mildly acidic water passing over them during their incorporation into the deposit mapped as Clay-with-flints on Wood Hill. The distribution of fossils in the 1993 trench can be summarised as follows:

- The larger fossil fragments were found in association with artefacts in spits 1 to 5 and then again in spits 10 and 11.
- Complete fossils were found in B8.
- A predominance of very small fossil fragments was confined to spits 6 to 9.
- Fossils or fossil fragments do not seem to be present in the lower levels below spit 12 in the Clay-with-flints *sensu stricto*.

Superficial deposits and fossils.

The fact that fossils and fossil fragments do not appear to be present below spit 12 raises an interesting question:

- Are the fossils and fossils fragments representative of, and derived from, the Chalk zone that is in direct contact locally with the overlying Clay-with-flints?

If the fossils and fossil fragments are representative of the Chalk zone that lies immediately beneath the Clay-with-flints, then the obvious explanation for their presence in the deposit is that they have eroded out of the Upper Chalk into the overlying Clay-with-flints. However, fossils or fossil fragments were not found below spit 12,

A distribution pattern such as this might be expected if the Upper Chalk underlying the Clay-with-flints was bereft of fossils or exhibited a localised inconsistency in the distribution of fossils

in the Upper Chalk on Wood Hill itself. A random distribution of fossils in the Upper Chalk may well explain the apparently non-random distribution pattern of the fossil and fossil fragments in the top spits of 1993 trench, as the sequence of grouped spits (Sub-section 6.2) indicate the input of material by soil creep from three different directions.

Because they occur in a known sequence, certain fossils within the Chalk have been identified as 'markers' (see Figure 68). These fossils can therefore be used to identify zonal classifications, lithological divisions and thicknesses in the Chalk formation. However, although the Wood Hill 1993 fossils and fossil fragments have been identified as coming from the Cretaceous periods, the Senonian stage and in the stratigraphical sub-division of the Upper Chalk, it has not been possible to determine with certainty the precise fossil zone.

It is generally agreed that nowhere in Britain is the Chalk succession complete, and in the Wealden area a large part of the Chalk is missing. Fordham and Green (1973, 1980: 23) suggest that up to 120m of Upper Chalk is present, that it is around 97 per cent calcium carbonate, and that the flints are mainly tabular and in bands along the bedding plane. Using data provided by Ian Slipper (pers. comms) it has been possible here to extrapolate the height of the Upper Chalk at Kingsdown (an area adjacent to Wood Hill but at a lower level) as Lower Senonian. It was agreed, however, that despite its greater height, Wood Hill was still likely to fall within the Lower Senonian stage and the *Micraster coranguinum* zone.

Lithic procurement and cortex colours

Over geological time, many different processes of erosion and deposition have acted upon Wood Hill, changing and reducing its shape and size, and facilitating the erosion of flints and fossils out of the Chalk as the hill-slopes weathered. This poses the following questions:

- Did the Palaeolithic people who made the artefacts at this site, use flint nodules from the Clay-with-flints and/or material found on the surface of the superficial deposit that may have covered much of Wood Hill?
- Were flint nodules collected from the weathered and eroding sides of the hills by Palaeolithic people, who then carried them up to the top of Wood Hill to provide the raw material for their stone tools?
- Were the fossils and fossil fragments in the 1993 trench genuinely associated with flint nodules?

The fossils and fossil fragments may have been in any chalky material adhering to the nodules how-

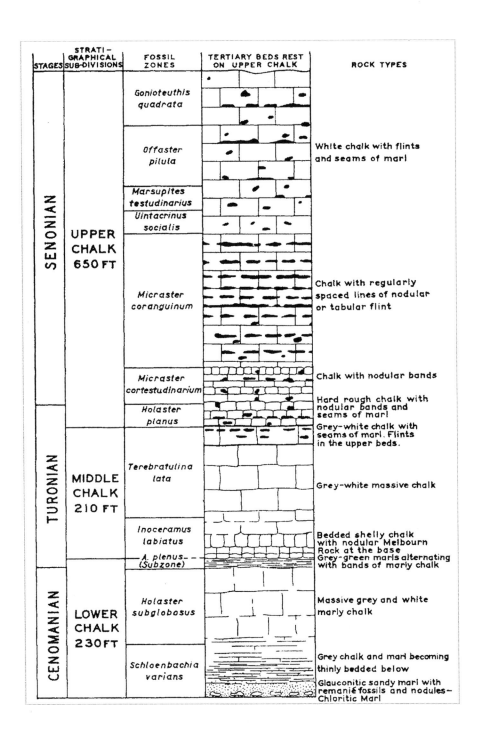

STAGES	STRATI-GRAPHICAL SUB-DIVISIONS	FOSSIL ZONES	TERTIARY BEDS REST ON UPPER CHALK	ROCK TYPES
SENONIAN	UPPER CHALK 650 FT	Gonioteuthis quadrata		
		Offaster pilula		White chalk with flints and seams of marl
		Marsupites testudinarius		
		Uintacrinus socialis		
		Micraster coranguinum		Chalk with regularly spaced lines of nodular or tabular flint
		Micraster cortestudinarium		Chalk with nodular bands
TURONIAN	MIDDLE CHALK 210 FT	Holaster planus		Hard rough chalk with nodular bands and seams of marl
				Grey-white chalk with seams of marl. Flints in the upper beds.
		Terebratulina lata		Grey-white massive chalk
		Inoceramus labiatus		Bedded shelly chalk with nodular Melbourn Rock at the base
		A. plenus (Subzone)		Grey-green marls alternating with bands of marly chalk
CENOMANIAN	LOWER CHALK 230FT	Holaster subglobosus		Massive grey and white marly chalk
		Schloenbachia varians		Grey chalk and marl becoming thinly bedded below
				Glauconitic sandy marl with remanié fossils and nodules— Chloritic Marl

Figure 68 *Generalised section of the Chalk of the Wealden district showing the zonal classification, lithological divisions and thicknesses. After Gallois and Edmunds (1978).Figure 69. Wood Hill 1993 excavation – Handaxe thinning flake (WH93.F11) with conjoining small flake (WH93.F13). Also small flake (WH93.F5) showing later stages of soft hammer working. (Drawn by J.Wallis)*

ever, fossils/fragments are also known to have been incorporated into flint during the formation of the nodules – then released during the process of knapping (see for example, Lord, 1993: plate 7a).

- Perhaps the fossils were collected by the Palaeolithic people and taken up to the top of the hill, deliberately, as objects of curiosity.

The appreciation/awareness of fossils by Palaeolithic peoples had been noted by Smith – two of his observation are quoted here,

> 'at Caddington ... a massive flint cast of a large oyster, *Inoceramus Cuvieri, Sby.*, from the chalk.... It is remarkable for having been picked up by a Palaeolithic man and slightly flaked, as if in an attempt to turn it into a chopping tool.' (*op. cit.*, 1894: 102). He also records that,

> 'A few years ago at Bedford I found a considerable number of examples of *Coscinopora globularis, D'Orb.*, showing an artificial enlargement of the natural orifice, which seemed to indicate that the fossils had been used for personal ornaments as beads' (*op. cit.*, 1894: 272).

A number of possibilities could therefore, account for the presence of the fossils found in association with the knapping debris. As for the flint nodules used for knapping, Catt suggests,

> 'The unworn nodules from the Clay-with-flints *sensu stricto* would have been more suitable as a raw material than most of the fragments in the upper layers of Plateau Drift. They would be found either by digging through the Plateau Drift on the interfluves or near the surface on upper valley sides, but in both situations nodules could almost equally well be obtained direct from the Chalk. The two can be distinguished by the colour of the cortex, as nodules from the Clay-with-flints are usually stained brown or black, but parts of the cortex are preserved on relatively few artefacts, so this rarely helps locate the source of the flint' (1986: 157).

Investigations

Using Catt's (*ibid.*) observations on cortex colour as a framework, a thorough search was made though all the material excavated, recorded and bagged during the 1993 excavation and the 1994 investigations (Material from the Halliwell and Parfitt excavations in 1984/85 awaits similar assessment in due course). It was necessary to sort through 1,501 numbered and bagged samples from the control spits and around the same number from unnumbered samples from the bulk samples. All samples entered in the site archive carried brief descriptions; however, the actual colour of the cortex on the nodules and nodule fragments could not usually be seen and was therefore not recorded (this was due to the tenacious quality of the clay combined with weather conditions on site in 1993 which were less than ideal). Initially, the material was sorted by spit and square into two main groups. One group consisted of Tertiary pebbles and the other of everything else. This second group was then divided up (again by spit and square) into three sub-groups; these included tabular flint, bullhead flint, and nodular flint, and a subgroup was also reserved for fossils and fossil fragments. All the nodular flints, nodular flint fragments, selected pieces of tabular and bullhead flint, and what appeared to be fossils, were then washed to remove the clay and to expose the cortex. This was not an easy task as the clay adhering to the flints and fossils would not readily dissolve. Soaking did not really help, as in this case it merely increased the tendency of the clay to stick or smear. Stiff brushes or solvents could not be used, as this would perhaps have damaged the surface of the flints and/or alter the colour. Removing the clay therefore involved holding each flint under warm running water and very gently rubbing the clay covered areas with a cloth or a very soft toothbrush. All the washed flints and fossils were then dried.

A pattern soon became apparent. The nodular flints and bullhead flints are small, with an average size of 50cm; the tabular flint pieces are very much smaller. The nodules are usually complete, with very little evidence of damage, but where damage has occurred the flints are deeply patinated on the damaged surfaces, an indication that the fracture is ancient. There is little evidence of frost pitting on the pebbles and nodules in spits 1 to 5 and even less below spit 5. Nodular flint was not found below spit 11 although small bullhead flints, tabular flint and pebbles were. The cortex of the nodular flints and nodular flint fragments are heavily stained black and brown, sometimes the staining is in large patches which cover most of the surface but on other nodules the staining is lighter, producing a mottled effect. Staining of the cortex was also observed on the bullhead nodules, bullhead fragments and tabular flint, both as patches and mottling. This posed the question:

- Were the black and brown stainings on the cortex of the flints, superficial staining which had not been removed by the simple washing procedures? or,
- Were the stainings the result of a (chemical) change that had produce a permanent stain which had penetrated the cortex of the flint?

In an attempt to answer these questions I selected a small heavily stained Chalk flint nodule (WH93. B7.N1079) and subjected it to sonic cleaning for 45 minutes! The nodule was put into a plastic beaker filled with (Oxford!) tap water; ultra sonic pressure waves were then directed at the sample causing particles not chemically bonded to the surface (cortex) of the nodule to be dislodged. Sonic cleaning is extremely effective, but although the experimental nodule had been processed for a much longer time than would normally be the case – all the staining remained.

The next stage of the investigation involved a cortex colour assessment of the flints and fossils using the internationally recognised Munsell Color charts (1992 revised edition). These charts standardise assessments and descriptions of colour, making it possible to compare with some accuracy material from various sources (note: the higher the number in each section, the lighter the colour). The cortex stainings were given the values of 10 YR 2/1 (black, for the darkest areas); 10 YR 3/3 (dark brown, medium staining); 10 YR 7/6 (yellow) and 10 YR 7/4 (very pale brown, for the lightest areas). The fossils' values are 2.5 YR 8/2 (pale yellow); 10 YR 8/2 (very pale brown).

The artefacts from Wood Hill are indicative of a Lower Palaeolithic working site. Many of the artefacts (flakes of all sizes) retain remnants of cortex – indeed, much of this debitage is over fifty per cent cortex, yet there is no black/brown staining on the artefacts. A colour assessment based on the Munsell Color charts has shown that, where cortex exists, the colour value is 10YR 8/4 (very pale brown). The colour range for the flint is 2.5YR 8/1 (white), 2.5YR 8/2 (pale yellow), 2.5Y 8/3 (pale yellow), 2.5Y 8/4 (pale yellow). The cortex colour of one small flake (F43) from square B spit 11 can be classed as 10YR 8/4 (very pale brown) and 10YR 7/4 (very pale brown).

Furthermore, many of the Lower Palaeolithic artefacts are larger than these black/brown stained nodular flints.

Conclusion

Clearly, then, these small black stained nodules did not provide the raw material for the Lower Palaeolithic knappers. If the raw material did not come from the deposits mapped as Clay-with-flints which cap the hilltop, then where did it come from? Scattered throughout the 1993 trench, particularly in the top spits and around spits 10 to 12, were several very large Chalk flint nodules (similar very large nodules were found in a number of the 1984/85 trenches but the depth of find was not recorded). The Munsell Color for the cortex of these very large Chalk flint nodules is 10YR 8/2 (very pale brown) and 2.5Y 8/2 (pale yellow). All the large nodules are unstained, as are the two fossils found at similar levels. Although the fossils would appear to be genuinely associated with the flint nodules, it is not possible to say whether they were an inherent part of the nodule or were adhering to the nodule's surface or were deliberately collected by the Palaeolithic people. If Catt's (1986: 157) analysis is valid (i.e. that nodules from the Chalk can be distinguished by the colour of the cortex, as nodules from the Clay-with-flints are usually stained brown or black) and there is no reason to think that it is not, then it would appear that the Lower Palaeolithic people who visited Wood Hill obtained flint nodules from the weathered and eroding Chalk hillsides. They then carried the nodules (and fossils) up to the hill-top plateau where they manufactured their stone tools.

Sub-section 6.8: Description and analysis of the Lower Palaeolithic artefacts recovered during the Wood Hill 1993 excavation and the Wood Hill 1994 resistivity survey

The results of the flint and fossil analysis, as set out in the previous Sub-section 6.7, strongly suggest that the excavated Lower Palaeolithic artefacts found on Wood Hill were manufactured from Chalk flint nodules transported up onto the hilltop by Lower Palaeolithic peoples. In this Sub-section, the Wood Hill artefacts (some of which are illustrated in figures 69, 70 and 71) from both 1993 excavations and 1994 auger pit are considered.

Nodules and flakes

Having acquired suitable nodules, the Lower Palaeolithic craftsmen set about turning them into usable tools. Stone tools were produced either by the shaping of a 'core tool' by the removal of waste flakes or, alternatively, flakes were removed from a core, for use or as blanks for tools. The flakes were removed from the stone by striking with a 'hammerstone' (a hard hammer) or with bone, antler and/or perhaps wood (a soft hammer). It is the way in which Palaeolithic peoples removed such flakes that provides the information which not only confirms the authenticity of Lower Palaeolithic artefacts but also identifies the stage of manufacture they represent (for detailed descriptions and illustrations of flint knapping techniques see, for example, Inizan *et al.*, 1992; Lord, 1993 and Whittaker, 1995).

Determining the condition of the artefacts

Over geological time, both mechanical and chemical processes have effected changes on the Wood Hill artefacts. The condition an artefact exhibits now can therefore be seen as a record of its post-depositional history. Patination, the colour change of the flint over time, is the result of weak alkaline solutions gradually corroding the surface of the flint (with the effect of breaking up the reflected light: see discussion in Section 4). The rate at which patination occurs appears to be dependent on the Ph of the soil surrounding the artefact. In addition, artefacts from both high and low-levels can be stained by the leaching of certain mineral and chemical reactions in the soil. The commonly seen 'iron staining' is an example of this. Palaeolithic artefacts recovered from the Downlands of southern England may be found in a wide range of colours from white/yellow through to dark ochreous orange/red/brown. The excavated Lower Palaeolithic artefacts from Wood Hill are mostly white/yellow, whereas a number of the Wood Hill, Lower Palaeolithic surface finds are ochreous. As previously noted, only Lower Palaeolithic artefacts have been found below the top soil on Wood Hill, but Bronze Age artefacts have been recovered as surface finds. This later material is very distinctive as it is patinated blue/grey/white. Clearly, the effects produced by chemical processes on the artefacts furnish much useful information. However, the effects produced by mechanical processes are arguably of greater value when it comes to assessing the 'history' of an artefact or 'status' of a site. The processes responsible for producing scratches (striations) have already been discussed in Section 4.

Artefact morphology – as a guide to original positions of deposition

The Downlands of southern England provided Palaeolithic people with many opportunities for the manufacture, as well as the use of stone tools, as there is much evidence of Palaeolithic activity in the form of waste flakes and debitage from artefact manufacture, along with discarded or dropped artefacts. Before considering in detail the context of any finds the artefacts themselves must be assessed. The morphology and technology of an artefact can on occasions provide at least a little information as to its industry type (see the General Introduction). The artefacts may also show the effects of natural wear processes that may have resulted in abrasion and/or fracture. The degree of abrasion exhibited by an artefact is generally seen as an important guide to interpreting movement patterns of that artefact (see Sub-section 6.8). It is reasonable to assume that an artefact recovered in a completely unworn condition is at, or very near to, its original place of deposition. Conversely, a very abraded artefact must have been subject to much wear and is, therefore, by implication, likely to have travelled some distance from its original place of deposition. An artefact may also exhibit varying degrees of weathering if it has been in an exposed position for a long time. That is quite a different matter, although an extreme degree of weathering can certainly be mistaken for heavy mechanical abrasion. Many of the artefacts recovered from high-level find-spots/sites in areas mapped as Clay-with-flints have in the past indeed been described as very worn, or even 'very rolled', which would imply fluviatile transport. However, I am of the considered opinion that often artefacts from these high-levels, when described as 'very worn', are in fact merely displaying extreme levels of weathering. The implications of this difference cannot be over emphasised: weathered artefacts need not have moved at all from their place of manufacture or use. A crucial element in any attempted interpretation of the relationship between find-spot/sites and activity patterns of Palaeolithic peoples is therefore the condition of each individual artefact recovered.

To assess the condition of the Wood Hill (1993 and 1994) Lower Palaeolithic artefacts, which range in size from tiny flakes measuring around 1mm to the plano-convex biface which measures 120mm × 66mm, I used the precept set out by Wymer (1968:5) who states that

> 'The degree of abrasion can be assessed visually, quite objectively, and the artefact placed into one of five categories'.

Although the five categories proposed by Wymer are intended for the assessment of artefacts recovered from a variety of environments, the areas mapped as Clay-with-flints are unique. Therefore, an additional category must be added, for as previously noted many of the artefacts recovered from areas mapped as Clay-with-flints are often very weathered. Roe (1981: 183–4), writing of the occurrences in North Hampshire states:

'At first sight the artefacts look somewhat abraded and even water-worn, but this is not in fact the case: their surfaces have merely been altered, and the ridges worn down, by weathering, presumably during long exposure on the surface or just below it'.

I propose, therefore, to add to Wymer's list the category of *'Weathered'*, but to include it in the same assessment bands used to define the degree of rolling. The full list of categories is as follows:

1. Mint – as fresh and sharp as a newly-struck flint.
2. Sharp – the ridges between the flake scars are dulled, but with no discernible blunting of the ridge visible with the naked eye. The surface of the artefact will be slightly lustrous.
3. *Slightly Weathered* – Slightly Rolled – the ridges between the flake scars have a distinct facet, but nowhere is it greater than 1mm wide. This weathering or rolling may be localised.
4. *Weathered* – Rolled – as above, but the facet is greater than 1mm wide but less than 2mm.
5. *Very Weathered* – Very Rolled – as above, but the facets are in places greater than 2mm. The flint may be almost unrecognisable as an artefact.

As artefacts from areas mapped as Clay-with-flints might, of course, be both weathered and rolled, I have examined (with a stereoscopic microscope, magnification ×100 and where necessary ×300) all the Wood Hill 1993 and 1994 artefacts from the smallest flakes (1mm) to the plano-convex biface, for features associated with movement of that artefact

on/in the deposit, or conversely the movement/s of the deposit on the artefact such as for example, striations produced by particular agents, e.g.: soil movement, without substantial lateral transport, and/or sand and/or pebble abrasion (see Section 4 and Sub-section 6.5). The Lower Palaeolithic artefacts found during the Wood Hill 1993 excavation and the 1994 resistivity survey are now considered.

Lower Palaeolithic artefacts from the 1993 excavation of Wood Hill

All the artefacts found during the 1993 excavation of Wood Hill measuring 20mm or more were assigned the site code WH93 plus an individual number and fully recorded (see Sub-section 6.1); smaller artefacts (<20mm) were recorded by square and spit only. All the larger artefacts were found within spits 1 to 5 and spits 11 to 13 (see Table 7) the significance of this distribution is discussed in detail in Sub-section 6.11.

The Wood Hill site-archive for 1993 has forty-four entries on the artefact list. Following off-site re-examination, eighteen doubtful entries (F3, F4, F8, F18 to F23, F25 to F29, F31, F39, F40, F42) were withdrawn from the artefact list, but all the appertaining data was included in the natural clasts record. The indubitable authenticity of twenty six Lower Palaeolithic artefacts measuring 20mm or more was confirmed. As previously noted, the site also yielded large numbers of smaller items of knapping debris.

	A	B	C
1	F1, F2,	F5, F6	F7, F9, F10, F11, F12, F13, F14, F15, F16, F17
2			F24
3			F30, F34
4	F35, F36, F37	F33	F44
5	F32		
6			
7			
8			
9			
10			
11	Shattered Chalk	F43	
12		F38 (biface)	
13		F41	
14			
15			
16			
17			
18			

Table 7 Wood Hill 1993: Spits and squares in which artefacts (listed by site code) were found.

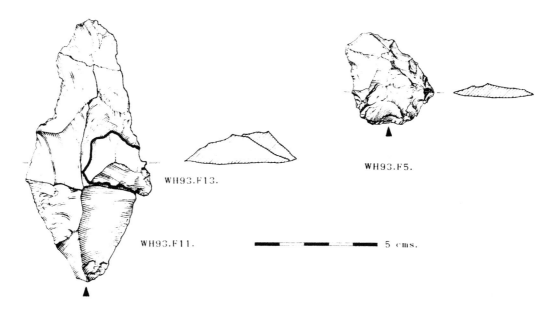

Figure 69 *Wood Hill 1993 excavation – Handaxe thinning flake (WH93.F11) with conjoining small flake (WH93.F13).
Also small flake (WH93.F5) showing later stages of soft hammer working. (Drawn by J. Wallis)*

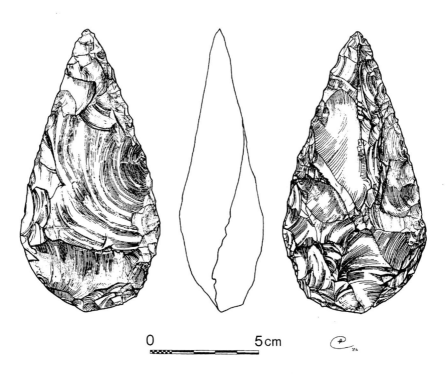

Figure 70 *Wood Hill 1993 excavation – Plano-convex biface (WH93.F38) from Square B spit 12.
(Drawn by M.H.R. Cook)*

Note: where artefacts are described as fragments, that is artefacts with one or more pieces missing, it is to be understood that the missing pieces are ancient losses. Some of these breaks may be 'mechanical' fracture, that is they occurred as the flakes fell to the ground during the various stages of stone tool manufacture, while others may be the result of freeze/thaw processes for example 'thermal' fractures and frost plucking (pot lid fractures) – the broken surfaces display a similar depth of patination to that found on the rest of the artefact.

Two artefacts from square C spit 1 conjoin, one is a biface thinning flake (WH93.F11) and the other a small flake (WH93.F13) – see Figure 69. A plano-convex biface (WH93.F38) found in square B spit 12 (see Figure 70) is briefly discussed here, but is also the subject of a separate Sub-section (see 6.9)

A summary of the 26 Lower Palaeolithic artefacts

Table 8 Summary of the 26 Lower Palaeolithic artefacts from the Wood Hill 1993 excavation

Types of artefacts form of percussion	Square, spit and artefact number	Total
– Biface	B12/F38	1
– Thinning flake (soft hammer)	C1/F11	1
– Trimming flakes (soft hammer)	A4/F36, B1/F5, B4/F33, C1/F9, C1/F10	1
– Trimming flake fragment	C1/F14	1
– Flakes (hard hammer)	A1/F2	1
– Flakes (soft hammer)	A5/F32, C1/F13, C2/24, C3/F30, C4/F44	5
– Flake fragments (soft hammer)	A1/F1, B13/F41, B11/F43	3
– Flake fragments (not definable)	C1F7, C1/F15, C1/F17	3
– Waste flakes (hard hammer)	C1/F12, C1/F16	2
– Debitage products (hard hammer)	A4/F35	1
– Debitage products (not definable)	A4/F37, B1/F6, C3/34	3
		26

from the Wood Hill 1993 excavation is given in the table (Table 8). In addition to the 26 excavated artefacts, all of which measured 20mm or more in maximum surviving dimension, 231 artefacts measuring less than 20mm were recovered from the sieved soil samples. These 231 artefacts represent a very conservative sample of positively identified material which I selected out of a total of over 700 possible small flakes and trimming flake fragments. All the small artefacts were examined using a stereoscopic microscope (at ×100 and ×300 magnification) and the type, size, condition, spit number and the square in which they were found recorded.

If the criteria used to judge the larger artefacts are extended to these smaller flakes and fragments, then the condition of 178 of the 231 artefacts can be described as sharp and slightly lustrous, the remaining 53 (8 of which are mostly cortex) as slightly weathered or slightly rolled. Very few striations were visible on these artefacts, frost plucking was conspicuous by its absence but thermal fracturing may well have produced a number of the fragments. The majority of the slightly weathered/slightly rolled artefacts came from Square C, spits 6, 7, 8, 9, 10, 11. With the exception of 7 flakes, which may possibly be Bullhead flint, all the remaining flakes are derived from Chalk Nodular flint. A summary of the relationship between squares A, B and C (spits 1 to 17) and these small artefacts measuring less than 20mm is shown in Table 9.

Table 9 Size distribution of Wood Hill artefacts measuring <20mm by square and spit.

Spit	A				B				C				Overall
	<5	5-10	10<>20	Total	<5	5-10	10<>20	Total	<5	5-10	10<>20	Total	Total
1	0	2	0	2	0	1	2	3	4	10	15	29	34
2	0	0	0	0	0	1	0	1	27	28	12	67	68
3	2	2	0	4	0	2	2	4	7	6	10	23	31
4	2	1	0	3	0	1	1	2	5	7	12	24	29
5	4	3	0	7	0	1	0	1	5	2	0	7	15
6	0	0	0	0	3	0	1	4	8	0	0	8	12
7	1	1	0	2	7	0	0	7	4	0	0	4	13
8	0	0	0	0	0	0	0	0	3	0	0	3	3
9	0	0	0	0	2	0	2	4	1	1	0	2	6
10					0	0	0	0	5	1	0	6	6
11					2	1	0	3	0	1	0	1	4
12					0	0	0	0	0	0	0	0	0
13		No data							0	1	0	1	1
14	CHALK				0	0	1	1	1	0	0	1	2
15					2	2	1	5	0	0	0	0	5
16					0	0	0	0	0	0	0	0	0
17					0	1	0	1	0	1	0	1	2
18					Maximum depth of excavation								
Total	9	9	0	18	16	10	10	36	70	58	49	177	231

Total for all squares	<5	5-10	10<>20	Total
	95	77	59	231

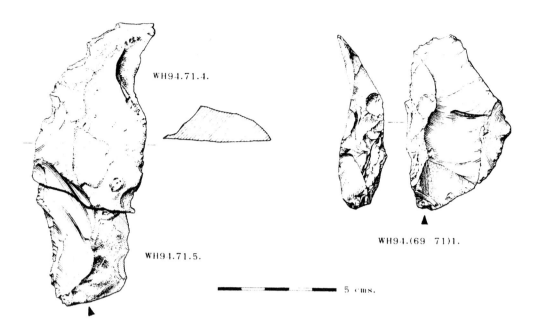

Figure 71 *Conjoining thinning flakes (WH94.71.4 and WH94.71.5) and rejuvenated flake (WH94. (69-71)1 from the 1994 auger pit. (Drawn by J.Wallis).*

Lower Palaeolithic artefacts from the Wood Hill 1994 auger pit

During the 1994 auger survey of Wood Hill it became necessary to dig out a 40cms × 40cms pit at survey point P5 (see Figures 61, 63 and Sub-section 6.6) to remove obstructing nodules (all nodules were fully recorded and retained). The augering brief did not include excavation *per se*, but as it was necessary to cut through the deposits and possible archaeological horizons, great care was taken. The pit was excavated in 5cm spits (as was the 1993 excavation). As soon as the passage of the auger was obstructed it was withdrawn until the obstruction was investigated, all features of the deposits and any finds were then recorded. Working in this way, in such a confined space, was not easy but the diligence of the workers was adequately rewarded by the recovery of a number of Lower Palaeolithic waste flakes – two of which conjoined (WH94.71.4 and WH94.71.5 shown in Figure 71).

The auger pit deposits

Although a brief description of the auger pit deposits is given here (see Figure 72), they are also considered in greater detail in Sub-section 6.11 where the auger pit stratigraphy and artefacts are discussed with those of the 1993 and 1984/85 artefacts and trenches. All the on-site measurements in the auger pit were taken from the surface of the top soil which at this point had a thickness of 25cms. This was in contrast to all the other Wood Hill excavations where the depths were measured from the base of the top soil. Therefore, to minimise confusion and to facilitate direct comparison between the auger pit deposit and artefacts, and the deposits and artefacts in other Wood Hill trenches, the depths from both the surface of top soil and the base of top soil are given.

The auger pit stratigraphy (see Figure 72) is as follows:

- 1 to 25cms of top soil;
- Between 25cms and around 40cms to 50cms (5cms to 15cms-20cms below the base of the top soil) was a layer of light coloured clay.
- Between 50cms and 70cms (20cms to 45cms below the base of the top soil) the clay graduated from an unmottled light colour to being mottled red. It contained several Bullhead flints as well as Tertiary pebbles (black, red and brown), the numbers of which increased with depth. Artefacts were found at 45cms from the surface of the top soil (see details below and Figure 72).
- At around 70cms to 80cms (45cms to 55cms below the base of the top soil) the deposit became very dark, almost black and red Tertiary pebbles were present. Artefacts were found at 71cm (see details below and Figure 72).
- At 80cms to 90cms (55cms to 65cms below the base of the top soil) was a layer containing nodules, and black (no other colours) well rounded pebbles averaging 1–2cms, which dipped slightly SE along the a-axis.
- Between 90cms and 110cms (65cms to 85cms

Table 10 *Lower Palaeolithic artefacts from the Wood Hill 1994 auger pit*

Types of artefacts and form of percussion	Square, spit and artefact number	Total
– Thinning flakes (hard hammer)	WH94.71.4 (conjoins with WH94.71.5	1
– Flakes (hard hammer)	WH94 (69–71)1. (rejuventated flake)	1
– Debitage products (percussion undefinable)	WH94.45.1, WH94.45.2, WH94.7.1, WH94.71.3	4

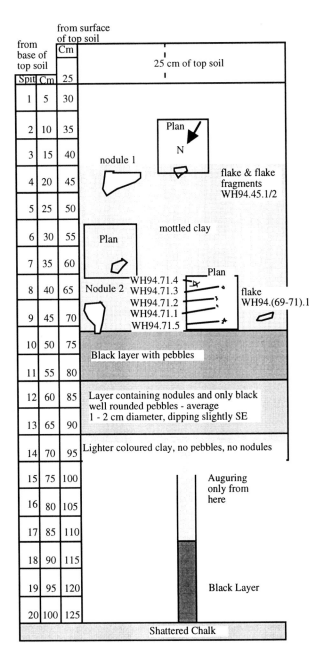

Figure 72 *Wood Hill 1994 auger pit, dug at survey point P5 to locate Chalk, which was expanded to 40x40cm to dig out obstructions.*

below the base of the top soil) was a continuous layer of very much lighter clay and no nodules.
- Between 110cms and 125cms (85cms to 100cms below the base of the top soil) was a black layer.
- Shattered Chalk was found at 125cms (100cms below the base of the top soil).

The 6 Lower Palaeolithic artefacts from the Wood Hill 1994 auger pit are summarised in Table 10.

Results and Interpretations

Data obtained from the examination of all the Wood Hill 1993 and 1994 artefacts support the view that the Lower Palaeolithic site at Wood Hill is indeed *in situ*. The condition of all the artefacts (measuring 20mm or more) recovered during the 1993 excavation and the 1994 auger pit, conform, to Wymer's 'Artefact Condition Assessment Category 2' (as described earlier in this Sub-section): all these artefacts can therefore be described as 'Sharp'. The ridges between the flake scars are dulled, but with no discernible facet on the ridge visible with the naked eye and the surface of the artefacts are slightly lustrous. Very few striations were observed on the artefacts at either ×100 or ×300 magnification; those that are present on the dorsal or ventral surfaces are shallow and measure between 1–2mm long; a few small striations were observed to be associated with a number of the damaged edges. Of the 231 smaller artefacts (i.e. those measuring <5mm to <20mm) from the 1993 trench, 178 could be described as 'Sharp' and 45 as 'Slightly Weathered/Slightly Rolled' a further 8 artefacts were mostly cortex. As with the larger artefacts, very few striations were observed at either ×100 or ×300 magnification and those that are present are shallow and measure around 1mm. The majority of the small Slightly Weathered/Slightly Rolled artefacts were found in square C, spits 6, 7, 8, 9, 10 and 11 of the 1993 trench. There are no data for small artefacts from the 1994 auger pit, as the small soil samples collected during auguring were placed in 'light fast' bags, for possible optical stimulated luminescence dating (OSL) dating at a later stage. Full data on small artefacts from the auger pit will therefore only become available when these small bags are eventually opened.

Discussion

Throughout this research I have stressed the need for a new approach and different criteria to be used to evaluate the Palaeolithic artefacts recovered from deposits mapped as Clay-with-flints. However, as the perceived worth of an occurrence depends on comparing and contrasting one site with another I am obliged at this stage of the discussion to use the existing methods (i.e. those developed for low-level sites) to assess the worth of the Wood Hill occurrences, and other similar high-level embedded artefacts.

An in situ site defined

To date, there are no criteria to evaluate the importance of a high-level Palaeolithic find-site in deposits mapped as Clay-with-flints on the Chalk downlands of southern England, other than those devised to assess low-level sites which are found in very different environments, for example, river-side, lakeside, beach-sites and cave-floors. The importance of a low-level site is judged essentially by how much or how little the artefacts have moved from their original place of deposition. Using these criteria then, the most important sites are those designated as being 'in situ' sites in 'primary context' – that is, where it can be shown conclusively that the artefacts/finds were in the same position when found, as they were when they were originally deposited by Palaeolithic people on the Palaeolithic landsurface. However, as the majority of low-level Palaeolithic occurrences do not come into this 'primary context' category, additional criteria are used to define the status of a site. These categories range from sites designated as *in situ*, via categories that allow for some movement of the artefacts within the deposit, through to sites where the artefacts/finds are found in a totally derived context, that is, a site where no real or demonstrable relationship exists between the artefacts and the deposit within which they were found. For example, occurrences at low-levels of Palaeolithic artefacts which had been manufactured on the Clay-with-flints capped hill tops and plateaux and subsequently moved, by one process or another from the high-levels to the low levels, would come into this category. Many low-level finds on the South Downs in Sussex, around Eastbourne, Seaford, and the Cuckmere Valley are good examples of this (see Woodcock, 1981).

Therefore, a 'sliding scale' of importance exists which is based on the condition of the artefacts found on the site. Moreover, the integrity of a site increases if recovered flakes that were struck in antiquity by Palaeolithic people can be refitted (conjoined) together again, since evidence of movement or gross disturbance of artefacts within a deposit is regarded as an undesirable devaluing factor of both the artefacts and the site. For a Palaeolithic occurrence to be categorised as an *'in situ'* site, the following conditions therefore apply:

1. The artefacts would be expected to exhibit little evidence of abrasion. However, abrasion and edge damage must be assessed with caution as the presence of such features may be the result of small movements generated by later freeze/thaw processes or, perhaps, worm activity, whether of the artefact within the deposit or the deposits over the artefact, rather than evidence of movement over a substantial distance (see Section 4). The condition of the artefacts may range from heavily patinated and weathered through to unpatinated and unweathered.

2. The number and type of artefacts/finds recovered should represent adequately the nature of the site. For example, an *in situ* working site assemblage should consist of a wide range of waste flakes from the smallest to much larger flakes. The maximum size of these humanly struck flakes would depend both on the size of the original nodules from which the flakes were struck and the stage of manufacture which took place at that site.

Conclusion

The detailed methods of excavation employed on Wood Hill during 1993 and 1994, combined with the post-excavation investigations, have produced a data-set for these Lower Palaeolithic artefacts found in relation to deposits mapped as Clay-with-flints on the Chalk downlands of southern England which is unique and unequalled. Using this information, and that derived from the 1984/85 excavations (see Section 5) the pattern of distribution of the Lower Palaeolithic artefacts across the Wood Hill site and the nature of the human occupation are examined and discussed in the final Sub-section (6.11).

Sub-section 6.9: The Wood Hill Biface (WH93.F38)

The Wood Hill 1993 excavation produced Lower Palaeolithic artefacts, which were found in two distributions (see Sub-section 6.8). Most of the artefacts came from the top of the trench in spits 1 to 5. These were various types of flakes, all the by-products of stone tool manufacture. In the lower levels of the trench, three artefacts were found (all in square B), two flakes in spits 11 and 13 respectively, and a handaxe in spit 12. This handaxe (WH93.F38) is a pointed-pyriform plano-convex biface with a twisted profile (see Figure 73).

Bifaces fitting this description display distinctive characteristics and have sometimes been described as 'slipper-shaped', as they are pointed, narrow, plano-convex (i.e. having a marked D-shape or flat triangular cross-section, especially at the distal end). The sides may be straight, convex or with one slightly concave side. The flake scar patterns are the result of soft-hammer percussion and the edges are often finely finished. The distinctive shape may reflect the fact that these bifaces were sometimes, but not always, made from large flakes which determined their shape, leaving them flatter on one face. However, Roe pointed out that there are instances where bifaces of this type are demonstrably made from nodules and

> 'the plano-convexity of the section undoubtedly reflects the maker's intentions and a distinctive manufacturing technique' (1968: 122).

Flakes are removed first from the ventral surface, leaving a comparatively small number of shallow scars. There are typically far more scars on the dorsal surface, and these have a tendency to truncate the proximal ends of the scars on the ventral surface. The finer trimming flake scars are almost always on the dorsal surface.

The Wood Hill plano-convex biface (WH93.F38)

This pointed-pyriform plano-convex biface with a twisted profile, was, as previously noted, discovered in square B, spit 12, 60cm. below the base of the top soil, in a small area of deposits with the characteristics of windblown material. When found, the biface lay on its left edge, dorsal side up and butt foremost. It could be argued that without conjoining flakes to the biface itself there is no way of determining whether this particular artefact was actually made on Wood Hill, however, all the available evidence indicates that it was.

On the basis of outline shape alone, this handaxe can be classified as belonging to the 'Pointed Tradition' (Roe, 1981: 156) of which there are three groups. Only one assemblage corresponds to the Pointed Tradition Group 3; this is the Wolvercote material, and this is the group to which the Wood Hill biface belongs.

WH93.F38 – Biface (pointed-pyriform plano-convex).
- length 120mm; breadth 66mm; maximum thickness 32mm; weight 200.52 grams.
- the proximal end is complete;
- the distal end is complete;
- both sides are complete;
- there are 58 flake scars on the ventral surface, and
- 94 flake scars on the dorsal surface;
- no cortex is present;
- 'Munsell Color' values for the flint are: 2.5Y 8/1 (white) and 2.5Y 8/2 (pale yellow) with grey inclusions;
- soft hammer percussion predominates.

The condition of the biface (WH93.F38)

Following cleaning with distilled water, distilled ammonia, and white spirit, the biface was examined under a microscope,

- at 100 × magnification; the edge of the implement exhibited some reflaking, edge rounding and a number of well polished areas and short striations on both faces;
- at 300 × magnification very short scratches were apparent on the edges.

Dr. John Mitchell (Microwear specialist, University of Oxford) concluded that all the observed features listed above were produced by natural processes; there are no microwear traces; the biface is patinated; it exhibits little evidence of movement on/within the deposit; the movements that have taken place have been over a very a short distance indeed.

Having examined the biface myself, at both ×100 and ×300 magnification, the only information I can add to that supplied by Mitchell is that none of these very few striations measures more than 1mm in length and that nearly all of these tiny scratches appear to be confined to one area at the distal end of the dorsal surface. The processes responsible for producing striations were previously discussed in detail in Section 4. I am of the opinion, which was first mooted by Boyd Dawkins (1916: 45) and restated by Wymer (1980: 2), that these very small striations were probably produced as the result of soil movement without substantial lateral transport, as opposed to sand abrasion, the soil being pressed against the surface of the biface, with freeze/thaw processes providing the movement which produced the abrasion.

British plano-convex bifaces and their European affinities

Typology, is no longer a reliable yardstick for classifying and dating artefacts. However, found amongst the various Lower Palaeolithic industry-types in Britain (but sparsely represented) is an industry-type that is characterised by distinctive plano-convex pointed bifaces. These British plano-convex pointed bifaces resemble plano-convex pointed bifaces found at La Micoque, level V1(Layer N) in the Dordogne, France (type-site of the Micoquian) and the plano-convex pointed 'Micoquian'

type bifaces found in Germany, for example at Bockstein 111 (Rammingen, near Ulm), Klausennische (Essing, near Leckheim (Bosinski 1967). Similar bifaces have also been found at other sites in both France and Germany and related forms occur across central Europe into Poland and Russia (Roe 1981: 123; Tyldesley 1986a).

The biggest collection of plano-convex bifaces in Britain comes from an ancient stream or river channel discovered at the turn of the century in a low-level brick pit (SP 498105) at Wolvercote, in the Upper Thames Valley (Bell 1904; Sandford 1924, 1926, 1939 in Tyldesley 1986a). The area is now an ornamental lake. A special study of the British plano-convex bifaces was made by Tyldesley (1986a; 1986b). In her assessment (1986a) there were 20 occurrences: some were single finds, others occurred as small assemblages. The finds are clustered into three areas; East Anglia, the Thames Valley and the Bournemouth

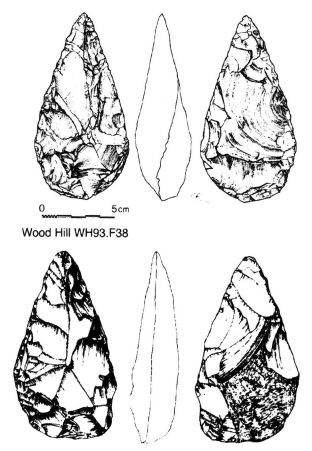

0 _____ 5cm

Wood Hill WH93.F38

Wolvercote Channel: (Tyldesley 1986a:40.No.23.Figure 2.23.)

Figure 73 Comparison of the plano-convex biface from Wood Hill (WH93.F38) with Fig.2.23. from Wolvercote Channel (Tyldesley 1986a:40, No.23. Fig 2.23).

to Portsmouth area of South Hampshire. It is now possible to expand this list. These additional finds are discussed later in this Sub-section.

The Wolvercote Channel material

Under Bordes' (1961) system of classification, all the plano-convex material from the Wolvercote Channel would be grouped as either 'Micoquian' or 'lanceolate', but neither class is quite appropriate to the Wolvercote bifaces. The 'classic' Wolvercote biface is defined by Tyldesley as an elongated pointed pyriform handaxe with no twist to the profile, and straight or slightly convex cutting edges; the butt may be roughly worked, but the upper third is invariably well made, being plano-convex in profile, often with a well-defined 'ridge' extending along the 'spine' of the dorsal face (*op. cit.* 1986b: 23).

There is, as can be seen in Figure 73, much similarity between the Wood Hill biface (WH93.F38) from East Kent (length 120mm; breadth 66mm; thickness 32mm; weight 200.52 grams) and one of the bifaces from the Wolvercote Channel, Oxfordshire (Tyldesley 1986a:40, No. 23 Figure 2.23) the measurements of which are: length 122mm; breadth 68mm; thickness 34mm; weight 225 grams. This latter artefact is described by Tyldesley as,

> 'A typically pyriform plano-convex handaxe with a definite "ridge" apparent at the tip of the convex face. The domed face has many more flake removals than the flatter face. The cutting-edge runs all round the implement and is more or less straight, although the butt is only roughly worked. The handaxe has been made from a nodule of flint, and there is a large cherty/cortex patch on the flatter face. The implement is unrolled and unpatinated and slightly shiny in appearance.'

On examining this biface in the Pitt Rivers Museum, Oxford, I noted that it has iron staining on the left edge, particularly on the dorsal surface, an indication perhaps, that the immediate environment of the left edge of the dorsal surface was at one time different to the rest of the artefact e.g. only this particular area was buried, exposed or lay close to an iron-pan horizon. The Wood Hill plano-convex pointed pyriform biface has a twisted profile: in this respect it does not conform to the 'classic' Wolvercote bifaces although it does in all others. Although the Wood Hill biface is patinated, while the Wolvercote one is not, there is a great the similarity between the two handaxes (barring the twisted profile of WH93.F38). Tyldesley states that

> 'All [British plano-convex handaxes] bear a certain resemblance to the typical Wolvercote plano-

convex bifaces, and their existence seems to indicate that the Wolvercote Channel industry is not unique in having plano-convex handaxes but rather in having so many deliberate pieces made in a definite style....' (*op. cit.* 1986a: 103).

The distribution of the British plano-convex bifaces

Earlier in this Sub-section it was noted that as result of this study more artefacts can be added to Tyldesley's original list of 20 British plano-convex bifaces. In addition to the Wood Hill plano-convex biface already discussed; bifaces reminiscent of Wolvercote material have also come from The Red Barns site at Porchester, South Hampshire (Gamble and ApSimon, 1986). Other finds, which also warrant inclusion, come from Limpsfield, Surrey and Dorneywood, Buckinghamshire (Figure 74).

The Red Barns site

The Red Barns site (SU 608063) lies on the western end of Portsdown Hill, near Porchester, Fareham, Hampshire. Following earlier investigations of the area by Draper in 1973, Woodcock, ApSimon and Shackley (1973) and Draper and Woodcock (1974), a rescue excavation was undertaken in 1975 in an area due for development. The excavations and the recovered artefacts, are described by Gamble and ApSimon (1986) thus:

> 'Among the retouched artefacts were two finely finished handaxes. The larger is a pointed plano-convex type similar to those from the Wolvercote channel ... A broken tip of another plano-convex handaxe and a further two roughouts were also recovered. The other complete handaxe is by contrast symmetrical, small and pointed' (*op. cit.* 1986: 10)

The environmental evidence is seen by the authors to suggest human activity on an open slope with sparse vegetation (*op. cit.* 1986: 12).

Bifaces from Limpsfield and Dorneywood

Much of the recorded information on the Palaeolithic handaxes found in relation to deposits mapped as Clay-with-flints is minimal. Sometimes artefacts are described in the original sources, as 'pointed' handaxes, but often the shape is not specified, it is therefore possible that other 'Micoquian', 'lanceolate' and 'Wolvercote' type bifaces have been found on the deposits mapped as Clay-with-flints and now

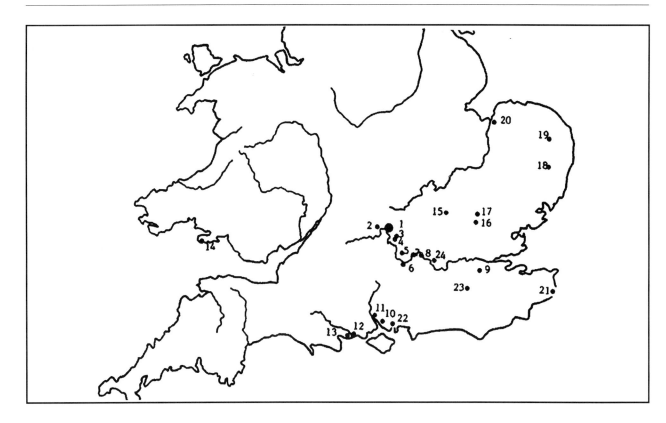

1	Wolvercote and Summertown	8	Maidenhead	16	Bishop's Stortford
2	Eynsham	9	Wilmington	17	Quendon
3	Chiselhampton	10	Warsash	18	Homersfield
4	Berinsfield	11	Southampton	19	Whitlington
5	Goring Heath	13	Bournemouth	20	East Winch
6	Tilehurst	14	Rhossilli		
7	Henley-on-Thames	15	Hitchin		

New entries (nos 21 to 24) as recorded by Scott-Jackson (1996)

21 Wood Hill, Kingsdown, Kent
22 Porchester, Fareham,
23 Limpsfield, Surrey
24 Doneywood, Bucks

Figure 74 *Showing the distribution of British plano convex bifaces – entries 1 to 20 are as recorded by Tyldesley (1986a) and new entries 21 to 24 (Scott-Jackson,1996).*

await positive identification in museums and private collections – as graphically illustrated by the following additions to Tyldesley's (1986a) original list of British plano-convex bifaces.

Recently discovered amongst an old collection of material from Limpsfield, Surrey is a plano-convex biface. The majority of the Limpsfield artefacts came from gravels and exhibited some MTA (Mousterian of Acheulian Tradition) influence, whereas this biface, marked 'found *in situ* 1903' seems to have come not from the gravels, but from high-level brickearth and is very reminiscent of the Wolvercote handaxes. Further conformation of the existence of 'Wolvercote' style material on high-level sites away from low-level gravels comes from the 'Records of Bucks' Vol. XV1, Part 4, 1959. In an article by A.C. Lacaille entitled 'Palaeoliths from the Brickearth in South-East Buckinghamshire', five bifaces are illustrated: these artefacts appear to be similar to material found at Wolvercote. Although not identified as such

in the article, certain links with the Wolvercote material seem apparent. In his account, Lacaille first notes that J. Reid Moir extracted Acheulian tools from brickearth at Hoxne. He then writes

'It was in this same brickearth that John Frere made his famous discovery in 1797. The hand-axes of evolved Acheulian facies of which this classic find consisted are exactly matched by the bifaces from Dorneywood. Though small, the series of flakes from Dorneywood is interesting not only on typology and technology ... As one interprets the evidence today, these flakes and derivatives, by reason of their delicate workmanship and circumstances of their discovery, appear to correspond to the beautifully executed flake-implements recovered from brickearth at High Lodge near Mildenhall, Suffolk ... they are held by some authorities to be products of an advanced phase of Acheulian craftsmanship. This typological parallelism was stressed by the late Reginald A. Smith in referring to the patinated scrapers worked on the edges of one face from the upper layer of Saint-Acheul. It was brought out again in many of the advanced Acheulian flake-tools, especially Acheulian V1–V11 (Micoquian) from the argile rouge [red clay] at sites around Amiens (Somme)' (*op. cit.* 1959: 275).

All the Dorneywood artefacts are recorded by Lacaille as being found,

'in brickearth [overlying Chalk] at about 200ft. O.D used, until the early years of this century, to be dug out of hollows on the plateau in what is now the picturesque Dorneywood Golf Course. Here about sixty years ago there were recovered a number of flint tools, some being delicate bifaces of the most advanced Acheulian type ... Patinated cream and lightest fawn, yet retaining their pristine sharpness' (*op. cit.* 1959: 275).

The five bifaces illustrated in the Lacaille (1959) paper, and the three Dorneywood bifaces from the Shrubsole collection (in the Museum of Reading, Berkshire) are comparable to a number of pointed plano-convex bifaces described and illustrated in Tyldesley's (1986a) study of the Wolvercote Channel (and other predominately plano-convex assemblages).

– Dorneywood biface (Lacaille, 1959, Fig. 1.1) is similar to – Wolvercote Channel biface (Tyldesley, 1986a, Fig.2.16);
– Dorneywood biface (Lacaille, 1959, Fig. 1.2) is similar to – Wolvercote Channel biface (Tyldesley, 1986a, Fig. 2.20);
– Dorneywood biface (Lacaille, 1959, Fig. 1.3) is similar to – Wolvercote Channel biface (Tyldesley, 1986a, Fig. 2.40);
– Dorneywood biface (Lacaille, 1959, Fig. 1.4) is similar to – Wolvercote Channel biface (Tyldesley, 1986a, Fig. 2.39);
– Dorneywood biface (Lacaille, 1959, Fig. 1.6) is similar to – Wolvercote Channel biface (Tyldesley, 1986a, Fig. 2.43);
– Dorneywood biface (Shrubsole collection, AE 8[2?] 04.120.46.2) is similar to – Wolvercote Channel biface (Tyldesley, 1986a, Fig. 2.25);
– Dorneywood biface (Shrubsole collection, ((AE 201) 120–46/4) is similar to – Wolvercote Channel biface (Tyldesley, 1986a, Fig.2.49);
– Dorneywood biface (Shrubsole collection, ((AE 286) 6/3/09) is similar to – Wolvercote Channel biface (Tyldesley, 1986a, Fig. 2.12).

Tyldesley (1986a) recorded plano-convex bifaces at 20 find spots/sites. With the exception of the one – Friar Park biface (discussed below), all these British plano-convex bifaces have been found in low-lying river and beach gravels or sand. The four additions I have made to Tyldesley's original (1986) records are bifaces from the higher-levels:

– The Red Barns plano-convex bifaces were recovered from a Chalk downland slope of Portsdown where the artefacts had been buried under a soliflucted chalk mudflow (see B.G.S. Sht.316).
– The Limpsfield plano-convex biface was found *in situ* in what is probably Head brickearth (see B.G.S. Sht.287 and Field and Nicolaysen in Lithics No 14/15).
– The Dorneywood plano-convex bifaces were found in high-level brickearth associated with the Boyn Hill Terrace and glacial sands and gravel (see B.G.S. Sht.287)
– The Wood Hill plano-convex biface recovered from deposits mapped as Clay-with-flints (which contain 'brickearth' see Sub-Section 6.3).

The Friar Park site at Henley-on-Thames (SU 750827) in southern England also produced a plano-convex handaxe that had come from a higher level. It is described as an isolated find from the brickearth (White 1908), at least 130ft above the River Thames. The brickearth at this point appears to be associated with Upper Chalk and Terrace Deposits (see B.G.S. Sheet.254). Wymer (1968: 201–2) notes that this handaxe is very similar to those found below the brickearth of the Wolvercote Channel and that it is the only biface definitely known to have come from high-level brickearth in the whole Thames Valley above Burnham, Bucks.

It is very significant, as far as this research is concerned, that in Britain none of the plano-convex bifaces, previously recorded, had been recovered from deposits mapped as Clay-with-flints. Only one Clay-with-flints site in France, Boisguillaume, near Rouen in the Northern Paris Basin has produced plano-convex bifaces (Callow 1976: 7, 34). However, these do not have the distinctive 'ridge' extending down from the tip, nor are they particularly plano-convex in profile (Tyldesley 1986a: 148). The Wood Hill 1993 plano-convex pointed pyriform biface is therefore unique in Britain, in that it is the first of such handaxes to come from a well documented, high-level, *in situ* hilltop site, capped with deposits mapped as Clay-with-flints on the Chalk downlands of southern England.

Chance variation or design?

The widespread occurrence of the Micoquian variants could suggest that these very distinctive plano-convex bifaces were not produced by chance. It may be argued that this form of handaxe was manufactured in response to a lack of good quality flint, but the form is also found where high-quality flint is in abundance. Perhaps plano-convex bifaces were originally developed in an area where good materials were scarce, but the distinctive shape may also have been found to provided additional facilities which could not be supplied by the 'usual' pointed handaxe.

Dates and origins

Although the classic Wolvercote bifaces cannot be considered as true 'Micoquian bifaces' (following Bordes, 1961 definition) there are several sites in north-west France (for example, La Mare-aux-Clercs, Bihorel; Bordes, 1954) that have produced plano-convex bifaces which are somewhat similar to those found in the Wolvercote Channel (Tyldesley, 1986a). However, in Germany, Micoquian sites do not appear to include any 'typical Wolvercote handaxes' and the handaxes are often small, barely bifacial and sometimes manufactured from rocks other than flint (Bosinski, 1967), while the Polish and Russian Micoquian sites are very different to the French Micoquian sites (Tyldesley, 1986a).

The available literature strongly suggests that a change of tool emphasis (a lower biface component in the assemblages compared to Wolvercote) in Micoquian sites continues eastwards across Central Europe. Also, all the British plano-convex bifaces (which includes the Wolvercote Channel assemblage) and the European Micoquian material are assignable to the Late Acheulian (Lower Palaeolithic) and perhaps to some facies of the earlier Middle Palaeolithic of Central and Eastern Europe. Tyldesley states,

'given the lack of uniformity amongst the sites designated 'Micoquian' by various authors, it must be concluded that the Wolvercote material would not be out of place within this wide Final Acheulian tradition, lying morphologically closest to the North French material. This would indicate a rather weak British Late Acheulian link with Central Europe' (*op. cit.* 1986a: 172)

Reassessments

As part of his general study of the Quaternary of the Thames, a stratigraphical reassessment of the Wolvercote gravel and Wolvercote Channel deposits was undertaken by Bridgland (1994). A simplified correlation of British Quaternary events and marine

Table 11 A simplified correlation of British Quaternary events and marine stages. After Gamble and Lawson (1996)

Pleistocene Sub-divisions	British Quaternary Stage	Climate	Possible correlations with deep-sea core Maritime stage	Possible date, years BP	Sites and events	Divisions of the Palaeolithic
HOLOCENE	FLANDRIAN	Warm	1	Present 12,000	Development of Postglacial environments	MESOLITHIC–MODERN
UPPER	DEVENSIAN	Mainly cold	2–4 5a–d	40,000 100,000	Maximum of ice sheet 18–20,000 BP reached N. Norfolk and S. Wales	UPPER
UPPER	IPSWICHIAN	Warm	5e	120,000	No certain occupation of Britain	MIDDLE
MIDDLE	WOLSTONIAN COMPLEX	Cold Warm Cold Warm Cold	6 7 8 9 10	352,000	*Pontnewydd: sparse occupation of Britain* *Hoxne* *Many Lower Palaeolithic sites*	LOWER
MIDDLE	HOXNIAN	Warm	11	428,000	*Swanscombe skull site*	LOWER
MIDDLE	ANGLIAN	Cold	12	472,000	Major glaciation of Britain	LOWER
MIDDLE	CROMERIAN COMPLEX	Warm	13	525,000	*High Lodge* *Boxgrove* *Westbury-sub-Mendip*	LOWER

stages (Gamble and Lawson, 1996) is shown in Table 11. The results of these investigations now suggest that,

> 'it is possible to accommodate the Wolvercote Channel in one of two temperate episodes between the Anglian (Oxygen Isotope Stage 12) and the older of the two Summertown-Radley interglacials (Oxygen Isotope Stage 7). Correlation of the Wolvercote Channel deposits is possible on this basis, with either Stage 11 or Stage 9 of the oxygen isotope record... Since the Wolvercote Formation clearly post-dates the rejuvenation event that followed the deposition of the Hanborough Gravel, correlation of the Wolvercote Channel deposits with Oxygen Isotope Stage 9 (rather than 11) is strongly indicated' (Bridgland 1994: 63–4).

Before this reassessment it could only be stated that the Wolvercote Channel and its industry belonged to a post-Wolstonian warm phase, possibly late Ipswichian/early Devensian, (Tyldesley 1986b: 23–4) – a time period which would now equate with oxygen isotope stage 5.

- Oxygen Isotope Stage 5 gives a date range of 75,000 to 128,000 yrs. B.P. whereas,
- Oxygen isotope stage 9 gives a date range of 297,000 to 330,000 yrs. B.P.

Discussion

Set out in this Sub-section is sufficient information to warrant a reassessment of the relative position of the British plano-convex industry within the European Micoquian variants. The relevant points are as follows:

1. The 'classic' Wolvercote refined pointed pyriform plano-convex bifaces with a ridge, but without a twisted profile have apparently not (to date) been found outside Britain;
2. The most prolific occurrence of the pointed pyriform plano-convex bifaces i.e. the greatest number of this type of biface in an assemblage, is (to date) that found in the Wolvercote Channel assemblage;
3. 'Non-classic' Wolvercote refined pointed pyriform plano-convex bifaces (i.e. with or without a ridge, and with a twisted profile) are found within the Wolvercote assemblage and also at other sites both in Britain and Continental Europe;
4. There is a lack of uniformity amongst the Continental European sites designated Micoquian;

5. The change of tool emphasis (i.e. a lower biface component in the assemblages compared to that found at Wolvercote) in the Micoquian sites continues EASTWARDS across Central Europe;
6. Bridgland's (1994) revised dates for the Wolvercote deposits make a much earlier date possible for this industry than had previously been anticipated.
7. The discovery of the plano-convex biface (WH93.F38) *in situ*, on a hilltop in Kent, in an area mapped as Clay-with-flints, on the Chalk downlands of southern England;
8. The 're-discovery' of plano-convex bifaces at Dorneywood, Buckinghamshire and Limpsfield, Surrey, both finds from brickearth;
9. The possibility that there are further unrecognised plano-convex bifaces in British museums and private collections.

As previously noted, the British pointed pyriform plano-convex bifaces (which includes the Wolvercote Channel material) and the Continental European Micoquian variants have been assigned to the Late Acheulian and Middle Palaeolithic. The lack of uniformity amongst the European Micoquian sites, but a supposedly consistent time period for these sites, both in Britain and across Continental Europe, has nurtured a pattern of distribution which has France as the centre, with the Micoquian influence radiating out into Britain, changing gradually as it passes through Germany and more so as it reaches Poland and Russia. As the Wolvercote material is by no means a 'classic' Micoquian industry, the British material is generally regarded as exhibiting a rather weak link with the Continental European Micoquian variants.

This, I believe, is no longer a viable scenario as Bridgland's (1994) revised date, now Oxygen Isotope Stage 9 for the Wolvercote Channel, effectively places the Wolvercote bifaces much earlier in the British Lower Palaeolithic, around 297,000 to 330,000 yrs. B.P and well outside the Late Acheulian/early Mousterian/Micoquian time frame of Oxygen Isotope Stage 5, a date range of 75,000 to 125,000 yrs. B.P 'For the Wolvercote Channel deposits to be as late as these comparable continental industries, they would have to post-date much, if not all, of the Summertown-Radley Formation' (Bridgland, 1994: 63) – a situation which does not equate with Bridgland's latest findings. Furthermore, while a uniformity of design is certainly the hallmark of the Wolvercote bifaces, within the assemblage there are a number of 'non classic' bifaces. Bifaces resembling both the 'classic' and 'non classic' Wolvercote forms have been found in various places in southern England.

Conclusion

Based on this current information I propose that, unless the date of ANY Continental European Micoquian variant is reassessed and shown to be at least as old as the Wolvercote Channel material, the technology which produced the pointed pyriform plano-convex biface may have been centred in Britain during the early/middle Acheulian (Lower Palaeolithic) and then radiated out of Britain, reaching France and then Central Europe during the Late Acheulian/ early Mousterian (late Lower Palaeolithic/early Middle Palaeolithic). If true, this suggestion is a reversal of previous thinking. As this technology dispersed throughout Continental Europe, the form of the resulting bifaces became more diverse and their importance in assemblages diminished.

Support for an early/middle Acheulian (Lower Palaeolithic) age for the British plano-convex bifaces comes, albeit in a convoluted way, from a number of other archaeological reports. For example, it is interesting to note that in his paper (reviewed earlier in this sub-section) Lacaille (1959: 276) states,

> 'Though small, the series of flakes from Dorneywood is interesting, not only on typology and technology, but because they are linked with the core-tools they strengthen comparisons with Worthington G. Smith's comprehensive and resemblant discoveries'.

Smith's finds, as we saw in Section 4, are definitely Lower Palaeolithic although the only similarity of many of the artefacts to 'Micoquian' style material is the flaking skill. Lacaille also makes the point that the Dorneywood material, 'by reason of their delicate workmanship' appears to correspond closely with the flake implements found at High Lodge near Mildenhall, Suffolk. The High Lodge artefacts were at one time thought to be the product of an advanced stage of Acheulian craftsmanship which, as we saw earlier, was equated with Acheulian V1–V11 (Micoquian). Based on recent stratigraphic reassessments, the High Lodge material has now been shown to be without doubt early Lower Palaeolithic with a date of around 500,000 yrs. B.P (Ashton *et al.* 1992: 174).

Lacaille also specifically compared the Dorneywood artefacts to the Hoxne handaxes which are now thought to be oxygen isotope Stage 11 (a date range 400,000 to 380,000 yrs. B.P), possibly 9 (a date range of 297,000 to 330,000 yrs. B.P). However, there is no known dating evidence for the brickearth of Dorneywood.

Finally, we have seen that the morphology of the Wolvercote Channel artefacts combined with the then generally accepted age of the Wolvercote Channel forced Roe (1981) and Tyldesley (1986) to categorise these bifaces as Late Acheulian/early Mousterian (Micoquian). Over a decade earlier Wymer (1968) had also rejected Bishop's (1958) suggestion that the Wolvercote Channel could be pre-Wolstonian, although he believed the channel-fill to be of late Hoxnian to early Wolstonian age. However, he noted the importance of the plano-convex bifaces from the Wolvercote Channel and felt that the Wolvercote artefacts could be seen as broadly comparable to those found in the Swanscombe Middle Gravel. The Middle Gravels at Swanscombe have now been assigned to the Hoxnian Interglacial, oxygen isotope stage 11, the Hoxnian dated around 400,000 to 380,000 yrs B.P.

The discovery of WH93.F38, a pointed-pyriform plano-convex bifacial handaxe in the Wood Hill deposits mapped as Clay-with-flints, has prompted questions in this Sub-section that not only relate to the Wood Hill site itself and the biface in particular, but also to the relative positions both temporal and spatial of all plano-convex bifaces in Britain and Continental Europe.

The position of the Wood Hill bifacial handaxe within the 1993 trench and such associations as there are with artefacts from the 1993 trench, 1994 auger pit and the 1984/85 excavations are explored in Sub-section 6.11. As a final point in this Sub-section, burnt flint was found during the excavation on Wood Hill: dates were obtained by thermoluminescence analysis of this material and the readings would indeed suit oxygen isotope Stage 9 or 11. These dates and their application to the Wood Hill artefacts and deposits are considered next in Sub-section 6.10.

Sub-section 6.10: Burnt flints, dates and discussions

Dating Lower and Middle Palaeolithic open sites and their artefacts is always fraught with many difficulties but the Palaeolithic sites on, and artefacts from, the deposits mapped as Clay-with-flint, present particular problems. Deposits mapped as Clay-with-flints are decalcified, acid deposits and, as such, are highly unlikely to preserve faunal or floral remains for analysis. Understanding and dating ancient environments and artefacts invariably depends on the good preservation of such materials.

There are two forms of dating, one relative, the other absolute. Relative time scales are usually based on correlations of paleontological and stratigraphic data in which a position within a stratigraphic time scale, a time sequence marked by presence of a particular fossil, mineral or rock, can be compared with others of its kind, no absolute age being implied. The various methods of 'absolute dating' depend mainly on the use of unstable radio active isotopes in selected samples of a wide range of materials; however, the dates obtained by these methods can still be subject to error. New methods of investigation and dating are constantly being developed. The application of different techniques to what are at present regard as the 'sterile' environment of deposits mapped as Clay-with-flints could 'unlock' much information which is stored in these ancient deposits. For example, with the use of sophisticated on-site equipment (ground probes) it might be possible to locate 'hidden' hearths and degraded bones by identifying specific chemical signals (residues) still present in the deposits as the presence of organic carbon and nitrogen in the soil may be indicative of charcoal and possibly therefore hearths, and the presence of phosphate indicative of bone material, both could equate with occupational layers.

Such information is currently usually obtained by the subsequent off-site analysis of sediment samples taken from selected areas in the trench. However, in the case of deposits mapped as Clay-with-flints identifying the areas from which to take such samples during excavation is problematic. Datable faunal/floral material is, as previously noted, unlikely to be present in deposits mapped as Clay-with-flints deposits (pockets of brickearth if located may provided useful samples). If we are to increase our understanding of Palaeolithic sites on such sediments, it is imperative therefore, that all future excavators in these areas employ the detailed three-dimensional recording procedure for the sediments, geology, geomorphology and archaeology (as described in Sub-section 6.1) in order to maximise data retrieval, as neither the deposits themselves nor the processes that have acted upon them over geological time, are well understood.

The Wood Hill burnt flints

During the 1993 excavation on Wood Hill two small pieces of burnt flint were found in square A, one in spit 1 (5cms below the top soil) and the other in spit 2 (10cms below the top soil – see Figure 75). Two large pieces of burnt flint had also been found during the 1984/85 excavations, one in Trench 10 (WHK-84–46/12) 6cms below the top soil and one in Trench 11(WHK-84–47/6) 48cms below the top soil – see Figure 75. All four pieces of burnt flint were dispatched for Thermoluminescence dating to Oxford University's Research Laboratory for Archaeology and the History of Art. Soil samples from the site to provide background data were also included.

Note: Newly identified problems associated with the TL dating of detailed decalcified deposits apply to recently decalcified deposits – not to the ancient high-level deposits mapped as Clay-with-flints (pers. comm. Dr N. Debenham, Quaternary TL dating specialist).

Thermoluminescence dating of the Wood Hill burnt flints

After visual examination in the Laboratory, it was decided that only two of the four samples were suitable for analysis. The two samples selected were:

– 1984/85 (WHK-84–46/12) from Trench 10 (lab. ref. 288b1) and
– 1984/85 (WHK-84–47/6) from Trench 11 (lab. ref. 288c1)

Both samples of burnt flint from the 1993 excavation were considered to be too small to be successfully dated. The selected flints were dated using the fine grained thermoluminescence (TL) method (Zimmerman, 1971) and the coarse grain fraction of the sample as described by Huxtable (1982). Agreement between the archaeological dose evaluated from coarse grains with that evaluated from fine grains acts as a check to ensure that spurious thermoluminescence has been eliminated, following the recommendations of Aitken (1985).

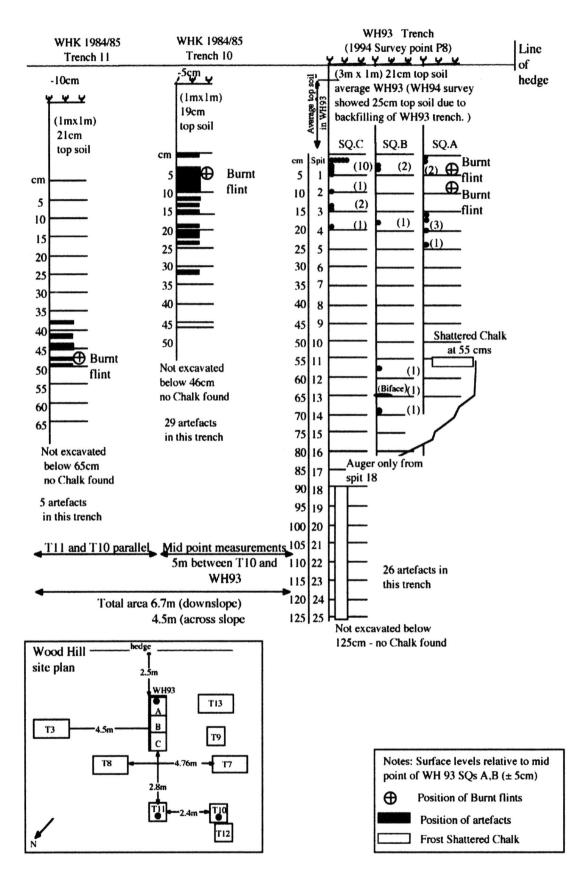

Figure 75 Diagram showing relative positions of the burnt flints and excavated artefacts in WH93 (SQ.A,B,C), WHK 1984/85 Trench 10 and WHK 1984/85 Trench 11.

Results

The TL ages obtained from these pieces of burnt flint suggested that they do indeed both date from the Lower Palaeolithic (the British Lower Palaeolithic dates from around 600,000–200,000 yrs. B.P). However, because of the radon emanation from the soil samples, the possible age range is large:

– WHK-84–46/12 from Trench 10 (lab. ref. 288b1) is 380,000±26,000 yrs. B.P.
  this gives a possible age range of 406,000–354,000 yrs. B.P.

– WHK- 84–47/6 from Trench 11 (lab. ref. 288c1) is 200,000± 33,000 yrs. B.P.
  this gives a possible age range of 233,000–167,000 yrs. B.P.

It is important to note that:

– For sample 288b1 – the older date, the fine grain archaeological dose agreed with that obtained from the coarse grain fraction within error limits. This agreement acts as a check to ensure that spurious TL has been eliminated and that there have been no problems in the preparation of the samples. However,

– For sample 288c1 – the younger date, the fine grain and coarse grain dates did not agree. The Research Laboratory concluded that the discrepancy was due to some loss of TL due to the grinding action on the sample during fine grain preparation. As a result, the date obtained from this sample is quoted as that obtained from the coarse grain fraction which would not have been subjected to such rigorous crushing as the fine grain. If anything, a date derived from the fine grain would have been marginally older than the actual reading obtained from the course grain fraction.

Discussion

As this TL data is derived from such a small sample size, considerable caution must be exercised in its application and ideally more burnt flints from Wood Hill are needed for a comparison. However, the proviso must not detract from the enormous significance of this important information.

Previous to this investigation, no dates (as opposed to broad categories, i.e. Lower and Middle Palaeolithic) existed for high-level Palaeolithic sites on deposits mapped as Clay-with-flints. The discovery and dating of this burnt flint has made it possible, for the first time, directly to link and compare (using more than just general categories) a high-level Lower Palaeolithic site on the deposits mapped as Clay-with-flints with dated low-level river, beach and cave sites (certain associations between the Wood Hill site

and various dated low-level sites are discussed later in this Sub-section). The two dates obtained from the burnt flint represent two occurrences widely separated in time within the Middle Pleistocene (refer to Table 11)

1. Taken at face value, Sample 288b1 from Trench 10 at 380,000±26,000 yrs. B.P. (date range, 406,000–354,000 yrs B.P.) can be assigned to the early part of the British Lower Palaeolithic at around oxygen isotope stage 11 (still sometimes referred to as the Hoxnian Interglacial) through to the early part of the middle of the British Lower Palaeolithic at around oxygen isotope stage 9 (an unnamed warm period within the 'Wolstonian' glacial complex). The sediments at Wolston, which gave rise to the Wolstonian stage, originally a period separating the Hoxnian and the Ipswichian, have been shown to predate the Hoxnian. Many workers now suggest that these sediments cannot represent the period between the Hoxnian and Ipswichian, and that evidence from other sites

'indicate that the pattern of glaciation and environmental change during this time interval was rather more complex than is suggested by the assumption of a single glaciation' (Green *et al.* 1984; Briggs, Coope and Gilbertson, 1985, quoted in Ballantyne and Harris 1994: 12–14).

2. Similarly, Sample 288c1 from Trench 11 at 200,000±33,000 yrs. B.P. (date range, 233,000–167,000 yrs. B.P) can be assigned to the late Lower Palaeolithic at around oxygen isotope stage 7 through to the late Lower Palaeolithic/early Middle Palaeolithic at around oxygen isotope stage 6, both within the latter part of the 'Wolstonian' Glacial complex, Stage 7 being a warm period and Stage 6, a cold one.

Pollen analysis

In addition to the TL dating of burnt flint, twelve soil samples were given to Dr Adrian Parker (University of Oxford) for pollen analysis but, as expected, the grains were too degraded to provide useful information. As noted earlier in this Sub-section, the deposits mapped as Clay-with-flints are decalcified. However, small pockets of windblown material (e.g. loess and coversands) do exist within the Clay-with-flints deposits. There is, therefore, the chance that pollen of suitable quality for analysis may be recovered from such a sample.

It would be fitting at this stage of the discussion to describe in detail how the Wood Hill burnt flint relates to the artefacts of this *in situ* Acheulian occupation: they suggest that there are two widely separated phases of human presence on the site. However, to do this would require at this stage, many explanations and discussions best suited to the following Sub-section (6.11), which includes three 'Models': the evolution of the Wood Hill site; the Lower Palaeolithic occupation of this site: patterns of artefact distribution – a reduction sequence, and the Conclusion to the Case-study. The relationships of the burnt flint to the artefacts and the deposits is, therefore, fully explored in Models 1, 2 and 3 (see Sub-section 6.11). Although in Figure 75 it may be seen that the data obtained are, in what might at first be considered, the 'wrong' order, we shall see that a full consideration of the stratigraphy shows this not to be the case.

Another site for British Lower and Middle Palaeolithic archaeological record

In the General Introduction it was noted that the British Lower and Middle Palaeolithic archaeological record is based almost exclusively on artefacts from low-level river, lakeside, beach and cave sites and that credence has invariable been given to artefacts often 'derived' from high-level sites but found in gravel environments whereas, artefacts from the high-level sites in areas mapped as Clay-with-flints have so often been rejected on the grounds that they are 'derived' material! The former have become part of the archaeological record, the latter have not ... until now. Wood Hill is therefore, a site of great interest and importance for those wishing to understand the earlier Palaeolithic of Britain.

Conclusion

There are a number of low-level, Palaeolithic sites which form the framework of the British Lower and Middle Palaeolithic archaeological record (much has been written about these sites, see for example: Wymer, 1974; Roe, 1981; Ashton *et al.* 1992). The key question here is: in the overall picture of the British Lower and Middle Palaeolithic where does Wood Hill fit in? A correlation shown in Table 12 below places the (288c1.T11) level of occupation within the

Table 12 The comparative context of Wood Hill in relation to the British Lower and Middle Palaeolithic.

Site	Stage	Boundary age yrsB.P.	Suggested site yrs B.P.	probable oxygen isotope stage	Site type	Artefacts
Bakers Hole	Wolstonian Complex	352,00–132000	?	stage 9, 8, 7?	valley	Levallois quarry site
Wood Hill (288c1) T11	Wolstonian Complex	352,000–132000	200000 ±33,000	stage 7	C-w-f hilltop	Acheulian
Wolvercote	Wolstonian Complex	352,000–132000	297,000–330000	stage 9	river channel	Acheulian
Barnham	Hoxnian Interglacial	352,000–428000	around 400000	stage 11	river	Clactonian (flake/core reduction) + biface debitage
Clacton	Hoxnian Interglacial	352000–428000	around 400000	stage 11	river	Clactonian (flake/core reduction)
Wood Hill (288b1) T10	Hoxnian Interglacial	352,000 428000	380000 ±26,000	stage 11	C-w-f hilltop	Acheulian
Swanscombe (Barnfield Pit)	Hoxnian Interglacial	352,000–428000	around 428000	stage 11	river	Acheulian Clactonian
Warren Hill	Late Cromerian	352,000–428000	around 400000	stage 13	river	Acheulian ovate, cordate bifaces and a crude handaxe industry
High Lodge	Cromerian Interglacial Complex	480,000–810000	around 500000	stage 13	river	Acheulian flake/core flake/core industry
Boxgrove	Cromerian Interglacial Complex	480,000–810000	around 500000	stage 13	foreshore coastal plain	Acheulian ovate and cordate bifaces

Wolstonian Complex, a date which also encompasses Bakers Hole and Wolvercote. Level (288b1.T10) corresponds to the Hoxnian Interglacial, oxygen isotope stage 11, which includes such sites as Barnham, Clacton and Swanscombe.

Wood Hill has, without doubt, been the scene of considerable Lower Palaeolithic activity. As previously noted in Section 5 and Sub-section 6.8: all the artefacts found during the 1984/85, 1993 and 1994 are indicative of handaxe manufacturing sites. Occupation of the site may of course, in addition to the TL dates suggested, have occurred at other times during the Lower and Middle Palaeolithic periods, however more excavation and more burnt flints would be required to substantiate this idea.

Sub-section 6.11: Conclusion to the Case-study, including three models: The evolution of the Wood Hill site; The Lower Palaeolithic occupation of this site; Patterns of artefact distribution – a reduction sequence

In the introduction to the Wood Hill Case-study (Section 5), I set out certain fundamental questions and hypotheses aimed at understanding the relationships between the Chalk Downlands of southern England, the deposits mapped as Clay-with-flints which cap them, and the presence of Lower and Middle Palaeolithic artefacts on these same high-levels which have evidently survived throughout both glacial and temperate periods. The two questions and one hypothesis were selected for this Case-study, are as follows:

Questions:

(a) How could Palaeolithic artefacts become incorporated into, and/or remain on the surface of the deposits mapped as Clay-with-flints over many hundreds of thousands of years?

(b) From the time Palaeolithic peoples manufactured and deposited their artefacts on the Palaeolithic high-level landsurfaces, southern England has undergone many climatic changes associated with both glacial and temperate periods. What has happened specifically to the deposits mapped as Clay-with-flints in these high-level areas where the artefacts are still to be found?

Hypothesis:

1. Given the state of restricted change of the deposits mapped as Clay-with-flints which cap the Chalk Downland, more or less *in situ* Palaeolithic sites should exist on some of these high-levels.

The expressed aims, therefore, of the Wood Hill Case-study were to provide a greater understanding, in particular, of the Lower Palaeolithic site of Wood Hill and, in general, of Palaeolithic artefacts found in relation to deposits mapped as Clay-with-flints on the Chalk Downlands of southern England. Each facet of the Case-study investigations has been the focus of a separate Sub-section – sometimes it has been possible to reach a firm conclusion within a particular area of investigations, sometimes not. The time has now come, in this the final Sub-section, to draw together these separate conclusions. Difficulties are inherent, as the Lower Palaeolithic site of Wood Hill can be likened to an old jigsaw puzzle, some pieces of which are now lost forever and there is no picture to serve as a guide. However, as in the case of the 'old puzzle,' those pieces which are left are solid, factual evidence of past processes and patterns. Reconstructing the picture is therefore a matter of proceeding with great care, fitting one result carefully to another, being ever mindful of the possibility of omissions and data distortions. Piecing together these conclusions also requires some courage, as preconceived ideas about the deposits mapped as Clay-with-flints and the associated Palaeolithic artefacts abound but, it is now necessary to hold such ideas in abeyance or our understanding of the deposits and the artefacts will advance no further forward. The two most important questions relating to the Wood Hill Lower Palaeolithic site can now be addressed, namely:

1. How did the Lower Palaeolithic site at Wood Hill evolve?
2. What is the significance of the distribution pattern of the Lower Palaeolithic artefacts across the site?

In the discussions that follow there is much information to be considered. For the sake of clarity, it is necessary to restate a number of ideas. However, where these depend on detailed discussions and conclusions, reference is made to the appropriate Sections and Sub-sections.

That the Chalk Downlands of southern England lay beyond the Anglian glacial maxima and have been subjected only to 'restricted change' since the late Cromerian (a date now estimated to be at least 500,000 yrs. B.P), is initially confirmed by the presence of frost shattered Chalk and the capping of deposits mapped as Clay-with-flints (see Explanatory Sections 1 and 2). Climatic fluctuations (including seasonal changes) over geological time, produced both temperate and glacial or periglacial environments. These changes generated predominately different types of erosion of the Chalk Downlands and their Clay-with-flints capping. During cold periods, mechanical erosion, such as that associated with frost action and freeze/thaw processes, dominated but, when the climate ameliorated, chemical erosion, in the form of solution and solifluction for example, occurred.

Previous studies of the deposits mapped as Clay-with-flints have been concentrated on numbers of small trenches dug in specific areas although, as we have seen, the deposits mapped as Clay-with-flints are extremely variable. Nevertheless, the results derived from data produced from these restricted investigations have been applied indiscriminately to all the deposits mapped as Clay-with-flints and the Chalk downlands of southern England. It is the type and the amount of erosion which is generally perceived to have affected the deposits mapped as Clay-with-flints and the Chalk Downland (and consequently to have distorted the value of the associated Palaeolithic artefacts) that have been challenged by this research. If the superficial deposits mapped as Clay-with-flints are thought to be heavily cryoturbated and/or very soliflucted, then the existence of Palaeolithic sites *in situ* in these deposits is just not a feasible proposition. All the Palaeolithic artefacts accordingly acquire the status of 'lag deposits' and are then considered to be 'derived,' with the result that they are effectively excluded from the British Lower and Middle Palaeolithic record. However, if this general theory can be shown to be false in its application to just one group of Palaeolithic artefacts from deposits mapped as Clay-with-flints then the status of ALL artefacts recovered from all the deposits mapped as Clay-with-flints would need to be reconsidered, since the uncritical general assumption might prove to be just as wrong elsewhere.

In Section 5 (hypothesis 2), I suggested that some current models used to explain patterns and levels of erosion and deposition on the high-level areas mapped as Clay-with-flints may require substantial adjustment, and several ideas have been explored in this study and remain subjects for further research. This research has also produced a 'Bench marks' system which will certainly facilitate an assessment of the type and amount of erosion of both the deposits mapped as Clay-with-flints and the Chalk in any one area, and for this Wood Hill was the pilot study (see Explanatory Section 1 and the General Conclusion).

Models

As the deposits mapped as Clay-with-flints are so variable and the effects of this variability so little understood (see Explanatory Section 2), it is inevitable that the proposals which have been set out in this study to explain the sequence of events on Wood Hill will, by their very nature, be contentious. These proposals are however derived from repeatable and testable data of the highest integrity, data which have been gathered as a result of good advice and using rigorous modern scientific methods. Also, as previously stated, this study is not intended to provide definitive answers but rather to be a springboard for much needed further investigations of both the deposits mapped as Clay-with-flints and the associated Lower and Middle Palaeolithic artefacts. The three models proposed are:

– Model 1: the evolution of the Wood Hill site, constructed from the sedimentological, geological and geomorphological data, illustrated in Figure 76 below.
– Model 2: a sequence for the Lower Palaeolithic occupation of Wood Hill. This model partly uses the data on which Model 1 depends but also uses evidence provided by the 1984/85, 1993 and 1994 investigations, illustrated in Figure 76 and Figure 35.
– Model 3: the distribution patterns of the Lower Palaeolithic artefacts on Wood Hill, with reference to Models 1 and 2, illustrated in Figure 36.

Background to Model 1

The 1994 Resistivity survey of Wood Hill (Sub-section 6.6) confirmed that the Lower Palaeolithic site (in the surveyed area) in Field 2 was effectively contained within a large solution feature in the Upper Chalk, which extended across the whole of that part of the hill, and that, the surface of this Upper Chalk was irregular. Furthermore, a deep 'basin like' depression also existed in an area of the Clay-with-flints itself. This 'basin' feature appeared in the 1993 trench at the edge of Square B and the whole of Square C (see Figures 39, 40, 41, 42) and was infilled with a deposit that was somewhat different to that in Square A (see Sub-section 6.3 and 6.5).

The 1993 trench was carefully positioned in the middle of a number of small scattered trenches dug during 1984/85 by the Dover Archaeological Group, since siting the trench in this position would make it possible, not only to address the questions set out by the 1993 excavation plan itself, but also to answer some of the questions posed by the 1984/85 excavations. Detailed descriptions of the Wood Hill 1993 excavation procedures are to be found in Sub-section 6.1, but to reiterate:

- A 3m × 1m trench was divided into three 1m × 1m squares (A. B. C) and was excavated in 18 horizontal spits.
- All the spits were dug at 5cm. vertical intervals throughout the trench.
- Stratified deposits were identified in the 1993 trench (see Sub-sections 6.2 and 6.3).

Grouped by spits, the sequence has a distinctive upper part (1 to 4/5) and a middle part (5/6 to 8/9). The lower spits (below 9/10) were not grouped, as the evidence was inconclusive.

Model 1: *The evolution of the Wood Hill site – as constructed from the sedimentological, geological and geomorphological data, collected during this research (refer to Figures 76a, 76b)*

1. The Chalk from which Wood Hill is composed was laid down on the sea-bed during the Cretaceous period (see Sub-section 6.7).
2. The Upper Chalk layer was then overlain with Sub-Palaeogene deposits, which may have formed in both deep and shallow water. The Sub-Palaeogene deposits in the Wood Hill area seem principally to consist of (deep water formed) Thanet/Bullhead Beds (see Sub-section 6.5). Tectonic activity then lifted and folded the Chalk, along with the Sub-Palaeogene capping deposits to create the Chalklands of southern England (see Explanatory Section 1).
3. The uplifted superficial Sub-Palaeogene deposits, overlying the Chalk, were then reworked during the Eocene to form Plateau Drift and, with the insoluble residue of the Upper Chalk, Clay-with-flints (see Explanatory Section 2). The

Clay-with-flints deposits have been subject to only restricted change since approximately the end of the late Cromerian, a date of at least 500,000 yrs. B.P. Over geological time, the sculpturing processes of solution, erosion and deposition produced the Chalk Downlands with the capping of deposits mapped as Clay-with-flints. The Chalk ridge, of which Wood Hill is a part, was therefore quite probably a much larger area than it is today. However, exactly when Wood Hill, with its capping of deposits mapped as Clay-with-flints, became a distinctive topographic entity or feature within the Chalk Downlands is not possible to say.

4. A layer of frost shattered Chalk was formed directly under the deposits mapped as Clay-with-flints before during and/or after the Anglian glacial period (shattering of the Chalk on exposed slopes may also have occurred, and if so layers of soliflucted material (colluvium, Coombe rock) around Wood Hill may be the testament to this).

Frost shattered Chalk is thus to be found on the top of Wood Hill and on the lower parts of the slopes (at P1 and P2 in Figure 63) and in patches within the solution hollows but also adjacent to areas of unshattered Chalk (see Sub-section 6.6).

These specific areas of frost shattered Chalk on Wood Hill may be places where the frost was able to penetrate to a deeper level through the overlying deposits, due perhaps to the exploitation of pre-existing conditions, for example differences in the thickness of the overlying deposits, particular variations in the deposits mapped as Clay-with-flints or indeed any features which facilitated an increased interplay between the particular characteristics of the Chalk at that point and the total porosity and moisture content (degree of saturation) at the onset of the freezing in the restricted area.

Below the cappings of the Clay-with-flints deposits, solution features formed in the Upper Chalk. One very large and deep solution feature extends across the top of the hill, effectively retaining in place the capping deposits mapped as Clay-with-flints (see Sub-section 6.6: Figure 67).

5. Lower Palaeolithic artefacts were found in the higher level of Trench 10, the TL dates for the burnt flint found here give a date of 380,000± 26,000 yrs BP (see Sub-Section 6.10).
6. Subsequently, the Lower Palaeolithic artefacts found in trench 10 were covered and 'sealed in' (possibly by a layer of material brought in by soil creep and wind blown deposits).
7. The hollow in the Clay-with-flints in Field 2

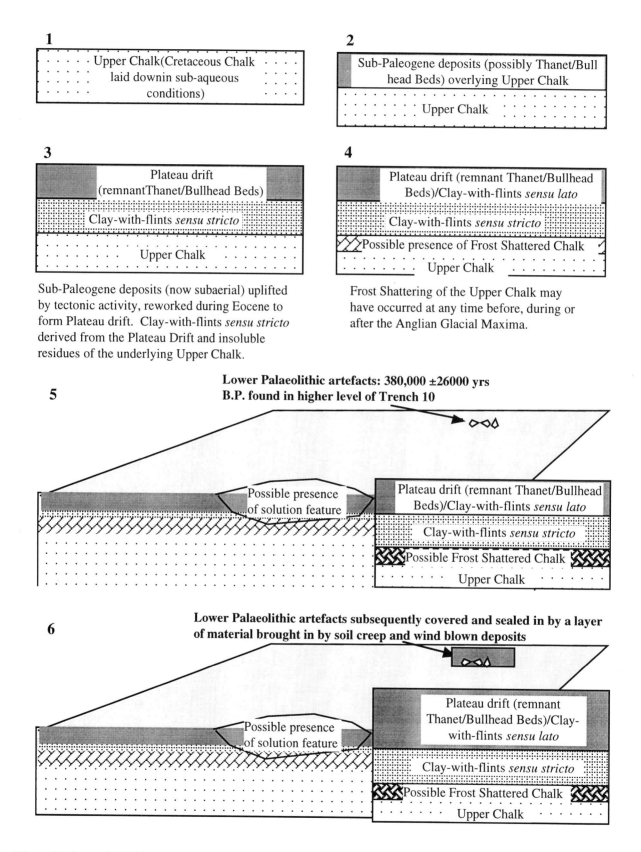

1
Upper Chalk(Cretaceous Chalk laid downin sub-aqueous conditions)

2
Sub-Paleogene deposits (possibly Thanet/Bull head Beds) overlying Upper Chalk

Upper Chalk

3
Plateau drift (remnantThanet/Bullhead Beds)

Clay-with-flints *sensu stricto*

Upper Chalk

Sub-Paleogene deposits (now subaerial) uplifted by tectonic activity, reworked during Eocene to form Plateau drift. Clay-with-flints *sensu stricto* derived from the Plateau Drift and insoluble residues of the underlying Upper Chalk.

4
Plateau drift (remnant Thanet/Bullhead Beds)/Clay-with-flints *sensu lato*

Clay-with-flints *sensu stricto*

Possible presence of Frost Shattered Chalk

Upper Chalk

Frost Shattering of the Upper Chalk may have occurred at any time before, during or after the Anglian Glacial Maxima.

Lower Palaeolithic artefacts: 380,000 ±26000 yrs B.P. found in higher level of Trench 10

5

Possible presence of solution feature

Plateau drift (remnant Thanet/Bullhead Beds)/Clay-with-flints *sensu lato*

Clay-with-flints *sensu stricto*

Possible Frost Shattered Chalk

Upper Chalk

Lower Palaeolithic artefacts subsequently covered and sealed in by a layer of material brought in by soil creep and wind blown deposits

6

Possible presence of solution feature

Plateau drift (remnant Thanet/Bullhead Beds)/Clay-with-flints *sensu lato*

Clay-with-flints *sensu stricto*

Possible Frost Shattered Chalk

Upper Chalk

Figure 76 (part a) Model 1: The evolution of Wood Hill - including the Lower Palaeolithic site in the 1994 surveyed area and showing two levels of Lower Palaeolithic occurrences.

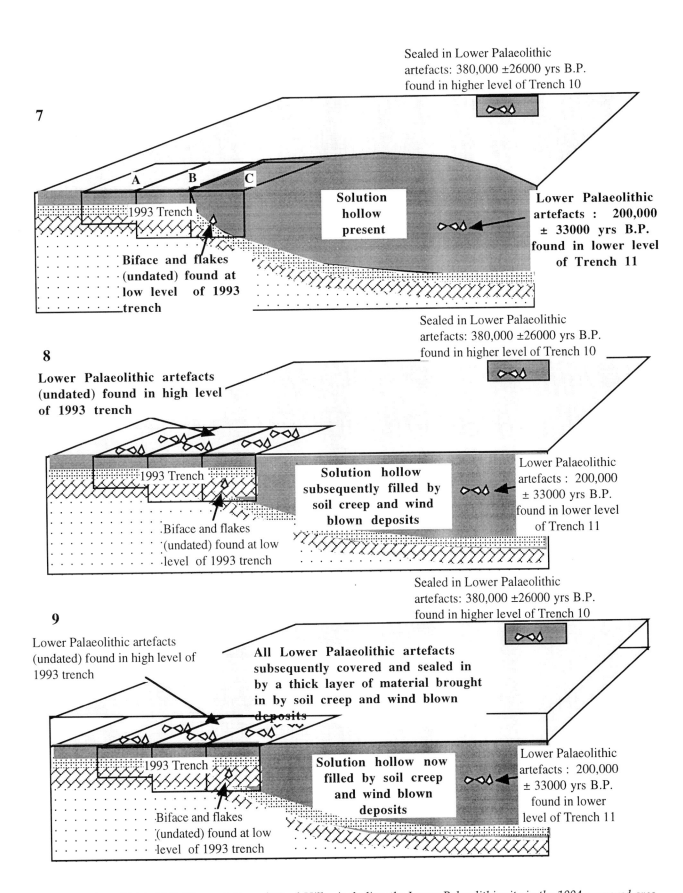

7

Sealed in Lower Palaeolithic
artefacts: 380,000 ±26000 yrs B.P.
found in higher level of Trench 10

A   B   C

1993 Trench

**Solution
hollow
present**

**Lower Palaeolithic
artefacts : 200,000
± 33000 yrs B.P.
found in lower level
of Trench 11**

Biface and flakes
(undated) found at
low level of 1993
trench

8

Sealed in Lower Palaeolithic
artefacts: 380,000 ±26000 yrs B.P.
found in higher level of Trench 10

**Lower Palaeolithic artefacts
(undated) found in high level
of 1993 trench**

1993 Trench

**Solution hollow
subsequently filled by
soil creep and wind
blown deposits**

Lower Palaeolithic
artefacts : 200,000
± 33000 yrs B.P.
found in lower level
of Trench 11

Biface and flakes
(undated) found at low
level of 1993 trench

9

Sealed in Lower Palaeolithic
artefacts: 380,000 ±26000 yrs B.P.
found in higher level of Trench 10

Lower Palaeolithic artefacts
(undated) found in high level of
1993 trench

**All Lower Palaeolithic artefacts
subsequently covered and sealed in
by a thick layer of material brought
in by soil creep and wind blown
deposits**

1993 Trench

**Solution hollow now
filled by soil creep
and wind blown
deposits**

Lower Palaeolithic
artefacts : 200,000
± 33000 yrs B.P.
found in lower
level of Trench 11

Biface and flakes
(undated) found at low
level of 1993 trench

*Figure 76 (part b) Model 1: The evolution of Wood Hill – including the Lower Palaeolithic site in the 1994 surveyed area
and showing two levels of Lower Palaeolithic occurrences.*

(shown in Figure 76 (part a) Model 1) gradually deepened and widened, with the result that by around 233,000 yrs.B.P it took the form of a 'basin like' depression (see Model 2 in this Sub-section, Explanatory Section 1 and Sub-sections: 6.2, 6.6 and 6.10). Because the solution process operates from below, the Clay-with-flints deposits merely sink into the solution hollow virtually undisturbed. The existence of a depression does NOT mean that areas of Clay-with-flints have been removed by erosion from above. Lower Palaeolithic artefacts were found in the lower level of Trench 11 – the associated burnt flint was assigned a date of 200,000±33000 yrs.B.P but as previously noted it may well be older (Sub-section 6.10). The undated biface and flakes found in the lower levels of Square B in the 1993 trench were also found at a similar level to those in trench 11.

8. This Clay-with-flints hollow was then 'infilled' with deposits brought in again by soil creep (see Sub-sections 6.2, 6.3 and 6.5) and with wind-blown deposits (coversands and loess). Lower Palaeolithic artefacts (undated) were found in the higher levels of the 1993 trench on the edge of the, now sealed, solution hollow (see Model 2 below).

    Clasts sampled from the Clay-with-flints deposits in the 1993 trench exhibit preferred orientations. Clasts from the Clay-with-flints at the lowest levels (spit 10 to 16) in the 1993 trench were orientated along the a-axis NE-SW. A change then occurs in the middle levels (spits 6 to 9): the preferred a-axis orientation of the clasts now becomes NW-SE, once again there is a change at the top of the trench between spits 1–5 where the preferred orientation becomes NNE-SSW (see Sub-section 6.2). Results from both the particle size analysis and the orientation data confirm that this is indeed a stratified deposit – a coherent sequence and that patterns such as this could not be produced by cryoturbation or a random mixing of the deposits; therefore soil creep seems the most likely process (see Sub-sections: 6.2, 6.3, 6.7).

9. The Lower Palaeolithic site was then sealed in again possibly by further incidences of soil creep (worm activity may have played a part – although there is very little evidence of this) and by windblown materials which covered Wood Hill as a whole. Easterly winds during the Devensian blew loess westward directly across the country from the source area in the North Sea basin, while the coversands were of local origin (see Sub-sections: 6.2, 6.3 and 6.5).

    The level of erosion on Wood Hill, certainly during the late Devensian was not as great as

that usually estimated for Chalk downland areas. The Devensian was just one of many glacial periods but it is generally agreed that, although it is likely that frost shattered Chalk was formed in previous periglacial periods, frost shattered Chalk exposed to erosional processes was sludged away before the end of the Devensian. It is highly significant, therefore, that the downslope layer of frost shattered Chalk on such an exposed site as Wood Hill at survey points P1 and P2, for example, is still present today (see Figure 61), as the frost shattered layer of the Chalk is broken into small fragments which often fit only loosely together. Movement within or on this surface could disturb these fragments, which would then be readily removed by erosion (see Explanatory Section 1 and Sub-section 6.6).

There is every indication that Wood Hill remained a 'sealed' area right up until the Bronze Age, for, although both Lower Palaeolithic and Bronze Age artefacts can be found in abundance as surface-finds scattered across the fields, no artefact that is not Lower Palaeolithic has been found in any of the many trenches dug by the Dover Archaeological Group in 1984/85, nor in the 1993 trench or during auguring in 1994 (see Section 5 and Sub-section 6.8). Alternatively, this could be seen as evidence of a 'lost horizon', whereby occupation 'horizons' subsequent to the Lower Palaeolithic 'horizon' on Wood Hill were lost to erosion before the Bronze Age.

Model 2: which provides a sequence for the Lower Palaeolithic occupation of Wood Hill – it is superimposed on Model 1 but uses additional data from derived from the 1984/85, the 1993 and the 1994 excavations and investigations

Background to Model 2

As previously noted, the Dover Archaeological Group 1984/85 excavations in Fields 2, 4 and 9 were restricted to the simple straightforward excavation of many small trenches, scattered across the hilltop, each measuring approximately 1m × 1m or 2m × 1m (Figure 34). This method of excavation had the unavoidable effect of producing fragmented site data, as each trench was considered principally as an entity in itself. Therefore the greatest of caution was needed when using this 1984/85 data to construct patterns of the relationship between these trenches.

In terms of Lower Palaeolithic artefacts, Field 2 proved to be the most productive but a number of artefacts were also found in Field 9 (see Section 5). Only one face of each trench, usually the SE one, is shown in the 1984/85 section drawings; also the colour of the deposits was described subjectively without the aid of the Munsell Color chart. As the chart was not used by the 1984/85 excavators, interpreting deposits described as 'orange', 'cream' or 'purple' is somewhat problematical, particularly as these colours are not used in the chart to describe soils. Deposits described as 'cream' may possibly be included in the 10 YR range (very pale brown); the 2.5 Y range (pale yellow) or maybe even the 5 Y range (pale yellow). Two hues may cover the 'orange' deposits: 5 YR (range, reddish yellow or yellowish red) and 7.5 YR (range, reddish yellow). 'Purple' is more difficult to categorise: it could be 2.5 YR 2 5/2 (very dusky red) or perhaps 5 YR 2 5/2 (dark reddish brown).

All references to the deposits in the 1984/85 trenches, both in the following discussions and on the diagrams, are as described in the 1984/85 site-archive. Consequently, the diagrams show a considerable variation in the colour of the deposits, probably far more than actually existed. However, the great variability of the colour of deposits mapped as Clay-with-flints in general dictates that even 'educated guesses' as to the 'actual' colour of the 1984/85 deposits are not applicable here. In the diagram which accompanies Model 2 (Figure 35), the 1984/85 and 1993 trenches plus the 1994 auger pit are shown as 'block sections' (SE face unless otherwise stated) superimposed on the 1994 Resistivity survey grid, with 'spot heights' given for the shattered Chalk. The level/s at which the Lower Palaeolithic artefacts were found within each trench are indicated by the turquoise line.

At this point in the discussion there is need to return momentarily to the analogy of 'the old jigsaw puzzle' – each trench can be equated with a piece of the puzzle but when the site plan is viewed it is clear that there are many areas (missing pieces) still to be excavated. There are therefore gaps in the picture: it is not possible for example, at this point in time, to determine with certainty the exact extent of the Clay-with-flints basin-like feature. It is clear, however, from the examination of the Wood Hill trenches in Figure 35 that there is a certain similarity in the type and depth of the deposits in particular trenches. Using both the type and depth of the deposits as 'markers', the grouping of the trenches is summarised in Table 13. Having grouped the trenches by geological similarities (and in consequence the differences) it can be seen that:

Table 13 The possible trench relationships based on type and depth of the deposits.

Trenches	1993 SQ.A	1993 SQ.B	1993 SQ.C	1994 Auger Pit	T2*	T3 L	T3 R	T7	T8 L	T8 R	T9	T10	T11	T12	T13 L	T13 R	T14* L	T14* R	T15*	(BS9)*	T19*	T20*
SQ.A		●		●											●				●		●	
SQ.B	●			O											●				O		O	
SQ.C				●				●	●				O	●	O		O					
Auger Pit			●				O		O				O		O		●					
T2*	ᴿO	O														●			●			
T3 R																●						
T3 L															●							
T7			●	O													●				O	
T8 R		●	●										O	O			O					
T8 L							●															
T9													●	●								●
T10				●									●	●								●
T11		●	O	Ⓞ					Ⓞ		●	●					Ⓞ					●
T12			●	●		O	O								O		●					
T13 R								●														
T13 L	●	●		●															O		●	
T14* R			●	●										●								
T14* L	●	●							●	●												
T15*	●	●			●	O															●	
(BS9)*				Ⓞ				●			O				O	●						
T19*	●	●		●											●				●			
T20*									●	●	O											

Key: *   Outside the 1994 surveyed area   R Right side of trench   L Left side of trench
      ●   Similar deposits
      O   Deposits with some resemblance

Note (within cells): T10 Auger Pit "Certain low areas"; T11 SQ.B "Small area in SQ B".

Table 14 *The relationship between both the number of Wood Hill Lower Palaeolithic artefacts and burnt flints and the depths (in cms) at which they were found. (Each artefact represented by *)*

cms	1993			1994			1984/85										
	SQ A	SQ B	SQ C	Aug.Pit	T2	T3	T7	T8	T9	T10	T11	T12	T13	T14	T15	T19	T20
1	**+BF	*	***				*	**	***	***			*******				
2	BF		**				***		*			*	***				
3		*	**				*		****						**		
4						*			*	*		**					
5			***			*			**	******			*		*		*
6							**		*	*****+ BF		*					*
7						*			*	*			*	*			*
8							*	***	*	*			*		**		
9						*		*		*		*					
10			*							**			**	*		*	*
11						**		*	**				*			*	*
12						***			*	*		*	*				
13						**			*			*	*	*			
14			*			**	*		**	*		*	**				
15	*		*			*	*					*				*	**
16										*							*
17						*	**										*
18	*	*			*	****	**					**		*			
19						*		*	*	*		**					
20			*	**								**					
21	*					**	*	**		*							
22						*	*			**				*			
23	*					*			**								*
24							*			*		*					*
25						*	*	**				*					**
26						*						**					
27																	
28						*											
29									*								
30									*			*					
31									*								
32							*			*							
33												*					
34												**					
35								**									
36																	
37												*					
38											*	**					
39												*					
40																	
41												*					
42											*						
43																	
44											*						
45				*							*						*
46				*****													
47																	
48											BF						
49																	
50											*						
51																	
52																	
53																	
54																	
55		*															
56																	
57																	
58																	
59																	
60																	
61		*															
62																	
63																	
64		*															
65																	

- the depth at which shattered Chalk was found is very variable;
- small solution (or possibly tree-throw) hollows are a common feature;
- the large Clay-with-flints 'basin' is a significant feature on Wood Hill;
- in many of the trenches, silty/sandy deposits were identified;
- there is a similarity in the depth at which the Lower Palaeolithic artefacts were found within the deposits, both in Field 2 and Field 9 (see Table 14).

When these Lower Palaeolithic artefacts and burnt flints are 'plotted out' by the depth at which they were found within each trench (see Section 5) an interesting pattern emerges. There appear to be two, just possibly three 'levels' of archaeological occurrences: 0.01m to around 0.20m; 0.01 to around 0.32m; and at a very much lower level, around 0.40m to 0.64m.

The level/s at which artefacts and burnt flints were found in the trenches are as follows (see also Table 14):

- 1993 Square A: artefacts from 0.01m-0.23m (burnt flint at approximately 0.03m & 0.08m);
- 1993 Square B: artefacts from 0.01m to 0.18m; then from 0.56m to 0.64m;
- 1993 Square C: artefacts from 0.01m to 0.20m;
- 1994 Auger pit: artefacts at 0.20m; then from 0.45m to 0.46m;
- T2: artefact at 0.18m;
- T3: artefacts at 0.04m to 0.28m;
- T7: artefacts from 0.01m to 0.32m;
- T8: artefacts from 0.01m to 0.35m;
- T9: artefacts from 0.01m to 0.31m;
- T10: artefacts from 0.01m to 0.32m (burnt flint at 0.06m);
- T11: artefacts at 0.38m to 0.50m (burnt flint at 0.48m);
- T12: artefacts at 0.02m to 0.41m;
- T13: artefacts from 0.01m to 0.14m;
- T14: artefacts at 0.07m to 0.22m;
- T15: artefacts at 0.03m to 0.08m;
- T19: artefacts at 0.10m to 0.15m;
- T20: artefacts at 0.05m to 0.24m.

Model 2: The Lower Palaeolithic occupation of Wood Hill

By combining the results of this artefact analysis and the information obtained from the 1993 and 1994 detailed surveys of Wood Hill it has been possible to construct a diagram showing the relationship between the various trenches in the surveyed area and the levels at which the Lower Palaeolithic

artefacts were found within these trenches (see Figure 77).

In order to do this, the 1984/85 artefacts have been grouped into 5cm spits, to facilitate easier comparison with the 1993 and 1994 artefacts and to standardise the data. Given a tolerance of ±5cm the surface levels of the trenches in the surveyed area have been determined relative to the SW corner of the 1993 trench, which is also the 1994 survey point P8 (see Figure 77 and Sub-section 6.6). Outside the surveyed area, the relative position of the Lower Palaeolithic artefacts and trenches could be determined by simple comparison only, but with special reference to the depth of the Chalk. Included for comparison, are the trenches in Field 9 that did not contain artefacts, in addition to those which did (see Figure 78). Even if allowances are made for a tolerance greater than the ±5cm already 'built in', it is clear from the diagrams (Figures 77, 78) that Lower Palaeolithic artefacts occur at two distinct and consistent 'levels' (one high and one low) across both Field 2 and Field 9 of the Wood Hill site. The trenches can be classified thus:

1. Trenches with one 'high level' of artefact distribution within the range of 0.01m down to 0.35m (equivalent to spits 1 to 7) are: T2, T3, T7, T8, T9, T10, T13, T14, T15, T19. Burnt flint was found in T10 at a depth of 0.06m (spit 2) and dated as 380±26,000 yrs. B.P (this gives a possible range of 406,000–354,000 yrs B.P. see Sub-section 6.10)
2. Trenches with two 'levels' of artefact distribution, one high and one low, within the ranges of 0.01m down to 0.24m (equivalent to spits 1 to 5) and between 0.45m and 0.64m (equivalent to spits 9 to 13) are:
   - the 1993 trench (Square A = spits 1 to 5; Square B = spits 1 to 3 and 11 to 13; Square C = 1 to 4). Burnt flint was found in spits 1 and 2 of Square A but the samples were too small to date (see Sub-section 6.10);
   - the 1994 auger pit at 0.20m (spit 4) and at 0.45m and 0.46m (spits 9/10);
   - T20 at 0.05m to 0.24m (spits 1 to 5) and at 0.45m (spit 9).
3. Trench T11 situated in the Clay-with-flints 'basin' is of particular interest as here the artefacts are confined to the lower level only, at a depth of 0.38m to 0.50 (spits 8 to 10). Burnt flint was found in T11 at a depth of 0.48m (spit 10) and dated as 200,000±33,000 yrs. B.P. (this gives a possible range of 233,000–167,000 yrs. B.P. see Sub-section 6.10).
4. Classifying T12 is somewhat problematical as the artefacts are continuously distributed down through the trench to a depth of 0.41m (spit 9) (see Table 13 above and Figure 77. However, the artefacts in T12 may represent more than the one

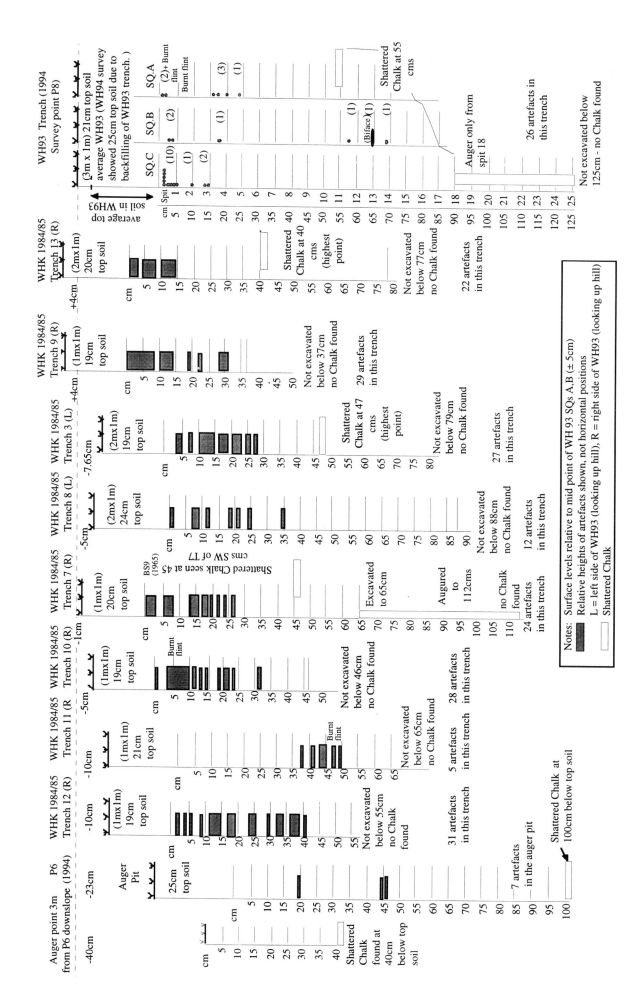

Figure 77 Showing relative heights of excavated artefacts in trenches in the 1994 surveyed area.

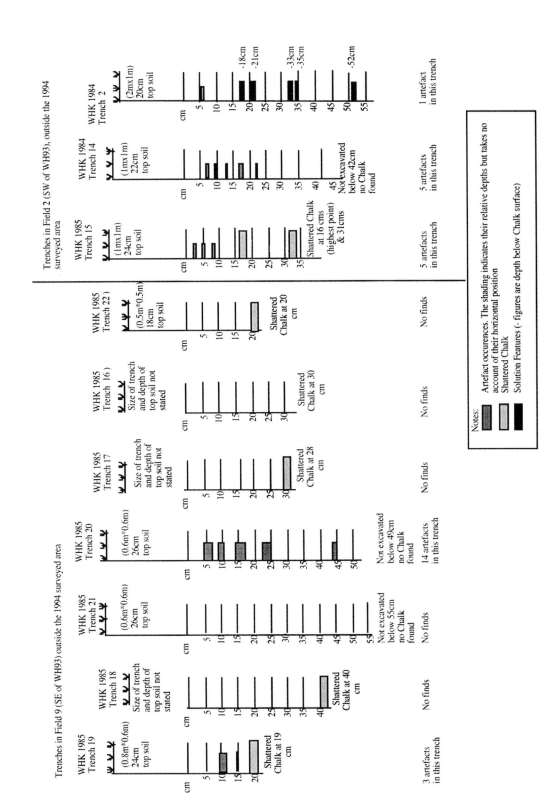

Figure 78 *Showing relative heights of excavated artefacts in trenches in Field 9 and Field 2 outside the 1994 surveyed area.*

level, as at 0.41m they 'overlap' the lower level of occurrences: a number of artefacts in T12 may therefore be regarded as being at the same level as certain artefacts in T11 (see Figure 77).

As the weight of evidence contained in this Wood Hill Case-study firmly supports the idea that the deposits mapped as Clay-with-flints in this specific area are indeed stratified, then the position which the Lower Palaeolithic artefacts held within the trenches and the significance of these positions can now be considered. Although no research is ever without its critics or dissenters, for no matter how objective the data is, opinions are invariably subjective, let us assume, for the sake of the argument, that the models proposed for the evolution of the Lower and Middle Palaeolithic at Wood Hill in this Sub-section are correct. This is not to say that these models are the only possible interpretations, but rather that they are the best of the options presented by the available data.

Using the Wood Hill geological and sedimentological data, the TL dates derived from the burnt flints and the available data on the Lower Palaeolithic artefacts recovered from trenches outside and within the Clay-with-flints 'basin'; a model for the Lower Palaeolithic occupation of Wood Hill can be constructed. To reiterate:

- 1993 Square A and most of Square B formed the 'backwall' of the Clay-with-flints 'basin' in this trench;
- All the artefacts in Square A came from the 'high level' (spits 1–5) with the two small pieces of undateable burnt flint coming from spits 1 and 2;
- Both the pieces of undateable burnt flint in Square A, align with the datable piece of burnt flint in T10, which was found at a depth of 0.06m (equivalent to spit 2);
- The T10 burnt flint is dated at 380,000±26,000 yrs. B.P;
- All the artefacts in T10 came from the 'high level' (spits 1–7). The nature of the deposits in T10 suggests that it too was outside the Clay-with-flints 'basin';
- All the T11 artefacts and one piece of burnt flint (dated at 200,000±33,000 yrs B.P.) came from a 'low level' (spit 8-10) silty-sandy deposit;
- The biface found in 1993 Square B also came from the 'low level' (spit 12), in a small area of silty/sandy deposits similar to the 1993 Square C 'infill' deposit WITHIN/ON THE EDGE OF the Clay-with-flints 'basin'. Two other artefacts were found at this low level in Square B, one in spit 11 and one in spit 13.

As we have seen, there are two distinct levels of Lower Palaeolithic artefacts found at Wood Hill. These levels, of course, could represent any number of occupation episodes or occurrences. It is thus perfectly reasonable that the older of the two pieces of burnt flint (380,000 ± 26,000 yrs. B.P) was found in the 'higher level' (0.06m) of Trench 10 in a trench situated OUTSIDE the Clay-with-flints 'basin', and that the younger piece of burnt flint (200,000 ± 33,000 yrs. B.P) was found at the 'low level' (0.48m) in Trench 11, since the latter appears to be situated WITHIN the Clay-with-flints 'basin'. Whether the Clay-with-flints 'basin' was in existence when the earlier group of Lower Palaeolithic people manufactured their stone tools and burnt the flint in the area occupied by T10, OUTSIDE the 'basin' cannot be known – if it was, perhaps it held water, an important resource on this high-level site. Whatever the reason, they seemed to have chosen not to work in the particular area of Wood Hill which we have designated as 1984/85 T11 and 1993 Square B. About 200,000 years later another Lower Palaeolithic group visited Wood Hill, but this time they burnt flint and manufactured stone tools WITHIN the 'basin like' depression in the ground. This Lower Palaeolithic site was then 'sealed in' by soil creep (and windblown materials). Subsequently, another Lower Palaeolithic manufacturing episode occurred this also was 'sealed in' (see Model 1.5; 1.6; 1.8 and Model 3 in this Sub-section).

Model 3: The distribution patterns of the Lower Palaeolithic artefacts on Wood Hill with reference to Models 1 and 2

Background to Model 3

From the information given in Section 5 and Sub-section 6.8, it is clear that Wood Hill was a Lower Palaeolithic working-site and that both Field 2 and Field 9 contained Lower Palaeolithic artefacts, principally knapping-waste, in a wide range of sizes. The 1984/85 excavations posed important questions, which were: do the Lower Palaeolithic artefacts on Wood Hill represent a single occurrence, i.e. a knapping area used by an unknown number of Palaeolithic people during one visit to the site, or do they represent a number of occurrences i.e. many visits to the site by one or several groups of people over a greater period of time? To some extent these questions have now been answered, as the TL dates for the burnt flint (see Sub-section 6.10) and other analysis have shown that Lower Palaeolithic peoples made (at least) three visits to Wood Hill, but what is not known at this stage of the research is whether Wood Hill was occupied at any time during the intervening period of 200,000 years.

The problems encountered when attempting to

separate 'background noise' from 'signals', both controlled by climatic change and geological processes, were previously discussed in Sub-section 6.2. Similar difficulties are involved when attempting to distinguish between the distribution patterns of Lower and Middle Palaeolithic artefacts produced as a result of the manufacturing process and any subsequent post-knapping disturbances resulting from bioturbation. The task of determining the patterns of artefact distribution on Wood Hill has been left to the final stages of this Case-study in order that all the relevant results of this research contained in both the Sections and Sub-sections could be later taken into consideration.

There are two alternative methods of analysing flake debris: individual and aggregate flake analysis (Ahler 1989). In this study the aggregate method was discounted as:

1. There is not, as yet, a complete recovered flake aggregate from the site, as only a limited number of trenches have been excavated.
2. The data set is further compromised, as data collection prior to 1993 was not aimed at aggregate analysis and therefore only flakes of approximately 10mm or above were collected.
3. The aggregate method cannot properly be used to analyse mixed samples – those where 'the archaeological sample reflects a mix of multiple, technologically discrete knapping episodes that occurred at the same location' (Ahler, 1989: 89). The Wood Hill assemblage has already been shown to reflect at least two episodes widely separated in time.

It was therefore decided to adopt the individual flake analysis method for this study.

To construct a complete 'reduction sequence' requires more information than is currently available at Wood Hill as many crucial areas remain to be excavated (see Figure 36 site plan). The term 'reduction sequence' which encompasses the many stages involved in the manufacture of stone tools from start to finish (as defined by Mellars, 1989: 241) is used here in preference to the French concept of 'chaîne opératoire' which has cultural implications in addition to a simple description of the stages of manufacture and is, therefore, at this stage of the investigations, inapplicable to a site such as Wood Hill (see Henry and Odell, 1989: 241). By considering each trench as an entity in itself and then as a sample of the whole, it has been possible to produce a 'limited' reduction sequence based on the types and sizes of the artefacts in the trenches and the depth at which they were found (as shown in the comprehensive descriptions of both artefacts and deposits in Model 2).

A reduction sequence

A flint nodule that is being shaped into a tool undergoes various stages of manufacture before the final product is achieved (a 'reduction sequence'). Each stage in the manufacture of the implement is marked by a change in either the shape and/or size of the flakes as they are removed from the nodule, the size of the nodule becoming progressively smaller until the desired shape has been reached.

– In **Stage 1** the 'roughing-out' hard hammer stage, the majority of the flakes would be relatively large, although some small flakes would also be present. Considerable amounts of cortex would be present on the dorsal surfaces.
– During **Stage 2** when hard and soft hammers are used, many of the resulting flakes may be relatively long and thin and are often curved in profile. Cortex amounts are much less, and some flakes may have none at all.
– In **Stage 3** the final shaping and finishing stage, small and very small, thin flakes are carefully removed with a soft hammer (knapping is discussed in more detail in Sub-section 6.8). Cortex would be very rare.

Lower and Middle Palaeolithic sites have been discovered where the evidence was in good order and complete enough for the reconstruction of reduction sequences. The knapping area at Boxgrove, Sussex, England (Roberts *et al.* 1995) is one example; another is the Maastricht – Belvedere site in The Netherlands (Roebroeks, 1988) and at the Late Palaeolithic site at Meer, Belgium. Larry Keeley (Van Noten *et al.* 1978; Cahen and Keeley, 1980) was even able to reconstruct the activities of two knappers, one left-handed. In theory, therefore, as the varying morphology of the knapping-waste reflects the predictable consecutive stages of stone-tool manufacture, it should be possible to use this to identify different stages and areas of stone-tool manufacture across the Lower Palaeolithic site of Wood Hill, albeit with the provisos previously discussed.

The flint nodules from which the Wood Hill artefacts were manufactured appear to have been obtained by the Lower Palaeolithic people from the nearby weathered and eroding Chalk hillsides. Selected flint nodules were then carried by these people to the hilltop plateau to be used for the manufacture of stone tools (see Sub-section 6.7). Having acquired a suitable nodule, the Lower Palaeolithic flint-knappers on Wood Hill set to work, this much we can be sure of. What is not so obvious is how much they may have moved around the hill in the course of manufacturing one implement or, indeed whether they always started in one place. Did they for example, 'rough-out' the implement in one place and then move to another area to complete the final stages of manufacture, or did they execute all the stages of manufacture in the same place? Many waste flakes are produced by one knapper making one single handaxe, as was shown by Newcomer's (1971) experiment in which he records the following by-products in the course of making 1 handaxe:

–   numbered major flakes 51;
–   unnumbered material dry sieved through a 1mm sieve gave 8.4 g of flint and cortex 'dust' and minute chips [flakes]
–   unnumbered chips that would not pass through the 1mm sieve gave a total of 4,618.

If a Lower Palaeolithic knapper, in the course of manufacturing a handaxe, worked in one place only, then the waste-flakes within that area would exhibit a wide range of types and sizes – from the largest to the smallest. If this was not the case, then the size and type of the flakes in any part of the site should, as we have seen, indicate the stage of manufacture that took place there. There is however, a problem with this theory, if it is applied without due caution to the Wood Hill data. Throughout all the stages of manufacture, as the knapper strikes the nodule, flakes fly out, and more often than not the larger and

heavy flakes fall to the ground around the knapper's feet, but the smaller flakes can radiate outwards a great deal further. If viewed as a whole, the 'epicentre' of the activity is identifiable; however, if the view is fragmented, as it is at Wood Hill, it becomes impossible to determine the boundaries and the epicentres with confidence. The problem is compounded if two (or more) knapping areas may lie within reasonable proximity to each other. One periphery combined with another periphery could give a distorted reduction sequence as shown in Figure 79).

In this hypothetical example, two separate knapping episodes have taken place close together. In each case, the knapper has remained in the same spot to complete the full manufacturing process. For purposes of the diagram, the waste flakes are shown with different sizes, which correspond to stages 1, 2 and 3 of the reduction sequence. However, the smaller flakes have combined at the boundaries. If a small trench was dug on this boundary it might be concluded erroneously that this was a single stage 3 and/or 2 manufacturing area only. Conversely, small (stage 2 and 3) material 'invading' a stage 1 only area would also have the potential to distort the reduction sequence, if the whole area were not uncovered.

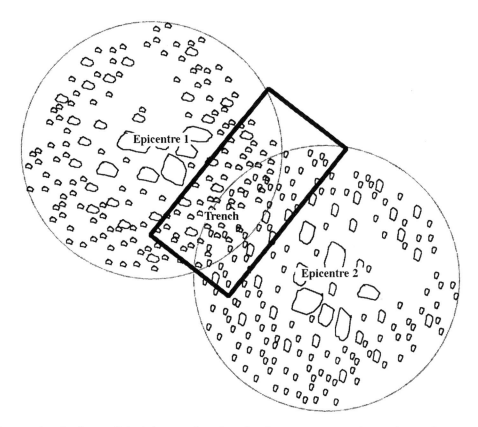

Figure 79 *Diagram showing how a distorted perception of a reduction sequence, seeming to show only a stage 2/3 epicentre, can be produced in a trench if it is cut through the periphery of two overlapping knapping episodes actually containing manufacturing stages 1, 2 and 3.*

Also to be considered is a distribution pattern described by Isaac (1989: 216) as 'scatter between the patches'. In this situation, a hill top might have accommodated many 'epicentres', with surrounding scatters of artefacts and waste, but it is unlikely that the areas between them were completely devoid of artefacts. Trenches dug in such places would produce little or perhaps no evidence of Palaeolithic occupation.

In this attempt to interpret the activities of the Lower Palaeolithic peoples, the concentration has so far, centred exclusively on the evidence of tool manufacturing on Wood Hill. However, burnt flint was also found on the site. This adds an additional dimension to the reduction sequence – why were pieces of burnt flint present? This, and correlations such as burnt flint equates with hearths; fires needed fuel and flint knappers required food and drink; are addressed in the latter part of this Sub-section.

Earlier (in this Sub-section), it was noted that most of the Wood Hill artefacts appear to be concentrated in two distinct and widely separated levels within the trenches, one high level and one low level (see Figures 77, 78). Artefacts were found at both the high and low levels in WH 1993, WH 1994 and T20, whereas in T11 artefacts were found only at the low level. In all the other trenches, artefacts were found only at the high level. A summary of these results is set out in Table 15 below:

A combination of the aforementioned data with the artefact distribution plan (Figure 36) and the diagram showing the distribution of the artefacts within the trenches (Figure 35) reveals the following points:

Trenches situated away from the 1993/1994 surveyed area:

– The T14 assemblage, found at the high level, correlates to manufacturing stages 2 and 3.
– In T15, artefacts were also found at the high level and correlate to manufacturing stage 1.
– In T19, artefacts were found at the high level and correlate to manufacturing stage 2.
– Artefacts in T20 were found mostly in the high level but one was found at the low level (at a depth of 0.49m the excavation of this trench stopped). The high level assemblage correlates to manufacturing stages 1, 2 and 3.

Trenches situated within the 1993/94 surveyed area, but OUTSIDE the Clay-with-flints 'basin'

WH 1993. (square A and most of square B) plus T3, T7, T9, T10, T12 and T13. Interestingly, all the artefacts in these trenches were found in the high level (but see description of square B below), and all have assemblages that correlate to manufacturing stages 1, 2 and 3. T10 produced the burnt flint which gave a TL date of 380,000±26,000 yrs. B.P.

Trenches situated INSIDE the Clay-with-flints 'basin'

A very small part of WH 1993 square B (adjacent to square C) was in situated in the 'basin'. Artefacts from square B were found at both the high level (see

Table 15. Manufacturing stages in each trench (H = high level, L = low level).

Trench no	Stages					
	1,2 & 3	1 & 2	2 & 3	1 only	2 only	Finished implements
T2 insuff.data						
T3	H					
T7	H					
T8		H				
T9	H					
T10	H					
T11				L		
T12	H					
T13	H					
T14			H			
T15				H		
T19					H	
T20	H				L?	
WH 1993 A	H					
WH 1993 B	L				H	SQ. B12
WH 1993 C	H					
WH 1994		H&L				

above) and the low level. This low level assemblage correlates with manufacturing stages 2, 3 (and stage 4 if the finished implement – the plano-convex biface – is considered as a stage and if some of the waste belongs to it, indicating it was made here (see earlier note in this Sub-section). The WH 1993 square C artefacts all came from the high level and correlated to manufacturing stages 1, 2 and 3. Other trenches within the basin were: T8, where the artefacts were found at the high level and the assemblage correlates to manufacturing stages 1 and 2; and T11, where all the artefacts came from the low level and correlated to manufacturing stage 1.

WH 1994 artefacts from the auger pit were also found in two distinct levels, some distance apart vertically, and appear at this stage of the research to correlate to manufacturing stages 1 and 2 only, but this may change at a later date when the small amount of sediments held in 'light-fast' bags becomes available for sieving.

Although no direct link can be made between WH 1993 and T11 (two trenches positioned close together) there are, nevertheless, several interesting facts to be reconsidered. T11, as we have seen, contained (at a low level) manufacturing stage 1 artefacts, and burnt flint which gave a TL date of 200,000 ± 33,000 yrs. B.P (see Sub-section 6.10.). Conversely WH 1993 square B (at low-level, spits 11–13) produced a small number of artefacts which correlate to manufacturing stages 2 and 3 and a plano-convex biface. This plano-convex biface could be ascribed to the Late Acheulian/ Micoquian; it could also be accommodated in the time period suggested by the Trench 11, burnt flint TL dates. However, it could also be substantially older (see discussion in Sub-section 6.9).

Conclusion

Without going into the realms of speculation, there is little more that can be said at this stage of the research regarding the reduction sequence on Wood Hill for, as we have seen, with the exception of the plano-convex biface (WH93.F38), there is a general absence in the excavated material of diagnostic stone implements but there are a great many waste-flakes. The 1984/85 excavators were restricted in the size of the artefacts they could retrieve; the smallest of the flakes measured around 0.10m.

Although the few attempts by the Dover Archaeological Group to conjoin the 1984/85 material proved unsuccessful, an exciting development has occurred, at the time of going to press (late 1999) Vicky Winton, a D.Phil. research student at the Unit for the study of Palaeolithic artefacts and deposits mapped as Clay-with-flints (PADMAC), University

of Oxford, has just started a technical analysis of the Wood Hill 1984/85 artefacts and has already successfully conjoined a number of flakes from one trench.

The method of excavation employed in 1993, and the subsequent investigations of the sediments taken from this trench, resulted in the recovery of the smallest flakes (down to around 1mm). In addition, humanly struck, conjoinable flakes were found in square C (see Sub-section 6.8). The importance of an archaeological site is determined by a number of 'measurable' factors:, these results, when considered together, categorise the site. As set out in Sub-section 6.8, the factors which define an *in situ* Palaeolithic site are as follows:

1. The 'sliding scale' of importance which is based on the type, number, size and condition of artefacts found on that site, the integrity of a site increases if recovered flakes, which were struck in antiquity by Palaeolithic people can be refitted (conjoined) together again. Such a situation suggests lack of disturbance, while evidence of movement or gross disturbance of artefacts within a deposit is regarded as an undesirable devaluing factor for both the artefacts and the site as a whole.

2. The need to assess with caution, all artefacts exhibiting features such as abrasion and edge damage for, while this damage may be the result of much movement, it may also be the result of either small movements of the artefact within the deposit, or conversely small movement of particular components of the deposits around the artefacts. Such movement may be indicative of local freeze/thaw processes rather than evidence of movement of the artefacts over a substantial distance.

3. The type and number of artefacts/finds recovered from a site should represent adequately the nature of the site. Therefore, an *in situ* working site assemblage should consist of a wide range of waste flakes from the smallest to the largest.

When aligning the Wood Hill assemblage against the criteria for an *in situ* Palaeolithic site based on the archaeological evidence, it is clear from the information set out in this, and the previous Sub-sections, that the site does indeed meet the stated requirement as the following summary shows:

Waste flakes were found in a wide range of sizes from the smallest (around 0.01m) to large primary flakes, thinning flakes and trimming flakes. A completed plano-convex biface in fresh condition was also found in WH 1993 square B. All the artefacts exhibit little evidence of abrasion. To date, two conjoinable, humanly struck flakes, were found in

WH 1993 square C. and two conjoinable, humanly struck flakes were also found in the 1994 auger pit and as noted above, conjoinable flakes have also be found in the 1984/85 assemblage.

As the Lower Palaeolithic *in situ* site at Wood Hill is one of the rare 'embedded' Clay-with-flints occurrences, it is useful briefly to compare this East Kent site with the other 'embedded' sites/finds, details of which were given in Sections 4, namely:

- The sites discovered in the middle of the 19th century by W.G. Smith on the borders of Bedfordshire/ Hertfordshire near Dunstable and Luton, notably at Caddington, Whipsnade, Gaddesden Row, Slip End, Round Green and Mixieshill pit and Ramridge End; – The 'embedded' finds at Lower Kingswood, Banstead, Surrey reported by L.W. Carpenter (1966) and Walls and Cotton (1980); – The finds from Folkington Hill, above Wannock, Sussex, reported by A.E. Todd (1932– 34).
- The site discovered on Hackpen Hill, Wiltshire, by the Reverend H.G.O Kendall (1916).

These important embedded sites represent a small proportion of the total of Palaeolithic find spots/sites on the deposits mapped as Clay-with-flints in southern England. However, before a comparison of these embedded sites can be made, two questions must be considered,

- do the find spots/sites represent Palaeolithic sites of all types – randomly scattered across the land? or,
- is it a non-random distribution pattern reflecting the seasonal hunting patterns of these Palaeolithic people?

Ethnographic examples – a glimpse into a Palaeolithic world

Definitive answers cannot of course be given at this stage of the research, nevertheless the following modern ethnographic example of the Nunamiut of Alaska (Binford, 1978) may provide us with a glimpse of the Palaeolithic world. The Nunamiut use a classic intercept strategy to hunt migrating caribou. This strategy results in three types of site: observation and hunting sites; butchering areas and consumption/resting areas. The observation and hunting sites contained much manufacturing debris as the hunters used the time waiting for the herds to make tools and other artefacts, also small hearths were often kindled in these sites (*op. cit.* 1978: 172). Binford (*ibid.*) reported that for monitoring and encounter hunting phase of strategy there are basically two types of sites:

- overnight camps and stopping places, and
- kill sites frequently associated with hearths and some refuse from food consumption.

The overnight camp locations are in places that offered optimal conditions for providing for the hunters comfort and needs and are a day's journey apart along a commonly used route through the mountains. The same locations may be used repeatedly during different seasons and for different purposes. Such locations are almost always

- in or near a good stand of willows for firewood,
- near a source of reliable water in summer and ice or overflow spring water in winter, and
- afford protection to some degree from high winds.

As these criteria are also used in the selection of locations for winter and summer residential camps, the hunting camps are frequently located at the site of the residential camps. Abandoned camps offer additional incentives to their subsequent use as stopping and camping places. First, there are frequently usable shelters, particularly in an abandoned winter camp. Second caches are commonly made at such locations so that emergency tool needs may be met there and other raw materials of use scavenged from such a location. Third, there are almost always usable facilities, racks for storage and for drying equipment, hearths, and well-dried firewood in the deteriorating structures. The best locations combine the preceding features with

- access to a prominent overlook from which a large area may be scanned for game, and
- a 'change of pace' factor such as a change of grade as at the top of a pass, or a marked change in slope such that walking or sledding increases or decreases with ease or a river crossing where the gear must be unloaded and reloaded after crossing (*op. cit.* 1978: 169–170).

Foley (1987: 185) proposed that the butchering and consumption areas would be necessary in order to share food, and that sharing which would not have been necessary in a purely gathering context. Also, an efficient method of exploiting carcasses would be to set up caches of stone tools to which the carcass would be transported for butchering. This model he suggests, uses less energy than taking the tools to the carcasses and is supported by the accumulations of stone and bone found at Plio-Pleistocene archaeological sites and is also observed in chimpanzees in West Africa (*ibid.*). The increase in density of artefact material and proximity of bones in anatomically human sites suggests that there may have been a shift from the scattered caches of earlier species to the use of a single central place where all activities except food procurement took place (*op. cit.*: 187).

Patterns of mobility could perhaps be extrapolated from stone tool assemblages if it were possible to identify differences due, for example, to seasonal hunting patterns. In the case of the Nunamiut, for example, Binford (1978: 483) observes that seasonal differences in food sources in summer and in winter caused differences in the types of tools in the assemblages and their size. Thus, if an assemblage was found to contain all the types of tools then it was used all year round whereas, if it only contained one type then it was used only seasonally. Similarly, where the assemblage gradually changed over time, then the presence of a variety of different examples might suggest a long-term occupation or a regularly used site. It is clear from these examples that there are particular features which marked out specific sites. A number of these same features are paralleled in the embedded hilltop/plateaux sites on the deposits mapped as Clay-with-flints – these sites are considered next.

Features that unify the Palaeolithic sites on deposits mapped as Clay-with-flints

The hilltops and plateaux edges of the Downlands were important to Palaeolithic people. From these high places they could (safely?) watch the movements of animals on both the hillsides and in the valleys below. They could also manufacture stone tools from the readily available flint or stone of a knappable quality. High-level vantage points and knappable flint or stone is a consistent, unifying feature of all the high-level occurrences on the deposits mapped as Clay-with-flints. The ease with which knappable flint and stone could be procured was no doubt a factor which also determined the precise position of the working area/s.

The presence of handaxe trimming flakes is quite frequent at these high-level sites, suggesting implement manufacture from immediately available flint: piles of raw material and many conjoinable flakes were found at Caddington (Smith, 1894). Wood Hill also provides good evidence for handaxe manufacture as very large nodules obtained from the Chalk slopes were found with the artefacts, and conjoinable flakes were also present.

The Wood Hill excavations produced four pieces of burnt flint, two of which were datable. The discovery of burnt flint, often referred to as fire crackled flint in the many of the early reports, was not confined to Wood Hill. It was also found at Lower Kingswood and Hackpen Hill, but W.G. Smith makes no mention of burnt flint being found at the sites near Dunstable and Luton. As Smith meticulously recorded and commented on what he

saw, this is indeed puzzling; Prof. D. Roe suggests (pers. comm.) that had Smith encountered burnt flint, he would have noticed it, and talked about 'the hearths and cooking places of the savages'. However, this material may have had little significance for Smith and was therefore not acknowledged, as it is only comparatively recently that the technique of thermoluminescence dating has been developed and successfully used to date burnt flint. It is also interesting to note that, to date, burnt flint has not been found at Boxgrove, although charcoal has been identified (M. Roberts pers. comm.).

All the available evidence suggests that Wood Hill, Lower Kingswood and Hackpen Hill (the evidence from Folkington Hill is somewhat inconclusive) were essentially manufacturing sites. These sites overlook deep valleys; they contain much manufacturing debris in the form of waste flakes and also burnt flint, which is usually associated with hearths. These sites exhibit features which are reminiscent of the hunting/observation sites studied by Binford (1978) which he described as 'strategically placed hunting and observation sites that contained much manufacturing debris, as the men used the time waiting for the herds to manufacture tools and other artefacts, small hearths were also kindled at these sites' (*op. cit.*: 172). Similarities such as these may be no more than a coincidence and the blurring of facts over time, however, they may also be close to the truth. The embedded high-level sites, which to date I have simply classified as manufacturing sites, may indeed be the Palaeolithic equivalent of the Nunamiut's hunting/observation sites.

Different types of Palaeolithic encampments may, or may not, be reflected in the artefact assemblages. For example, the type of artefacts recovered from a butchery site may differ from a manufacturing site; however, at the Lower Palaeolithic coastal site at Boxgrove, Sussex, (Roberts *et al.* 1995) both manufacturing and butchery took place in close proximity. Defining the status and character of the Boxgrove site was dependent on a number of factors, which include the type, number and condition of the artefacts, along with other evidence such as cut marks on the bones of the associated fauna, and microwear analysis of the stone tools. Much of this evidence is (as yet) unavailable for the high-level sites.

Palaeolithic peoples had one need above and beyond stone tools, and even food, namely fresh water. It is this resource which may determines the differences between these sites. As previously noted in Section 4, the sites discovered by Smith were situated on a high plateau. During the Lower Palaeolithic period, a lake, swamp, bogs, or a series of ponds existed in this particular area and it was around these water sources that the Lower Palaeolithic people lived (Smith 1894:64). This plateau is now dissected by deep valleys. Due to the decalcified nature of much of the deposits mapped as Clay-with-flints, there is no evidence available to suggest that Palaeolithic peoples actually lived, as opposed to making implements, on the top of Wood Hill, Lower Kingswood, Folkington Hill or Hackpen Hill, but equally there is no evidence to the contrary. The source of fresh water in these areas may then have been the valley streams. Any evidence of Lower and Middle Palaeolithic camps sited at the foot or sides of these hills would probably by now have been swept away or buried under colluvium (Coombe Rock).

A feature of the Chalk Downlands capped with deposits mapped as Clay-with-flints is the solution features (and tree-throw hollows, see Sub-section 6.3). Lower Palaeolithic artefacts were recovered from solution hollows, not only at Wood Hill, but also at Hackpen Hill and the sites around Dunstable and Luton (see Section 4 and Sub-sections 6.6 and 6.8). Many of the solution hollows are/were filled with 'Brickearth', notably as far as this study is concerned, the sites around Dunstable and Luton, and Hackpen Hill. Interestingly, there are reports that in these examples, following the removal of the brickearth for commercial brick-making, ponds formed in the hollows (see Section 4). For ponds to form in hollows on the plateaux and hilltops of the Chalk Downlands, the Clay-with-flints lining the hollow must be very deep or the Chalk saturated or else the water will readily drain away. If small ponds were a general feature of the hilltops and plateaux in Palaeolithic times, a wider range of activities may have been undertaken on these high levels than the assemblages suggest: home bases in addition to working and/or butchery sites may be represented in some assemblages; Hackpen Hill is one such possibility (see Section 4).

The importance of solution features in preserving *in situ* the Lower Palaeolithic site on Wood Hill has been adequately demonstrated in this Case study. As archaeological material is clearly retained within these features, it may be possible, here and elsewhere with the use of specialist on-site technology, to search them for the chemical signatures associated with organic phosphates and carbons in an attempt to identify traces of hearths, bones and ponds, thereby adding another dimension to the study of Palaeolithic artefacts found in relation to deposits mapped as Clay-with-flints.

General Conclusion. Lower and Middle Palaeolithic artefacts found in relation to deposits mapped as Clay-with-flints on the Chalk Downlands of southern England

It may be remembered that, in addition to the problems generated by the Harrisonian 'eolith' debate that took place around the turn of the century and which centered on the positive identification of humanly struck artefacts, the main objections to the inclusion of high-level artefacts into British Palaeolithic archaeological record were based on a general misunderstanding of the effects of climate change over geological time both on the deposits mapped as Clay-with-flints and the Chalk Downlands.

In this the final Section, the point has now been reached where a re-assessment of the results of this research can be made in the context of both the variety of reasons that have been given – or sometimes not given – over the years for this exclusion of artefacts from the deposits mapped as Clay-with-flints from the British Palaeolithic archaeological record, and the research aims as set out in the 'Questions' and 'Hypotheses' in the General Introduction.

For the sake of clarity in the summaries which follow, a statement and answer format has been adopted i.e. after the reiteration of each main objection, pertinent question or hypothesis, the results and conclusions of that specific area of research is immediately addressed.

The inclusion of artefacts from deposits mapped as Clay-with-flints into the British Palaeolithic archaeological record

1. Original objection: 'None of the assemblages, however apparently discrete, can be considered in any way to be *in situ*'.

Results of research: The combined results of the investigations undertaken as part of the Case-study of the Lower Palaeolithic site at Wood Hill have shown that the 1993 assemblage is indeed *in situ*, thereby negating this long held view (see Sub-sections 6.1 to 6.11).

2. Original objection: 'It is impossible to date this material either by relative or absolute dating methods'.

Results of research: The successful TL dating of the burnt flint which was found in association with the Lower Palaeolithic artefacts effectively dismisses this objection (see Sub-section 6.10).

3. Original objection: 'Processes operating in cold and temperate environments have effectively removed any useful stratigraphic or environmental evidence that might once have existed'.

Results of research: The presence of measurable/observable stratigraphy in the Wood Hill 1993 trench and observable stratigraphy in the 1984/85 and 1994 excavation trenches refutes this opinion (see Sub-sections 6.2, 6.3, 6.11).

The Case-study – which was designed to answer a number of questions and test particular hypotheses

Of the three questions which were set out in the General Introduction, (see also Section 5), two have been addressed by the Case-study:

Questions:
(a) 'How could Palaeolithic artefacts have become incorporated into, or remained on the surface of the deposits mapped as Clay-with-flints over tens of thousands of years, during both glacial and temperate periods?'

(b) 'What has happened to the sediments since the artefacts were deposited?'

Results of research: The results of the Wood Hill Case-study show that Palaeolithic artefacts are retained in solution features and effectively 'sealed in' by agents such as soil creep, windblown material and (perhaps to a much lesser degree) worm activity (see Sub-section 6.11).

(c) The third question 'is there a correlation between particular facies of deposits mapped as Clay with-flints and the occurrence of Lower and Middle Palaeolithic artefacts on/in these deposits in southern England?' – is very important and demands an answer but that unfortunately requires more time and funding than were available at this stage of the research.

Hypotheses

In addition to the questions, the three hypotheses listed below were postulated. The original intention was to address only hypothesis 1 in the initial research; however, certain data derived from the investigations also proved applicable to hypotheses 2 and 3. But both hypotheses 2 and 3 could still provide future case-studies for archaeologists and other Quaternary researchers.

Hypothesis 1: 'Given the state of restricted change of the deposits mapped as Clay-with-flints which cap the Chalk Downland hilltops and plateaux, more or less *in situ* Palaeolithic sites should exist on some of these high-levels.

Results of research: Hypothesis 1 is directly supported by the Wood Hill Case-study (see Sub-section 6.11), and I also commented on the extent to which material was *in situ* at some of the previously known embedded sites (see Section 4)

Hypothesis 2: 'Some current models which are used to explain patterns and levels of erosion and deposition on the hilltops/plateaux mapped as Clay-with-flints may require substantial adjustment'.

Results of research: Hypothesis 2 is certainly supported by the Wood Hill Case-study (see Sub-sections 6.2, 6.3 and 6.11), most notably in the results of the various excavations described in Section 4.

Hypothesis 3: 'There are a number of factors that should indicate whether any given hilltop and plateau capped with deposits mapped as Clay-with-flints would warrant detailed archaeological survey or excavation. Some of these features are the presence or absence of stone artefacts on these high-levels; the shape and location of these high-levels, as a feature of both the ancient and modern general topography of the immediate area; the geographical relationship between the various hill-tops and plateaux capped with deposits mapped as Clay-with-flints that have produced surface finds of stone artefacts within a specific area; the pattern and distribution of these high-level surface-finds relative to the local distribution of the Palaeolithic finds at lower levels; and the proximity in Palaeolithic times of essential resources such as good quality flint and/or fresh water'.

Results of research: A combination of two different areas of investigation undertaken as part of this study, has produced important data directly related to Hypothesis 3. These data indicate that 'frost shattered Chalk' and 'asymmetric valley side slopes' can provide standard 'Bench-marks,' against which levels of change/erosion of the Chalk on any specific downland hill-top/plateau can be measured, and hence it can be shown how much, or how little, the deposits mapped as Clay-with-flints and any Lower and Middle Palaeolithic artefacts in these areas would have been affected (Figure 8). These are crucial considerations from the point of view of the archaeologist in search of Palaeolithic artefacts on the hilltop areas of deposits mapped as Clay-with-flints, hoping that they have been relatively unaffected by surrounding hill-slope processes. The use of geological and geomorphological data to solve archaeological problems is not new. What is new, however, is this use of frost shattered Chalk and valley side slope asymmetry as 'Bench marks' for use in an area where there is no existing framework for Palaeolithic archaeological investigations (see Explanatory Section 1).

The results of these investigations must not be regarded as having yet provided the definitive answer, but they do provide a useful 'tool', which enables practical decisions to be made in the field based on good scientific data. With its valley side slope asymmetry, frost shattered Chalk and Lower Palaeolithic artefacts as surface and embedded finds and presence of high quality flint nodules from the Upper Chalk, the Case-study site of Wood Hill provided an ideal area for the 'bench mark's pilot study.

All Palaeolithic artefacts found on or in the deposits mapped as Clay-with-flints are important, be it a fine handaxe of a small worn waste flake, as each artefact reflects an action of a Palaeolithic person and a geological process or processes at, and subsequent to, a certain point in time. For the closer an artefact is found to its original place of deposition, the greater the amount of information it is likely to reveal about its Palaeolithic manufacturers, whereas an artefact moved from its original position of deposition may act as a 'marker' and provide clues to the process or processes that have affected that area/site over geological time. Viewed in this way, even the most worn and damaged artefacts can take on a value, not usually accorded them.

Future research – recommendations and cautions

The use of the scientific methods described in this study have established Wood Hill as an *in situ* Lower

Palaeolithic site, situated at a high level on deposits mapped as Clay-with-flints, and have fully justified its inclusion in the British Lower and Middle Palaeolithic archaeological record.

Clearly, there is a great need for further research on both the deposits mapped as Clay-with-flints and also on the associated Palaeolithic artefacts, therefore,

- I do not believe that any future studies of Palaeolithic artefacts found in relation to deposits mapped as Clay-with-flints should proceed in isolation without parallel investigations of the deposits themselves and the associated Chalk. This is essential as both the existence of the deposits and the presence of the artefacts on the Downland high-levels are inextricably linked. To attempt to study the artefacts in isolation would compromise the integrity of the assemblages and leave the sites open once again to criticisms similar to those associated with the Harrisonian 'eolith' debate.

- If further *in situ* sites are to be found on the deposits mapped as Clay-with-flints, and the integrity of these high-level sites maintained, then the level of detail and range of investigations employed at each site *must be at least equal* to those which I employed in the Wood Hill 1993 and 1994 excavations and investigations.

Given the great variability of the deposits mapped as Clay-with-flints and the distribution patterns of Palaeolithic artefacts across the Downlands, there is a need for a structured, overall plan for the investigation and excavation of these Palaeolithic sites – rather than the uncoordinated excavation of perhaps interesting-looking but randomly situated areas. With the use of both the Gazetteer and 'Bench marks' as guides, future investigations would ideally be widely distributed over the Chalk Downlands (as opposed to exclusively targeting a few areas), with each site forming a coherent link in what would eventually become a grid-like system of investigation.

Some recommendations for future research in north-western France

Although, the expressed aim of this research was to focus attention on a much neglected area of the British Palaeolithic, namely Lower and Middle Palaeolithic artefacts found in relation to deposits mapped as Clay-with-flints, there is value in suggesting that results of this research would also be directly applicable to other areas, notably the Paris Basin area in northwestern France. Here, as in southern England, deposits of a very similar nature

to those mapped as Clay-with-flints (Argile 'a Silex) cap the Chalk hills and plateaux.

Recent discoveries during excavations in advance of construction work for the A28 and A29 motorways in Haute-Normandie (see Delagnes and Ropars, 1996), revealed two open air sites from the Middle Palaeolithic: one at Pucheuil, Saint-Saëns (Seine-Maritime), conserved in an Upper Chalk doline in a Argile à Silex area on the very edge of the Caux plateau, and the other at Etoutteville (Seine-Maritime), also located at the edge of a karstic depression. The French excavators (*ibid.*) record that the context of these finds was hitherto unknown, that the potential of such locations was largely underestimated and that these finds bring new data to our knowledge of ancient prehistory at a regional level as well as in the larger framework of north-west Europe. Their comments are particularly interesting in the light of the stated aims of this research, as the Palaeolithic record of continental northwestern Europe is, according to Tuffreau and Antoine (1995: 147):

'characterised by sites in a loess- and fluvial deposits context, usually preserved in the form of loess covered river terraces'.

Clearly, what is now needed is a Gazetteer of Lower and Middle Palaeolithic artefacts found in relation to the deposits mapped as Argile 'a Silex in north-west France – comparable to the one I have compiled for southern England. Also required, as in southern England, are further investigations and excavations using the guidelines and methodology expounded in this study.

An international problem – seeing the landscape as a whole, the relationship between high and low level sites

An important aspect highlighted by this research, which is applicable to all Palaeolithic sites world wide, but is so often marginalised, is the relationship between the high and low level sites in any one area. All sites are important, whether they are situated at a high or low level. Naturally, those sites which provide the best examples of Palaeolithic industries and/or contain other notable finds will command the greatest attention, however, it is essential that the Palaeolithic landscape is considered as a whole, or the local/national archaeological record will be distorted. This is particularly important where there is much variation in the deposits, both within and between areas, substantial variation can occur even within small areas. Furthermore, as this research has shown, the problem is amplified if the local deposits are not well understood.

One of the best examples (and earliest) of the complex interaction of hominid groups between high and low level sites over a wide area and on very different deposits, is that provided by the sites at East Turkana, Kenya in East Africa. The following site details are taken from the Koobi Fora, Research Project Report Vol. 5 (Isaac 1997).

> 'The well-dispersed distribution of findspots clearly implies much human movement across the landscape, but we certainly do not have all of the scatter between patches, which might help us to understand how the principal places related to each other from the point of view of those who frequented them. It may also be that the sets of patches we have is itself biased in some way' (*ibid.*).

The East Turkana region is described in the report as a mosaic of local environmental situations. Many of the sites in East Turkana are related to stream courses, the position of the stream channel giving rise to variability in the archaeological evidence. The gravels in the sites situated further away from the volcanic highlands and nearer to the lake do not contain rock clasts of a workable size. It appears therefore, that at sites such as FxJj 1, 3 and 10, and FwJj 1, the knappable rock could only have been brought in from several kilometres away, in the form of cobbles and clasts to be flaked on the site. Alternatively,

> 'it could also have come in the form of ready made artefacts or roughouts, requiring only minor subsequent reshaping or resharpening when blunted in use' (*ibid.*).

From the archaeological evidence, its seems that both modes occurred and that in addition, the hominids took at least some of the stone artefacts away with them when they vacated these lake side sites. At site GaJj 5 (in particular) all the artefacts were taken away leaving only cut-marked bones. Such evidence suggests a purposeful, planned expedition to process meat-bearing bones. Moving away from the low level sites around the lake and upwards to the basin rim -

> 'the further one goes, the easier it is to obtain rock in larger units; but the sites are harder to find, under a heavy superficial mantle, and more liable to have suffered disturbance in this higher-energy environment' (*ibid.*).

Well away from the lake, in an area with suitable large clasts for knapping, were the youngest of the three Acheulian-related sites. Although their state of survival precluded the recovery of much behavioural information, other than that related to knap-

ping, the archaeological evidence suggested that these sites were specialised places for making tool blanks (the 'mega-cores' at FxJj 33) and where the secondary stages of large bifacial tool manufacture took place (*ibid.*).

It could be argued that the question of lithic procurement at any one site might be sufficient to expand the Palaeolithic archaeologist's awareness of the landscape to a wider area than the site itself. However, the key issue here is not just a question of determining the source of knapping material (important as this is), but the fundamental appreciation of the equal importance of the sites in a specific area, whether situated at high or low levels. For, as we have seen in the foregoing East Turkana example, sites may be interrelated with a variety of activities being undertaken at the different sites, e.g. roughing out at one site; finishing the tools at another; butchery at another. Provided we see Palaeolithic people as hunter/scavenger/gatherers, then we must consider the landscape as a whole and in consequence accept that no one site, in any one area, is likely hold all the clues to the activities of a particular group, or groups, of Palaeolithic people.

Conclusion

If the importance of considering the entire archaeological evidence in any one area/region is clearly demonstrated by the complex interrelationships found in such early occupations in East Turkana, dated around 1.5 million years ago, then the importance of this approach in later contexts, for example, the Continental European Lower Palaeolithic, from around 800,000 years B.P. and the British Lower Palaeolithic, from around 500,000 years B.P., is difficult to deny.

In summary, the results of this research have shown the importance of the Lower and Middle Palaeolithic artefacts found in relation to deposits mapped as Clay-with-flints on the Chalk Downlands of southern England, (similar factors will apply elsewhere as I have indicated in these closing pages) and has demonstrated the value of a new methodological approach to these sites. If future investigations and excavations were to proceed in a controlled manner, then a comprehensive picture of the relationship between the Palaeolithic artefacts, the different types of deposits mapped as Clay-with-flints, and the Chalk downlands of southern England would start to take shape and add greatly to our knowledge of the Lower and Middle Palaeolithic periods in Britain, and indeed in north-west Europe as a whole.

Bibliography

Ahler, S.A. (1989). Mass analysis of flaking debris: studying the forest rather than the tree. In: D.O. Henry and G.H. Odell (eds), Alternative approaches to lithic analysis, *Archeological Papers of the American Anthropological Association, 1.*

Aitken, M.J. (1985). *Thermoluminescence Dating*, Academic Press Inc, London.

Anderson, K.E. and Furley, P.A., (1975) An assessment of the relationship between the surface properties of chalk soils and slope using principle component analysis, *Journal of Soil Sciences.* 26, 130–143

Ashton, N.M., Cook, J., Lewis, S. G. and Rose, J. (1992). *High Lodge – Excavations by G, de G. Sieveking 1962–1968 and J. Cook 1988*, British Museum Press, London.

Ashton, N.M. and McNabb, J. (1994). Bifaces in perspective. In: N.M. Ashston and A. David (eds), Stories in Stone, *Lithic Studies Occasional Paper, No. 4.* London, Lithic Studies Society. 182–191.

Atkinson, R.J.C. (1957). Worms and weathering, *Antiquity*, 31, 219–233.

Atkinson, T.C. and Smith, D.I. (1974). Rapid groundwater flow in fissures in the chalk: an example from South Hampshire. *Quarterly Journal of Engineering Geology*, 7, 1971–205.

Avery, B.W. (1958). A sequence of beechwood soils on the Chiltern Hills, England, *Journal of Soil Science*, 9 (2), 210–14.

Avery, B.W. (1964). The Soils and Land Use of the District round Aylesbury and Hemel Hempstead (Sheet 238), *Memoir of the Soil Survey of Great Britain: England and Wales.* HMSO, London.

Avery, B.W. (1980). System of Soil Classification for England and Wales (Higher Categories), *Soil Survey Technical Monograph No. 14*, Harpenden.

Avery, B.W. (1990). *Soils of the British Isles*, C.A.B. International, Wallingford.

Avery, B.W., Stephen, G., Brown, G. and Yaaldon, D.H. (1959). The origin and development of Brown Earths on the Clay-with-flints and Coombe Deposits, *Journal of Soil Science*, 10, (2), 177–95.

Ballantyne, C. K. and Cornish, R. (1979). Use of the Chi-Square test for the analysis of orientation data, *Journal of Sedimentary Petrology*, 49. (3), 773–776, fig. 1.

Ballantyne, C.K. and Harris, C. (1994) *The Periglaciation of Great Britain*, Cambridge University Press

Barrow, G. (1919). Some future work for the Geologists' Association, *Proceedings of the Geologists' Association*, 30, 2–48.

Bell, M. (1977). Excavation at Bishopstone. *Sussex Archaeological Collections* 115. Lewes.

Bell, M. (1992). The prehistory of soil erosion. In: M. Bell, and J. Boardman. (eds) *Past and present soil erosion.* Oxbow monograph, 22. Oxbow, Oxford.

Binford, L.R. (1978). *Nunamiut Ethnoarchaeology*, Academic Press, New York

Bishop, W.W. (1958). The Pleistocene geology and geomorphology of three gaps in the Midland Jurassic Escarpment, *Phil. Trans. Roy. Soc. (series B)*, 241, 255–306.

Bonte, A. (1955). Age et Origine des formations superficielles'a silex, *C. R. hebd. seanc. Acad. Sci.* 241, 1318–1320.

Bordes, F. (1954). Les limons quaternaires du Bassin de la Seine. Stratigraphie at archéologie Paléolithique, *Archives de l'Institut de Paléontologie Humaine*, Mem 26, Masson, Paris.

Bordes, F. (1961). *Typologie du Paléolithique Ancien et Moyen*, Institut de Préhistoire de L'université de Bordeaux, 1–2.

Bosinski, G. (1967). *Die mittel paläolithischen Funde im Westlichen Mitteleuropa*, Fundamenta, Reihe A, Band 4, ed., H Schwab-edissen, Bohlau, Köln.

Boulton, G.S. (1978). Boulder shapes and grain-size distributions of debris as indicators of transport paths through a glacier and till genesis, *Sedimentology*, 25, 773–99.

Brajnikov, B. (1937). Recherches sur la formation applee 'Argile à Silex' dans le Bassin de Paris, *Revue Geogr. phys, Geol. Dyn*, 10, 7–90, 109–130.

Bridgland, D.R. (1986). *Clast Lithological Analysis, Technical Guide No.3*, Quaternary Research Association, Cambridge.

Bridgland, D.R. (1994). *Quaternary of the Thames*, Chapman and Hall, London.

Briggs, D.J. (1977). *Sediments, Sources and Methods in Geography*, Butterworths, London.

Briggs, D.J., Coope, G.R. and Gilbertson, D.D. (1985). The chronology and environmental framework of early man in the upper Thames Valley, *British Archaeological Series*, 137.

Briggs, D.J. and Griffin C.M. (1986). Sediment provenances in the Creswell Caves. In: D.J. Briggs, D.D. Gilbertson and R.D.S. Jenkinson (eds), *Peak District & Northern Dukeries*, Quaternary Research Association, Cambridge, 139–50.

Bullock, P. and Murphy, C.P. (1979). Evolution of a paleo-argillaceous brown earth (Paleudalf) from Oxfordshire, England, *Geoderma*, 22, 225–253.

Cahen, D. and Keeley, L.H. (1980). Not less than two, not more than three. In: D.A. Roe (ed), Early Man: some precise moments in the remote past. *World Archaeology*, Routledge and Kegan Paul Ltd. Vol. 12, No. 2, 166–179. Callow, P. (1976). *The Lower and Middle Palaeolithic of Britain and adjacent areas of Europe*, unpublished Ph.D. thesis, University of Cambridge.

Carpenter, L.W. (1956). The palaeoliths of Walton and Banstead Heaths, *Proceedings of the Leatherhead and District Local History Society*, 1, 6–10.

Carpenter, L.W. (1960). A Palaeolithic floor at Lower Kingswood, *Proceedings of the Leatherhead and District Local History Society*, 2, 99–101.

Catt, J.A. (1977). Loess and Coversands. In: F.W. Shotton (ed), *British Quaternary Studies, recent advances.* Oxford University Press.

Catt, J.A. (1979). Soils and Quaternary geology in Britain, *Journal of Soil Sciences*, 30, 607–642.

Catt, J.A. (1986a). The nature, origin and geomorphological significance of Clay-with-flints. In: G. de G. Sieveking and M.B. Hart (eds), The Scientific Study of Flint and Chert. *Proceedings of the Fourth International Flint Symposium*, Cambridge University Press, 151–156.

Catt, J.A. (1986b). *Soils and Quaternary Geology: A Handbook for Field Scientists*. Clarendon Press. Oxford.

Catt, J.A, and Hodgson, J. M. (1976). *Soils and geomorphology of the Chalk in south-east England*, Earth Surface Processes. 1. 181–93.

Catt, J.A. and Weir, A.H. (1976). The study of archaeologically important sediments by petrographic techniques. In: D.A. Davidson and M.L, Shackley, M.L. (eds), *Geoarchaeology*, 65–91.

Chartres, C. J. (1980). A Quaternary soil sequence in the Kennet Valley, central southern England. *Geoderma*, 23, 125–146.

Chartres, C.J. (1984). The micromorphology of net valley, Berkshire, England, Earth *Surface Processes and Landforms*, 9, 343–55.

Clark, D.V. and Hansel, A.K. (1989). Clast ploughing, lodgement and glacier sliding over a soft glacier bed, *Boreas*, 18, 201–207.

Clark, M.J. (1965). The form of chalk slopes, *University of Southampton, Research Series in Geography*, 2, 3–4.

Clark, M.J., Lewin, J. and Small, R.J. (1967). The sarsen stones of the Marlborough Downs and their geomorphological implications, *University of Southampton Research Series in Geography*, 4, 3–40.

Clayden, B. and Hollis, J.M. (1984). Criteria for differentiating soil series, *Soil Survey Technical Monograph*, 17, Harpenden.

Codrington, T. (1866). The geology of the Berkshire and Hampshire extension and the Marlborough Railways, *Wiltshire Archaeological and Natural History Magazine*, 9, 167–193.

Coleman, A. (1952). Some aspects of the development of the Lower Stour, Kent, *Proceedings of Geol. Association*, 63, 63–86, 75.

Conway, B., Ashton, N. and McNabb, J. (1996). *Excavations at Barnfield Pit, Swanscombe 1968–72*, British Museum Press, London.

Crabtree, R.W. (1986). Spatial distribution of solutional erosion. In: S.T. Trudgill, (ed), *Solute Processes*, Wiley Interscience, Chichester.

Dawkins, W.B. (1916). Comments on – H.G.O. Kendall's (1916) Excavations at Hackpen Hill. *Proceedings of the Society of Antiquaries of London*. 2nd. series. 28. 44–46.

Delagnes, A. and Ropars, A. (1996). Paléolithique moyen en pays de Caux (Haute-Normandie). *56 Documents d'Archéologie Française*. Éditions de la Maison des Sciences de L'Homme. Paris.

Dobkins, J.E. and Folk, R.L. (1970). Shape development on Tahiti-Nui, *Journal of Sedimentary Petrology*, 40, 1167–1203.

Domack, E.W. and Lawson, D.E. (1985). Pebble fabric in a ice-rafted diamicton, *The Journal of Geology*, 93, 577–591.

Dowdeswell, J.A., Hambrey, M.J. and Ruitang, W. (1985). A comparison of clast fabric and shape in late Precambrian and modern glacigenic sediments, *Journal of Sedimentary Petrology*, 55, 691–704.

Draper, J.C. (1951). Stone industries from Rainbow Bar, Hants, *Archaeological Newsletter*, 3, 147–149.

Dyer, J. (1978). Worthington George Smith and other studies, *Bedfordshire Historical Record Society*, 57. 141–179.

Edmonds, C.N. (1983). Towards the prediction of subsidence risk upon the Chalk outcrop, *Quaterly Journal of Engineering Geology*, 16, 261–266.

English Heritage (1991–1994). The Southern Rivers Palaeolithic Project, *Wessex Archaeology*

Evans, J. (later Sir John) (1872). *The Ancient Stone Implements, Weapons and Ornaments of Great Britain (1st edn)*, Longmans, Green and Co., London.

Evans, Sir John (1897). *The Ancient Stone Implements, Weapons and Ornaments of Great Britain (2nd.edn, rev.)*, Longmans, Green and Co, London.

Foley, R. (1987). *Another Unique Species*, Longmans.

Fordham, S.J. and Green, R. D. (1973). Soils of Kent 2, (Sheet TR35, Deal), *Soil Survey Record No. 15*. Harpenden, Soil Survey and Land Research Centre, Bedford.

Fordham, S.J. and Green, R.D. (1980). Soils in Kent, *Soil Survey Bulletin No. 9*. Harpenden, Soil Survey and Land Research Centre, Bedford.

French, H.M. (1972). Asymmetrical slope development in the Chiltern Hills, *Biuletyn Peryglacjalny*, 21, 51–73.

French, H.M. (1973). Cryopediments on the chalk of southern England, *Biuletyn Peryglacjalny*, 22, 149–56.

French, H.M. (1976). *The Periglacial Environment*, Longman, London.

Friedman, G.M. and Sanders, J .E. (1978). *Principles of Sediment-ology*, Wiley, New York.

Gale, S.J, (1984). The hydraulics of conduit flow in carbonate aquifers, *Journal of Hydrology*, 70, 309–327.

Gale, S.J. (1990). The shape of beach gravels, *Journal of Sediment-ary Petrology*, 60, 787–789.

Gale, S.J. and Hoare, P.G. (1991). *Quaternary Sediments: Petrographic Methods for the Study of Unlithified Rocks*, Belhaven, London.

Gallois, R.W. and Edmonds, F.H. (1978). *The Wealden District, British Regional Geology*, Natural Environment Research Centre, Institute of Geological Sciences, 4th. edition, H.M.S.O.

Gamble, C.S, (1994). Time for Boxgrove man, U.K. *Nature*, 369, (6478), 275–276.

Gamble, C.S and ApSimon, A. (1986) In: S.N. Collcutt (ed.), *The Palaeolithic of Britain and its nearest neighbours: recent trends*, Sheffield University, Department of Archaeology and Pre-history, Sheffield, 8–12.

Gamble, C.S and Lawson, A.J. (1996). *The English Palaeolithic Reviewed*, The Trust for Wessex Archaeology, vii.

Gaunt, J., Parfitt, K. and Halliwell, G. (1977). Surveys along the Dover by-pass, *Kent Archaeological Review*, 48, 196–200.

Goudie, A.I. (1988). *The Encyclopaedic Dictionary of Physical Geography*, Basil Blackwell Ltd. Oxford.

Goudie, A.I. (1993). *The landforms of England and Wales*, Blackwell, Oxford.

Graham, J. (1991). Collection and analysis of field data. In: M Tucker (ed), *Techniques in Sedimentology*, Blackwell, Oxford.

Green, C.P., Coope, G.R., Currant, A.P., Holyoak, D.T., Ivano-vich, M., Jones, R.L., Keen, D.H., McGregor, D.F.M. and Robin-son, J.E. (1984). Evidence of two temperate episodes in Late Pleistocene deposits at Marsworth, U.K. *Nature*, 309, 778–781.

Griffiths, J.C. (1967). *Scientific method in analysis of Sedimentary*, McGraw Hill, New York.

Halliwell, G. and Parfitt, K. (1993). Non-river gravel Lower and Middle Palaeolithic discoveries in East Kent, *Kent Archaeological Review*, Council for Kentish Archaeology, 114. 80–89.

Harms, J.C., Southard, J.B. and Walker, R.G. (1982). Structures and sequences in clastic rocks, *Society of Economic Paleon-tologists and Mineralogists*, Short Course, 9, 249.

Harrison, Sir Edward R. (1928). *Harrison of Ightham: a book about Benjamin Harrison, of Ightham, Kent, made up principally of extracts from his notebooks and correspondence*, Oxford University Press, London.

Henry, D.O. and Odell, G.H. (1989). Alternative approaches to lithic analysis, *Archeological Papers of the American Anthropological Association*, 1.

Hodgson, J.M., Catt, J.A. and Weir, A.H. (1967). The origin and development of Clay-with-flints and associated soil horizons on the South Downs, *Journal of Soil Science*, 18, 85–102.

Hodgson, J.M., Rayner, J.H, and Catt, J.A. (1974). The geomorphological significance of the Clay-with-flints on the South Downs, *Transactions of the Institute of British Geographers*, 61, 119–129.

Holdings, C. S. (1973). Resilience and stability of ecological systems, *Annual review of ecology and systematics* 4, 1–23.

Holmes, C.D. (1941). Till fabric, *Bulletin of the Geological Society of America*, 52, 1299–1354.

Hull, E. and Whitaker, W. (1861). The geology of parts of Oxfordshire and Berkshire, *Memoir of the Geological Survey of Great Britain*. ii, 1–57.

Huxtable, J. (1982). Fine grain thermoluminescence (TL) techniques applied to flint dating, *PACT 6*, 346–352.

Inizan, M-L., Roche, H. and Tixier, J. (1992). *Technology of knapped stone*, C.R.E.P, Meudon.

Isaac, G. Ll. and Isaac, B. (1997) *Koobi Fora. Research project. Vol. 5*. Clarendon Press, Oxford

Isaac, G. Ll. (1989). *The archaeology of human origins*. Cambridge University Press.

John, D.T. (1980). The soils and superficial deposits on the North Downs of Surrey. In: D.K.C. Jones, (ed), The Shaping of Southern England, *Institute of British Geographers Special Publication*, 11, 101–130.

Jones, D.K.C. (1974). The influence of the Clabrian transgression on the drainage evolution of south-east England. In: E.H. Brown and R.S. Walters (eds), *Progress in Geomorphology, Institute of British Geographers, Special Publication*, 7, 139–58.

Jones, D.K.C. (1980). The Tertiary evolution of south-east England with particular reference to the Weald, *The Shaping of Southern England*, 13–47, London Academic Press.

Jones, D.K.C. (1981). *The Southeast and Southern England*, London, Methuen.

Jukes-Browne, A.J. (1906). The Clay-with-flints; its origin and distribution, *Quarterly Journal of the Geological Society of London*, 62, 132–64.

Kemp, R.A. (1990). Soil Micromorphology and the Quaternary, *Quaternary Research Association Technical Guide No. 2*. Cambridge.

Kendall, H.G.O. (1916). Excavations on Hackpen Hill, Wilts, *Proceedings of the Society of Antiquaries of London*, 2nd. series, 28, 26–48.

Kennedy, B.A. (1976). Valley-side Slopes and Climate in E. Derbyshire, *Geomorphology and Climate*, Wiley, Chichester. 171–201.

King, C.A.M. (1966). *Techniques in geomorphology*, Arnold, London.

Kovach W. L. (1994). *Oriana Users Manual*. KCS, Wales. (published on the Internet).

Krumbein, W.C. (1934). Size frequency distributions of sediments, *Journal of Sedimentary Petrology*, 4, 65–77.

Lawson, D.E. (1979a). Sedimentalogical analysis of the western terminus region of the Matanuska Glacier, Alaska, *Cold Regions Research and Engineering Laboratory Report*, 79–9, 122.

Lawson, D.E. (1979b). A comparison of pebble orientations in the ice and deposits of the Mantanuska Glacier, Alaska, *The Journal of Geology*, 87, 629–645.

Lacaille, A.D. (1959). Palaeoliths from Brickearth in South-East Buckinghamshire, *Records of Bucks*, XVI, (4), 274–288.

Lacaille, A.D. (1971). Some Wiltshire Palaeoliths, *Prehistoric and Roman studies, The British Museum Quarterly*, 35, 1–4.

Lehmann, E. (1975). *Nonparametrics*, Holden-Day, San Francisco, U.S.A.

Lindholm, R. (1987). *A Practical Approach to Sedimentology*, Allen and Unwin, London.

Lord, J. W. (1993). *The Nature and Subsequent Uses of Flint*, John Lord.

Loveday, J. (1958). *A study of the soils and their relation to landscape form in the southern Chilterns*, Ph. D. thesis, London University.

Loveday, J. (1962). Plateau deposits of the southern Chiltern Hills, *Proceedings of the Geologists' Association*, 73, 83–102.

Luedtke, B.E. (1992). An Archaeologist's Guide to Chert and Flint, *Archaeological Research Tools 7*, Institute of Archaeology, University of California.

Macphail, R.I. (1992). Soil micromorphological evidence of ancient soil erosion. In: M. Bell, M. J. Boardman. (eds) *Past and present soil erosion*. Oxbow monograph, 22. Oxbow, Oxford.

Matthews, B. (1977). Clay-with-flints on the Yorkshire and Lincolnshire Wolds, *Proceedings of the Yorkshire Geological Society*, 41, 231–239.

May, R.M. (1973). *Stability and complexity in model ecosystems*, Princeton N.J. Princeton University Press.

McGowan, A. and Derbyshire, E. (1974). Technical developments in the study of particulate matter in glacial tills. *The Journal of Geology*, 82, 225–235.

McManus, J. (1991). Grain size determination and interpretation. in Tucker, M. (ed.), *Techniques in Sedimentology*, Blackwell, Oxford.

Mellars, P. (1989). Technological changes at the Middle-Upper Palaeolithic transition: explanatory approaches. In: D.O. Henry and G.H. Odell (eds), Alternative approaches to lithic analysis, *Archeological Papers of the American Anthropological Association*, 1.

Melville, R.V. and Freshney, E.C. (1982). The Hampshire Basin and adjoining areas, *British Regional Geology*, Natural Environment Research Council. Institute of Geological Sciences, 4th. edition. H.M.S.O.

Morrison, R.B. (1978). Quaternary soil stratigraphy – concepts, methods and problems. In: W.C. Mahaney (ed), Quaternary soils, *GeoAbstracts*, Norwich, 77–108.

Mortimer, R.N. (1986). Controls on Upper Cretaceous sedimentation in the South Downs, with particular reference to flint distribution. In: G. de G. Sieveking and M.B. Hart (eds), The Scientific Study of Flint and Chert, *Proceedings of the Fourth International Flint Symposium* Cambridge University Press, 161–167.

Munsell, (1992). *Soil Color Charts*, Macbeth, New York.

Murton, J. B. (1988). Stratigraphy, Isle of Thanet. In: J.B. Murton, C.A. Whiteman, M.R. Bates, D.R. Bridgland, A.J. Long, M.B. Roberts, and M.P.Steel (eds.), *The Quaternary of Kent and Sussex, Field Guide*, Quaternary Research Association, 2.1, 21, 26, 30.

Murton, J. B., Baker, C., Bateman, M., Whiteman, C. (1988). Pegwell Bay, Cliffsend. In: J.B. Murton, C.A. Whiteman, M.R.Bates, D.R.Bridgland, A.J. Long, M.B.Roberts, and M.P.Steel (eds), *The Quaternary of Kent and Sussex, Field Guide*, Quaternary Research Association, 2.7, 36.

Nemec, W. (1988). The Shape of the Rose, *Sedimentary Geology*, 59, 149–152.

Nemec, W. and Steel, R.J. (1984). Alluvial and coastal conglomerates: Their significant features and some comments on gravelly mass flow deposits. In: E.H.Koster and R.J. Steel (eds), Sedimentology of gravels and conglomerates, *Canadian Society of Petroleum Geologists Memoir*, 10, 1–31.

Newcomer, M.H. (1971). Some quantitative experiments in handaxe manufacture, *World Archaeology*, 3, 1.

Ollier, C.D, and Thomasson, A.J. (1957). Asymmetrical valleys of the Chiltern Hills, *Geographical Journal*, 123, 71–80.

Parsons, A.J. (1988). *Hillslope form*, Routledge, London.

Paterson, K. (1970). *Aspects of the geomorphology of the Oxford Region*, (unpublished) Ph.D. thesis, University of Oxford.

Pemberton, F.F. (1971). Lower Kingswood: excavations at Rookery Farm, *Surrey Archaeological Collection*, Surrey Archaeological Society, 68, 190.

Pepper, D.M. (1968). *A contribution to the geography of the Clay-with-flints of southern England and Northern France*, unpublished Ph.d. thesis. London University, 714.

Pepper, D.M. (1973). A comparison of the 'Argile'a Silex' of Northern France with the 'Clay-with-flints' of Southern England, *Proceedings of the Geologists Association*, 84 (3), 331–352.

Pettijohn, E.J. (1975). *Sedimentary Rocks* (3rd ed.), Harper & Row.

Pinchemel, P. (1954). *Les Plaines de Craie du Nord- ouest du Bassin Parisien et du Sud-est du Bassin de Londres et leur bordeurs*. These lettres, Paris, A. Colin, édit.

Potts, A.S., Browne, T.J. and Rendell, H.M. (1983) Hydrology and water supply in Sussex. In Geography Editorial Committee (eds) *Sussex: Environment, Landscape and Society*, Sutton, Gloucester

Powers, M.C. (1982). Comparison chart for estimating roundness and sphericity, *AGI Data Sheet 18*, American Geological Institute.

Prestwich, J. (1858). 'On the age of some sands and iron-sandstones on the North Downs' *Quarterly Journal of the Geological Society of London*, 14, 333–335.

Ragg, J. M. and Clayden, B. (1973). The Classification of some British soils according to the Comprehensive System of the United States, *Soil Survey Technical Monograph No. 3.*, Harpenden.

Reid, C. (1898). The geology of the country around Eastbourne, *Memoirs of the Geological Survey of England and Wales*.

Reid, C. (1899). The geology of the country around Dorchester, *Memoirs of the Geological Survey of England and Wales*.

Reid, C. (1903). The geology of the country around Chichester, *Memoirs of the Geological Survey of England and Wales*.

Roberts, M.B., Stringer, C.B. and Parfitt, S.A. (1994). A hominid tibia from Middle Pleistocene sediments at Boxgrove, U.K. *Nature*, 369, (6478), 311–313.

Roberts, M.B., Gamble, C.S. and Bridgland, D.R. (1995). The earliest occupation of Europe: the British Isle. In: W. Roebroeks and T. Van Koltschoten (eds), *The earliest occupation of Europe*, European Science Foundation. University of Leiden

Roe, D.A. (1968). A Gazetteer of British Lower and Middle Palaeolithic Sites, *Council for British Archaeology (Research Report no. 8)*. London.

Roe, D.A. (1981). *The Lower and Middle Palaeolithic periods in Britain*, Routledge and Kegan Paul, London.

Roe, D.A. (1996). Summary and Overview. In: G.LL. Isaac. and B. Isaac (eds). *Koobi Fora, Research Project Report: Plio-Pleistocene Archaeology*. 5, Clarendon Press. Oxford.

Roebroeks, W. (1988). From find scatters to early hominid behaviour: A study of Middle Palaeolithic riverside settlements at Maastricht-Bélvedère (The Netherlands). *Analecta Praehistorica Leidensia*, University of Leiden.

Rose, J. and Allen, P. (1977). Middle Pleistocene stratigraphy in South-east Suffolk, *Journal of the Geolgical Society of London*, 133, 83–102.

Röttlander, E. (1975). The formation of patina on flint, *Archaeometry*, 17, 106–110.

Sampson, C. Garth. (1978). *Palaeoecology and archaeology of an Acheulian site at Caddington, England*, Dept. of Anthropology, Southern Methodist University, Dallas. U.S.A.

Schaetzl, R.J. (1990). Effects of treethrow microtopography on the characteristics and genesis of spodosols, Michigan, USA. *Catena* 17, 111–126.

Scott-Jackson, J.E. (1991a). *A study of Palaeolithic find-spots on the North Hampshire Downs*, (unpublished) B.Sc.(Hons.) thesis, Oxford Brookes University.

Scott-Jackson, J.E. (1991b). *Gazetteer of the Palaeolithic find-spots on the North Hampshire Downs*, (unpublished).

Scott-Jackson, J.E. (1994). Lower Palaeolithic finds at Wood Hill, East Kent: A geological and geomorphological approach to an archaeological problem, *Lithics*, 13, 11–16.

Scott-Jackson, J.E. (1996). *A study of Lower and Middle Palaeolithic artefacts found on relation to deposits mapped as Clay-with-flints on the Chalk Downlands of southern England*, (unpublished) D.Phil. thesis, University of Oxford.

Scott-Jackson, J. E. (1999). *Gazetteer of Lower and Middle Palaeolithic artefacts found in relation to deposits mapped as Clay-with-flints on the Chalk downlands of southern England*. (on-going unpublished study).

Selby, M.J. (1982). *Hillslope materials and processes*, Oxford University Press.

Shackley, M. (1981). On the Palaeolithic archaeology of Hampshire: In The Archaeology of Hampshire, S. J. Shennan and R.T. Schadla-Hall (eds), *Monograph No.1 Hampshire Field Club and Archaeological Society*, 4–9.

Small, R.J. and Fisher, G.C. (1961). The morphology of Chalk escarpments: a critical discussion, *Transactions of the Institute of British Geographers*, 29, 71–90.

Small, R.J and Fisher, G.C. (1970). The origins of the secondary escarpment of the South Downs, *Transactions of the Institute of British Geographers*, 49, 97–107.

Smart, J.G.O., Bisson, G, and Worssam, B.C. (1966). Geology of the country around Canterbury and Folkestone, *Memoirs of the Geological Survey of Great Britain*, H.MS.O. London.

Smart, J.G.O., Bisson, G. and Worssam, B.C. (1975). *The Geology of the County around Canterbury and Folkstone*, Institute of Geological Sciences, Natural Environmental Research Council. H.M.S.O. London.

Smith, D.I. and Atkinson, T.C. (1976). Process, landform and climate in limestone regions. In: E. Derbyshire (ed) *Geomorphology and climate*, Wiley, Chichester, 367–409.

Smith, R.A. (1915). Plateau Deposits and Implements, *Proceedings of the Prehistoric Society of East Anglia*, 2, part 1.

Smith, R.A. (1916). Comments on H.G.O.Kendall's (1916) Excavations at Hackpen Hill, Wilts. *Proceedings of the Society of Antiquaries of London*, 2nd. series, 28, 47–48.

Smith, R.A. (1918). Flint Implements from the Palaeolithic floor at Whipsnade, Beds, *Proceedings of the Society of Antiquaries of London*, 2nd. series, 31, 39–50.

Smith, W.G. (1892). Primitive Man: a Palaeolithic floor near Dunstable, *Natural Science*, 1:9, 664–670.

Smith, W.G. (1894). *Man, the Primeval Savage: his haunts and relics from the hilltops of Bedfordshire to Blackwall*, Stanford, London.

Smith, W.G. (1906). Human skeleton of Palaeolithic Age, *Man*, Royal Anthropological Institute, 6:10–11.

Smith, W.G. (1908). Eoliths, *Man*, Royal Anthropological Institute, 8, 26:49–53, plate D.

Smith, W.G. (1916). Notes on the Palaeolithic Floor near Caddington, *Archaeologia*, Society of Antiquaries of London, 2nd series, 17.

Sparks, B.W. (1949). Denudation chronology of the dip slope of the South Downs, *Proceedings of the Geologists Association*, 60, 165–215.

Sparks, B.W. (1960). *Geomorphology*. Longman, London.

Spencer, D.W. (1963). The Interpretation of Grain Size Distribution Curves of Clastic Sediments, *Journal of Sedimentary Petrology*, 33, (1) 180–190.

Stapert, D. (1976). Some natural surface modification on flint in the Netherlands, *Palaeohistoria* 18, 7–41.

Stephens, E.P. (1956). The uprooting of trees: a forest process. *Soil Science Society of America Proceedings* 20, 113–116.

Stratten, T. (1974). Notes on the application of shape parameters to differentiate between beach and river deposits in Southern Africa, *Transactions of the Geological Society of South Africa*, 77, 59–64.

Swan, A.R.H. and Sandilands M. (1995). *Introduction to Geological Data Analysis*, Blackwell, Oxford.

Tanner, W.F. (1969). The particle size scale, *Journal of Sedimentary Petrology*, 39, 509–512.

Te Punga, M.T. (1957). Periglaciation in southern England, *Tijdchr. Kon. ned. aardrijksk. Genoot*, 64, 401–12.

Thomasson, A.J. (1961). Some aspects of Drift Deposits and geomorphology of South-East Hertfordshire, *Proceedings Geol Association*, 72, 287–302.

Thorez, J., Bullock, P., Catt, J, and Weir, A. (1971). The petrography and origin of deposits filling solution pipes in the Chalk near South Mimms, Hertfordshire, *Geological Magazine*, 108, 413–423.

Todd, A.E. (1934). Early flake implements from the Clay-with-flints on the Eastbourne Downs, *Proceedings of the Prehistoric Society of East Anglia*, 7, 419–420.

Todd, A.E. (1935). Early Palaeoliths from the Summit of the South Downs, *Proceedings of the Prehistoric Society of East Anglia*, 9, 140–143.

Trudgill, S.T. (1986). Solute processes and landforms: An assessment. In: S.T. Trudgill (ed), *Solute Processes*, Wiley, Chichester.

Tuffreau, A. and Antoine, P. (1995). The earliest occupation of Europe: Continental Northwestern Europe. In: W. Roebroeks and T. Van Koltschoten (eds), *The earliest occupation of Europe*, European Science Foundation. University of Leiden.

Tyldesley, J.A. (1986a). *The Wolvercote Channel handaxes assemblage: a comparative study*, BAR, British Series, Oxford.

Tyldesley, J.A. (1986b). A re-assessment of the handaxe assemblage recovered from the Wolvercote channel, Oxford. In: S.N. Collcutt (ed), *The Palaeolithic of Britain and its nearest neighbours: recent trends*, Sheffield University, Department of Archaeology and Prehistory, Sheffield.

Van Noten, F., Cahen, D., Keeley, L.H. and Moeyersons, J. (1978). Les Chasseurs de Meer. In: S.J. de Laet (ed), *Dissertationes Archaeologicae Gandenses*, de Tempel, Brugge, Vol.XVIII.

Veneman, P.L., Van Veen, J.A. and Paul, E.A. (1981). Organic C dynamics in grassland soils 2: Model validation and simulation of the long term effects of cultivation and rainfall erosion. *Canadian Journal of Soil Science* 61, 211–224.

Walls, T. and Cotton, J. (1980). Palaeoliths from the North Downs at Lower Kingswood, *Surrey Archaeological Collections*, Surrey Archaeological Society, 72, 15–36.

Washbourne, A.L. (1973). *Periglacial processes and environments*, Edward Arnold, London.

Watt, A. (1988). *Longman illustrated dictionary of geology*, Longman, Essex.

Weir, A.H. and Catt, J.A. (1965). The mineralogy of some Upper Chalk samples from the Arundel area, Sussex, *Clay Minerals*, 6, 97–100.

West, R.G. (1958). The Quaternary deposits at Hoxne, Suffolk, *Philosophical Transactions of the Royal Society of London*, 239, 265–356.

Whitaker, W. (1867). On subaerial denudation, and on cliffs and escarpments of the Chalk and the Lower Tertiary Beds, *Geology Magazine*, 4, 447–83.

Whitaker, W. (1872). The geology of the London Basin, *Memoirs of the Geological Survey of Great Britain*, xi., 1–619.

Whitaker, W. (1889). The geology of the London and part of the Thames Valley, *Memoirs of the Geological Survey of Great Britain*.

White, H.J.O. and Jukes-Brown, A.J. (1908). The geology of the country around Henley-on-Thames and Wallingford, *Memoirs of the Geological Survey*, England, H.M.S.O. London.

White, H.J.O. (1909). The geology of the country around Basingstoke, *Memoirs of the Geological Survey of Great Britain*.

White, M.J. (1995). Raw materials and Biface Variability in Southern Britain: A preliminary Examination, *Lithics*, 15, 1–20.

White, M.J. (1997). The earlier Palaeolithic occupation of the Chilterns (southern England): re-assessing the sites of Worthington G. Smith. *Antiquity*, 71, 912–931.

White, M.J. and Pettitt, P.B.(1995). Technology of early Palaeolithic Western Europe: Innovation, variability and a unified framework. *Lithics*, 16:27–40.

Whittaker, J. C. (1995). *Flintknapping: making and understanding stone tools*, University of Texas Press, Austin.

Williams, R.B.G. (1971). Aspects of the geomorphology of the South Downs, *Guide to Sussex Excursions*, Institute of British Geographers.

Williams, R.B.G. (1975). The British climate during the Last Glaciation: an interpretation based on periglacial phenomena. In: A.E. Wright and F. Moseley (eds), Ice Ages: Ancient and Modern, *Geological Journal, Special Issue*, 6, 95–120.

Williams, R.B.G. (1980). The weathering and erosion of Chalk under periglacial conditions. In: D.K.C. Jones (ed), *The shaping of Southern England*, Academic Press, London, 225–248.

Williams, R.B.G. (1986). Periglacial phenomena in the South Downs. In: G. de G. Sieveking and M.B. Hart (eds), The Scientific Study of Flint and Chert, *Proceedings of the Fourth International Flint Symposium* Cambridge University Press., 161–167.

Williams, R.B.G. (1987). Frost weathered mantles on the Chalk. In: J. Boardman (ed), *Periglacial processes and landforms in Britain and Ireland*, Cambridge University Press., 153–62.

Williams, R.B.G. and Robinson, D.A. (1983). The landforms of Sussex. In: *The Geography Editorial Committee Sussex: Environment, Landscape and Society*, Alan Sutton, Gloucester, 33–49

Willis, G.W. (1947). Hampshire palaeoliths and the Clay-with-flints, *Proceedings of the Hampshire Field Club and Archaeological Society*, Gilbert and Son, London, 16. (3). 253–256.

Willman, H.B. and Frye, J.C. (1970). Pleistocene stratigraphy of Illinois, *Illinois State, Geological Bulletin*, 94.

Wilson, D.R. (1982). *Air Photo Interpretation for Archaeologists*, Batsford, London.

Woodcock, A. (1981). The Lower and Middle Palaeolithic periods in Sussex, *B.A.R. British Series*, 94.

Woodcock, N.H. and Naylor, M.A. (1983). Randomness Testing in Three-Dimensional Orientation Data. *Journal of Structural Geology*, 5 (5), 539–548.

Woodward, H.B. (1887). *The Geology of England and Wales*, 2nd. edn., Philip, London.

Woodward, H.B. (1912). *The Geology of Soils and Substrata*, Arnold, London.

Wooldridge, S.W. (1927). The Pliocene history of the London Basin, *Proceedings of the Geologists' Association*, 38, 49–132.

Wooldridge, S.W. and Goldring, F. (1953). *The Weald*, London.

Wooldridge, S.W. and Linton, D.L. (1955). *Structure, Surface and Drainage in South-east England*, 2nd. edn., Philip. London. xiii, 1–76.

Wymer, J.J. (1974). Clactonian and Acheulian industries in Britain – their chronology and significance, *Proceeedings of the Geologists' Association*, 85,391,421.

Wymer, J.J. (1968). *Lower Palaeolithic Archaeology in Britain as represented by the Thames Valley*, John Baker, London.

Wymer, J.J. (1980). The excavation of the Acheulian site at Gaddesden Row, *The Bedfordshire Archaeological Journal*, Bedfordshire Archaeological Council, 14. 2–4.

Wymer, J.J. (1987). The Palaeolithic period in Surrey. In: J. Bird and D.G. Bird (eds), *The Archaeology of Surrey*, Surrey Archaeological Society, Adlard and Son. Ltd, Surrey.

Zimmerman, D.W. (1971). Thermoluminescence dating using fine grains from pottery, *Archaeometry* 13, 9–52.